Drug Prohibition and the Conscience of Nations

Arnold S. Trebach

and

Kevin B. Zeese

Editors

The Drug Policy Foundation
Washington, D.C.

© 1990 by The Drug Policy Foundation

All rights reserved. No part of this book may be reproduced or transmitted in any form or by any means, electronic or mechanical, including photocopying, recording or by any information storage and retrieval system, without permission in writing from the Publisher.

ISBN 1-87-9189-00-3

Drug Policy Foundation books and materials are available at special discounts for bulk purchases for sales promotions, premiums, fundraising or educational use.

Drug Prohibition and the Conscience of Nations was published by the Drug Policy Foundation, an independent forum for drug policy alternatives.

The Foundation is a charitable corporation under the laws of the District of Columbia and section 501(c)(3) of the U.S. Internal Revenue Code. Thus, all contributions to the Foundation are tax-deductible. To maintain its independence, the Drug Policy Foundation neither seeks nor will it accept government funding. The Foundation is supported by the contributions of thousands of private citizens and organizations.

Drug Policy Foundation
4801 Massachusetts Ave., N.W., Suite 400
Washington, D.C. 20016-2087 U.S.A.
(202) 895-1634 u fax (202) 537-3007

Whatever we have been doing in the area of drug abuse should be immediately modified. Legislation aiming at regulation and decriminalization (not "legalization") should be formulated as novel efforts that could be quickly modified if unsuccessful. The panel suggests that this legislation be formulated following four principles. First, separately consider the different drugs involved and not consider that there is one massive drug problem; second, distinguish between the effects of drugs and the associated criminal activity; third, design the legislation being aware that these are initial efforts subject to change with experience; and fourth, think of "drugs" as including alcohol and nicotine.

Twentieth Annual Report of the Research Advisory Panel 1989. Commentary Section. Prepared for the Governor and Legislature of California. The attorney general of California attempted to suppress this official report.

Also by Arnold S. Trebach

The Rationing of Justice
The Heroin Solution
The Great Drug War
The Reformer's Catalogue

Also by Kevin B. Zeese

Drug Testing Legal Manual
The Reformer's Catalogue

Contents

Preface 1

Chapter One • War Songs 7

Chapter Two • The Drug War Is Fundamentally Unsound 23

Chapter Three • The Dutch Do It Better 45

Chapter Four • Crack: A Disaster of Historic Dimensions? 61

Chapter Five • The Denial of Medical Marijuana To Sick People 83

Chapter Six • Why Make Narcotic Addicts Suffer? 107

Chapter Seven • Forcing People to Face Death From AIDS 125

Chapter Eight • Why Make Criminals Of Marijuana Users? 151

Chapter Nine • Imprisoning Our Children to Save Them From Drugs 163

Chapter Ten • The Soldier's Bayonet and the Headman's Axe 177

Chapter Eleven •. The Growing Army of Dissenters 199

Chapter Twelve • Winding Down the War on Drugs 229

References 243

Index 249

Detailed Contents

	1 Preface
Chapter 1	7 Introduction
War Songs	8 The President Tells A White Lie About Crack
	George Bush
	11 First, Get The Casual Users
	Office of National Drug Control Strategy
	14 The Drug Czar Tells Off The Intellectuals
	William J. Bennett
	20 Last Year's Hopeless Cause Is This Year's Opportunity For Victory
	William J. Bennett
Chapter 2	23 Introduction
The Drug War is	24 The Conceptual Base Of Drug Prohibition Is Flawed
Fundamentally	*George P. Shultz*
Unsound	25 The Solution Becomes The Problem
	Ethan Nadelmann
	28 The Important Thing About A Holy War Is To *Fight* It Not To *Win* It
	Arnold S. Trebach and Kevin B. Zeese
	30 Ignoring The Lessons Of Drug Wars Past
	Kevin B. Zeese
	34 Ignoring The Great Commission Reports
	Arnold S. Trebach
	38 The Whole Deal Is As Shabby As The Trick With The Bag Of Cocaine
	Lewis H. Lapham
	43 Mr. Butts Runs Into An Old Friend
	G. B. Trudeau

Chapter 3	45	Introduction
The Dutch Do It Better	46	The U.S. Ambassador Tells The Truth About Holland! *John Shad*
	49	The Pragmatic Strategies Of The Dutch "Drug Czar" *Eddy L. Engelsman*
	55	Their Spirit Of Moderation And Experimentation Is Unmatched *Arnold S. Trebach*
Chapter 4	61	Introduction
Crack: A Disaster of Historic Dimensions?	62	Crack: Crime, Blood, And Monster Mothers *A.M. Rosenthal*
	64	The Plague Among Us *Arnold S. Trebach*
	69	Women And Crack: What's The Real Story? *Marsha Rosenbaum, Sheigla Murphy, Jeanette Irwin, and Lynn Watson*
	71	How Many Crack Babies? *Dale Gieringer*
	75	Prohibition May Be More Toxic Than Crack *Paul Goldstein, Henry H. Brownstein, Patrick J. Ryan and Patrick A. Bellucci*
	78	It's Not All It's Cracked Up To Be *Jefferson Morley*
Chapter 5	83	Introduction
The Denial of Medical Marijuana to Sick People	84	A Harvard Medical School Professor Tells About His Son Who Suffered From Cancer *Lester Grinspoon*
	86	A Michigan Mother Tells About Her Two Sons Who Suffered From Cancer *Mae Nutt*
	97	Their Government Tells Them All To Get Lost *John Lawn*
	103	Politics Is The Real Issue *Jim Hankins*
	104	How Cancer And AIDS Patients Suffer At The Hands Of The DEA *Robert Randall*

Chapter 6
Why Make Narcotic Addicts Suffer?

- 107 Introduction
- 108 Milton Polansky: We Pronounced His Death Sentence
  Arnold S. Trebach
- 113 My Father's Life Was Redeemed In This Writing
  Lisa Polansky
- 115 I Feel That I Am A Responsible Person
  Lawrence Cushing
- 122 Barbra: I Don't Understand. Why Do I Have To Do This?
  D. Keith Mano

Chapter 7
Forcing People To Face Death From AIDS

- 125 Introduction
- 126 Needles And The Conscience Of A Nation
  Edward M. Brecher
- 129 AIDS: We Have No Strategy. No Program. No Policy.
  Cherni Gillman
- 133 Dead People Can't Get Into Drug Treatment
  Dulcey Consuelo Davidson
- 138 Bravery In Australia
  Alex Wodak
- 141 Compassion And Success In Liverpool — The Mersey Harm Reduction Model Today
  Pat O'Hare
- 146 When They Visit New York They Say They Want to Cry
  Arnold S. Trebach

Chapter 8
Why Make Criminals of Marijuana Users?

- 151 Introduction
- 152 Let Us Not Punish The Millions Who Choose A Different Path
  Marvin D. Miller
- 157 Marijuana Enhances The Lives Of Some People
  Lester Grinspoon

Chapter 9
Imprisoning Our Children To Save Them From Drugs

- 163 Introduction
- 165 Arrest (Even Lobotomize) My Child
  Arnold S. Trebach
- 166 Straight Rides Over Kids Again... And Some Say They Love It
  Skip Hollandsworth

Chapter 10
The Soldier's Bayonet and the Headman's Axe

177 Introduction

178 It Is Becoming A Real War
Kevin B. Zeese

183 When Will We Learn The Lesson Of Ayatollah Khalkhali?
Arnold S. Trebach

187 Keep The Troops In The Barracks
Jonathan Marshall

189 Overkill In Panama
Tom Wicker

192 Waging War On America's Poor
Kevin B. Zeese

195 Rural Citizens Under The Guns And Helicopters
Ronald M. Sinoway

Chapter 11
The Growing Army of Dissenters

199 Introduction

200 The Mayor Of Baltimore Continues His Challenge
Kurt L. Schmoke

205 A Federal Judge Enlists
Robert W. Sweet

208 The Anger Of A Retired Chief Detective
Ralph F. Salerno

210 The Despair Of The Foot Soldiers
Arthur McBride and John T. Shuler

217 The American People Are Starting To Question The Drug War
Richard J. Dennis

Chapter 12
Winding Down the War On Drugs

229 Introduction

233 The Expert Report That The California Government Tried To Suppress
California Research Advisory Panel

References 243

Index 249

Preface

If there is a human symbol of what this volume and the Drug Policy Foundation are all about, it is Francis L. Young. He is a federal employee in his early 60s, courtly, reserved, has never even seen a marijuana cigarette, and has no association with the reform movement. Yet, he is reported to be a pariah within his agency, the Drug Enforcement Administration.

Francis Young's offense was that he went against the prevailing official dogma and listened with an open mind to all the conflicting facts presented to him in a recent dispute. Mr. Young is the chief administrative law judge of the DEA. This means that he has the power to preside over contested fact-finding inquiries and to issue decisions which, however, are not binding on his boss, the Administrator of the DEA. The issue in the dispute was whether or not marijuana could be a helpful and safe medicine in cases such as cancer and multiple sclerosis.

For many years, the U.S. government has fiercely fought off repeated legal attempts to change the legal status of marijuana. This included dogged resistance to allowing its use even in medicine and even for dying patients. Two major reasons were cited. One, it really is not such a good medicine. Two, somewhat more quietly, reclassifying it as a medicine again will send the message to our youth that this terrible drug is really not so terrible after all.

After several platoons of reform-minded lawyers, including the two editors, finally bludgeoned the government into actually holding hearings and listening to evidence on all sides, happenstance put Judge Young in charge of the proceedings. We can testify that he never gave a hint of partiality; indeed, there were times when we felt that he was too kind to his fellow employees, the lawyers from the DEA General Counsel's office, representing the government — and when he was much too harsh on us. During 1987 and 1988, throughout 13 days of hearings and 18 volumes of evidence, the powerful U.S. government presented every scintilla of information and every conceivable expert supporting the official view that marijuana is a bad medicine. The government also sought to show, even though it was not an issue, that the drug was a destructive presence in society and that to cease the all-out war on that plant was to shake hands with the devil.

It is fair to say that never in modern history has one drug been subjected to greater impartial analysis where the power of cross-examination had full play before an impartial judge.

In the end, Judge Young issued a decision that upheld virtually every point we reformers had been making, in and out of court, for years. He declared, to the utter dismay of the leaders of DEA, that there has never been a documented death in the 5,000-year history of marijuana use, that it is far safer than many foods we commonly consume, and that it can be a helpful and safe medicine for multitudes of suffering patients.

Yet, marijuana and medicine are not the main points here. Courage and integrity by government officials are. Time after time, both of us have been quietly told by government officials that the extremism of the drug war was a snare and a destructive folly — but that they could not speak out for fear of destruction themselves by the hysteria that ruled government drug policy. Such officials in the drug-war closet have included members of Congress, heads of federal agencies, DEA agents, medical researchers, and front-line city cops. (Not included in the list was Francis L. Young, with whom we have never had a private, substantive discussion).

We cannot provide these officials and their counterparts in private life with courage and integrity. They will have to summon that up from some inner places within their own consciences. We can, however, keep providing them and the general public with new evidence of the destructive folly of drug-war extremism. We can also provide fresh insights on how we can extricate ourselves from this situation which so much resembles the debacle of Vietnam. And we can provide emotional support for those officials now struggling with the decision to emerge from the closet.

This book continues the efforts of the Drug Policy Foundation to shed some calm light on the emotional, chaotic drug situation in America and around the world. So much is happening so fast that we often cannot understand events when they happen and soon forget them when they are a few weeks old.

Through its newsletters, books, conferences, and television productions, the Foundation seeks to both chronicle and interpret for the general public the course of the drug war and of the reform movement that opposes its harshest manifestations. And make no mistake about it: we in the Foundation view all too many of the efforts of leading drug warriors, in government and in private organizations, to be extreme, impractical, and counterproductive.

Thus, we have developed a deep suspicion of drug prohibition and of the excessive reliance on the police, prisons, and now even the military to enforce the drug laws. Unlike federal employee

Preface

Young, President George Bush has continued the dominant tradition of extremism and factual distortions that have for so long characterized U.S. drug policy — and which too many world leaders seem, perversely, to admire. We gasped in disbelief when President Bush, in apparent violation of a number of laws and in utter disregard of the deservedly raw sensibilities of millions of Latin Americans, sent 24,000 troops to arrest the president of a sovereign country. We do not have to grant an iota of sympathy to Manuel Noriega, very probably a major drug trafficker and all-around bad guy, to be saddened, even aghast, at the lowest official estimated toll of the Panama adventure: major parts of this small country ravaged, 202 Panamanian civilians and 314 soldiers killed, and 23 American soldiers killed. As Tom Wicker observed in a trenchant editorial in *The New York Times*: "539 people lost their lives as the primary human cost of putting handcuffs on one thug."

That seemingly mad chapter in drug-control history took place within the past year, during the Christmas season of 1989. It had been proceeded by the first Bush-Bennett *National Drug Control Strategy*, a harsh document mandated by the harsh drug law of 1988. Mr. Bush's September speech on nationwide television announcing the strategy fit within the mainstream of American drug-control efforts during this century (and showed again just how rare Judge Young's decision was). While many parts of the speech sounded reasonable, in the end, it promised war on drug users and sellers, a war without mercy. The kinder, gentler president justified his anger by holding up a bag of crack which, he said somberly, had been purchased in the park right across the street from the White House. The message was clear: the dealers are practically invading the presidential mansion! Sound the alarm! But, like so much in the drug war ideology, it was a false alarm.

A resourceful reporter, perhaps helped by shame-faced police, uncovered the truth. The young black dealer had to be repeatedly lured to Lafayette Park. He had never knowingly been there and did not even know where the White House was. It was an event staged for the speech. In other words, a lie. When confronted by press, the president of the free world shot back: "I don't understand. I mean, has somebody got some advocates here for this drug guy?"

The answer, of course, should be not advocates for the drug guy but for truth and compassion by the leading officials of a democratic society. The outrage that greeted that typically demagogic performance is fading into the mists of the past as more drug-control events overwhelm our senses. We do not want to let that happen. Nor do we want to forget a myriad of other important events, books, articles, and court decisions that took place within the last year or so and that made an important difference in the drug policy debate.

We want everyone to remember that event and the fact that some people simply could not believe our president could get away with it. We want to remember, for example, the response of Lewis Lapham, the erudite editor of *Harper's Magazine*, who wrote in an essay featured on the December 1989 cover: "I see no reason why I can't look forward to hearing him declare a war against cripples, or one-eyed people, or red geraniums. It was a genuinely awful speech, rooted at the beginning in a lie, directed at an imaginary enemy, sustained by false argument, proposing a policy that has already failed, playing to the galleries of prejudice and fear."

Nor do we want to forget that the main answer to this searing, factual attack was a curt wave of the hand from Drug Czar William Bennett that same month at Harvard University. In a much-heralded address, Mr. Bennett attacked the intellectual essays and op-ed pieces criticizing his drug war, specifically mentioning the *Harper's* article as being written "with an ignorant sneer."

Last but not least, we do not want anyone to forget that Drug Czar Bennett, with the full support of the Bush White House, announced on April 13, 1989, that the U.S. government would make the nation's capital city a test case of its ability to enforce the drug laws. Since that brave announcement, the drug and crime situation in Washington, D.C. has deteriorated. Open-air drug markets flourish on Washington streets. Drug-trade homicides reached approximately 260 during 1989. Those 260 drug-trade homicides in this small city of 622,000 souls surpasses the number of such homicides that occurred throughout any industrialized *nation* during 1989. During 1990, the second full year of the Bush Administration, this small holocaust continues in Washington. Indeed, it appears that the grisly record of 1989 may well be surpassed.

The trial of Mayor Marion Barry in 1990 documented how the chief executive of the city was able to buy and use drugs repeatedly over the past decade even though he was surrounded by a phalanx of police. The failure of the jury to render guilty verdicts on most charges showed how resistance to reliance on the criminal law to control drug use was growing, especially among minorities.

In September of 1990, President Bush and Drug Czar Bennett issued a report claiming significant progress in their war on drugs. No mention was made of the Washington test case. Within days of their report, it was discovered that a cocaine ring had been operating partly from a House of Representatives office garage. A few days later, Mr. Bennett admitted that no progress was being made on the test case in Washington, primarily because "There is just no consuming passion against drugs in D.C."

So that we all may remember these important events and the ideas surrounding them, we have produced this volume and intend to continue to produce similar volumes in the years ahead. We produced a somewhat similar book last year entitled *Drug Policy 1989-1990: A Reformer's Catalogue*. This book builds on that one but has its own distinct style: it is shorter and contains a balanced mix of wholly new materials as well as significant writings of the recent past including the views of some of the most important supporters of the drug war.

The inspiration for the title was an article by the late, wonderful Edward Brecher entitled "Needles and the Conscience of a Nation." In that article, contained herein, Mr. Brecher made the case for expanding our sense of national morality to include deviants, law breakers, even prostitutes and addicts. "Don't protect only the rich and the middle classes or only the law abiding: for the infection will sooner or later spread from the unprotected to the protected," he wrote. Ed was referring to the American public health strategy developed over a century ago. He said that it was a "scientific rule that is also a moral precept." He argued that it should now be applied to AIDS and anti-needle laws.

We believe that this rule ought to apply to the entire drug problem. If we treat deviants and law breakers as enemies of the state to be destroyed in a harsh war, then the rest of us are placed in serious danger, often from enemies as devious and deadly as the AIDS virus. That combined good scientific rule and moral precept, moreover, ought to apply to all aspects of modern societies, not simply the arena of drug control.

The young staff of a young, vibrant organization, the Drug Policy Foundation, again pitched in and produced yet another publication in record time. We particularly want to thank Carolyn B. Shulman, who effectively took the lead in organizing mate-

Preface

rials and staff for this project. In addition, we wish to thank Kennington Wall, Pamela Griffin, Michael Elsner, and Rachel Donaldson for their fine contributions in this regard.

Arnold S. Trebach
and
Kevin B. Zeese

Washington, District of Columbia
October 1990

This — this is crack cocaine seized a few days ago by Drug Enforcement agents in a park just across the street from the White House. It could easily have been heroin or PCP.

—*President George Bush*

The non-addicted casual or regular user is likely to have a still-intact family, social and work life. These are the users who should have their names published in local papers. They should be subject to drivers' license suspension, employer notification, overnight or weekend detention, eviction from public housing, or forfeiture of the cars they drive while purchasing drugs.

—*Drug Czar William Bennett*

Chapter 1
War Songs

Introduction

The lyrics extolling the drug war have become so embedded in the national psyche that they are almost as familiar as the national anthem. Yet, those lyrics are often rewritten to explain past failures and to reinforce the drug prohibition ethic.

Passed in the regular biennial wave of drug emotion, the Anti-Drug Abuse Act of 1988 came up with a few allegedly new lyrics. One person would be given the job of coordinating all of the anti-drug abuse activity of the federal government and he would be required to submit periodic written strategy reports aimed at making the nation drug free. The official would be called the Director of the Office of National Drug Control Policy (informally, the Drug Czar) and would be responsible for coordinating all drug-control activities. The law required the first plan to be released on September 5, 1989, the second in January 1990, and annual reports thereafter every September.

As we shall see, very little of all of this was actually new — and very few new strategies have emerged.

In this chapter we look at how President Bush explained the first strategy report in his speech involving the infamous bag of crack; how William Bennett, the first Drug Czar, justified the targeting of casual users and how he lambasted the intellectuals who opposed him; and the declaration of partial victory by Mr. Bennett one year after the first plan was released.

The President Tells A White Lie About Crack[*]

Good evening. This is the first time since taking the oath of office that I felt an issue was so important, so threatening that it warranted talking directly with you, the American people. All of us agree that the gravest domestic threat facing our nation today is drugs.

Drugs have strained our faith in our system of justice. Our courts, our prisons, our legal system are stretched to the breaking point. The social costs of drugs are mounting. In short, drugs are sapping our strength as a nation. Turn on the evening news or pick up the morning paper and you'll see what some Americans know just by stepping out their front door: Our most serious problem today is cocaine and, in particular, crack.

Who's responsible? Let me tell you straight out.

Everyone who uses drugs. Everyone who sells drugs. And everyone who looks the other way.

Tonight, I'll tell you how many Americans are using illegal drugs. I will present to you our national strategy to deal with every aspect of this threat. And I will ask you to get involved in what promises to be a very difficult fight.

---
[*] George Bush, Address by the President on National Drug Policy, the Oval Office, Sept. 5, 1989.

This — this is crack cocaine seized a few days ago by Drug Enforcement agents in a park just across the street from the White House. It could easily have been heroin or PCP. It's as innocent-looking as candy, but it's turning our cities into battle zones, and it is murdering our children. Let there be no mistake; this stuff is poison. Some used to call drugs harmless recreation. They're not. Drugs are a real and terribly dangerous threat to our neighborhoods, our friends and our families.

No one among us is out of harm's way. When 4-year-olds play in playgrounds strewn with discarded hypodermic needles and crack vials — it breaks my heart. When cocaine — one of the most deadly and addictive illegal drugs — is available to school kids — school kids — it's an outrage. And when hundreds of thousands of babies are born each year to mothers who use drugs — premature babies born desperately sick — then even the most defenseless among us are at risk.

These are the tragedies behind the statistics. But the numbers also have quite a story to tell. Let me share with you the results of the recently completed Household Survey of the National Institute on Drug Abuse. It compares recent drug use to three years ago. It tells us some good news and some very bad news. First, the good.

As you can see in the chart, in 1985, the government estimated that 23 million Americans were using drugs on a "current" basis — that is, at least once in the preceding month. Last year, that number fell by more than a third. That means almost nine million fewer Americans are casual drug users. Good news.

Because we changed our national attitude toward drugs, casual drug use has declined. We have many to thank: our brave law enforcement officers, religious leaders, teachers, community activists, and leaders of business and labor. We should also thank the media for their exhaustive news and editorial

War Songs

"This — this is crack cocaine..."

AP/Wide World Photo

coverage and for their air time and space for antidrug messages. And finally, I want to thank President and Mrs. Reagan for their leadership. All of these good people told the truth — that drug use is wrong and dangerous.

But as much comfort as we can draw from these dramatic reductions, there is also bad news — very bad news. Roughly eight million people have used cocaine in the past year; almost one million of them used it frequently — once a week or more.

What this means is that, in spite of the fact that overall cocaine use is down, frequent use has almost doubled in the last few years. And that's why habitual cocaine users — especially crack users — are the most pressing, immediate drug problem.

What, then, is our plan? To begin with, I trust the lesson of experience. No single policy will cut it, no matter how glamorous or magical it may sound. To win the war against addictive drugs like crack will take more than just a federal strategy. It will take a national strategy: one that reaches into every school, every workplace, involving every family....

Our weapons in this strategy are the law and criminal justice system, our foreign policy, our treatment systems, and our schools and drug prevention programs. So the basic weapons we need are the ones we already have. What's been lacking is a strategy to effectively use them.

Let me address four of the major elements of our strategy.

First, we are determined to enforce the law, to make our streets and neighborhoods safe. So to start, I'm proposing that we more than double federal assistance to state and local law enforcement. Americans have a right to safety in and around their homes. And we won't have safe neighborhoods unless we're tough on drug criminals — much tougher than we are now. Sometimes that means tougher penalties. But more often it just means punishment that is swift and certain. We've all heard stories about drug dealers who are caught and arrested — again and again — but never punished. Well, here the rules have changed. If you sell drugs, you will be caught. And when you're caught, you will be prosecuted. And once you're convicted, you will do time. Caught. Prosecuted. Punished.

I'm also proposing that we enlarge our criminal justice system across the board — at the local, state and federal levels alike. We need more prisons, more jails, more courts, more prosecutors....
The second element of our strategy looks beyond our borders where the cocaine and crack bought on America's streets is grown and processed. In Colombia alone, cocaine killers have gunned down a leading statesman, murdered almost 200 judges and seven members of their Supreme Court. The besieged governments of the drug-producing countries are fighting back, fighting to break the international drug rings. But you and I agree with the courageous President of Colombia, Virgilio Barco, who said that if Americans use cocaine, then Americans are paying for murder. American cocaine users need to understand that our nation has zero tolerance for casual drug use. We have a responsibility not to leave our brave friends in Colombia to fight alone....

And our message to the drug cartels is this: the rules have changed. We will help any government that wants our help. When requested, we will for the first time make available the appropriate resources of America's armed forces. We will intensify our efforts against drug smugglers on the high seas, in international airspace and at our borders. We will stop the flow of chemicals from the United States used to process drugs. We will pursue and enforce international agreements to track drug money to the front men and financiers. And then we will handcuff these money launderers and jail them — just like any street dealer. And for the drug kingpins, the death penalty.

The third part of our strategy concerns drug treatment. Experts believe that there are two million American drug users who may be able to get off drugs with proper treatment. But right now, only 40 percent of them are actually getting help. This is simply not good enough.

Many people who need treatment won't seek it on their own. And some who do seek it are put on a waiting list. Most programs were set up to deal with heroin addicts, but, today, the major problem is cocaine users. It's time we expand our treatment systems and do a better job of providing services to those who need them....

Fourth, we must stop illegal drug use before it starts. Unfortunately, it begins early — for many kids, before their teens. But it doesn't start the way you might think, from a dealer or an addict hanging around a school playground. More often, our kids first get their drugs free, from friends, or even from older brothers or sisters. Peer pressure spreads drug use. Peer pressure can help stop it....

To start, Congress needs not only to act on this national drug strategy, but also to act on our crime package announced last May: a package to toughen sentences, beef up law enforcement and build new prison space for 24,000 inmates....

First, Get The Casual Users*

Drug Use: Source and Spread

...Drug use usually starts early, in the first few years of adolescence. But notwithstanding popular mythology about shadowy, raincoated pushers corrupting young innocents on school playgrounds, children almost never *purchase* their first drug experience. Generally speaking, drug dealers still make most of their money from known, regular customers, and they still — all things being equal — prefer to avoid the risk of selling their wares to strangers, however young. Similarly, new and novice users themselves are typically reluctant to accept an unfamiliar substance from an unfamiliar face. In fact, young people rarely make any independent effort to seek out drugs for the first time. They don't have to; use ordinarily begins through simple personal contact with other users. Where drugs are concerned, as with so much else, young people respond most immediately and directly to the blandishments of peer pressure. And so first use invariably involves the free and enthusiastic offer of a drug by a friend.

This friend — or "carrier," in epidemiological terms — is seldom a hard-core addict. In the terminal stage of an uninterrupted drug use career, the addict is almost completely present-minded — preoccupied with finding and taking his drug; other planning and organizational skills have largely deserted him. He very often cannot maintain anything resembling a normal family or work life. Some addicts may attempt to become dealers to earn money, but most fail at this work, too, since they lack sufficient self-control to avoid consuming their own sales inventory. What's more, an addict's active enthusiasm for his drug's euphoric high or soothing low tends significantly to recede over time; for biochemical reasons, that high or low becomes increasingly difficult to reproduce (except at risk of a lethal overdose), and drug taking becomes a mostly defensive effort to head off the unpleasant psychological effects of a "crash" — or the intensely painful physical effects of actual withdrawal.

In short, the bottomed-out addict is a mess. He makes the worst possible advertisement for new drug use. And he is not likely to have much remaining peer contact with non-users in any case, as he isolates himself in the world of addicts and dealers necessary to maintain his habit. Simply put, a true addict's drug use is not very contagious.

The non-addicted casual or regular user, however, is a very different story. He is likely to have a still-intact family, social and work life. He is likely still to "enjoy" his drug for the pleasure it offers. And he is thus much more willing and able to proselytize his drug use — by action or example — among his remaining non-user peers, friends and acquaintances. A non-addict's drug use, in other words, is *highly* contagious. And casual or regular use — whether ongoing or brand new — may always lead to addiction; again, we have no accurate way to predict its eventual trajectory.

These facts about drug use phenomenology are both a problem and an advantage for any intelligent national drug control campaign. Unfortunately, they mean that those specifically addict-directed efforts of law enforcement and treatment — though urgently required for neighborhood safety and reasons of simple compassion — will remain difficult, time-consuming, and labor in-

---

* Office of National Drug Control Policy, *National Drug Control Strategy*, Government Printing Office, 1989, p.10.

tensive, and will promise to reduce the number of American drug users only, for the most part, on a one-by-one, case-by-case basis. They also mean that non-addicted casual and regular use remains a grave issue of national concern, despite NIDA's report of recent dramatic declines in its prevalence. Non-addicted users still comprise the vast bulk of our drug-involved population. There are many millions of them. And each represents a potential agent of infection for the non-users in his personal ambit.

But there is good news, too. Though compared to addiction, non-addicted drug behavior is the more common and contagious form, it is also more susceptible to change and improvement. The same general techniques employed to slow and mixed effect with addicts may achieve markedly better results with non-addicts. Casual and regular drug users are much more easily induced to enter treatment, for example, and they are much more likely to reduce or cease their use as a result of it.

In fact, all the basic mechanisms we use against illegal drugs — to raise their price; to restrict their availability; to intensify legal and social sanctions for their sale, purchase, and use; and to otherwise depress general demand for them — have a more immediate and positive behavioral effect on non-addicts than on addicts. And in the search for long-term solutions to epidemic drug use, this fact works to our benefit. Any additional short-term reduction in the number of American casual or regular drug users will be a good in itself, of course. But because it is their kind of drug use that is most contagious, any further reduction in the non-addicted drug user population will also promise still greater future reductions in the number of Americans who are recruited to join their dangerous ranks....

Criminal Sanctions

Making streets safer and drug users more accountable for their actions requires the criminal justice system to expand and reform in an unprecedented way. Effective street-level enforcement means dramatically increasing the number of drug offenders arrested. But unless there is a system ready to absorb them, drug control will end at the police station.

A true addict's drug use is not very contagious.

Expansion does not merely mean more police or more prisons (though it surely requires both). It means enlarging the system as a whole so that drug offenders can be dealt with swiftly, justly and efficiently through every step of the judicial and correctional process. Further necessary expansion efforts must not perpetuate imbalances in our present system. Again, a large police force may be able to double the number of drug-related arrests it makes, but unless there is a sufficient number of jails, prosecutors, judges, courtrooms, prisons, and administrative staff, a point of diminishing returns is soon reached: more arrests mean less thorough and effective punishment.

If state and local officials wish to expand their capacity to prosecute and sentence drug offenders they must broaden their notions of what constitutes punishment. In many jurisdictions, the choice of criminal sanctions is between prison or nothing at all. Dealers involved in large-scale drug traffic and violent predatory crime are obvious candidates for prison sentences that will both take them off the streets for significant periods of time and deter other potential offenders. Such sentences put a strain on the system, but the demands of justice and domestic security require them.

Other types of offenders, however, can be dealt with in more efficient and often less expensive ways. Military-style boot camps, with their rigorous regimes and austere conditions, bring a sense of order and discipline to the lives of youthful, non-violent first-time offenders, and perhaps serve as a deterrent against future crimes. Halfway houses and strictly supervised addiction recovery programs can meet the demands of offenders who require treatment. A number of states have successfully experimented with various house arrest programs that keep an offender incapacitated at his own expense. "Casual" users who maintain a job and a steady income should face stiff fines — much stiffer than they do now — and, where appropriate, property forfeiture. The 1988 Anti-Drug Abuse Act further broadens the array of penalties a judge has at his disposal by providing courts with the power to deny or withhold certain federal benefits from convicted drug offenders. The Administration will encourage the regular application of that provision to ensure that it becomes a more widely used tool for penalizing drug use.

These are the sorts of alternative sanctions that the criminal justice system must explore if it is successfully going to deter and contain drug use. But such measures can be — and must be — complemented by a host of less formal sanctions aimed specifically at those first-time and occasional users who, because their activities are too often viewed as relatively inconsequential, now avoid any penalty whatsoever. These are the users who should have their names published in local papers. They should be subject to drivers' license suspension, employer notification, overnight or weekend detention, eviction from public housing, or forfeiture of the cars they drive while purchasing drugs. Whatever the extent of their offense, if they use drugs they should be held accountable.

Young offenders in particular must be confronted with penalties that both deter them from future drug use and embarrass them among their peers. Today, many young drug offenders boast about their lenient treatment in the hands of the authorities and wear it as a badge of pride; corrections officials must make sure that when juveniles are caught using or selling drugs, their punishment becomes a source of shame. We need a mix of sanctions for juvenile drug use that includes school suspension, parental notification, and postponement of driver's license eligibility, and extends to weekends of "community service" that involve arduous and unenviable public chores.

Other aspects of our state criminal justice systems also need reform. Our probation systems provide a vivid example of the need for more accountability. In many jurisdictions, the probation system is so overcrowded and so loosely managed that it can barely be said to exist in any meaningful sense. Offenders who violate the conditions of probation often go unpunished, remaining at liberty until they are arrested again for yet another drug offense. Probation, like parole, court-supervised treatment, and some release programs, should be tied to a regular and rigorous program of drug testing in order to coerce offenders to abstain from drugs while integrating them back into the community. Such programs make prison space available for those drug offenders we cannot safely return to the streets. But unless they rigidly enforce drug abstinence under the threat of incarceration, these efforts lose their teeth. Drug tests should be a part of every stage of the criminal justice process — at the time of arrest and throughout the period of probation or incarceration, and parole — because they are the most effective way of keeping offenders off drugs both in and out of detention.

The many available alternatives to incarceration should not lead us to conclude that states and localities don't need more prisons and jails. They do. And they need them immediately and urgently. Most state prisons are already operating far above their designed capacity: the most recent surveys show Pennsylvania's correctional facilities operating at 138 percent capacity; Oklahoma at 142 percent; and Massachusetts at 173 percent. During 1986, 16 percent of New Jersey's prison population had to be housed in local jails due to overcrowding in state facilities. And, most notoriously, many states have been forced under court order to release prisoners before their terms have been served whenever a court-established prison population limit has been exceeded.

Recognizing the dimensions of this crisis, several states have embarked on ambitious plans to expand the capacity of their correctional facilities. Those plans should be carried out without delay, and the Administration will further this expansion by providing funds and technical assistance for the design and planning of other new and enlarged state prisons. The task of building them, however, remains with state governments, who poorly serve their constituents when prison construction is stalled or resisted.

So, clearly, effective local drug enforcement very much depends on the creation of more prison space.

The Drug Czar Tells Off The Intellectuals[*]

...The issue I want to address is our national drug policy and the intellectuals. Unfortunately, the issue is a little one-sided. There is a very great deal to say about our national drug policy, but much less to say about the intellectuals — except that by and large, they're against it. Why they should be against it is an interesting question, perhaps more a social-psychological question than a properly intellectual one. But whatever the reasons, I'm sorry to say that on properly intellectual grounds the arguments mustered against our current drug policy by America's intellectuals make for very thin gruel indeed.

I should point out, however, that in the fields of medical and scientific research, there is indeed serious and valuable drug-related work going on. But in the great public policy debate over drugs, the academic and intellectual communities have by and large had little to contribute, and little of that has been genuinely useful or for that matter mentally distinguished.

The field of national drug policy is wide open for serious research and serious thinking on both the theoretical and the practical levels; treatment and prevention; education; law enforcement and the criminal-justice system; the proper role of the federal government versus state and local jurisdictions; international diplomacy and foreign intelligence — these are only a few of the areas in which complex questions of policy and politics need to be addressed and resolved if our national drug strategy is to be successful. But apart from a handful of exceptions — including Mark Moore and Mark Kleiman here at the Kennedy School, and

---

[*] William J. Bennett, "Drug Policy and the Intellectuals," speech, Kennedy School of Government, Harvard University, Dec. 11, 1989.

Harvard's own, or ex-own, James Q. Wilson — on most of these issues the country's major ideas factories have not just shut down, they've hardly even tooled up.

It's not that most intellectuals are indifferent to the drug issue, though there may be some of that, too. Rather, they seem complacent and incurious. They've made up their minds, and they don't want to be bothered with further information or analysis, further discussion or debate, especially when it comes from Washington. What I read in the opinion columns of my newspaper or in my monthly magazine or what I hear from the resident intellectual on my favorite television talk show is something like a developing intellectual consensus on the drug question. That consensus holds one or both of these propositions to be self-evident: (a) *that the drug problem in America is absurdly simple, and easily solved; and b) that the drug problem in America is a lost cause.*

As it happens, each of these apparently contradictory propositions is false. As it also happens, both are disputed by the *real* experts on drugs in the United States — and there are many such experts, though not the kind the media like to focus on. And both are disbelieved by the American people, whose experience tells them, emphatically, otherwise.

The consensus has a political dimension, which helps account for its seemingly divergent aspect. In some quarters of the far Right there is a tendency to assert that the drug problem is essentially a problem of the inner city, and therefore that what it calls for, essentially, is quarantine. "If those people want to kill themselves off with drugs, let them kill themselves off with drugs," would be a crude but not too inaccurate way of summarizing this position. But this position has relatively few adherents. On the Left, it is something else, something much more prevalent. There we see whole cadres of social scientists, abetted by whole armies of social workers, who seem to take it as catechism that the problem facing us isn't drugs at all, it's poverty, or racism, or some other equally large and intractable social phenomenon. If we want to eliminate the drug problem, these people say, we must first eliminate the "root causes" of drugs, a hopelessly daunting task at which, however, they also happen to make their living. Twenty-five years ago, no one would have suggested that we must first address the root causes of racism before fighting segregation. We fought it, quite correctly, by passing laws against unacceptable conduct. The causes of racism was an interesting question, but the moral imperative was to end it as soon as possible and by all reasonable means: education, prevention, the media, and not least of all, the law. So too with drugs.

What unites these two views of the drug problem from opposite sides of the political spectrum is that they issue, inevitably, in a policy of neglect. To me that is a scandalous position, intellectually as well as morally scandalous. For I believe, along with those I have named as the real experts on drugs, and along with most Americans, that the drug problem is not easy but difficult — very difficult in some respects. But at the same time, and again along with those same experts and with the American people, I believe it is not a lost cause but a solvable one. I will return to this theme, but let me pause here to note one specific issue on which the Left/Right consensus has lately come to rest; a position around which it has been attempting to build national sentiment. That position is legalization.

It is indeed bizarre to see the likes of Anthony Lewis and William F. Buckley lining up on the same side of an issue; but such is the perversity that the so-called legalization debate engenders. To call it a "debate," though, suggests that the arguments in *favor* of drug legalization are rigorous, substantial, and serious. They are not. They are, at bottom, a series of superficial and even disingenuous ideas that more sober minds recognize as a recipe for a public policy disaster. Let me explain.

Most conversations about legalization begin with the notion of "taking the profit out of the drug business." But has anyone bothered to examine carefully how the drug business works? As a recent *New York Times* article vividly described, instances of drug dealers actually earning huge sums of money are relatively rare. There are some who do, of course, but most people in the crack business are the low-level "runners" who do not make much money at all. Many of them work as prostitutes or small-time criminals to supplement their drug earnings. True, a lot of naive kids are lured into the drug world by visions of a life filled with big money and fast cars. That's what they think the good life holds for them. But the reality is far different. Many dealers, in the long run, wind up smoking more crack than they sell. Their business becomes a form of slavery: long hours, dangerous work, small pay, and, as *The Times* pointed out, no health benefits either. In many cases, steady work at McDonald's over time would in fact be a step *up* the income scale for these kids. What does straighten them out, it seems, is not a higher minimum wage, or less stringent laws, but the dawning realization that dealing drugs invariably leads to murder or to prison. And that's exactly why we have drug laws — to make drug use a wholly unattractive choice.

Legalization, on the other hand, removes that incentive to stay away from a life of drugs. Let's be honest, there are some people who are going to smoke crack whether it is legal or illegal. But by keeping it illegal, we maintain the criminal sanctions that persuade most people that the good life cannot be reached by dealing drugs.

The big lie behind every call for legalization is that making drugs legally available would "solve" the drug problem. But has anyone actually thought about what that kind of legalized regime would look like? Would crack be legal? How about PCP? Or smokeable heroin? Or ice? Would they all be stocked at the local convenience store, perhaps just a few blocks from an elementary school? And how much would they cost? If we taxed drugs and made them expensive, we would still have the black market and crime problems that we have today if we sold them cheap to eliminate the black market cocaine at, say, $10 a gram — then we would succeed in making a daily dose of cocaine well within the allowance budget of most sixth-graders. When pressed, the advocates of legalization like to sound courageous by proposing that we begin by legalizing marijuana. But they have absolutely nothing to say on the tough questions of controlling other, more powerful drugs, and how they would be regulated.

As far as marijuana is concerned, let me say this: I didn't have to become drug czar to be opposed to legalized marijuana. As Secretary of Education I realized that, given the state of American education, the last thing we needed was a policy that made widely available a substance that impairs memory, concentration and attention span; why in God's name foster the use of a drug that makes you stupid?

> *I didn't have to become drug czar to be opposed to legalized marijuana.*

Now what would happen if drugs were suddenly made legal? Legalization advocates deny that the amount of drug use would be affected. I would argue that if drugs are easier to obtain, drug use will soar. In fact, we have just undergone a kind of cruel national experiment in which drugs became cheap and widely available: that experiment is called the crack epidemic. When powder cocaine was expensive and hard to get, it was found almost exclusively in the circles of the rich, the famous, or the privileged. Only when cocaine was dumped into the country, and a $3 vial of crack could be bought on street corners did we see cocaine use skyrocket this time largely among the poor and disadvantaged. The lesson is clear: if you're in favor of drugs being sold in stores like aspirin, you're in favor of boom times for drug users and drug addicts. With legalization, drug use will go up, way up.

When drug use rises, who benefits and who pays? Legalization advocates think that the cost of enforcing drug laws is too great. But the real question — the question they never ask — is what does it cost not to enforce those laws. The price that American society would have to pay for legalized drugs, I submit, would be intolerably high. We would have more drug-related accidents at work, on the highways, and in the airways. We would have even bigger losses in worker productivity. Our hospitals would be filled with drug emergencies. We would have more school kids on dope, and that means more dropouts. More pregnant women would buy legal cocaine, and then deliver tiny, premature infants. I've seen them in hospitals across the country. It's a horrid form of child abuse, and under a legalization scheme, we will have a lot more of it. For those women and those babies, crack has the same effect whether it's legal or not. Now, if you add to that the costs of treatment, social welfare, and insurance, you've got the price of legalization. So I ask you again, who benefits, who pays?

What about crime? To listen to legalization advocates, one might think that street crime would disappear with the repeal of our drug laws. They haven't done their homework. Our best research indicates that most drug criminals were into crime well before they got into drugs. Making drugs legal would just be a way of subsidizing their habit. They would continue to rob and steal to pay for food, for clothes, for entertainment. And they would carry on with their drug trafficking by undercutting the legalized price of drugs and catering to teenagers, who, I assume, would be nominally restricted from buying drugs at the corner store.

All this should be old news to people who understand one clear lesson of prohibition. When we had laws against alcohol, there was less consumption of alcohol, less alcohol-related disease, fewer drunken brawls, and a lot less public drunkenness. And contrary to myth, there is no evidence that Prohibition caused big increases in crime. No one is suggesting that we go back to Prohibition. But at least we should admit that legalized alcohol, which is responsible for some 100,000 deaths a year, is hardly a model for drug policy. As Charles Krauthammer has pointed out, the question is not which is worse, alcohol or drugs. The question is can we accept both legalized alcohol *and* legalized drugs? The answer is no.

So it seems to me that on the merits of their arguments, the legalizers have no case at all. But there is another, crucial point I want to make on this subject, unrelated to costs or benefits. Drug use — especially heavy drug use — destroys human character. It destroys dignity and autonomy, it burns away the sense of responsibility, it subverts productivity, it makes a mockery of virtue. As our Founders would surely recognize, a citizenry that is perpetually in a drug-induced haze doesn't bode well for the future of self-government. Libertarians don't like to hear this, but it is a truth that everyone knows who has seen drug addiction up close. And don't listen to people who say drug users are only hurting themselves: they hurt parents, they destroy families, they ruin friendships. And let me remind this audience, here at a great university, that drugs are a threat to the life of the mind; anyone who values that life should have nothing but contempt for drugs. Learned institutions should regard drugs as the plague.

That's why I find the surrender of many of America's intellectuals to arguments for drug legalization so odd and so scandalous. For the past three months, I have been traveling the country, visiting drug-ridden neighborhoods, seeing treatment and prevention programs in action, talking to teachers, cops, parents, kids. These, it seems, are the real drug experts — they've witnessed the problem first hand. But unlike some prominent residents of Princeton, Madison, Cambridge or Palo Alto, they refuse to surrender. They are in the community, reclaiming their neighborhoods, working with police, setting up community activities, getting addicts into treatment, saving their children.

Too many American intellectuals don't know about this and seem not to want to know. Their hostility to the national war on drugs is, I think, partly rooted in a general hostility to law enforcement and criminal justice. That's why they take refuge in pseudo-solutions like legalization, which stress only the treatment side of the problem. Whenever discussion turns to the need for more police and stronger penalties, they cry that our constitutional liberties are in jeopardy. Well, yes, they are in jeopardy, but not from drug *policy:* on this score, the guardians of our Constitution can sleep easy. Constitutional liberties are in jeopardy, instead, from drugs themselves, which every day scorch the earth of our common freedom. Yes, sometimes cops go too far, and when they do they should be held accountable. But these excursions from the law are the exception. Meanwhile drug dealers violate our rights everyday as a rule, as a norm, as their *modus operandi.* Why can't our civil libertarians see that?

When we are not being told by critics that law enforcement threatens our liberties, we are being told that it won't work. Let me tell you that law enforcement does work and why it must work. Several weeks ago I was in Wichita, Kansas, talking to a teenage boy who was now in his fourth treatment program. Every time he had finished a previous round of treatment, he found himself back on the streets, surrounded by the same cheap dope and tough hustlers who had gotten him started in the first place. He was tempted, he was pressured, and he gave in. Virtually any expert on drug treatment will tell you that, for most people, no therapy in the world can fight temptation on that scale. As long as drugs are found on any street corner, no amount of treatment, no amount of education can finally stand against them. Yes, we need drug treatment and drug education. But drug treatment and drug education need law enforcement. And that's why our strategy calls for a bigger criminal justice system: as a form of drug *prevention.*

To the Americans who are waging the drug war

> *Contrary to myth, there is no evidence that Prohibition caused big increases in crime.*

in their own front yards every day, this is nothing new, nothing startling. In the San Jose section of Albuquerque, New Mexico, just two weeks ago, I spoke to Rudy Chavez and Jack Candelarla, and police chief Sam Baca. They had wanted to start a youth center that would keep their kids safe from the depredations of the street. Somehow it never worked — until together they set up a police station right in the heart of drug-dealing territory. Then it worked. Together with the cops, the law-abiding residents cleared the area, and made it safe for them and their children to walk outside their homes. The youth center began to thrive.

Scenes like this are being played out all across the country. I've seen them in Tulsa, Dallas, Tampa, Omaha, Des Moines, Seattle, New York. Americans — many of them poor, black or Hispanic have figured out what the armchair critics haven't. Drugs may threaten to destroy their neighborhoods, but *they* refuse to stand by and let it happen. *They* have discovered that it is possible not only to fight back, but to win. In some elite circles, the talk may be only of the sad state of the helpless and the hopeless, but while these circles talk on, the helpless and the hopeless themselves are carrying out a national drug policy. They are fighting back.

When I think of these scenes I'm reminded of what John Jacob, president of the Urban League, said recently: drugs are destroying more black families than poverty ever did. And I'm thankful that many of these poor families have the courage to fight drugs now, rather than declaring themselves passive victims of root causes.

America's intellectuals — and here I think particularly of liberal intellectuals — have spent much of the last nine years decrying the social programs of two Republican administrations in the name of the defenseless poor. But today, on the one outstanding issue that disproportionately hurts the poor — that is wiping out many of the poor — where are the liberal intellectuals to be found? They are on the editorial and op-ed pages, and in magazines like this month's *Harper's*, telling us with an ignorant sneer that our drug policy won't work. Many universities, too, which have been quick to take on the challenges of sexism, racism and ethnocentrism, seem content on the drug issue to wag a finger at us, or to point it mindlessly at American society in general. In public policy schools, there is no shortage of arms control scholars. Isn't it time we had more drug control scholars?

The current situation won't do. The failure to get serious about the drug issue is, I think, a failure of civic courage — the kind of courage shown by many who have been among the main victims of the drug scourge. But it betokens as well a betrayal of the self-declared mission of intellectuals as the bearers of society's conscience. There may be reasons for this reluctance, this hostility, this failure. But I would remind you that not all crusades led by the U.S. government, enjoying broad popular support, are brutish, corrupt and sinister. What is brutish, corrupt, and sinister is the murder and mayhem being committed in our cities' streets. One would think that a little more concern and serious thought would come from those who claim to care so deeply about America's problems.

So I stand here this afternoon with a simple message for America's pundits and academic cynics: get serious about drug policy. We are grappling with complicated, stubborn policy issues, and I encourage you to join us. Tough work lies ahead, and we need serious minds to focus on how we should use the tools that we have in the most effective way.

I came to this job with realistic expectations. I am not promising a drug-free America by next week, or even by next year. But that doesn't mean that success is out of reach. Success will come — I've seen a lot of it already — in slow, careful steps. Its enemies are timidity, petulance, false expectations. But its three greatest foes remain surrender, despair and neglect. So, for the sake of their fellow citizens, I invite America's deep thinkers to get with the program, or at the very least, to get in the game.

Last Year's Hopeless Cause Is This Year's Opportunity For Victory*

One year ago today, President Bush announced his first National Drug Control Strategy. In support of that strategy, federal spending on drugs has already jumped 50 percent since the beginning of this Administration. And the second funding phase of the President's strategy, due to begin the first of next month pending Congressional approval, would boost federal drug spending still further — to more than $10.6 billion, almost 70 percent higher than last year's level.

More money, attention, thinking, research, legislative and government action, cooperative effort, and manpower are now being applied to the drug problem than at any time in American history. In every relevant area, more work is now being done than ever before: against drug production and trafficking overseas; against smuggling at our borders; against drug crime in our streets and communities; against the medical problems of addiction; and against the encroachment of drugs into our schools and families and neighborhoods.

The logical question to ask today is: Where has this work left us? What is the status of the drug war, one year later?

It helps to remember where we were when we began. When I was confirmed for this job, most commentators — friends and critics, both — described the work ahead in almost apocalyptic terms. The drug crisis was "hopeless," "beyond control," "getting worse with no end in sight." It's fair to say that this was not simply "conventional wisdom" in the *Newsweek* sense of the term. It was backed up by almost every conceivable objective analysis and available statistic.

Drug cartels in Latin America appeared invincible; their profits and power and production were at a peak. Unprecedented amounts of cocaine and other drugs were flowing through our streets, at historically low prices and historically high purity. Drug-related medical emergencies had doubled, tripled, and quadrupled through the last years of the 1980s — every few months, without a break.

Truth be told, I was never persuaded that the drug problem was beyond control, nor was the President when he promised that "this scourge will stop." Late last summer, in fact, the National Institute on Drug Abuse released results of a survey that demonstrated actual declines in overall American drug use beginning as early as 1985. But even last summer, the thorniest aspects of the drug problem — overseas production, smuggling, wholesale domestic marketing, numbers of addicts and overdoses — all seemed still to be intensifying, and predictions flew that nothing the President contemplated doing could or would have any meaningful effect.

Since last summer, however, almost every piece of news and hard evidence we've seen — including those concerning the toughest specific drug

---

* Statement of Director William J. Bennett, Office of National Drug Control Policy, Press Conference on the Status of the Drug War in connection with the release of *Leading Drug Indicators*, Washington, D.C., Sept. 5, 1990.

problems — has told a different story. I won't bother reviewing this material in much detail right now. The latest results of our leading statistical indicators and research measures are collected and analyzed in the white paper you've been given, and many of you have been reporting this news piecemeal for many months.

Cartel operations in Latin America have been significantly disrupted. A number of major anti-smuggling victories have recently been achieved. For the first time in many, many years, wholesale cocaine prices in major metropolitan areas have risen quite sharply — doubled in some areas — and purity is down, indicating supply shortages. And hospital emergency room data — widely considered the best available indicator of trends in addictive behavior — seem finally to be showing measurable declines nationwide.

In short, last year's hopeless cause is this year's revived opportunity for victory. I think a prudent and cautious judgment on our present circumstances would be that the drug problem — in general, nationwide — is no longer getting worse, and in some very significant respects is now getting better.

Credit for progress made so far should not be at issue, and is widely shared. In broad brush, the President's Drug Strategy has enjoyed bipartisan political and funding support in Congress. Our strategy has also been joined and complemented by comprehensive and necessary state and local efforts across the country. And I would underscore once again, above all, that American public opinion has turned hard against drug use in any form, and in favor, instead, of concerted and consistent national effort toward further success in a continued drug war. Just yesterday, the Partnership for a Drug Free America released new survey research that confirms what we've already seen in our High School Senior Survey and other indicators: the turn away from drugs in American attitudes and behavior — especially among young people.

Perseverance — organized government and private-sector effort — will be the key. And easy satisfaction is grossly premature. The drug problem is still far too big. Too many communities, families, and individuals still suffer the terrible consequences of drug use and drug crime. The drug situation in too many neighborhoods has not improved, and now is precisely *not* the time to trim sails, reduce effort, or cut funding. The evidence of the past year suggests that progress is possible — not that it is inevitable. And so we will be looking for continued national and international support of our work. I believe we will find it. And I believe it will, before long, make a definitive difference.

I have to tell you that it seems to me that the conceptual base of the current program is flawed and the program is not likely to work.

—George P. Shultz

Imagine if every time you took an aspirin, you didn't know if it was 5 milligrams or 500 milligrams.

—Ethan Nadelmann

Chapter 2

The Drug War Is Fundamentally Unsound

Introduction

The recent escalation in punitive drug policies has led to a growing number of drug war dissenters. Contrary to Mr. Bennett's Harvard speech, such opposition is no longer merely the province of intellectuals and liberals. Strong dissent has come from politicians and from the ranks of the drug warriors themselves.

Most of the remainder of this book is devoted to demonstrating that these dissenters are correct and that many of the passionate and well-intentioned theories of the president, the drug czar, and multitudes of experts are unsound and destructive. In this chapter, we seek to deal with fundamental arguments that raise serious questions about the facts and ideas that lie at the very base of current dominant drug-control strategies.

This chapter begins with the viewpoint of one of the most important people to join the ranks of the drug war dissenters, former Secretary of State George Shultz. In 1984 while serving under the Reagan Administration, Mr. Shultz advanced, much as President Bush did in 1989, a coordinated five-part plan to fight the drug problem. That same year Mr. Shultz stated: "We are confronting the threat and making significant progress." Five years later and coincidentally, the same year Bush announced his drug control strategy, Mr. Shultz went public with his belief that not only were we not making significant progress in controlling drugs, but drug prohibition was and is fundamentally flawed.

The Conceptual Base Of Drug Prohibition Is Flawed*

I was struck a couple of years ago by the drug-interdiction effort in the Bahamas. We had intercepted during the year an estimated $5 billion street value of cocaine. I don't know how much got through. Nobody has any credible estimate. The total gross national product of the Bahamas is probably somewhere between $1-2 billion. So you get an idea of the leverage there and elsewhere that our market for drugs has brought about.

I welcome the emphasis that is now being put on the drug problem. The efforts —
- to get to the people who are addicted, try to rehabilitate them (if they cannot be rehabilitated, at least contain them);
- to educate people;
- to strongly discourage use of drugs by people who are casual users and first users;
- to stop this process among the young
    — are extremely important.

But I have to tell you that it seems to me that the conceptual base of the current program is flawed and the program is not likely to work. The conceptual base — a criminal justice approach — is the same that I have worked through before, in the Nixon administration when I was budget director and secretary of the Treasury with jurisdiction over Customs. We designed a comprehensive program, and we worked hard on it. In the Reagan administration we designed a comprehensive program; we worked very hard on it. Our international efforts were far greater than ever before. You're looking at a guy whose motorcade was attacked in Bolivia by drug terrorists, so I'm personally a veteran of this war.

What we have before us now is essentially the same program but with more resources plowed into all the enforcement and control efforts. These efforts wind up creating a market where the price vastly exceeds the cost. With these incentives, demand creates its own supply and a criminal network along with it. It seems to me we're not really going to get anywhere until we can take the criminality out of the drug business and the incentives for criminality out of it. Frankly, the only way I can think of to accomplish this is to make it possible for addicts to buy drugs at some regulated place at a price that approximates their cost. When you do that you wipe out the criminal incentives, including I might say, the incentive that the drug pushers have to go around and get kids addicted, so that they create a market for themselves. They won't have that incentive because they won't have that market.

---

* George P. Shultz, Adapted from an informal talk on Oct. 7, 1989, by the former Secretary of State (under President Reagan) and Secretary of the Treasury (under President Nixon) to an alumni gathering at Stanford Business School. A version of this talk appeared in *The Drug Policy Letter*, November/December 1989, p.3.

So I think the conceptual base needs to be thought out in a different way. If I am catching your attention, then read a bold and informative article in this September's issue of *Science* by Ethan Nadelmann on this subject. We need at least to consider and examine forms of controlled legalization of drugs.

I find it very difficult to say that. Sometimes at a reception or cocktail party I advance these views and people head for somebody else. They don't even want to talk to you. I know that I'm shouting into the breeze here as far as what we're doing now. But I feel that if somebody doesn't get up and start talking about this now, the next time around, when we have the next start of these programs, it will still be true that everyone is scared to talk about it. No politician wants to say what I just said, not for a minute.

The Solution Becomes The Problem*

Fundamentally, we need to consider legalization because the criminal justice approaches of the past have failed, and those of the present and future are likewise largely doomed to failure. This has nothing to do with squabbles with law enforcement agencies, or corruption in Third World countries, or whether or not we have a Drug Czar, or whether or not his name is William Bennett. Rather, it reflects the nature of the commodity, the nature of the market, and the lucrativeness of it all.

Criminal justice approaches have not only failed to solve the problem, they have made matters far worse. Most of what people identify as part and parcel of the drug problem are in fact the result of drug prohibition, just as when people talked about the alcohol problem 60 years ago, most of what they identified were the results of alcohol prohibition.

Let's look very quickly at some of these approaches: international enforcement, interdiction, and domestic enforcement (of high-level traffickers as well as their street-level sellers).

Can we keep drugs from being exported to the United States? No, we can't. These drugs can be grown virtually everywhere, and to try preventing export from any one place results in "push down, pop up." Push down heroin coming out of Turkey, and it pops up in Mexico. Push it down in Mexico, and it pops up in Southeast Asia. Push down there and it comes from Southwest Asia. We have pushed down in so many places that it pops up virtually everywhere now. The United States is a multi-source heroin-importing country. The same is true with regard to marijuana and cocaine.

Another reason is that international law enforcement has but a tiny effect on the ultimate domestic price of drugs. Even if you double, triple, or quadruple the foreign price, it has almost no impact on the streets.

And finally, this is a business from which hundreds of thousands, if not millions, of people in Latin America and Asia are earning a very good living. The drugs are usually indigenous to their areas — opium in parts of Asia, for example, cannabis in Jamaica and parts of Africa, and coca that goes back thousands of years in Latin America — and cause few local problems. Moreover, they appear to bring in much more money than any alternative would provide.

Thus if you spray Latin America peasants' drug crops and try to persuade them to grow macadamia nuts instead, they respond by hiding their crops. And if you go down there, as William Bennett's people have done, and say, "Don't you understand how immoral you are being? You are poisoning

---

* Ethan Nadelmann, "Should Some Illegal Drugs Be Legalized?" *Issues in Science and Technology*, Summer 1990, p. 43.

the youth of America," the peasants are unimpressed. "Don't lecture us about morality," they say. "Our moral obligation is to do the best we can for ourselves, our families, and our communities. If that means selling this drug, which is native to our country anyway, then so be it." And they might well add another point: "While you Nortamericanos are talking to us about morality, your trade representatives are going around the world shoving down tariff barriers so that your farmers can export more tobacco. Are you so much on a moral high ground?"

Costs of Enforcement

What about interdiction? I don't know anybody who believes anymore that it makes a difference. Drugs can come into the country in any which way, and in small amounts — arriving by boat, plane, and car, hidden in flowers, chocolates, and statues. Looking for drugs is like looking for a needle in a haystack.

Interdiction has worked somewhat with respect to marijuana. But the success has proven counterproductive. The Coast Guard found that as it realized a few successes in interdicting marijuana, the drug lords seemed to be switching to cocaine. And why not? It is less bulky, less smelly, more compact and more lucrative. This pretty much parallels the responses of bootleggers during Prohibition, who switched from beer to hard liquor.

The other consequence of the marijuana interdiction "success" was to transform the country into perhaps the number-one producer of marijuana in the world. Some people think that the United States now produces the world's best marijuana, in fact, and that if the dollar were to drop lower, we would become a major exporter of marijuana.

What about domestic enforcement? If you go after the big traffickers — the people who most profitably and egregiously violate the drug laws — it makes little difference. Every time you arrest Mr. Number One, there is Mr. Number Two to fill his shoes. Indeed, it is often from Number Two that the police get the information to arrest Number One.

Similarly, with street-level enforcement, you can clean up some neighborhoods — at least for a while — but can you, for very long, keep drugs out of the hands of people who really want them? You have the same push-down, pop-up effect on the streets as there is on the global scale. Push down on 102nd Street and guess what pops up on 104th Street?

Now, law enforcement does accomplish something. It reduces availability a little, increases the price, and deters some people. But the costs and other negative consequences of continuing to focus on criminal justice end up making a lot of things much worse.

Consider the direct costs. In 1987, we spent something like $10 billion just enforcing drug laws. It may be close to $20 billion this year. Drug-law violators — and here I am not talking about drug-related crimes but drug-law violations such as possession, dealing, distribution, and manufacturing — are the number one cause of imprisonment in New York state prisons, in Florida prisons as well. They accounted for about 40 percent of all felony indictments in New York City Courts last year and for 52 percent in Washington, D.C. — quadruple what it was four years ago.

When cops say that the urban criminal justice system is becoming synonymous with drug enforcement systems, they are increasingly correct. In the federal prisons, 40 percent of the people there are there on drug-law violations; between three-quarters of a million and a million people were arrested last year on drug charges. We now have one million people behind bars in the United

The Drug War is Fundamentally Unsound

States, practically double what the number was 10 years ago. And a rapidly rising percentage of them are there for violating drug laws.

Living Dangerously

But although the direct costs are enormous, the indirect costs are far more severe. Drug prohibition is responsible for all sorts of violence and crime — from street-level theft to high-level corruption — that seemingly have little to do with drugs *per se.*

Consider this: tobacco is at least as addictive as heroin and cocaine, but have you ever been worried about being mugged by a tobacco addict? Of course not, because it is cheap — too cheap, in my view. Heroin and cocaine cost much more to buy, even though they don't cost much more to produce. They are expensive because they are illegal, and addicts are obliged to raise the income, typically illegally, to pay for them. That would change under a maintenance system, or other forms of drug legalization, in which prices were lower.

And the systematic violence of the drug-crime connection would also change. There would be far less need for illicit drug traffickers, and thus far fewer occasions for them to settle disputes among themselves by shooting one another, shooting cops and innocent bystanders (including kids) along the way.

Another cost, not much talked about, is the impact of prohibition on drug quality. Simply stated, drugs are more dangerous because they are illegal. Just as tens of thousands of people died or were blinded or poisoned by bad bootleg liquor 60 years ago, perhaps the majority of overdose deaths today are the result of drug prohibition.

Ordinarily, heroin does not kill. It addicts people and makes them constipated. But people overdose because they don't know what they're getting; they don't know if the heroin is 1 percent or 40 percent, or if it is cut with bad stuff, or if it is heroin at all — it may be a synthetic opiate or an amphetamine-type substance.

Just imagine if every time you picked up a bottle of wine, you didn't know whether it was 8 percent alcohol or 80 percent alcohol, or whether it was ethyl alcohol or methyl alcohol. Imagine if every time you took an aspirin, you didn't know if it was 5 milligrams or 500 milligrams.

Life would be a little more interesting, and also a little more dangerous. Fewer people might take those drugs, but more would get sick and die. That is exactly what is happening today with the illicit drug market. Nothing resembling an underground Food and Drug Administration has emerged to regulate the quality of illicit drugs on the streets, and the results are much more deadly.

My strongest argument for legalization, though, is a moral one. Enforcement of drug laws makes a mockery of an essential principle of a free-society — that those who do no harm to others should not be harmed by others, particularly not by the state. The vast majority of the 60 to 70 million Americans who have violated the drug laws in recent years have done no harm to anybody else. In most cases, they have done little or no harm to even themselves. Saying to those people," You lose your driver's license, you lose your job, you lose your freedom," is, to me, the greatest societal cost of our current drug prohibition system.

The Important Thing About A Holy War Is To *Fight It* Not To *Win* It*

The long-awaited National Drug Control Strategy, which the Bush administration unveiled on Sept. 5, 1989, will bring us more invasions of personal rights, more AIDS and AIDS deaths, more drug abuse, more drug trade murders, more assassinations of political leaders, more instability in producer countries, and more erosions of basic democratic traditions. Sadly, the only major criticism from within the Washington establishment comes from congressional Democrats who want to spend more money on the drug war.

Perpetuating Holy War

Why in the world would the leaders of a modern government continue and even expand such a harmful policy? As Ed Leuw, a Dutch government researcher, explained a few years ago, the drug war can only be understood as a holy war — and the important thing about a holy war is to *fight* it not to *win* it. While it is not generally recognized, therefore, it would help our understanding if we accepted that American society is now engaged in the equivalent of a holy war over differences in chemical tastes. The level of barbarism has not yet been as widespread as other holy wars, but barbarism is growing. And remember what is at the core of all of this violence. As many as 60 million or about 1 in 4 Americans sometimes perform a seemingly non-threatening act: *they imbibe certain drugs that the majority of the society does not like or even hates.*

The majority of citizens have enacted, through their elected representatives, laws making these substances illegal for seemingly good reasons in line with previous enactments imposing a government religion for the good of the whole people (before the First Amendment outlawed an official church). The rationale for the new chemical religion laws is that the drugs are mind-altering, harmful to health, and even fatal. While these reasons are, to an extent, supported by objective facts, millions of our citizens have persisted in taking these hated chemicals, in part because they personally do not believe them to be worse than the approved chemicals. (Support for their heretical position is found in the fact that deaths from all illegal drug overdoses total approximately 7,000 annually compared to well over 500,000 for tobacco and alcohol.)

Eliminating Heretics to Save Them

While the new holy war plan, which was authored by National Drug Control Policy Director William Bennett, promises help to some people, the major thrust of the multi-billion dollar package is hate, not help. That hatred is directed with full, virulent force at casual users of drugs, the most numerous of the heretics. The plan intends to eliminate, in a sense, casual users of drugs from American society. Casual users of, for example, marijuana and cocaine could be imprisoned for months in boot camps or hospitalized against their will through civil commitment procedures in psychiatric institutions. The plan also urges that casual users lose their cars and homes, be fired from their jobs under the drug-free workplace ideology, have their driver's licenses suspended for 1-5 years, be prohibited from obtaining student loans and grants, and suffer other penalties for "using or possessing even small amounts of drugs." States that do not pass such repressive statutes could lose hundreds of millions in federal benefits.

---

* Arnold S. Trebach and Kevin B. Zeese, "A Holy War by Any Other Name," *The Drug Policy Letter*, September/October, 1989, p.1.

The Drug War is Fundamentally Unsound

The high priests of the American holy war have managed to sell the notion that casual users of drugs must suffer these penalties because they are criminal co-conspirators of the drug barons and their murderous henchmen. Thus, when drug-trade thugs kill a police officer in New York or the wife of a policeman in Colombia, Mr. Bennett's rationale holds, American casual cocaine and marijuana users helped pull the triggers.

If there were no customers, of *course* the drug barons could not sell drugs and would not be able to hire killers. But if we accept the argument that casual users are actually involved in a murderous conspiracy, then we must perforce throw out centuries of Anglo-American legal doctrine and political philosophy. It has become central to civilized, democratic legal systems that individuals are liable only for the proximate results of their actions and only for those results they cause directly and intentionally to specific individuals. While there are some circumstances under which an individual might be liable to unknown third parties, these are rare exceptions to the general rule. Under the new logic there could be other bizarre persecutions: tobacco manufacturers could be nailed as accomplices to over 390,000 predictable cancer and coronary "homicides" a year, liquor producers as the ultimate cause of over 150,000 "homicides" due to heart disease and cirrhosis of the liver.

Ignoring Rational Government Reports

In preparing the strategy, Mr. Bennett also ignored a vast body of scientific facts and impartial reports. President Nixon's own drug commission, for example, in 1972 recommended that possession and small sales of marijuana would no longer be a criminal offense. In 1982, a distinguished panel of the quasi-governmental National Academy of Sciences reiterated the Nixon commission's findings and went further by recommending a national experiment wherein, as in 1933 regarding alcohol, federal marijuana laws would be repealed allowing the states freedom to enact their own, including legalization. In 1988, Judge Francis L. Young, the chief DEA administrative law judge, ruled that "Marijuana...is one of the safest therapeutically active substances known to man."

President Ford's White House task force report on all illegal drugs stated in 1975 that the government should be more calm in its approach, "stop raising unrealistic expectations of total elimination of drug abuse," and that excessive reliance on law enforcement will have significant adverse effects, including: "young, casual users of drugs are stigmatized by arrest; the health of committed users is threatened by impure drugs...and crime rates increase." No such worries about stigmatizing casual drug users or about harming the health of addicts appears anywhere in this new strategy. Nor is there anything of significance about controlling AIDS, a disease now threatening the entire society.

Rational Options

In the wake of the release of the Bush-Bennett strategy, the Drug Policy Foundation and other groups have been making the case against the continuation of this destructive, divisive war on the American people, and on the peoples of other countries. Some members of the loyal opposition are so appalled by the extremism of the drug warriors that they are advocating rapid legalization and the regulated sale of virtually all currently illegal drugs. That is only one of many options that have been proposed. Others include allowing states greater freedom to legalize and regulate marijuana; providing medicinal drugs and clean needles to addicts through doctors; granting treatment on demand; allowing doctors to prescribe marijuana and heroin to cancer and glaucoma sufferers; and leaving all the drugs laws on the books but enforcing them with great restraint as we do the sex laws.

Irrational Future

Nevertheless, the Bennett strategy may well dominate American society for the remainder of this century. As Jan. 1, 2000, dawns on Washington, one could make rational projections, based upon current trends, that would envision the following scene:

- American prisoners serving one year or more total at least 1.38 million. (This projection is based upon the 7.4 percent rate of annual increase at the end of the Reagan Era. However, the government just announced that the rate almost doubled during the first six months of 1989 with the result that from Jan. 1, 1981, to June 30, 1989, the prison population went up a mind-boggling 104 percent from 329,821 to 673,565. If the new rate continues, the prison population at the beginning of the next century will be 2.8 million.)
- Inmates of jails, juvenile institutions, boot camps, and psychiatric hospitals total a number equal to that of the long-term prisoners.
- Drug trade murders amount to 10,000 annually, up from approximately 2,000 in 1989.
- AIDS kills tens of thousands of addicts and non-addicts every year. The major vehicle for the transmission of the disease remains the heterosexual, injecting addict, especially since they still cannot get legal drugs or enough clean needles.
- Crime on the streets is worse than ever. Troops and tanks patrol the center of Washington and most major cities.
- The major protections of the Bill of Rights are, for all practical purposes, repealed during the continuing drug emergency.
- Drug abuse is rampant. New synthetic designer drugs have come on the market that are more potent and more deadly than crack or PCP.
- The federal drug abuse budget is $78 billion (almost a ten-fold increase from 1989).
- William Bennett is President of the United States.

Ignoring The Lessons Of Drug Wars Past*

The president has declared that he is committed to an all-out war on drugs promising to provide money to local law enforcement, build more jails and interdict and eradicate drugs before they reach our shores. He also promised to provide treatment to those who needed it.

These were not only the promises of President Bush but also the promises of President Nixon in 1969. This year marks the 20th anniversary of the modern war on drugs. Successive drug wars have been fought by each president. Even President Carter, who often is described as a weakling, took the aggressive action of spraying herbicides on marijuana and heroin growing in Mexico. The development of national strategies is also not new. President Reagan developed national strategies each year he was in office. The Bush administration has not created any dramatic new policy; it has merely tinkered at the fringes of the policies of the past.

There are many lessons we could learn from our two-decade-old drug war. Perhaps the greatest weakness of Mr. Bush and National Drug Control Policy Director William Bennett is their failure to examine and learn from the history of the war on drugs. Unfortunately, the administration plan seems

---

* Kevin B. Zeese, "Ignoring the Lessons of Drug Wars Past," *The Drug Policy Letter*, September/October 1989, p.3.

to ignore the successes of the past and builds on its failures.

A Prison State Will Not Make a Drug-Free Society

The Bush-Bennett Plan places its greatest emphasis on prisons, promising an 85 percent expansion of federal prison capacity. During the Reagan war on drugs the number of people incarcerated made it greatest jump in modern history.

No one claims that the doubling of our prison population in 8 1/2 years has made our streets safer or reduced the adverse health effects of drug abuse. Even Mr. Bennett's report acknowledges that emergency room mentions of drug abuse increased by 121 percent from 1985-1988. The current national drug control strategy does not explain why increased incarcerations will work this time.

Six months ago Mr. Bennett dramatically announced that Washington, D.C., would be the "test case" to see whether the nation could control drugs and crime. The capital city presents strong evidence that incarceration will not solve the drug problem. In the last few years, the District of Columbia has arrested over 40,000 people for drug offenses, its judges have given some of the longest sentences in America, and its prisons are bulging. Indeed, incarceration has become the norm for some segments of the population. Currently, 20 percent of black males ages 18-29 are either in prison or under government supervision. Yet, the city is breaking last year's record-setting homicide rate, and drug abuse has not decreased.

For some reason, the Bush administration plan follows the "D.C. model" of more arrests and more incarcerations even though it is not safe to walk on the streets of the capital, and drug abuse is more dangerous than ever before. The administration's proposal to spend millions of dollars to increase rates of incarceration should not be implemented until it is able to explain why the spiraling increase in incarceration over the last two decades has failed.

Eradicating One Crop Creates Another

The Bush-Bennett Plan, acknowledging the failure of the Reagan administration's interdiction program, places great emphasis on eradication, or what is now called the "Andean strategy." Once again, this has been tried repeatedly during the last two decades of drug war. It has not only failed, it has created new problems.

The most aggressive eradication program was the spraying of herbicides on marijuana growing in Mexico in the mid-70s. After spending millions of dollars on helicopters, manpower and equipment, the herbicide spraying program merely created a more diverse marijuana supply.

The U.S. marijuana crop is the direct result of eradication programs in Mexico. Marijuana has been a leading cash crop in the United States throughout the 1980s. According to Mr. Bennett's report, the U.S. crop now accounts for 25 percent of the domestic market. Indeed, America has become an exporter of marijuana.

In addition to expanding the U.S. crop, the eradication program spurred marijuana production in other Latin American countries producing the drug lords who are now behind the cocaine and crack markets. Even Mexico, according to Drug Enforcement Administration intelligence estimates, remained a major producer as the second largest exporter of marijuana to the United States last year.

Eradication of cocaine is going to be even more difficult. The hardy coca bush cannot be eradicated by herbicides; it must be done manually. Coca growers have laughed at U.S. efforts to cut the coca bushes without uprooting them. It has saved the farmers many hours of work in pruning the plants. To be successful the plants must be uprooted. Only a small percentage of land available for coca cultivation is currently being used. According to Dr. Lester Grinspoon of Harvard Medical School, the hardy coca plant will grow in many other countries, especially in areas that have warm winters. "The Andean strategy is stupid in terms of botany," Dr. Grinspoon said at a recent Drug Policy Foundation press conference at the National Press Club. When the economic and cultural realities of Latin America are considered along with the past record of eradication programs, it is absurd to waste resources on eradication.

Unable to Seal Off Borders

In 1969, President Nixon launched Operation Intercept, which militarized the Mexican border. One of every three cars entering the country from Mexico was searched for illegal drugs, chiefly marijuana. As a result, the pot market in Southern California temporarily dried up. But users began experimenting with other drugs, among them amphetamines, which quickly became a widely used drug.

In response to the border searches, smugglers switched from cars and trucks to boats and planes, thus expanding the drug war to sea and air. The marijuana market grew as well.

The Reagan administration focused its interdiction efforts in South Florida. High-tech military surveillance aircraft were recruited in the war on drugs. Colombia's traffickers quickly realized that marijuana was too bulky to ship undetected. But they also discovered that cocaine could be transported in briefcases, suitcases, even within human bodies. These methods of moving cocaine easily penetrated the government's high-tech net, resulting in cocaine becoming cheaper and more plentiful.

Interdiction has become less and less cost effective. The General Accounting Office recently reported that the Navy and Coast Guard spent a combined $40 million in 1988 and seized only 17 ships. The Air Force, meanwhile, used AWACS surveillance, at a cost of $8 million in 1987-88, to arrest 26 suspected smugglers.

Felony convictions did not work for the Nixon drug war. What evidence does Mr. Bennett have that indicates denying a driver's license will work for President Bush?

Coercion Fails to Convince Users

Twenty years after the drug war was first declared we are seemingly returning to the original strategy. The original war on drugs focused on going after the users; today, it is called "user accountability."

When President Nixon declared the war on drugs, it was a felony in virtually every state to possess any amount of marijuana. During the 1970s, American police arrested one person every two minutes for marijuana offenses. Nevertheless, marijuana use tripled, and the drug warriors changed the strategy to going after traffickers. Now the Bush administration is returning to the original plan.

William Bennett has yet a new strategy: deny driver's licenses to drug offenders. Felony convictions did not work for the Nixon drug war. What evidence does Mr. Bennett have that indicates denying a driver's license will work for President Bush? Does he believe that people who break the law selling drugs, when facing arrest and incarceration, will be concerned about losing their driver's license?

The other break from the past is widespread testing of bodily fluids for evidence of drug use. The fact that our free society is willing to resort to this type of strategy demonstrates the desperation of the failed drug prohibition. Drug testing requires mass searches of individuals almost always without any suspicion of drug use. That was exactly the type of government invasion of privacy our forefathers fought the American Revolution to prevent. As a result of our failed drug policies, we are destroying the freedoms that make this country special in human history.

Successes in the War on Drugs

Over the last two decades of drug wars there have been three notable successes from which we could learn a great deal and create a successful national strategy.

At the beginning of the drug war, the great drug scare was glue sniffing. This was actually seen as a very serious threat to our society. There were reports throughout the United States of young people sniffing glue, getting high and killing their brain cells.

Today glue sniffing is no longer a drug problem. This great threat has disappeared. We succeeded without eradicating glue at its source, without interdicting it and without mass incarcerations. We did not take away the driver's licenses of convicted glue sniffers. Indeed, glue remains legal and widely available throughout the United States, but is no longer a drug problem.

Another surprising success has been the decriminalization of marijuana. By 1978, 11 states encompassing one-third of the population had decriminalized marijuana, and over 30 other states had made a first offense punishable without incarceration and without a criminal record. Since 1978, there has been a dramatic decline in marijuana use among all age groups including our adolescents. Relaxing law enforcement did not result in increased use. While it is impossible to say what caused the dramatic decline in marijuana use, it is fair to say that relaxing the laws did not prevent the decline. Not only does Mr. Bennett ignore this success, but his report incorrectly claims that this change increased marijuana use and urges states to adopt harsher sanctions.

The other success is perhaps the most startling because it involves a legal drug, tobacco. At the beginning of the modern drug war, 40 percent of the U.S. population was regularly using tobacco; today regular use is down to 29 percent. Almost half of all living American adults who have ever smoked tobacco have quit. This has also been accomplished without mass incarcerations, eradication programs and without any reduction in tobacco availability.

Tobacco is particularly interesting because not only is it legal, but its farmers are subsidized by the government, and the drug is available in vending machines or over-the-counter throughout the United States. According to the Surgeon General, tobacco is as addictive as cocaine and heroin. Even with mass availability of a highly addictive drug we have seen a dramatic drop in use.

Learning the Lessons of the Past

The lessons of these victories and failures of the last 20 years is that law enforcement is not all that important in controlling drug abuse. Our only successes have been in areas where we have reduced law enforcement and encouraged social controls to come to the fore. Not only do these experiences demonstrate the failure of law enforcement, they demonstrate that law enforcement actually makes matters worse. Relying on criminal laws creates the "forbidden fruit" glamorization of illegality, the huge black market profits, the widespread corruption of public officials and the empowerment of wealthy, violent drug criminals.

If history teaches us that we can avoid all of these negative consequences and still reduce drug abuse, should not we at least try it? Does it not make more sense to build on the successes of the last two decades rather than building on the failures?

Drug Czar William Bennett can be criticized for many reasons including minimizing the effects of prejudice, poverty and poor education as root causes of drug abuse. He proposes massive expenditures for law enforcement without explaining where the funds will come from. He can also be criticized for advocating a policy of rhetoric over reason. However, the greatest criticism of Mr. Bennett may be that he is ignoring all of the drug war defeats of the past 20 years and is planning more of the same.

Ignoring The Great Commission Reports[*]

In preparing the new drug strategy William Bennett and the Office of National Drug Control Policy staff somehow managed to ignore the findings of virtually every impartial scholarly commission that has objectively researched the subject during the past century. This is a remarkable but familiar omission which accounts in large part for the remarkably destructive impact of American policy.

Many of these objective reports come from the United States but some of the most insightful come from other countries. None call for full legalization of drugs or views any of the drugs, including marijuana, as harmless, but each of the reports without fail calls for a gentle, humane approach to dealing with drug users and abusers. None of these great commission reports call for a war on drugs, on users or on addicts. Some countries, notably Britain and Holland, have followed much of the advice of these non-partisan expert reports. Others, most notably the United States, have consistently ignored them. Following are summaries of the key findings of these reports.

Indian Hemp Drugs Commission, *Marijuana,* **1893-94.** This 3,281-page, seven-volume classic report on the marijuana problem in India by British and Indian experts concluded: "Viewing the subject generally, it may be added that the moderate use of these drugs is the rule, and that the excessive use is comparatively exceptional. The moderate use produces practically no ill effects." Nothing of significance in the report's conclusions has been proven wrong in the intervening 95 years.

The Panama Canal Zone Military Investigations, **1916-1929.** After an exhaustive study of the smoking of marijuana among American soldiers stationed in the zone, the panel of civilian and military experts recommended that "no steps be taken by the Canal Zone authorities to prevent the sale or use of Marihuana." The committee also concluded that "there is no evidence that Marihuana as grown and used [in the Canal Zone] is a 'habit-forming' drug."

Departmental Committee on Morphine and Heroin Addiction, *Report,* **1926 (The Rolleston Report).** This landmark study by a distinguished group of British doctors codified existing practices regarding the maintenance of addicts on heroin and morphine by individual doctors and recommended that they continue without government or medical society interference. In coming to this conclusion,

---

[*] Arnold S. Trebach, "Ignoring The Great Commission Reports," *The Drug Policy Letter,* September/October, 1989, p.5.

these physicians displayed a humane regard for the addicts in their care, perhaps due to their view of the nature of narcotic addiction: "the condition must be regarded as a manifestation of disease and not as a mere form of vicious indulgence." The British addiction experts took pains to state that they did not agree with the opinions of "some eminent physicians, especially in the United States" that addicts "could always be cured by sudden withdrawal."

Mayor's Committee on Marihuana, *The Marihuana Problem in the City of New York*, 1944 (La Guardia Report). This study is viewed by many experts as the classic study of any drug viewed in its social, medical and legal context. The committee covered thousands of years of the history of marijuana and also made a detailed examination of conditions in New York City. Among its conclusions: "The practice of smoking marihuana does not lead to addiction in the medical sense of the word." And: "The use of marihuana does not lead to morphine or heroin or cocaine addiction and no effort is made to create a market for those narcotics by stimulating the practice of Marihuana smoking." Finally: "The publicity concerning the catastrophic effects of marihuana smoking in New York City is unfounded."

Interdepartmental Committee, *Drug Addiction*, 1961 (The First Brain Report). When the Brain Committee first met at the invitation of the Minister of Health, its mission was to review the advice given by the Rolleston Committee in 1926. That advice had been to continue to allow doctors to treat addicts with maintenance doses of powerful drugs when the doctors deemed it medically helpful for the patient. Brain I reiterated that advice and in this first report recommended no changes of any significance on the prescribing powers of doctors. This report expanded on one important point alluded to in Rolleston: the authenticity of the existence of "stabilized addicts." While many American experts doubt their existence, this report explained, "careful scrutiny of the histories of more than a hundred persons classified as addicts reveals that many of them who have been taking small and regular doses for years show little evidence of tolerance and are often leading reasonably satisfactory lives." Six "case histories of known stabilized addicts" were included in an appendix. They were mature, older patients, functioning normally on what would be huge doses of drugs by American standards. "Mr. F.," for example, a clerical worker, was receiving the equivalent of 200 milligrams of morphine tablets each day. It is likely that these patients and their doctors would be dealt with as criminals in parts of the United States, especially today.

Joint Committee of the American Bar Association and the American Medical Association on Narcotic Drugs, *Drug Addiction: Crime or Disease? Interim and Final Reports*, 1961. This report was the result of the only major combined study of drug policy made by two of the most important professional societies in the country. Chaired by attorney Rufus King of Washington, D.C., the committee presented a direct challenge to the tough policies of Federal Bureau of Narcotics Director Harry Anslinger, a philosophical ancestor of the current drug czar. The blue-ribbon committee included a senior federal judge and was advised by Indiana University's Alfred Lindesmith, one of the most distinguished addiction scholars in history. The report observed, "drug addiction is primarily a problem for the physician rather than the policeman, and it should not be necessary for anyone to violate the criminal law solely because he is addicted to drugs." The report concluded that drug addiction was a disease not a crime, that harsh criminal penalties were destructive, that drug prohibition ought to be re-examined, and that experiments should be conducted with British-style maintenance clinics for narcotic addicts.

Interdepartmental Committee, *Drug Addiction, Second Report*, 1965 (The Second Brain Report). Brain II has been consistently misinterpreted by leading American scholars and officials. It did not recommend the dismantling of the British prescription system nor the compulsory registration of addicts, as has been claimed. Instead, Brain II urged that (1) doctors who wished to prescribe "restricted drugs" to addicts for the purpose of maintenance be required to obtain a special license from the Home Office, (2) treatment centers be established for treating addicts who were to be regarded as sick and not criminal, and (3) doctors and other medical personnel be mandated to "notify" the Home Office when they encountered an addict in the course of their professional work. Originally, the category of restricted drugs included heroin and cocaine; now, dipipanone has been added.

However, the core of the British system remains, and in recent years, has been reinvigorated. Approximately 200 doctors with special licenses are free to prescribe all drugs, including the restricted medicines, for maintenance of addicts. Also, any doctor, unlike in the U.S., may prescribe all of the other drugs for maintenance, including, say, injectable morphine and methadone. Brain II in the end was aimed at controlling a few overprescribing doctors, not at adopting the American system of treating addicts as the enemy.

Advisory Committee on Drug Dependence, *Cannabis*, 1968 (The Wooton Report). This study report on marijuana and hashish was prepared by a group that included some of the leading drug abuse experts of the United Kingdom. These impartial experts worked as a subcommittee under the lead of Baroness Wooton of Abinger. The basic tone and substantive conclusions were similar to all of the other great commission reports. The Wooton group specifically endorsed the conclusions of the Indian Hemp Drugs Commission and the La Guardia Committee. Typical findings included the following. "There is no evidence that in Western society serious physical dangers are directly associated with the smoking of cannabis." "It can clearly be argued on the world picture that cannabis use does not lead to heroin addiction." "The evidence of a link with violent crime is far stronger with alcohol than with the smoking of cannabis." "There is no evidence that this activity...is producing in otherwise normal people conditions of dependence or psychosis, requiring medical treatment."

Canadian Government's Commission of Inquiry, *The Non-Medical Use of Drugs, Interim Report*, 1970 (The Le Dain Report). The distinguished Canadian experts on this governmental commission were led by law school dean, later Supreme Court Justice, Gerald Le Dain. The report was similar to the other great commission reports in terms of its non-martial, calm approach to the facts and in its belief that marijuana use did not constitute a great threat to the public welfare. The official governmental commission was remarkable in the extent to which its report portrayed casual drug users as decent, thoughtful citizens whose views deserved the fullest possible hearing by the government in the process of developing drug control strategies.

A mother of four and a school teacher was

quoted in the report as saying: "When I smoke grass I do it in the same social way that I take a glass of wine at dinner or have a drink at a party. I do not feel that it is one of the great and beautiful experiences of my life; I simply feel that it is pleasant and I think it ought to be legalized." The commission did not ask for that change immediately but instead recommended that serious consideration be given to legalization of personal possession in the near future. The report also urged that police and prosecutors go easy on casual users and keep them out of jail as often as possible.

National Commission on Marihuana and Drug Abuse, *Drug Use in America: Problem in Perspective*, **1973.** This commission was directed by Raymond P. Shafer, former Republican governor of Pennsylvania, and had four sitting, elected politicians among its 11 members. The commission also had leading addiction scholars among its members and staff. It was appointed by President Nixon in the midst of the drug war hysteria at that time. While the commission supported much existing policy, it produced two reflective reports, this being the final comprehensive document, which recommended research, experimentation and humane compromise. The first recommendations of the commission were:

"1. Possession of marihuana for personal use would no longer be an offense, but marihuana possessed in public would remain contraband subject to summary seizure and forfeiture.

"2. Casual distribution of small amounts of marihuana for no remuneration, or insignificant remuneration not involving profit, would no longer be an offense."

National Research Council of the National Academy of Sciences, *An Analysis of Marihuana Policy*, **1982.** This is the most recent American entry into the pantheon of ignored great commission reports.

The NAS Committee on Substance Abuse and Habitual Behavior was composed of some of the leading American experts on medicine, addiction treatment, law, business and public policy. These experts reviewed all of the available evidence on every aspect of the marijuana question. The committee then recommended that the country experiment with a system that would allow states to set up their own methods of controlling marijuana as is now done with alcohol. Under this approach, federal criminal penalties would be removed and each state could decide to legalize the drug and impose regulations concerning hours of sale, age limits and taxation.

In the same vein as all the previous major objective studies, this report stated that excessive marijuana use could cause serious harm, that such use was rare, and that on balance the current policy of total prohibition was socially and personally destructive. The report placed great emphasis on building up public education and informal social controls, which often have a greater impact on drug abuse than the criminal law. Regarding the possibility of disaster for our youth under legalization,

> *They were mature, older patients, functioning normally on what would be huge doses of drugs by American standards.*

the report observed: "...there is reason to believe that widespread uncontrolled use would not occur under regulation. Indeed, regulation might facilitate patterns of controlled use by diminishing the "forbidden fruit" aspect of the drug and perhaps increasing the likelihood that an adolescent would be introduced to the drug through families and friends, who practice moderate use, rather than from their heaviest-using, most drug-involved peers."

Advisory Council on the Misuse of Drugs, *AIDS and Drug Misuse,* **Part 1, 1988; Part 2, 1989.** "The spread of HIV is a greater danger to individual and public health than drug misuse," declared the leading drug abuse and health experts of the United Kingdom who sit on this distinguished quasi-governmental advisory group. This concept operated as the guiding principle in this, the most recent great commission report, one part issued in 1988, one in 1989. In stark contrast to the Bush-Bennett war plans just issued, the British council provided a comprehensive health plan that seeks to prevent the use of drugs, as is the American goal. However, the plan has realistic goals regarding drug abusers: abstinence in the American mode, where possible, but above all else, health and life. Thus, the Advisory Council accepted the lessons of the "harm reduction" programs of the Liverpool area and recommended that they be spread to the entire United Kingdom. Some of these lessons involve needle exchanges and prescribed drugs for addicts.

The report even went beyond the Liverpool experience when these leading British experts quietly observed "we believe that there is a place for an expansion of residential facilities where drug misusers may gain better health, skills and self-confidence whilst in receipt of prescribed drugs." Thus, while the United States is planning more prison space for drug addicts, the United Kingdom is contemplating more hostels where addicts could be taught to live more healthy, more self-confident and more productive lives in the community *whilst in receipt of prescribed drugs.*

The Whole Deal Is As Shabby As The Trick With The Bag Of Cocaine*

If President Bush's September address to the nation on the topic of drugs can be taken as an example of either his honesty or his courage, I see no reason why I can't look forward to hearing him declare a war against cripples, or one-eyed people, or red geraniums. It was a genuinely awful speech, rooted at the beginning in a lie directed at an imaginary enemy, sustained by false argument, proposing a policy that already had failed, playing to the galleries of prejudice and fear. The first several sentences of the speech established its credentials as a fraud. "Drugs," said Bush, "are sapping our strength as a nation." "The gravest domestic threat facing our nation," said Bush, "is drugs." "Our most serious problem today," said Bush, "is cocaine." None of the statements meets the standards either of minimal analysis or casual observation. The government's own figures show that the addiction to illegal drugs troubles a relatively small number of Americans, and the current generation of American youth is the strongest and healthiest in the nation's history.

In the sixth paragraph of his speech, the president elaborated his fraud by holding up a small plastic bag, as distastefully as if he were holding a urine specimen. "This is crack cocaine," he said,

---

*.Lewis H. Lapham, "A Political Opiate — The War on Drugs is a Folly and a Menace," *Harper's Magazine,* December 1989, p. 43. Copyright (c) 1989 by *Harper's Magazine.* All rights reserved. Reprinted from the December issue by special permission.

"seized a few days ago by Drug Enforcement Administration agents in a park just across the street from the White House. It could easily have been heroin or PCP." But since nobody, ever, has been known to sell any kind of drug in Lafayette Park, it couldn't possibly have been heroin or PCP. The bag of cocaine wasn't anything other than a stage prop: The DEA was put to considerable trouble and expense to tempt a dealer into the park in order to make the arrest at a time and place convenient to the president's little dramatic effect.

Bush's speechwriters ordered the staging of the "buy" because they wanted to make a rhetorical point about the dark and terrible sea of drugs washing up on the innocent, sun-dappled lawns of the White House. The sale was difficult to arrange because the drug dealer in question had never heard of Lafayette Park, didn't know how to find the place on a map, and couldn't imagine why anybody would want to make such complicated travel arrangements in order to buy rocks of low-grade crack.

Two days later, confronted by the press with the mechanics of his sleight of hand, Bush said, "I don't understand. I mean, has somebody got some advocates here for this drug guy?" The surprised and petulant tone of his question gave away the nature of the political game that he was playing, playing on what he assumed was the home field of the nation's best-loved superstitions. After seven months in office, he had chosen to make his first televised address on a topic that he thought was as safe as mother and the undesecrated flag. He had politely avoided any and all of the "serious problems facing our nation today" (the deficit, say, or the environment, or the question of race) and he had done what he could to animate a noncontroversial platitude with a good visual. He expected people to be supportive and nice.

Apparently it never occurred to him that anybody would complain about his taking a few minor liberties with the facts. Nor did he seem to notice that he had seized upon the human suffering implicit in the drug trade as an occasion for a shabby political trick. He had exploited exactly the same device in his election campaign by transforming the image of Willie Horton, a black convict who committed violent crimes after being released on furlough from a Massachusetts prison, into a metaphor for all the world's wickedness. I can imagine his speech writers explaining to him that the war on drugs was nothing more than Willie Horton writ large.

The premise of the war is so patently false, and the hope for victory so obviously futile, that I can make sense of it only by asking the rhetorical question *cui bono?* Who stands to gain by virtue of Bush's lovely little war, and what must the rest of us pay as tribute?

The question is a political one. But then, the war on drugs is a political war, waged not by scientists and doctors but by police officers and politicians. Under more fortunate circumstances, the prevalence of drugs in American society — not only cocaine and heroin and marijuana but also alcohol and tobacco and sleeping pills — would be properly addressed as a public-health question. The American Medical Association classifies drug addiction as a disease, not as a crime or a moral defeat. Nor is addiction contagious, like measles and the flu. Given the folly and expense of the war on drugs (comparable to the folly and expense of the war in Vietnam), I expect that the United States eventually will arrive at some method of decriminalizing the use of all drugs. The arguments in favor of decriminalization seem to me irrefutable, as do the lessons of experience taught by the failed attempt at the prohibition of alcohol.

But for the time being, as long as the question remains primarily political, the war on drugs serves the purposes of the more reactionary interests within our society (i.e., the defenders of the imagined innocence of a non-existent past) and transfers the costs of the war to precisely those individuals whom the promoters of the war say they wish to protect. I find it difficult to believe that the joke, although bitter, is unintended.

To politicians in search of sound opinions and sustained applause, the war on drugs presents itself as a gift from heaven. Because the human craving intoxicants cannot be suppressed — not by priests or jailers or acts of Congress — the politicians can bravely confront an allegorical enemy rather than an enemy that takes the corporeal form of the tobacco industry, say, or the Chinese, or the oil and baking lobbies. The war against drugs provides them with something to say that offends nobody, requires them to do nothing difficult, and allows them to postpone, perhaps indefinitely, the more urgent and specific questions about the state of the nation's schools, housing, employment opportunities for young black men — i.e., the conditions to which drug addiction speaks as a tragic symptom, not a cause. They remain safe in the knowledge that they might as well be denouncing Satan or the rain, and so they can direct the voices of prerecorded blame at metaphors and apparitions who, unlike Senator Jesse Helms and his friends at the North Carolina tobacco auctions, can be transformed into demonic spirits riding north across the Caribbean on an evil wind. The war on drugs thus becomes the perfect war for people who would rather not fight a war, a war in which the politicians who stand so fearlessly on the side of the good, the true, and the beautiful need do nothing else but strike noble poses as protectors of the people and defenders of the public trust.

> *Bush's speechwriters ordered the staging of the "buy" because they wanted to make a rhetorical point about the dark and terrible sea of drugs washing up on the innocent, sun-dappled lawns of the White House.*

Their cynicism is implicit in the arithmetic. President Bush in his September speech asked for $7.9 billion to wage his "assault on every front" of the drug war, but the Pentagon allots $5 billion a year to the B-2 program — i.e., to a single weapon. Expressed as a percentage of the federal budget, the new funds assigned to the war on drugs amount to .065 percent. Nor does the government offer to do anything boldly military about the legal drugs, principally alcohol and tobacco, that do far more damage to the society than all the marijuana and all the cocaine ever smuggled into Florida or California.

The drug war, like all wars, sells papers, and the media, like the politicians, ask for nothing better than a safe and profitable menace. The campaign against drugs involves most of the theatrical devices employed by "Miami Vice" — scenes of crimes in progress (almost always dressed up, for salacious effect, with cameo appearances of one or two prostitutes), melodramatic villains in the Andes, a vocabulary of high-

The Drug War is Fundamentally Unsound

tech military jargon as reassuring as the acronyms in a Tom Clancy novel, the specter of a crazed lumpenproletariat rising in revolt in the nation's cities.

Like camp followers trudging after an army of crusader knights on its way to Jerusalem, the media have in recent months displayed all the garish colors of the profession. Everybody who was anybody set up a booth and offered his or her tears for sale — not only Geraldo and Maury Povich but also, in much the same garish language, Dan Rather (on "48 Hours"), Ted Koppel (on "Nightline"), and Sam Donaldson (on "Prime Time Live"). In the six weeks between August 1 and Sept.13, [1989] the three television networks combined with *The New York Times* and *The Washington Post* to produce 347 reports from the frontiers of the apocalypse-crack in the cities, cocaine in the suburbs, customs agents seizing pickup trucks on the Mexican border, smugglers named Julio arriving every hour on the hour at Key West.

Most of the journalists writing the dispatches, like most of the columnists handing down the judgments of conscience, knew as much about crack or heroin or cocaine as they knew about the molecular structure of the moons of Saturn. Their ignorance didn't prevent them from coming to the rescue of their own, and the president's big story. On "World News Tonight" a few days after the president delivered his address, Peter Jennings, in a tone of voice that was as certain as it was silly (as well as being characteristic of the rest of the propaganda being broadcast over the other networks), said, "Using it even once can make a person crave cocaine for as long as they [sic] live."

So great was the media's excitement, and so determined their efforts to drum up a paying crowd, that hardly anybody bothered to question the premises of the drug war, and several of the more senior members of the troupe took it upon themselves to write diatribes against any dissent from the wisdom in office. A.M. Rosenthal, on the op-ed page of *The New York Times*, denounced even the slightest show of tolerance toward illegal drugs as an act of iniquity deserving comparison to the defense of slavery. William Safire, also writing in *The New York Times*, characterized any argument against the war on drugs as an un-American proof of defeatism. Without notable exception, the chorus of the big media tuned its instruments to the high metallic pitch of zero tolerance, scorned any truth that didn't echo their own, and pasted the smears of derision on the foreheads of the few people, among them Milton Friedman and William Buckley, who had the temerity to suggest that perhaps the war on drugs was both stupid and lost...

An opinion poll conducted during the week following the president's September address showed 62 percent of the respondents "willing to give up some freedoms" in order to hold America harmless against the scourge of drugs. The government stands more than willing to take them at their word. The war on drugs becomes a useful surrogate for the obsolescent Cold War, now fading into the realm of warm and nostalgic memory. Under the familiar rubrics of constant terror and ceaseless threat, the government subtracts as much as possible from the sum of the nation's civil liberties and imposes de facto martial law on citizenry that it chooses to imagine as a dangerous rabble.

Anybody who doubts this point has only to read the speeches of William Bennett, the commander-in-chief of the Bush administration's war on drugs. Bennett's voice is the voice of an intolerant scold, narrow and shrill and mean-spirited, the voice of a man afraid of liberty and mistrustful of freedom. He believes that it is the government's duty to impose on people a puritanical code of behavior best exemplified by the discipline in place at an unheated boarding school. He never misses the chance to demand more police, more jails, more judges, more arrests, more punishments, more people serving more millennia of "serious time...."

The militarization of the rhetoric supporting the war on drugs rots the public debate with a corrosive silence. The political weather turns gray and pinched. People who become accustomed to the arbitrary intrusions of the police also learn to speak more softly in the presence of political authority, to bow and smile and fill out the printed forms with the cowed obsequiousness of musicians playing waltzes at a Mafia wedding.

And for what? To punish people desperate enough or foolish enough to poison themselves with drugs? To exact vengeance on people afflicted with the sickness of addiction and who, to their grief and shame, can find no other way out of the alleys of their despair.

As a consequence of President Bush's war on drugs, society gains nothing except immediate access to an unlimited fund of resentment and unspecific rage. In return for so poor a victory, and in the interests of the kind of people who would build prisons instead of schools, Bush offers the nation the chance to deny its best principles, to corrupt its magistrates and enrich its most vicious and efficient criminals, to repudiate its civil liberties and repent of the habits of freedom. The deal is as shabby as President Bush's trick with the bag of cocaine. For the sake of a vindictive policeman's dream of a quiet and orderly heaven, the country risks losing its constitutional right to its soul.

The Drug War is Fundamentally Unsound

Mr. Butts Runs Into An Old Friend

Drug Prohibition and the Conscience of Nations

Doonesbury — BY GARRY TRUDEAU

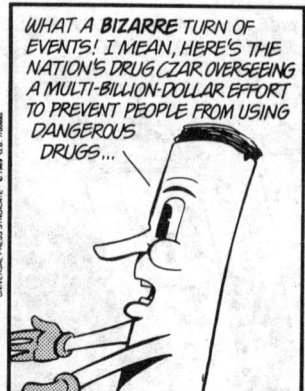

Doonesbury — BY GARRY TRUDEAU

Doonesbury — BY GARRY TRUDEAU

DOONESBURY COPYRIGHT 1989 G.B. Trudeau. Reprinted with permission of Universal Press Syndicate. All rights reserved.

This policy is often mistranslated and misinterpreted as "indulgent" or "permissive." In fact, in this society, it operates as a powerful social control.

—*John Shad*

The care system has no waiting lists. It is easily accessible, free of charge and it treats addicts respectfully as fellow citizens.

—*Eddy L. Engelsman*

Chapter 3

The Dutch Do It Better

Introduction

The Dutch are a calm people. In recent years, however, some of their leading officials and academic experts have become repeatedly agitated over the persistent slandering of their system of drug control by foreigners, especially by American politicians and drug enforcement officials. It has become almost a reflex action for leading drug warriors, such as U.S. Rep. Charles Rangel (D-N.Y.), chairman of the House Select Committee on Narcotics Abuse and Control, to reject calls for law reform by pointing to the alleged failures of Holland — and, of course, England. To make matters worse, and even more confusing, some leading English officials have periodically launched roughly similar attacks on the Dutch.

As we shall see later in this book, the English play an interesting game which finds their top ministers, led by the Prime, loudly proclaiming their allegiance to the drug war of their American cousins — all the while pouring millions of good English pounds into compassionate "harm reduction" programs. Current English policies are based in part upon their compassionate history of drug control and in part upon the truly successful work of their neighbors just across the channel.

The English talk American and act Dutch. The Dutch talk Dutch and act Dutch.

Unlike the minions of Mrs. Thatcher, and most of the ministers of the world, the leaders of the Dutch government, politicians all, stolidly refuse to enlist in the American war on drugs. Indeed, the Dutch government is the only one on record which officially states the truth which should be obvious to anyone who does not live in a cave: a war on drugs is actually a war on your own citizens.

Such attitudes cause a sense of disorientation, analogous to lack of oxygen when landing on a strange planet, to those committed to tough drug strategies. Even more disorienting is that there is almost no political conflict in Holland over the country's unique drug policies. Politicians across the spectrum simply agree on the major outlines of these non-war strategies partly because there is a broad belief that they work and partly because there is broad support among the people at the political grassroots.

It is even more remarkable that some American experts and officials have been reporting regularly on the Dutch success — and have been just as regularly ignored by those leading American politicians who simply do not want to hear inconvenient facts which suggest that any other nation could do better at drug control. Yet, the authoritative reports continue. One of the latest was the annual narcotics report for 1988 submitted in 1989 by John Shad, the U.S. Ambassador to The Netherlands. In a courageous analysis he suggested that it might well be "educational" for American policy makers to study Dutch drug policy for the insightful lessons it might provide in dealing with the harsh situation at home. Of course, there are many lessons to be learned in the Dutch school by everyone.

The United States Ambassador Tells The Truth About Holland!*

Dutch perceptions of the contrast between the dramatic worsening of the American drug situation and that of the Netherlands tend to reinforce their attitudes and convictions, regarding the drug phenomenon, that their national policy to confront it is on a true course. There is virtually no market for crack. Authorities are confident that local conditions, general knowledge of the American experience, and the national policy have forged barricades against the development of a major crack market here. Dutch policymakers attribute the perceived successes of their drug policy to its public-health orientation; to its extensive system of addict identification, therapy, counseling, and social reintegration; to the national social welfare regime; and to their prioritized enforcement of the narcotics laws.

The fundamental difference in Dutch drug policy is its demand-oriented approach to the problem which focuses on the drug abuser. He (or she) is dealt with more as a health and social problem than as a criminal. The Ministry of Public Health estimates the population of "hard drug addicts" at 15,000. Thirty to forty percent of those addicted are foreign nationals resident here.

There is some manufacture of synthetic illicit drugs in the Netherlands, but the major drug

---

*John Shad, U.S. Ambassador to the Netherlands, *Annual Narcotics Status Report for 1988*, May 26, 1989.

The Dutch Do It Better

problem is the volume of trafficking through the country to other destinations. The Dutch topography and its extensive transport network present formidable interdiction challenges. Around 130 criminal organizations in the Netherlands deal in drugs and traffickers are ethnically differentiated. Chinese, Turkish, and Pakistani organizations deal most of the heroin, Latin Americans and Surinamese service the growing cocaine traffic, and Dutch nationals dominate the marijuana and hashish trade.

There have been numerous calls for legalization of "hard drugs" (heroin, cocaine, and the psychotropics) on the one extreme and strict enforcement against all drugs, including "soft" cannabis products, on the other. Thus far, the Netherlands has chosen a middle way: Enforcement against hard drugs, official tolerance of soft drugs, and "decriminalization" of users....

Trafficking and Local Consumption

Dutch perceptions of illicit narcotics activities are divided into two distinct categories: those regarding trafficking into and through their country and those surrounding the question of domestic substance abuse.

Dutch attitudes toward trafficking closely mirror those of the U.S. government and of neighboring states in the European community. Dutch enforcement authorities consider their country particularly vulnerable to trafficking. They recall the complex and infinitely permeable coastline, the immense volume of maritime and riverine cargo flowing through the port of Rotterdam, the vast rail and highway networks distributing goods all over Europe, and the numbers of passengers and amount of air freight transiting Amsterdam's Schiphol International Air Terminal. These officials — who already often feel overwhelmed — express anxiety over the abolition of internal borders within the 12 states of the European Community, scheduled for the beginning of 1993. The necessary strengthening of the European outer perimeter and gateways — including the Dutch coast, the port of Rotterdam, and Schipol Airport — implies an EC-wide standardization and toughening of enforcement policy. This in turn will require formidably higher levels of financial, manpower, material, and technical resources.

In terms of dealing with the issue of internal demand and substance abuse, Dutch perceptions and policy vary radically from those held by the U.S. government and indeed by most other European states. Drug and other substance abuse is recognized here as one among many social problems...certainly not the most serious. Alcohol and tobacco abuse and traffic accidents, for example, claim far larger annual numbers of deaths in the Netherlands than does drug abuse. Incest, child abuse, petty crime, euthanasia, homosexual issues, prostitution, and AIDS all claim shares of public attention and resources as well.

Demand-Oriented Policy

The fundamental difference in Dutch drug policy is its demand-oriented approach to the problem as opposed to the supply-oriented approach favored by the United States and many other countries. The latter centers on substance eradication, law enforcement, and punitive considerations. Dutch policy focuses on the drug abuser. It views him primarily as an unfortunate with health and social problems rather than primarily as a criminal. It attempts to keep him "above ground" and it wants him within reach of medical authority. The policy attempts to stabilize his life and to limit the damage he causes to society, to family and to himself. It encourages and provides immediate therapy —

virtually upon demand whenever he is ready for it — including methadone maintenance, free needle-exchange to reduce the risk of AIDS and hepatitis infection if he is an intravenous abuser, counseling, and residential or out-patient long-term treatment. Finally, and when possible, it assists his eventual reintegration into society. The policy is often mistranslated and misinterpreted as "indulgent" or "permissive." In fact, in this society, it operates as a powerful social control. Speaking to local audiences a senior official of the justice ministry expressed the Dutch position this way:

If you think about drugs in a dogmatic way, assistance of course remains a form of heresy. AIDS is the only reason why other countries are joining us, very cautiously.

Other significant features of the Netherlands' social and economic landscape which differentiate Dutch drug perceptions and policy are the presence of a pervasive national social-welfare network...and the absence of anything approaching slum conditions anywhere in the country. Dutch authorities perceive high profile anti-drug campaigns to be counterproductive. They believe that such efforts tend to stimulate "perverse demand" in adventurous youth. Therefore, drug education is kept low-key. Educators mix the topic into a broad matrix of other social survival information: sex education, teenage pregnancy and its prevention, venereal disease, child abuse and incest, AIDS prevention, alcohol and tobacco abuse.

Separation of Markets

Finally, the system attempts to maintain a wall between the market for "soft drugs" (cannabis products) and that for "hard drugs" (all others). This facet of the policy derives from evidence that substances exist on a continuum ranging from the relatively benign to the highly dangerous. Tobacco, marijuana, hashish, and alcohol repose on the relatively less risky side of the scale; on the more dangerous end lie hashish oil, the psychotropics, cocaine and heroin. Enforcement resources are prioritized from the lowest (adult users of soft drugs) to the highest (hard-drug drug dealers operating near school grounds). The separation of markets policy is a classic channeling technique: it acknowledges pharmacological differences between drugs, it "deromanticizes" drug use by creating tolerated outlets for youthful marijuana smokers while minimizing their exposure to hard-drug channels, and it concentrates enforcement and judicial resources against the most serious classes of drug offenders.

Public Support for Current Policy

In a vigorous participatory democracy such as the Netherlands which enjoys a free and inquisitive press, there appears to be little daylight between official and popular perceptions of the drug issue. Significantly, the narcotics policy is not and has not been a political issue within the country. A broad social and political consensus seems to endorse its efficacy and favor its continuation. However, some groups do oppose it vociferously and lobby against it, usually on moral or religious grounds. Justified protests have arisen recently among Amsterdam residents against the nuisance of open drug use in their neighborhoods. In typical pragmatic fashion, local officials likely will endeavor to find a less public and objectionable venue for the addicts rather than overhaul the policy.

American and Dutch Contrasts

Dutch authorities, who often visit the United States, view the current drug situation in American metropolitan areas with acute sympathy and dismay.

They contrast their own national experience — and policy — with ours. Their convictions are reinforced by their reading of the evidence which convinces them that, up to now, U.S. drug policy has been a spectacular failure. They sometimes express annoyance with visitors to the Netherlands bearing pre-set agendas who credit the unique history, society, and culture of the Netherlands for its relative immunity from the drug scourge... but then condemn the policy.

Virtually No Crack Abuse

Dutch enforcement and policy authorities reject prophecies of tidal waves of cocaine and crack soon to come crashing over Holland. They readily grant the formidable trafficking and interdiction challenge presented by these drugs, most of which are destined for other markets. But they are convinced that their policy has insulated the Netherlands from significant new demand for crack and cocaine. They point to the relatively small local market for cocaine and virtually none for crack, the low cocaine-to-heroin abuse ratio, declining numbers of young people experimenting with any form of drugs, the rising average age and stable number of the resident addict population, and the negligible numbers of drug overdose deaths (60 to 80 per year) and AIDS cases (currently around 800, of which about 65 are intravenous drug abusers). They do express concern about increases in any of these drug use indicators. But increases are registered over extraordinarily low benchmarks for a population of nearly 15 million.

The Dutch play unwilling host to thousands of West German addicts...nearly 40 percent of the Dutch national total. Not surprisingly, the Dutch consider these visitors to have been pushed across the border by the FRG's tough enforcement policy. The Germans, in turn, point to the "magnetic pull" of Dutch policy for addicts.

United States Interests

The primary goal for the United States is to encourage and enhance, by all feasible means, ongoing cooperative efforts with the Dutch in anti-trafficking activities. In light of our own problems, a secondary goal for United States policymakers might be an educational one. It is unlikely that many elements of Dutch drug policy successfully could be wrenched out of their social and cultural contexts. However, certain of the mechanics such as low threshold therapy, mobile treatment units, and needle exchange might well be adaptable to the American reality.

The Pragmatic Strategies Of The Dutch "Drug Czar"*

It may be surprising to some that in the Netherlands, possessing and trafficking in drugs, including cannabis products, are illegal activities.

The Netherlands is a small country. Bounded by the North Sea on the West and North, by Germany on the East and by Belgium on the South, it covers a land area of almost 13,000 square miles — about one-fourth of the size of New York State. Within this territory live more than 14.5 million people, including some 600,000 foreigners, making the Netherlands one of the most densely populated countries of the world. In the past hundred years the country has developed into a modern industrial society. The city of Rotterdam exemplifies the importance of foreign trade in that it is the largest port in the world. Even such a seemingly ahistoric factor as geography should be interpreted in the light of history and culture.

---

*Eddy L. Engelsman is the Head of the Alcohol, Drugs and Tobacco Branch; Ministry of Welfare, Public Health, and Cultural Affairs; The Netherlands. Mr. Engelsman rejects the title "czar" as inappropriate in a democratic nation. Certainly, no one calls him that, except an occasional American.

To foreign observers the most striking feature of the Netherlands has always been the abundance of water: water constituting both a threat and a means of livelihood, necessitating the building of dams and dikes, and drawing the people toward seafaring and trade. The Dutch have never conquered the sea but succeeded in controlling this enemy. A parallel can thus be drawn between the Netherlands' response to the sea and its often misunderstood drug policy.

Effects of Prohibition

In the Netherlands we hold the view that drug use is not primarily a problem for police and the courts, but rather a matter of social well-being and public health. Therefore, we have opted for a realistic and pragmatic approach to the drug problem. The aim of our policy is the reduction of health damages and risks.

From the beginning of the 1980s, Dutch political leaders have acknowledged the existence of primary and secondary effects of illicit drug use. Primary effects, such as tolerance, mood swings and addiction, are those caused by drug use itself. Secondary effects, such as drug-related crimes, prostitution and AIDS, are at least partly induced by the mere illegality of the drug. Unfortunately, the secondary and primary effects of drug use are often confused with one another. In other words, the effects of drug use are often mistaken for the effects of drug policies.

On the social level, the international community faces the problems of organized crime, erosion of the judicial system and high costs for police, justice and the prison apparatuses. In the Netherlands and elsewhere, the nature of the secondary effects of the drug problem has also blinded our view of the primary effects of drug use. Not surprisingly, this confusion has made the fight against international drug trafficking the main focus of national and international drug policies.

Social Security System

Under the Dutch system of social security, the State ensures the social rights of its citizens. It guarantees a minimum income to every citizen on the basis of the National Assistance Act and on the basis of several other Acts by supplying old age pensions, widow's and orphan's pensions, family allowances, and insurance benefits in case of sickness, disability, or unemployment. It sets minimum standards of housing and food and sees to it that these standards are met. The State also sponsors a system of medical care covering health insurance for all wage earners below a certain income level. Furthermore, the Dutch government provides school education at minimum costs, and it grants scholarships if necessary.

All these arrangements are not regarded as acts of charity that might be revoked at will, but as inalienable attributes of social justice. The more a society succeeds in protecting its members from poverty and hopelessness, being a breeding ground for drug use, the more it will succeed in reducing the demand for drugs.

The high level of social security in the Netherlands contributes to the overall efforts in containing the level of addiction and to the relatively good health of Dutch drug addicts. The position of the Dutch is that if these multifactorial socio-economic aspects are not taken into account, efforts to reduce demand will have little chance of success. In effect, the symptoms would be treated while the sickness would be ignored. Consequently, rather than waging a "war on drugs," the Dutch prefer to wage a "war against underdevelopment, deprivation, and lack of socio-economic status."

General Principles of Dutch Drug Policy

Dutch drug policy is often considered as an "experiment" by foreigners. Although Dutch drug policy is deliberately designed, it should not be seen as a specific policy that is different from policies of other areas in society. For instance, non-conformity in thought and behavior, such as prostitution and homosexuality, is tolerated as long as it does not harm other citizens. The drug policy of the Netherlands is just an example of the way in which the Dutch try to control or to solve their social and medical problems. This approach fits into Dutch culture and society and that is why it works in the Netherlands. If the Dutch would give up their drug policy, they would give up their historical and cultural identity. Because the Dutch see the problem of drug abuse not as a concern of the police and the justice system, but as a matter of public health and social well-being, the responsibility for coordinating drug policy in the Netherlands lies with the Minister for Welfare and Public Health.

It should be emphasized that the role of the penal system and law enforcement in the Netherlands is not as prominent as in many other countries. In the Netherlands, criminal law and its enforcement are meant to reduce the supply of drugs, not to criminalize use. In general, the Dutch do not rely heavily on criminal law and law enforcement. They prefer a policy of encirclement, adaptation and integration to a policy of criminalization, stigmatization and punishment. Drug legislation remains supplementary to informal mechanisms which for centuries have been established on traditional family structures and Calvinistic lifestyles.

Present day drug policy in the Netherlands has largely been determined by the 1972 publication of the recommendations of the Narcotics Working Party, entitled *Backgrounds and Risks of Drug Use*. The Working Party concluded that the basic premises of drug policy should be congruent with the extent of the risks involved in drug use. These risks, or the likelihood of harmful effects, are categorized according to the properties of the substances taken. However, the social background of the users, the circumstances in which the drugs are taken, the subjective expectancies and the reasons why people use drugs are at least as important as the pharmacological properties. Especially the reasons of use are of decisive importance as it makes a big difference whether one takes a drug for relaxation and recreation (think of alcohol and marijuana) or with the aim to overcome problems or to cope with a hard life, as a form of self-medication. The effects are also different.

The function of Dutch criminal law is an instrument of social control rather than an instrument for expressing moral values. Therefore, the Dutch make a distinction between policies aimed

> *The Dutch are very pragmatic and try to avoid a situation in which consumers of cannabis suffer more damage from the criminal proceedings than from the use of the drug itself.*

at drug users and policies aimed at drug traffickers. The Dutch believe that for drug users, the penal approach should be left aside as much as possible and ought to be substituted by other methods of prevention, such as health education.

The 1976 Opium Act and Prosecutorial Discretion

The differentiation in risks is reflected in the amended 1919 Opium Act, which came into force in 1976. Thus the Amended Opium Act draws a distinction between "drugs presenting unacceptable risks" such as opiates, cocaine, LSD, amphetamines on the one hand, and "hemp products," such as hashish and marijuana on the other hand. The maximum penalties for illicit trafficking in drugs with an unacceptable risk were considerably increased to a maximum of 12 years imprisonment and/or a fine approximating $600,000; (under certain conditions, e.g. when a crime was committed more than once, this maximum may go up to 16 years or higher). Maximum penalties for possession of small quantities (up to 30 grams) of cannabis preparations for personal use were reduced from an offense to a misdemeanor, that is one month detention or an approximately $3,000 fine.

The Dutch do care about the related health hazards and therefore try to address the next obvious question: what policy could lead to the lowering of drug consumption? In this regard the Dutch are very pragmatic and try to avoid a situation in which consumers of cannabis suffer more damage from the criminal proceedings than from the use of the drug itself.

This requires a restrained attitude on the part of the state. The pragmatic intentions enable such attitudes to be effectuated. Prosecutors are empowered to refrain from instituting criminal proceedings if there are weighty public interests to be considered. New guidelines with priorities have therefore been established for investigating and prosecuting offenses under the Opium Act. Investigation of the import and export of "drugs presenting unacceptable risks" takes priority above investigation of the possession of "hemp products" for personal use.

In a nutshell, the application of the expediency principle implies a pragmatic prosecution policy. If criminal proceedings against cannabis users do not eliminate the drug problem but aggravate it, the law steps aside. The same principle accounts for the sale of limited quantities of hashish in youth centers and coffee shops. This aims at a separation of the markets in which hard drugs and soft drugs circulate. According to the Minister of Justice, this restraint policy succeeds in keeping the sale of hashish out of the ambit of "hard" crime as much as possible.

This practice also prevents young people from going underground. If that were the case, the social surroundings in which hashish circulates and those in which heroin and cocaine appear, would mix up. This somewhat controversial Dutch practice should not be misinterpreted as a tolerant or lenient policy. It is, on the contrary, a well-considered and a very practical policy. The Dutch do not want to hide the problems of their society as they do not want them to get out of control.

Normalization: The Dutch Compromise

The Dutch have adopted their own, alternative way within the boundaries of the internationally prohibitive approach. It is a compromise between legalization and the war on drugs. It should be stressed that this orientation is a desirable approach in the cultural circumstances of The Netherlands.

The Dutch government feels the need to contain the *additional* (secondary) problems as much as possible. A gradual process of controlled integration of the drug phenomenon in society may teach its members to cope better with this happening. The addiction problem will continue to exist but it could be reduced from one on a collective, social level to one on the individual level. It is another way of looking at things, not by denying that drug addiction may cause severe individual and family problems, but by demystifying the popular views on drug use. Integration does not mean acceptance, but discouragement of use is not identical with criminalizing the consumer. This approach could be compared to the alcohol and tobacco control policies and particularly to Dutch policy on cannabis. During a recent year out of 14.5 million inhabitants in the Netherlands about 18,000 people died from tobacco smoking, about 2,000 deaths were directly related to alcohol abuse, and less than 100 Dutch citizens died from drug use. The reaction of society to these figures is rather surprising. It is able to cope with alcohol and smoking problems without emotional overtones and fear that the survival of our western civilization and society are at stake, but it is not prepared to accept drugs as the cause of an even insignificant number of deaths. The Dutch government wants to remain credible and does not want to encourage messages to youngsters such as "your drugs are killers, but ours are pleasures." Young people are very sensitive to such moral double standards.

The above mentioned line of thought was worked out in the memorandum of the Interministerial Steering Group on Alcohol and Drug Policy, entitled: *Drug Policy in Motion: Toward a Normalization of the Drug Problem*. This policy has been adopted by the Dutch government. A process of normalization of the drug phenomenon was advocated, which could possibly lead to a destigmatization of drug users. This does not mean that this phenomenon has been spirited away, but it has been put in another perspective in order to enable society to face the problems from a realistic point of view, unobscured by moralistic coloring. The process of normalization implies a change of climate. The pragmatic aspects of drug policy must be emphasized: that is a more factual and realistic approach instead of an over-dramatized one. A sound approach also means that the drug problem should not be considered as a specific social issue.

International Concerns

The Netherlands are relatively alone in their explicit belief that drug addiction is a problem of public health and welfare. While we recognize that drug addiction is a permanent phenomenon in our society, it can be controlled.

The pragmatic question of efficiency which the Netherlands are accustomed to ask for in measures and instruments, therefore, is not the most important principle of policy in many other countries. It often is not a point of discussion; drug use is simply forbidden. In fact, drug use is seen more as a sin than as behavior involving risks and harm which may be decreased. The objective of almost all countries is that drugs should be banned from society. And a drug free society and a drug free life are only attained by aiming at a total eradication of drugs. Of course, it is realized that this is not completely attainable, but the higher goal may not be affected. In the United States the attitude of zero-tolerance against users, user accountability and the refusal to make the supply of clean syringes to intravenous drug users legal, are symptoms of such a stand.

Dutch Experiences

Criminal law enables the Dutch government, by means of so-called prosecutorial discretion, to pursue a pragmatic drug policy regarding the possession and sale of small quantities of drugs. Criminal proceedings against consumers would not solve the problem but would aggravate it. This policy prevents users from going underground and sliding into the fringes of society where we cannot reach them and where the risks may increase.

Much attention to all drugs is paid in school education programs, albeit as a part of an integrated approach aimed at the promotion of healthy lifestyles. It is apparent that youngsters are acting responsibly since the vast majority are not interested in drugs. In the age group between 10-18 years, current cannabis use was 2.7 percent in 1989. (Current use is expressed in last month prevalence.) For heroin and cocaine current use was less than half a percent (last month prevalence: respectively 0.35 percent and 0.25 percent).

Apart from the poly-drug users, cocaine use in Amsterdam is embedded in non-marginalized social settings where confrontation with the police is rare. Consequently, since no additional risks are introduced to non-problematic users, enabling an open communication about drug use experiences, some kinds of informal use-control rules could be developed. There is very little violence. From 1983-84, we saw waves of free base cocaine use; mainly among "regular" heroin users. But, very few problems have arisen from these "waves" and crack use is still very low.

The number of drug addicts has stabilized and in some cities even decreased. Today, approximately 0.15 percent of the population are drug addicts. Their state of health is reasonably good. This may be regarded as a result of our harm reduction approach, by which both users and addicts are taught how to diminish the risks of drug use. It is not so much a "don't-do-it" message, but rather the message: "it's better not to do it, but if you do, these are the things you should know." The result is more health consciousness and the majority of the heroin and cocaine-using population are not injecting drugs. In Amsterdam this is less than 40 percent. In some smaller cities injecting is an absolute taboo among users. Another indication is the number of Dutch drug related-deaths, which is stable at about 60 cases per year. In Amsterdam, the 1989 statistics showed only 11 deaths out of the estimated 5,000 to 7,000 drug addicts.

One of the most striking features is the wide range of treatment and counseling services, which is capable of reaching the major part of the population of addicts. This is a success in itself! One can only succeed by adopting realistic treatment approaches, primarily directed at improving addicts' physical and social functioning, without requiring abstinence immediately. Low-threshold methadone-maintenance is one of the many modalities. Our entire system is sometimes called the harm reduction approach. Addicts are encouraged to try to retain relations with "normal" society as long as possible. The existence of harm reduction facilities does not prevent an increasing number of addicts who do want to kick their habit from making use of drug-free facilities, which are also widely available. The care-system has no waiting lists. It is easily accessible, free of charge and it treats addicts respectfully as fellow-citizens. Field studies among methadone clients and "street addicts" have shown that this approach has proved to be successful and that the "typical" addict is in no way an antisocial "junkie." It shows the importance of harm prevention strategies as primary mobilizers of health and harm reduction.

AIDS

Keeping close contact with drug addicts is also a prerequisite for an effective AIDS prevention policy; an important element in drug policy. I stress that action to contain the overall drug problem should go hand in hand with realistic, appropriate measures to stop the spread of AIDS. Our policy aims at changing the risky behavior of addicts as much as possible. The supply and use of sterile needles and syringes in exchange for used ones and the supply of condoms is one way of dealing with the problem, but is not a panacea. It must be embedded in a broader health care system. Persuasive face-to-face counseling is essential, if we are to change the addicts' behavior in favor of safer practices. Syringe programs do not lead to more drug use or to more injecting, but to less people sharing syringes. It may be surprising, but addicts are apparently able to act responsibly if the government allows them to do so. Addicts are indeed willing and able to change their behavior. The percentage of intravenous drug users among the total group of AIDS patients in the Netherlands is relatively low, namely 9.14 percent, or 120 people.

I don't know whether our experience is transferable to other countries. Our policy fits into Dutch culture and society and that is why it works in the Netherlands. But I think the experience is worth bringing to the attention of people in the United States. Although closer cooperation in this field is indispensable, we have to take into account the limitations posed by different legal systems, anchored in centuries of cultural and legal history. Attempts to reach an internationalization of drug policies in the sense of a single non-differentiated global approach is bound to prove counter-productive for many countries.

The problem of drug abuse is here to stay. I see no realistic prospect for its total eradication. But it can be successfully contained. This is an important fact, because it demonstrates that there is a feasible or possible middle ground between the extreme options of militarization and total legalization. Policy changes ought to be sought in this direction. Our thinking is that if demand reduction and realistic treatment approaches are given substantial attention, a more positive perspective would be created with regard to the future of drug policies.

Their Spirit Of Moderation And Experimentation Is Unmatched*

The Dutch actually set out to attempt a courageous experiment in drug-policy reform. I was able to observe it myself during July 1977 and again in September 1986. My last visit was particularly dramatic because I left my own country during the scared summer of 1986 and went to another that seemed as if it were in some distant, more peaceful galaxy. The Dutch have not solved their drug problems but they have gone further in rational control than any nation of which I am aware. They have consciously adopted a series of peaceful compromises and have rejected the idea of a war on drugs.

During the early 1970s, they commenced seemingly risky reforms that were based upon a view of drug use quite different than that held in America and most European countries. The Dutch saw marijuana "as a stepping stone to hard drugs" but not, according to Frits Rüter, Director of the Institute of Criminal Law at the University of Amsterdam, because of the qualities of the drug itself. Rather, Professor Rüter explained, it was because the law forced marijuana "into the criminal sphere in common with hard drugs and...it was sold in the same place and frequently by the same dealers." Through changes in the substantive law and detailed written guidelines for police and

---

*Arnold S. Trebach, *The Great Drug War*, Macmillan Publishing Company, 1987, pp. 103 and 375.

prosecutors, the Dutch set about to break that connection. The legal reforms reduced penalties for simple possession of pot and increased them for large scale dealing. Yet, possession and small sales of marijuana still remained, technically speaking, illegal. It was the sophisticated use of police and prosecutorial discretion that made the difference.

Indeed, these experiments could not have worked without the strong support of enforcement officials. It was disorienting for me, after talking to so many American police, to be sought out by police leaders at an Amsterdam Conference in September 1986 and to be told how much they believed in the use of discretion in allowing possession and small sales of marijuana, while vigorously pursuing organized crime figures and large traffickers who were involved in the trade of any drug, including marijuana. Such was the outspoken position expressed to me by, for example, two of the highest police executives in the Netherlands: W.F.K.J.F. Frackers, Inspector-General, Dutch National Police, and G.F. de Gooyer, the head of the National Criminal Intelligence Service. Both saw themselves as committed police leaders who could be more effective by taking a calm, flexible approach to the drug problem, which had to commence with distinguishing between marijuana and harder drugs. Both resented the attitude of the police of other nations, including those from the American Drug Enforcement Agency, who saw them as soft on drugs. They were not soft, they told me; they were smart. I agree with them.

I have seen with my own eyes how "house dealers" in youth clubs are allowed to sell marijuana and hashish and also how coffee shops all over Dutch cities sell these products right off the menu. The symbol of a marijuana plant on a sign tells the public that the products are for sale inside. The key is moderation and control, not prohibition and repression. I saw a coffeehouse with a marijuana plant painted on its sign within sight of the Ministry of Justice building in The Hague, the seat of government for the country. Any youth can walk in at any time and make a purchase under the eyes of the police. At the same time, I saw that the coffee shops were usually half empty and the youth centers were busy mainly on weekends. One American told me that he lived in Holland for six months near both a school with teenage students and a coffeehouse that sold marijuana. He never saw a single student in the coffeehouse during school hours.

Both resented the attitude of the police of other nations, including those from the American Drug Enforcement Agency, who saw them as soft on drugs. They were not soft, they told me; they were smart.

While Dutch criminal-justice and drug-abuse experts are independent characters and openly disagree on many things, there is almost universal agreement among them — including police leaders — that they have largely solved the marijuana problem. Their optimism and my personal observations from wandering the streets and coffee-

The Dutch Do It Better

houses of Dutch cities are supported by objective survey research. The use of marijuana by Dutch youth has dropped since the 1970s. Today, it seems to be substantially less than in those countries — especially West Germany, Norway, and the United States — that have undertaken a campaign to castigate the Dutch with the objective of forcibly enlisting them in the war on drugs.

Although the statistics are by no means precisely comparable, those collections of data that are available suggest dramatic contrasts. For example, the National Institute on Drug Abuse reports for 1983 stated that 5.5 percent of American high school seniors interviewed said that they used pot daily. In 1983 the prestigious Foundation for the Scientific Study of Alcohol and Drug Use, located in Amsterdam, released a study of use throughout the country. A total of 1,306 residents between the ages of 15 and 24 were interviewed in 1983, with the great majority in the 15-19 age category. Seven youngsters replied that they used pot or hashish daily — 1/2 of 1 percent of the 1,306 young people who had full access to these drugs without fear of legal sanction. This rate was less than 10 percent of the rate for the United States where marijuana remains illegal and where the government is waging a war against use of the drug, especially by youth.

I do not know if that low comparative rate would be supported precisely by other studies today. I do know that the youth of the Netherlands have not been harmed by one of the most tolerant drug policies of any country in the world.

Thus, the Dutch seem to have created a good model for that world. They have not gone to war on drugs and have been tolerant of those who have used them. They took away from youth the weapon of marijuana as a symbol of defiance. Most important, whether they planned to or not, they succeeded in making pot a boring subject to most of the youth of the country.

The Dutch seem to have dealt largely with the marijuana issue but have still not solved all of their difficulties with drugs. Yet, their spirit of moderation and experimentation is unmatched. They have tried a variety of approaches to supplying legal drugs to addicts through doctors and have kept adjusting their methods. A few years ago, the city government of Amsterdam came up with a proposal to experiment with medicalized heroin for addicts. The national government resisted and stopped it for the time being. When I was in Amsterdam in September 1986, however, Mayor Ed van Thijn sought me out at a reception he was holding at the Vincent van Gogh Museum to tell me that his government was going to propose the experiment again.

The city government is already showing its support for innovation in a variety of ways. I saw a small piece of that experimentation when I visited the Amsterdam chapter of the national addict union, or "Junkie Bond." The very existence of the union was breathtaking proof of how refreshingly different many Dutch leaders were in thinking about the fundamental nature of the drug problem. The union and another organization devoted to the interests of addicts, known by the initials MDHG, are greatly assisted by an annual contribution of approximately $80,000 from the city government. These related organizations, working side-by-side, provide a form of day hostel for using addicts, along with information, advice, and friendly support of all kinds. On the day of my visit in 1986, members told me of a small book they were writing, which contained the reminiscences of addicts who had kicked the habit. The tentative title: "Each In His Own Way."

While at their headquarters in a decent looking house not far from my hotel in downtown Amsterdam, I was seated in a room with three

Substance Use Among Students in Secondary Schools (13–18) in the Netherlands and United States of America (In %)

	13–14 years				15–16 years				17-18 years	
	m		f		m		f			
	USA	NL	USA	NL	USA	NL	USA	NL	USA	NL
Lifetime prevalence										
tobacco	–	–	–	–	–	–	–	–	66	72
alcohol	77	72	78	66	89	85	89	86	91	92
cannabis	15.3	2.8	14.0	2.4	40.2	12.2	29.8	9.3	43.7	17.7
inhalants	20.1	3.9	21.1	2.0	20.4	4.4	20.7	2.8	17.6	3.5
cocaine	3.3	0.5	3.9	0.8	8.4	1.6	7.0	0.7	10.3	1.6
heroin	–	–	–	–	–	–	–	–	1.3	0.5
stimulants	6.8	1.0	7.5	0.8	10.9	1.9	12.8	0.7	19.1	1.1
sleeping tablets	–	–	–	–	–	–	–	–	7.4	3.6
tranquilizers	–	–	–	–	–	–	–	–	7.6	4.3
Last month prevalence										
tobacco	15	15	17	16	24	26	29	33	29	32
alcohol	32	37	32	33	54	65	50	64	60	68
cannabis	6.3	1.5	5.4	1.0	17.1	6.6	12.6	3.8	16.7	4.6
inhalants	7.0	1.7	5.4	0.9	4.7	1.1	4.2	1.0	2.3	0.5
cocaine	1.5	0.4	1.7	0.0	3.0	0.5	2.4	0.4	2.8	0.2
heroin	–	–	–	–	–	–	–	–	0.3	0.3
stimulants	1.1	0.3	2.3	0.2	3.5	0.6	3.7	0.2	4.2	0.4
sleeping tablets	–	–	–	–	–	–	–	–	1.6	0.8
tranquillizers	–	–	–	–	–	–	–	–	1.3	1.1
N	2887	847	2972	773	2795	881	2765	854	16700	1797

Source: NL-data: Plomp.e.a. (1990): Roken, alcohol-en druggebruik onder scholieren vanaf 10 jaar, resultaten vierde Peilstationsonderzoek 1988/1989.

Source USA-data: American Health Association,1989; Lloyd Johnston, et als., "Monitoring The Future," The National High School Senior Survey, NIDA, 1990 members of the group: Thijs van den Boomen, a nonuser and the organization's administrative director, and Willem Jonkers and Mike Wittenkampf, both drug addicts. As we talked about all of the services offered by the organization, I was surprised to see a picture of Martin Luther King Jr. looking out over high stacks of big cardboard boxes. I was told that the organization was started by a Dutch man who was a disciple of King's because of the minister's great respect for human rights.

As for the boxes, they happened to contain "shooters," Mike told me. Many thousands of them. "Hypodermic needles?" I asked. Mike replied, "Yes, we call them 'shooters.'" All three then proceeded to explain that they conducted a major educational campaign to prevent disease among injecting addicts and prostitutes in the city. In addition, they provided free needles which could be obtained by turning in used ones. For the prostitutes, they also provided free condoms.

Children of crack addicts are at extreme risk of neglect and abuse, and child welfare agencies are reeling from crack-related cases.

—*A.M.Rosenthal*

These women are not monsters. They do not hate their kids, and they do not hit their kids any more than their counterparts who do not use crack. And given the high cost of drugs, they certainly do not share that expensive commodity with their kids.

—*Marsha Rosenbaum*

Chapter 4

Crack: A Disaster Of Historic Dimensions?

Introduction

Every so often, our elected officials feel the need to blame a whole host of social horrors on the existence of one illegal drug. In recent years cocaine and its derivative, crack, have been chosen as that scapegoat drug. There is no doubt that crack is highly addicting and dangerous to many people. Yet, while we believe that anyone who tries crack is playing with fire, we do not believe the hysterical claims made about the alleged epidemic of deaths and damage caused directly by crack.

It is a testament to the distorting power of drug-war fever that the hype about crack has been spread by leaders of the most respected institutions in

American society — and from them to the leaders of other nations. We have already seen that President Bush and Drug Czar Bennett placed a great deal of the blame for our current problems on the advent of crack. Even *The New York Times* seems to have lost a good deal of its normal moderation and balance when it comes to cocaine and crack.

A.M. Rosenthal and other members of *The Times* editorial page seemed consumed with the need to report on crack in terms more suitable to tabloids like *The National Enquirer.* In one editorial on May 28, 1989 the sub-leads included such startling phrases as, "Crime and Blood, in the Streets," "Mothers Turned into Monsters," and "Ripping the Fabric of Society." Aptly, that editorial was entitled, "Crack — A Disaster of Historic Dimensions, Still Growing."

The hysteria affected the news pages as well. *The New York Times'* distinguished health reporter, Jane E. Brody, helped spread the claim in a September 1988 story that the drug was causing "an epidemic of damaged infants." Prominently quoted in the article was the research of Dr. Ira J. Chasnoff, Director of the National Association for Perinatal Addiction Research and Education. Soon Dr. Chasnoff and the association were being quoted in newspapers around the world as sources for the assertion that perhaps one in ten new babies born in America or 375,000 every year were damaged by crack.

Crack: Crime, Blood, And Monster Mothers*

Crime, and Blood, in the Streets

America once thought of drug-related crime in terms of heroin. Stable organized crime groups managed distribution. Junkies stole for the price of a fix, then nodded off. The crack high, by contrast, reinforces feelings of power and aggression rather than blissful lassitude. Crack is distributed by younger, wilder, more heavily armed gangs. They arrogantly intimidate whole communities and make war on each other to control the lucrative business. In community after community, crack violence has overwhelmed law enforcement.

A 1986 survey of state prisoners found that 1 in 10 was under the influence of cocaine at the time of the crime, more than twice the number in 1979. More than half the males arrested in nine major cities last year tested positive for cocaine. In Washington, D.C., the figure was 59 percent up from 14 percent in 1984. In Manhattan, the figure was more than 80 percent. A 1987 survey found that police classified more than a third of murders and two-thirds of robberies and burglaries as drug-related.

Meanwhile, urban emergency rooms report a surge of injuries — crushed bones, blasted organs, floods of internal bleeding — once known only on the battlefield. They are the gory aftermath of shootouts among drug gangs armed for war.

Criminal Justice, Distorted

As an outraged public demands action, crack has forced criminal justice to spend furiously for police, prosecutors, courts and judges in a futile effort to keep up. The most horrendous cost comes at the end of the line. California now has 81,000

---

* A.M. Rosenthal, "Crack: A Disater of Historic Dimensions, Still Growing," *The New York Times*, May 28, 1989.

Crack: A Disaster of Historic Dimensions?

people locked up; since 1983, it has built 21,000 new prison beds and plans 16,000 more. Total cost: $3.2 billion. Since 1983, New York has spent about $900 million to build 17,780 cells. But state officials say they will need at least 9,000 more cells by March. President Bush recently pledged $1 billion to build 24,000 federal prison cells, largely for drug violators.

The billions aren't enough: federal penitentiaries would still be overcrowded by 25 percent. And at the state level, crack-caused crowding forces jurisdictions to release inmates in order to maintain minimal standards. That undermines all pretense of stern law enforcement.

Mothers Turned into Monsters

Unlike heroin, crack is popular with women. When they abuse it, they devastate their children as well as themselves. A recent study of 1,226 pregnant inner-city women in Boston found that 20 percent had used cocaine. Between 1986 and 1988, the number of newborn children in New York City testing positive for drugs — mostly cocaine — almost quadrupled, going from 1,325 to 5,088.

Babies born to crack addicts tend to suffer low birthweight, brain damage and malformation. A recent report in *The Times* described such a child: "a mere patch of flesh with a tangerine-sized head and limbs like splinters." Intensive hospital care for *each* crack baby costs about $90,000. That translates to $190 million a year in New York. For the nation, the figure is $2.5 billion.

Children of crack addicts are at extreme risk of neglect and abuse, and child welfare agencies are reeling from crack-related cases. In New York since 1987, reports of drug-related neglect and abuse have tripled. Meanwhile, urban child welfare workers estimate that 70 percent of children they see are raised by grandmothers or other relatives after parents abandon them for drugs.

Strain, and Fear, in Hospitals

Injuries, overdoses, or other health emergencies caused by smoking crack increased an astonishing 10 times between 1985 and 1987, according to a federal survey. The result is rising strain on urban health care systems already struggling with AIDS and a nursing shortage — with dire consequences for the quality of care given all patients.

Crack has even begun to destroy whatever civility was left to daily hospital life. One New York hospital reports that crack-addicted patients leave their beds to purchase the drug on the street, smoke it in their rooms, and routinely commit thefts and assaults. The routine of doctors and nurses, already harried and tense, now is filled with fear.

Health officials also blame crack for a new outbreak of syphilis in cities. The disease is spread by prostitution for drug money and casual sex with many partners in crack houses. Because syphilis also facilitates the spread of AIDS, crack has become an alarming new factor in the AIDS epidemic.

Ripping the Fabric of Society

The most profound damage of crack may be to social values. Crack dealing involves more adolescents than the heroin trade ever did, offering them money enough to realize the most alluring teenage fantasies — clothes, jewelry, cars, guns, power. Adults, who ought to be exerting authority, shrink in fear of such youngsters.

At the same time, vigilantism has begun to flare. After crack dealers took over an abandoned house on a working-class street in Detroit, the neighborhood "changed to a place where bands of teenagers shot at each other in daylight, sold drugs from the curb and sneered at people who threatened to call the police." Fed up, two residents burned the house down. At their trial, rather than deny involvement, they proudly admitted it. The jury quickly acquitted them. That was one of 100 similar fires in Detroit. In a two-week period in Miami last year, 35 suspected crack houses burned down.

Vigilantism, observes Gary Marx, a sociologist, "is a bargaining chip for the citizens, who are saying to the authorities, 'Unless you take action, we will.'" Crack forces upon America a question once limited to Third World societies beset by guerrilla terror: How can citizens respect a government that can't even provide basic security?

The crack-induced strains on American life are spreading. Residents of Seaford, Del., population 5,500, describe it as "a conservative, God-fearing community" and an "Ozzie and Harriet kind of place." But since crack dealers arrived in 1985, according to *The Wall Street Journal*, the rural town has seen brutal murders, robberies, burglaries, assaults, prostitution, syphilis and a cocaine-positive baby. There are other Seafords as drug dealers seek new markets in smaller cities and towns.

Even as the crack poison spreads to middle America, a federal government grown used to budget deficits and constricted social policies remains leery of any concerted response. Last year, Congress authorized a few billion in a drug bill that also created a drug "czar."

But those are diffident gestures against a murderous industry worth tens of billions a year. The administration acts as though the American people fear taxes and big government more than drug gangs that are seizing control of their communities.

The Plague Among Us*

When 1986 began, relatively few people had heard either of crack or of Len Bias. Soon, they were to become tragic household words. They dominated headlines and national fears, often pushing aside such concerns as Soviet espionage, nuclear war, terrorism, poverty, and crime in the streets.

Crack may well have existed for decades in various quiet back rooms of the drug world. More widespread use of the drug was first noticed by a few experts during the 80s. Public concern grew with stories of bizarre behavior by users, especially among our youth.

Few drug abuse experts knew anything about the drug because it was, comparatively speaking, so rarely used. I certainly was ignorant. On April 24, I admitted as much to a nationwide television audience during a heated discussion on the "MacNeil/Lehrer Newshour." Barbara Taylor, the editor of *Essence* magazine, shot back from New York that I certainly wasn't much of a scholar and that it was time to get hysterical about crack in order to save our children. Five weeks later, on another television interview show, Dr. Arnold Washton, a nationally renowned physician in the cocaine treatment business, countered my plea for calm measures by declaring, twice, that we should get hysterical about crack. Dr. Washton had been quoted frequently in the media to that effect, declaring at times that "crack is the most addictive drug known to man right now" and that it caused "almost instantaneous addiction."

Virtually every major print and electronic media vehicle, including the most respected and influential, joined in the emotional stampede. *The Washington Post* commenced a news story on the drug with a report of a New York City youth who had stabbed his mother to death in a crack-induced

---
* Arnold S. Trebach, The Great Drug War, p. 5.

frenzy. The prestigious paper gave no explanation of the details nor did it inquire into how many recent homicides were related to alcohol or handguns or the illegal drug trade. Reports were frequently made and repeated that females, including young girls, would go into houses where crack was sold, find that they were unable to stop taking the stuff, and would sell their bodies to man after man in order to buy more and more crack. The stories were never balanced with an inquiry into the extent to which drugs, mainly alcohol, and sex were intertwined in legal establishments known as bars.

Newsweek magazine seemed particularly hooked on the compulsion to run story after story on the drug, emphasizing the most sensational aspects of its impact on society and individuals. While it might be argued that such stories served the public interest by scaring off potential users, that was not always the case. One young, though mature college student, with some modest drug experience, told me much later that after reading a story on crack in a March issue of *Newsweek*, "I had never heard of it until then but when I read that it was better than sex and that it was cheaper than cocaine and that there was an epidemic, I wondered what I was missing. I questioned why I seemed to be the only one not doing the drug. The next day I asked some friends if they knew where to get some."

One of the most hysterical issues of a major American publication in recent history was the June 16, 1986, *Newsweek*, which rivaled the sensationalism of the *Reefer Madness* movie about pot in the 30s. Editor-in-chief Richard Smith unburdened himself of a lead editorial entitled "The Plague Among Us," in which he compared the drug problem to medieval plagues and to the Japanese attack on Pearl Harbor. Mr. Smith saw all of these drugs but now especially crack — "the ... most addictive commodity now on the market" — as creating a crisis that threatened the survival of the nation. The drugs themselves, mind you, not the governmental and social reaction to them.

A few days later, in one of those sad and unpredictable events that changes the course of history, Len Bias died suddenly in his room at the University of Maryland. Bias was 22, black, a star basketball player at the university, liked and admired by his friends and those fans in his region who knew him, a nice American kid, a model of clean living. The Boston Celtics (one of the most prestigious teams in all of American sports) had drafted him to play in the Na-

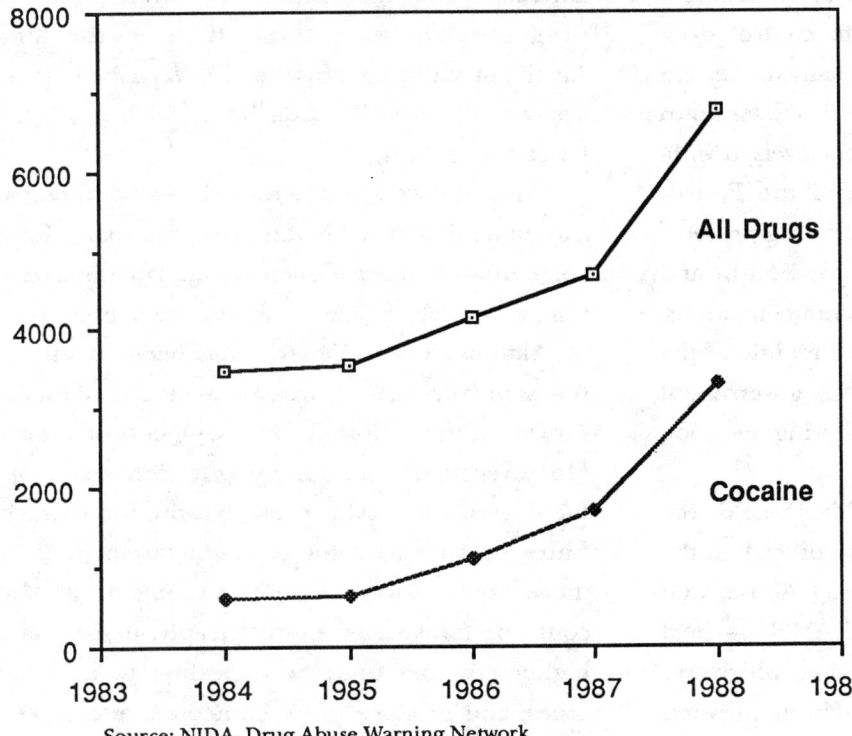

U.S. Deaths Due to Drug Abuse

Source: NIDA, Drug Abuse Warning Network

tional Basketball Association and he had just signed a rich contract. The kid even had a jersey number. Total strangers with no interest in basketball were elated for him. The young man from the other side of the tracks had his foot on the first step of the American glory trail.

Headlines in June suggested that crack might have killed Len Bias. Before the end of the month, another young black sports star, professional football player Don Rogers, died of a cocaine — many people heard that as "crack" — overdose. Coming on top of all of the previous hysteria, the tragic deaths of these two young Americans pushed the governmental and social leadership of the most powerful nation on earth into frenzied action in all directions at once.

Bills were tossed into legislative hoppers all over the country as if they were sandbags heaved onto dikes being hastily erected to control a rampaging flood. Measures were proposed on both ends of Pennsylvania Avenue in Washington to demand mass random urine tests of government officials, to deploy the military to control drug trafficking, to impose the death penalty for certain homicides connected with drug sales, to water down the exclusionary rule so that evidence seized without a warrant and in violation of the Fourth Amendment could be introduced in drug prosecutions so long as the officer had good faith, and dozens of other more repressive recommendations. It was a scary time to sit here in the middle of the national capital and sense my own government coming apart, losing its guts, blowing its cool, prostituting itself, or all four.

On July 10, Dr. Donald Ian MacDonald, the top operational federal drug abuse official — the Administrator of the Alcohol, Drug Abuse, and Mental Health Administration or ADAMHA — held a major press conference on cocaine, which was reported in all the major media. The impression given by the television network anchormen and by leading reporters on national newspapers was that Dr. MacDonald had produced shocking new data proving that there had been an explosion in cocaine and crack deaths during recent months. In a typical front-page story in July, *USA Today* reported (in error, as it later turned out) that there had been 563 cocaine-related deaths during the first six months of 1986.

On July 15, it was dramatically revealed that armed American helicopters crews had arrived with their planes in Bolivia to transport local police on raids against cocaine laboratories in the jungles. Later, President Reagan said that the deaths of young Bias and Johnson had been important factors influencing his decision to send off other young Americans in uniform to get the drugs at the source. It was also revealed that our troops had already been secretly involved in such missions, in, for example, Colombia — and that more drug raids would be launched in other countries if the Bolivian attacks were successful. These overseas military drug missions were tragic firsts in the long American antidrug crusade. They pushed us all across a chemical Rubicon from which it will not be easy to return.

What do we know about the drug that has caused all this furor? Not much, even today; I can come up with only rudimentary information. What follows, therefore, are cautious observations.

Almost every major drug has been, at various times in our history, treated as a threat to the survival of the nation by some segments of society. Moreover, there seems nothing terribly new about the type of chemical process that produced crack. Entrepreneurs have for eons sought to produce more potent forms of mind-altering drugs that could be transported more cheaply, be sold at a higher cost per unit, be appealing to different tastes, and produce more immediate effects. Fermented grapes and grains were and are fine for many millions of people. Distilling, however, produced spirits, sometimes called brandywine, that were more potent. Wine and beer create trouble for many people, but the greatest difficulty seems to come from the more concentrated distilled spirits of alcohol. The less natural the drug the more trouble for humans.

The same for opium. Smoking the dried powder that comes from the opium-poppy sap is both calming and potentially addicting — not nearly so alluring or dangerous, however, as using morphine, the main active ingredient in opium. Neither is as thrilling or as dangerous as diacetylmorphine, which could, for convenience, be called the essence of morphine plus a bit of vinegar-like acid; this concentrated and refined drug is also known as heroin.

Chewing the leaves of the South American coca plant produces, along with numbness of the mouth and tongue, a mild sensation of stimulation and good feeling. When chemists managed to isolate what might be called the essence of coca, the most powerful ingredient in the leaf, they produced a very potent white powder: cocaine hydrochloride. Largely ignored for years, cocaine, as it is usually called, suddenly became very popular to millions of Americans who now like to snort it through their noses.

For many thrill-seekers (and that is what is truly involved here) both the stimulation and the risks of the cocaine powder were enough. Then some bored soul decided to refine the powder further for smoking, which is *the* most rapid way to get drugs to the brain, being even quicker than injection. Thus, freebasing was born.

Traditional freebasing involves heating the powder with volatile chemicals, such as ether, which sometimes results in explosions and fires. This, apparently, is what injured comedian Richard Pryor several years ago. The preparation of crack is easier and safer. Cocaine powder is mixed with water and baking soda or ammonia. The result is a highly concentrated chemical that looks like bits of coagulated soap powder, often slightly off-white, about the size of large green peas. It is frequently smoked in a pipe and makes a crackling sound when lit. In some cities, it is known as rock or cooked cocaine.

A gram of cocaine, less than a teaspoonful, costs at least $100 in many communities. Crack pellets are sometimes sold for as little as $10 each in the same neighborhoods.

It was a scary time to sit here in the middle of the national capital and sense my own government coming apart, losing its guts, blowing its cool, prostituting itself, or all four.

That this form of the drug is more addicting than powdered cocaine should come as no surprise. Any drug that is more refined and then smoked will be more potent than its less concentrated relatives.

However, it is premature and perhaps misleading to call it the most addictive drug now known. While I believe that anybody who tries this relatively unknown compound is a fool, my guess is that it is no more addicting than smoked tobacco or smoked heroin. I also believe, in passing, that anyone who uses either of those latter substances in any form is a fool. As with those dangerous drugs, however, some foolish people use crack and do not get hooked.

It is also misleading to view this as a plot to hook our children with a cheap drug, as many alleged experts and commentators have been doing. Those people susceptible to the allure of crack will often spend roughly as much as those who use cocaine powder. While the high of crack is immediate, it is also of short duration, perhaps a few minutes, necessitating repeated purchases for those at risk. Many adults with money and curiosity are users.

We do not know how many addicted customers there are out there. One is too many in my book, but if there is truly a national epidemic, I have yet to see the hard proof.

That hard proof would exist, in my eyes, in the records of federal agencies such as the Drug Enforcement Administration of the Department of Justice or the National Institute of Drug Abuse (the NIDA) of the Department of Health and Human Services. When I heard and read the major news stories during July on the crack epidemic and related deaths, I was confused because they were inconsistent with my reading of the available federal data. My calls to officials in NIDA and DEA brought honest humility and responses like: we really don't know very much about crack but what we read in the newspapers. There is not even a separate listing for crack, they told me, in NIDA's authoritative Drug Abuse Warning Network (DAWN), which collects data on drug abuse deaths and injuries. Crack injuries and deaths are listed under cocaine.

When I finally obtained a copy of the materials passed out at that sensational July 10 news conference, I discovered that Dr. MacDonald had made a disclaimer from the start to the effect that the federal experts had no new data on cocaine and crack. The disclaimer was not reported by the media. Why, then, call this major news conference? Dr. MacDonald explained that he wanted "to underscore the great potential risk we know is involved in cocaine use." In the demagogic atmosphere of Washington at that time, this should have been interpreted: We, the leading national medical scientists, have nothing new to tell you about the dangers of cocaine, but everyone else is getting press attention from crack, and we deserve some too, by gosh.

All during the public hysteria of the summer of 1986, the only complete annual DAWN data available was that for 1984, which showed 604 mentions of cocaine in reports by medical examiners. (A "mention" signifies that a medical examiner or coroner found indications of the drug in the body of a person who died suddenly from drug abuse, normally from an overdose. Coroners reporting to DAWN may provide mentions of up to three drugs for each sudden drug abuse death.) That was a significant rise above the 195 mentions of 1981, an increase that was heralded from one end of the country to the other. Even if each of those 604 mentions involved a death caused by cocaine, which is not the case, and as tragic as each death was, it is difficult to see the destruction of a nation of 240 million in 604 cocaine deaths when so many more of our people are being killed by other drugs, especially the legal ones.

Totally ignored in the cries to save our children from crack were the NIDA data which showed that the total number of children who died from cocaine in 1984 was eight. Yes, eight, from all forms of cocaine, including crack. And these at the time of the greatest hysteria were the latest complete data from the federal government, which also showed 14 mentions of cocaine for ages 18 and 19, and 273 for young people in their 20s, or a total of 295 mentions for all Americans under age 30.

No data are available as of this writing, the fall of 1986, for this year. Thus, all of the claims about the great rise in crack deaths *for the first months of 1986*, such as that reported by *USA Today* and other major media voices, were false. Even more significant, none of the leading government drug abuse officials, who knew the claims for 1986 to be false, felt any responsibility to tell the public the truth during the scared summer of '86.

During that summer, preliminary information *was* available for 1985 on all cocaine deaths. The significance of this information was either ignored or reported in a misleading fashion by the government and the media. While the end of America from drugs was being declared, the number of known cocaine deaths in those preliminary figures had actually declined from 1984 to 1985. Because there had been a slight rise in recorded cocaine, including crack, *use* in those years, a fair headline might have been "Cocaine and crack use rise while deaths decline!" I would have settled for no headlines at all on the matter....

How many reported cocaine deaths have been laid at the door of crack, alone or in combination with other drugs? I have searched. My assistants have searched. We have gone through many government reports. We have quizzed government statistical experts. We have yet to discover one death in which the presence of crack was a confirmed factor. In time, I am sure that we will because it is such a potent and addicting drug, but up to now, we have not.

Women And Crack: What's The Real Story?*

Crack cocaine has given the media material for many sensational stories. This supposed inherently evil substance very quickly became the scourge of the nation by the late 1980s. The white powder that is being converted into "rocks" has been given exclusive credit for the social and personal downfall of "inner city" (a term that has become synonymous with "black") youth. Although most Americans have never seen — up close and in person — cocaine (or any other illegal drug), the media has provided, on a daily basis, all they need to know. When President Bush himself showed them a bag of crack on TV, the public's concern-turned-hysteria provided unquestioning support for intensifying the war on drugs.

Media Myth

Women's use of crack has provided even better media stories. The moral fiber of society, it is argued, is threatened by the violation of two powerful cultural mores that women are supposed to protect: sexual virtue and motherhood. We are told that women who use crack become sex-crazed; "toss-ups" or "strawberries" who lie around crack houses indulging in all kinds of promiscuous sex, including bestiality. Journalists tell us that men crack users report crack makes women so sexually excitable they will do anything. The implications for sexually transmitted diseases are obvious.

After sex comes babies, and with babies, motherhood. On this subject we have learned, through the media, that crack mothers abuse their children. They give their children drugs. Some even put crack in the baby's bottle!

---
* Marsha Rosenbaum, Ph.D., Sheigla Murphy, Jeanette Irwin and Lynne Watson, "Women and Crack: What's the Real Story?" *The Drug Policy Letter*, March/April 1990, p.2.

In sum, we "know" from reading the paper and watching TV that after one hit of crack, women take off their clothes and have sex with anyone, including the family pet. Subsequently, they beat their children, add crack to their babies' formulas; and for those children who are not already using it, they blow crack smoke in their faces. To make a long story short, women crack users are amoral animals, lacking a conscience.

As sociologists, we are suspicious of media reports and stereotypes about crack. Over the past decade, we have observed the often vast differences between media reports and our research findings about women heroin addicts, methadone maintenance, "ecstasy" (recently outlawed by the U.S. Drug Enforcement Administration), and middle-class cocaine use. Last summer, we set out to do a three-year study (funded by the National Institute on Drug Abuse) of women and cocaine. Unlike journalists, we have the luxury of taking our time. We do in-depth interviews that last three hours. By the end of the study, we will have completed 125 such interviews. Currently, we have interviewed 45 women, and although our analysis is preliminary, it merits some attention.

Crack and Sex

Do women lose control sexually? Most of our respondents do not admit to sexual abandon, but usually know others who do. Women's motivation, however, seems to be financial rather than physiological. The majority of our respondents report that crack actually reduces their desire to have sex, rather than the other way around. Those women who admit to "toss-up" behavior express feelings of extreme embarrassment and humiliation. They are aware of the stigma associated with the "sex-for-crack" dynamic and would rather not be participating in it. Yet they feel helpless to resist the urge to do more crack once they are high and will trade almost anything for it once they have started.

The power structure, hence the interpersonal dynamic, in the crack world is male-dominated. The men hold the drugs and have the money. Women crack users, rather than sexually stimulated, are stimulated by the desire for more crack. When they run out of money, if (and this is variable) they want to go on using crack, they cash in on the only remaining commodity left to them — their bodies. Those women who exchange sex for crack are prostituting themselves, and this occupation is not new, particularly among drug abusers and addicts. The only new twist is that prostitutes traditionally exchange sex for money and then use the money to buy drugs. With crack, some women cut out the money, exchanging sexual favors directly for drugs. Prostitution is, of course, the "oldest profession." It is not gender-specific, and men will do the same, given equal conditions and opportunities. These fellows are called "raspberries," but they have not as yet been the subject of media reports.

Crack and Mothering

As mothers, crack users share basic American parenting values. They express a great deal of concern for their children, even if they cannot always demonstrate techniques commonly agreed upon as exhibiting good mothering. A major problem faced by crack-using mothers is financial. Mothers receiving Aid to Families with Dependent Children benefits experience problems endemic to raising children in poverty. They live in inadequate, unsafe housing, have no respite and receive negative or non-existent social support. They cannot simultaneously support a crack habit and children. Yet they often try, for a period, to do both. The problem is not always simply financial.

The crack scene is all-consuming, and women become inundated in it. Thus even when they have money (albeit meager amounts), they become enveloped in the lifestyle — "cracked" — and their entire orientation centers around cocaine.

It is our impression, based on these preliminary findings, that non-deliberate neglect is a more appropriate term for the mother-child relationship than abuse. We have not found evidence of exceptional physical abuse. These women are not monsters. They do not hate their kids, and they do not hit their kids any more than their counterparts who do not use crack. And given the high cost of drugs, they certainly do not share that expensive commodity with their kids. Sadly, while on a crack binge, the children are ignored. These women are aware that they are hurting their children, as evidenced by the fact that many in our population voluntarily gave their children to relatives because they doubted their own ability to take care of them.

Like women heroin addicts a decade before them, women crack users are considered to be more "deviant" than their male counterparts. They are perceived to be not only loose women, but bad mothers — a stigma transcending time and culture. We wondered what they were really like. Could they be this bad? We learned from the women that they are tough. They are neither stupid nor pushovers. They do not like to talk about sex, but do maintain that men — both crack-using men and those men reporting on the crack scene — are exaggerating its importance as the motivation behind women's sexual activities. It is not that the stories about sex do not have some credibility, but they are exaggerated. They do not represent all women all of the time.

Although certainly a powerful substance, crack's main role in the lives of many of these women is to exacerbate a situation that is already terrible. Life is difficult for anyone who is single, trying to survive on AFDC and living in a small, often unfurnished, apartment in a housing project, homeless shelter or hotel. With no job or job skills and little education, they are locked into poverty.

Once again, it is not simply drugs that account for incidences of prostitution and child neglect. (Ten years ago it was heroin that was to blame, now it's crack, and 10 years from now it will be something else.) Crack may aggravate the situation, but take drugs away, and these conditions still exist. Thus, these socioeconomic conditions, not drugs, drive women (and men) to act in ways counter to society's sense of how people should live their lives.

How Many Crack Babies?*

No drug tragedy is more appalling than babies handicapped by their mothers' cocaine abuse in pregnancy. The figure of 375,000 "crack babies" has been widely reported in the media and recited by drug warriors such as William Bennett to warn of the perils of legalized drugs. Columnists Jack Anderson and A.M. Rosenthal speak of 300,000-400,000 "addicted" or "crack-addicted" babies.

These are mind-boggling numbers: one in 10 births. They are also incredible, given that the 1988 National Household Survey on Drug Abuse found that the number of women who used crack in the year was just 474,000, or less than 1 percent of the childbearing population, while just one million used cocaine of any kind on a monthly basis! No doubt the survey, conducted annually by the National Institute on Drug Abuse, underreports drug use. But there are also good grounds to investigate the source of the supposed "375,000 crack babies."

The source is a 1988 survey of 36 hospitals by Dr. Ira Chasnoff, director and founder of the

---

* Dale Gieringer, "How Many Crack Babies?" *The Drug Policy Letter*, March/April 1990, p. 4.

National Association for Perinatal Addiction Research and Education. Dr. Chasnoff makes it clear that 375,000 is not a count of crack-addicted babies, but rather a rough estimate of babies exposed to illicit drugs during pregnancy. The hospitals surveyed included both private and public institutions across the country, but were not a scientific, demographic sample. In fact, a glance at the list shows that it is weighted toward leading metropolitan areas where drug abuse is more prevalent. They reported rates of prenatal exposure to illicit substances ranging from 0.4-27 percent with an average of 11 percent — in round numbers, one in 10 — which works out to about 375,000 nationwide.

The meaning of Chasnoff's estimate is unfortunately obscured by the fact that different hospitals reported different statistics in their surveys. Some surveyed mothers' own self-reports of drug usage; others looked at urine samples of mothers (which are sensitive to cocaine for 2-3 days) or of babies (which are sensitive up to a week). A few hospitals counted marijuana and other illicit drugs along with cocaine, though Dr. Chasnoff maintains that cocaine accounted for most drug exposure. Like most studies, the survey did not distinguish between cocaine and crack, which, according to NIDA, accounts for about one-fifth of cocaine use. Estimates from Associate Professor Richard Barth of the School of Social Work at Berkeley have put the number of crack-exposed babies at around 1-4 percent.

Yet, however many babies are exposed to cocaine, the crucial question remains: how many are actually harmed by it? After all, one might well speak of a million-plus alcohol and tobacco babies. In fact, while crack-exposed babies run a high risk of premature birth and other problems, the U.S. Department of Health and Human Services estimates that over 2 in 3 suffer no obvious problems at birth.

However, there is concern that many may be at risk of more subtle, behavioral problems that are difficult to detect at birth and become evident only in later years. According to findings released last September by Dr. Chasnoff and Dr. Judith Howard of the University of California at Los Angeles, cocaine-exposed infants may suffer deficits in their ability to concentrate, interact socially and cope with unstructured environments at the age of 2-3 years. Such infants have been widely publicized in the media as "crack babies," though the nature and severity of their affliction is not entirely clear.

Professor Barth released a study in February that disputes Chasnoff's findings on long-term ef-

> *These are mind-boggling numbers: one in 10 births. They are also incredible, given that the 1988 National Household Survey on Drug Abuse found that the number of women who used crack in the year was just 474,000, or less than 1 percent of the childbearing population.*

fects. Barth found that these babies, who were observed from 1-4 years, compete quite well and will live among their peers in a healthy way. Unlike fetal alcohol babies, they are not born mentally retarded and are as bright as normal children. The study involved children in Los Angeles, San Francisco and Oakland.

Chasnoff's observations on the effect of maternal cocaine use on infants have been well documented. He says that physiologically, the most noticeable reproductive hazard of cocaine is a markedly higher risk of preterm delivery, low birthweight and growth retardation, occurring in up to 25-30 percent of exposed infants. He also says cocaine has also been linked to an increased incidence of miscarriage, sudden infant death syndrome, fetal strokes and certain deformities. The severity of these problems is highly variable. Preterm and low-birthweight babies are at greater risk of numerous life-threatening and debilitating complications, but in most cases their growth deficits are reversible with reasonable care. Fetal strokes and other birth defects may cause lasting impairment, but are more rare. Women who stop using cocaine early in pregnancy reduce the risk of fetal harm, though permanent damage may conceivably occur from a single intensive session. Fetal "addiction" to cocaine is not a major issue; rather, the danger is that cocaine may harm the fetus by constricting blood vessels, raising blood pressure, cutting fetal blood flow and interfering with the brain's neurotransmitters.

In addition, of course, some say there is good reason to worry about cocaine's effects on maternal behavior. Dr. Robert ten Benzel, a pediatrician at the University of Minnesota, says there is enough anecdotal evidence that proves some women use crack to induce abortions.

A major difficulty in judging the risk of prenatal cocaine use is that its symptoms can also be caused by other factors that are seldom fully controlled in studies. For example, low-birthweight and preterm babies can be caused by inadequate nutrition, poor prenatal care and polydrug abuse, all of which are more common in cocaine-abusing mothers. An important, new factor is syphilis, which has become a problem among crack users because some trade sex for drugs, according to Dr. Richard Fulroth, chief of newborn services at Highland Hospital in Oakland, California.

Controlling for other drug use, it has been estimated that women have a four times greater risk of low-birthweight babies if they use cocaine throughout pregnancy, or 1.8 times if they use it less often. The risk factor for smoking throughout pregnancy is three, and for drinking three or more drinks per day 1.7, according to the January issue of *American Journal of Public Health.* Thus cocaine seems comparable to other, legal drugs as a risk factor in problem pregnancies. Barth's study shows children with low birth weights catch up in overall growth by age two.

As for the mental and behavioral symptoms reported by Chasnoff and Howard, their incidence has not yet been statistically determined and remains controversial. Among the most worrisome evidence is a study published in the November issue of *The Journal of Pediatrics* that reported abnormal brain encephalograms in 35 percent of infants of cocaine-positive mothers, seven times the normal incidence. However, other investigators have failed to detect this, including Dr. Fulroth.

The horrors of crack baby syndrome have been sensationalized in the press. One researcher was quoted in *Newsweek* recently saying, "It's as if the part of the brain that makes us human beings capable of discussion or reflection is wiped out."

However, Chasnoff maintains that crack babies develop "within the normal range for cognitive development and are not, as some people have stated, brain damaged," whatever their behavioral differences. Experts note that cocaine-exposed babies show a wide range of outcomes, and cannot be automatically presumed to be defective or irremediable. Most agree that the prognosis for crack babies is hopeful, provided they receive attentive post-natal care and nurturing — which are, of course, apt to be sorely lacking within crack-using families.

Many observers think that the physical dangers of cocaine have been overblown by drug war hysteria. Some privately suggest that pressure for government funding has created an anti-cocaine bias. A study of research papers on prenatal cocaine use by Dr. Gideon Koren found that positive findings were significantly more likely to be accepted for publication than negative ones, even though the negative studies were better controlled and had more subjects. Professor Barth and other experts emphasize the many adverse economic, behavioral and cultural factors that put cocaine babies at risk.

Crack's greatest danger to most babies may come not from pharmacological harm, but rather from the lack of prenatal and postnatal care.

In Oakland's Mandela House, which provides addict mothers with attentive prenatal and postnatal care, Dr. Fulroth reports no problem births among its residents. Fulroth calls cocaine a "red flag" of broader problems. He says, "cocaine in my opinion is a symptom of what's happening to our society when you take away opportunity for education, housing [and] health care...."

Just how widespread is the problem of crack babies? A recent Household Survey of welfare agencies reported 8,974 crack-exposed babies in eight cities: New York, Los Angeles, Chicago, Miami, Phoenix, San Francisco, Tacoma and Fort Wayne. In his first National Drug Control Strategy, President Bush spoke of 100,000 crack babies — instead of 375,000 — making a somewhat loose extrapolation from eight cities to the entire nation and equating crack-exposed babies with crack babies.

A gauge of the HHS survey may be found in epidemiological birth statistics since crack was introduced in 1985. These show a true epidemic at some inner-city hospitals. At Highland Hospital, the rate of low-birthweight deliveries soared from 7 percent in 1985 to 11.2 percent in 1989. In Los Angeles from 1987-88, infant mortality among blacks jumped from 16.3-21.1 per 1000, and in Washington, D.C., from 21.4-25.1 — a worse rate than in some Third World countries. Looking at all races, Los Angeles County reported a 17 percent increase in low-birthweight infants from 5.3 percent-6.2 percent between 1988 and 89, which translates to an excess of 36,000 if projected nationally. This trend has been blamed on a combination of factors, including cocaine, syphilis and poor prenatal care. Nationwide, the most recent data from the Centers for Disease Control show a mere 2.2 percent increase in the rate of low-birth weight babies from 1985-87, corresponding to an excess of 6,000 births per year. The CDC data show no noticeable increase in other birth defects.

In sum, babies harmed by crack exposure may well represent the single greatest public health cost of cocaine, but the casualties are much less than the 375,000 commonly claimed in the media. In terms of fetal damage, cocaine may be comparable to alcohol, which claims some 4,000-12,000 cases of fetal alcohol syndrome per year, according to the National Institute on Alcohol Abuse and Alcoholism in 1987. On the other hand, as a cause of low birthweight, cocaine seems less troublesome than tobacco, which is somewhat less toxic but more widely used. Unfortunately, the pharmacological dangers of cocaine are greatly compounded by prenatal and postnatal neglect. This is plenty enough to be concerned about, without exaggerating the problem with spurious claims to defend the bankrupt, punitive policies that have brought it about.

Prohibition May Be More Toxic Than Crack*

The "crack epidemic" and an ensuing wave of violence began in New York City in late 1984. Criminal justice researchers, practitioners and private citizens argued that crack was different from other drugs because it caused a significant increase in the homicide rate. In New York, the total number of homicides committed in 1988 reached 1,896. This was an increase of more than 13 percent over the 1987 total of 1,672 and an apparent single-year record for the city.

We examined the relationship between use and trafficking of crack and homicide in New York City. The analysis is based on data directly collected from the New York City Police Department during the peak homicide year of 1988. The data includes 414 homicides that occurred March 1-October 31. These 414 homicide events created a database including 490 perpetrators and 434 victims.

Who are the Killers?

With regard to location, 45 percent of the 414 homicide events occurred in the street. An additional 35 percent occurred in residences, primarily the residence of the victim. The remainder of the homicides were distributed between bars, abandoned buildings, the transit system, and commercial or other public areas.

Sixty-eight percent of the homicides involved the use of firearms. The vast majority of these were handguns, with .38 caliber and 9 mm. weapons being the most prevalent. About 20 percent of the homicides were committed with knives or other cutting instruments. Physical force, such as strangulation, was the means used in 7 percent of the homicides.

In those homicides where data were available, 95 percent of the perpetrators were male, 83 percent were black, and the mean age was about 27 years. About 23 percent of the perpetrators were also identified as Hispanics. Eighty-four percent of the homicide victims were male, 83 percent were black, and the mean age was about 30 years.

A total of 140 perpetrators (29 percent) were identified by the police as being drug traffickers. A somewhat higher proportion (34 percent) of the victims were classified as drug traffickers (148). Police detectives who completed the forms were asked to distinguish between "high-level" and "low-level" dealers. The vast majority of perpetrators and

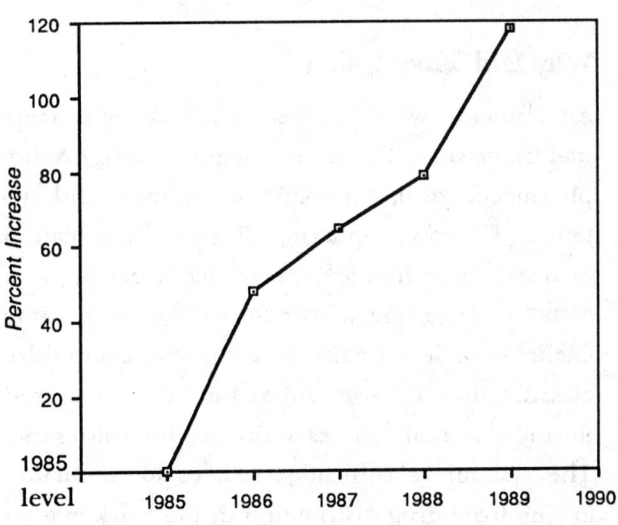

Percent Increase in Drug Related Murders Since 1985 in U.S.

Source: FBI *Uniform Crime Reports*.

---

* Paul J. Goldstein, Henry H. Brownstein, Patrick J. Ryan and Patricia A. Bellucci, "Most Drug-Related Murders Result From Crack Sales, Not Use," *The Drug Policy Letter*, March/April 1990, p. 6.

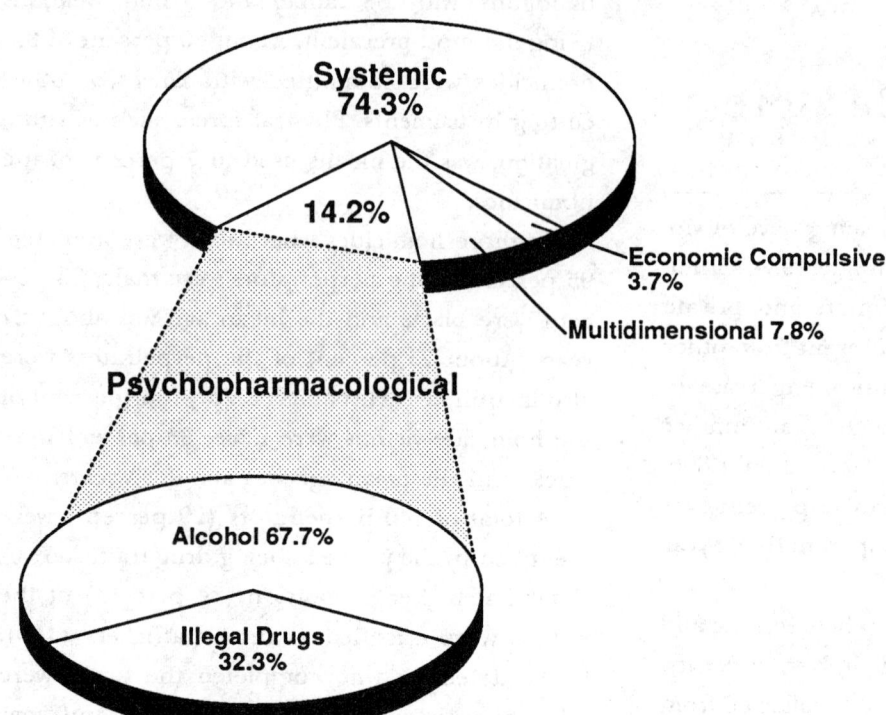

Majority of Drug-Related Murders due to the Drug Trade; Majority of Murderers who were Intoxicated were on Alcohol

victims were labeled as low-level traffickers. Only 16 perpetrators and 15 victims were considered to be high-level traffickers.

Why Did They Kill?

All homicides were classified in a tripartite conceptual framework. The three categories were psychopharmacological, economic, compulsive and systemic. The psychopharmacological classification involved those homicides in which a person, as a result of ingesting a specific substance, became excitable or irrational. The economic compulsive classification involves homicides that occurred during economic crimes to finance their drug use. The systemic classification relates to homicides arising from drug distribution or the black market drug trade.

A total of 218 (52.7 percent) of the 414 homicide events were classified as being primarily drug-related. Cases were defined as "drug-related" only when it was believed by both the police and the researchers that drugs contributed to the outcome in an important and causal manner. Homicides were only classified as drug-related in those cases where sufficient information was available to clearly make that determination. Thus, the finding that 52.7 percent of the homicides were drug-related must be viewed as a conservative approximation. The majority (162) of the drug-related homicides, about 74 percent, were classified as systemic.

The specific drug or drugs associated with each primary classification were also recorded. Crack was the leader in all homicide events and led in each category except for psychopharmacological, where alcohol was the leader. All 21 alcohol-related homicides were psychopharmacological. Alcohol-related murders constituted about 68 percent of the 31 psychopharmacological homicides.

In-Depth Analysis of Crack Homicides

Below is a more detailed review of the 118 "crack-only" homicides and the 13 "crack-in-combination" homicides.

Psychopharmacological. A total of 31 (7.5 percent) of the 414 homicide events were classified as being psychopharmacological. Only five of these homicides involved the use of crack. Of these five, one involved crack/alcohol combination and one involved crack/cocaine/alcohol combination. The other three involved crack only. Two of the three crack-only homicides were considered to be victim-precipitated. The single crack-only psychopharmacological homicide that was not victim precipitated involved a 22-year-old black male who, while high on crack, beat his infant daughter to death.

The crack/alcohol homicide involved a 26-year-old black male and a 56-year-old Hispanic woman who was babysitting for the perpetrator. While high on both alcohol and crack he tried to rape her. She resisted, and he struck her numerous times in the head with a blunt instrument, causing death. The perpetrator reported to the police that his alcohol use was the primary motivating factor in his violent behavior.

The crack/cocaine/alcohol homicide event involved a 47-year-old black male who stabbed his 21-year-old black girlfriend to death during a dispute of unknown origin. The perpetrator was high on all three substances. The victim was a reported user of crack, but it was unknown whether she was using at the time that she was murdered.

While these events were tragedies, they are hardly the basis for claims that crack induces violent behavior.

Economic Compulsive. Only about 2 percent of the homicides that were studied were economic compulsively motivated. However, all eight of these economically motivated murders were classified as crack-related. Six of the eight cases involved the murder of elderly persons ranging from 64 to 98 years old, during robberies or burglaries by crack users seeking money to finance their crack use. Of the two economically motivated murders not involving robbery of an elderly person, one occurred between crack users. Police report the perpetrator knew the victim possessed drugs and money, and killed him during a robbery undertaken to finance his personal drug use. The other incident appears to have been victim-precipitated. The police believe that an automobile owner surprised the victim while he was committing theft of his automobile. The owner chased the victim/auto thief into the park, and hit him with the automobile jack handle, killing him.

Systemic Homicides. About 39 percent (162) of all the homicide events studied were classified as systemic. Sixty-five percent (106) of these systemic homicides were classified as being primarily crack-related. These included 100 crack-only cases, with four cases involving crack/marijuana combinations. Twenty-eight percent (45) of the systemic cases were primarily cocaine-related. Only 7 percent (11) of the systemic cases involved drugs other than cocaine or crack.

Systemic homicides included a variety of black market drug business-related incidents. The most common were territorial disputes (44 percent of crack systemic homicides) followed by robberies of dealers (18 percent). Other incidents included assaults to collect debts, punishment of workers, disputes over drug thefts and the dealer selling bad drugs.

Is Prohibition More Dangerous Than Crack?

Several findings emerged rather clearly. First, the majority, 52.7 percent, of the homicide events that occurred during an eight-month study period were classified as drug-related. Second, most of the drug-related homicides, 60 percent, involved the use or trafficking of crack. Cocaine, in all its forms, including crack, was the primary drug involved in about 84 percent of the drug-related homicides. Third, most of the drug-related homicides, 74 percent, were classified as systemic — related to the drug trade — not drug use. This was true with all drugs except alcohol.

A substantial proportion, 26 percent, of the homicides that took place in New York City in 1988 may be projected from this study to have been crack-related systemic events. The most common sort of crack-systemic homicide was shown to be territorial disputes between rival dealers. Clearly, the emergent popularity of crack, combined with an unstable distribution system, produces a high level of violence.

Crack may be produced with relative ease, thereby bringing into the marketplace many small-scale entrepreneurs. These persons, with comparatively small amounts of cocaine, are able to begin their own businesses. Some of these small dealers are independent of established organizations and the normative controls evidenced in more traditional dealing hierarchies do not exist.

The entry of many small dealers into the crack marketplace has created a number of boundary disputes leading to violence. In an area as small as an apartment house, a tenement stoop, or a street corner, two or more crack dealers may be competing for the same customers. Dealers and customers interact in a highly volatile environment in which disputes and conflicts are routinely settled by a resort to physical force in which one or both of the parties tend to be carrying firearms. There appear to be efforts toward consolidation of these independents into larger organizations, and this trend toward consolidation may involve considerable violence also.

The crack distribution scene is undoubtedly violent. However, the crack phenomenon does not appear to have greatly influenced the overall homicide rate in New York City as reported in the Uniform Crime Reports. This rate did rise steeply in 1988 by about 13 percent. Yet crack first appeared in late 1984, and the homicide rates between 1984 and 1987 were still below the then peak years of 1979-81. In both nature and volume, crack-related homicides largely appear to be replacing other sorts of homicides rather than just adding to the existing homicide rate. The fact that only three of the 414 homicide events surveyed in this report were primarily related to the use or trafficking of heroin is certainly indicative of a decline in heroin-related homicides.

The foregoing data should clearly focus attention on the black market crack distribution "system" as the primary source of crack-related homicide violence. There were few cases of psychopharmacological or economic compulsive homicides involving crack. These data support earlier findings that drug users are more likely to finance their drug use by working in the drug business than by engaging in violent predatory theft.

It's Not All It's Cracked Up To Be*

I smoked crack and wrote an article about it for *The New Republic*. As I had hoped, "What Crack Is Like" instigated many debates within the Washington political class and attracted more than a little interest outside that cloistered group. The article made three points, all of which will strike some people as self-evident: Crack is a pleasurable drug with unpleasant side effects; crack can "make sick sense to demoralized people" and the spread of crack capitalism is related to the phenomenon of Reaganism. That same week I published a historical-economic analysis of the drug problem in *The Nation* ("Contradictions of Cocaine Capitalism," Oct. 2, [1989]) which initially drew little media attention, no doubt because it was a more substan-

---

* Jefferson Morley, "Aftermath of a Crack Article," *The Nation Magazine*/The Nation Company, Inc., Nov. 20, 1989, p. 592.

tive article. In fact, the reactions to *The New Republic* piece were more interesting than the piece itself. The peculiarities of our so-called drug war and the desire for a new debate about the problem have never been more evident.

By noon of the day *The New Republic* rolled off the presses William Bennett had described my piece as "garbage" and called me "a defector in the drug war." In this compliment I resented only Bennett's implication that I was a soldier, not a citizen, and somehow bound to salute his efforts. Over the weekend, the usual suspects from the Sunday morning talk shows — Pat Buchanan, Robert Novak, Al Hunt — reiterated Bennett's criticisms, often word for word: "garbage, irresponsible" and so on.

What especially galled the pundits was my remark that "if all you have in life is bad choices, crack may not be the most unpleasant of them." No one said this was untrue, as Michael Kinsley, editor of *The New Republic,* pointed out in my defense — only that it was "unhelpful." Indeed, R. Emmett Tyrrell Jr., editor of *The American Spectator,* expressed a journalistic philosophy no longer current, even at *Pravda.* Tyrrell said my article was "contemptible" because I did not express support for benevolent state efforts to wipe out market activity.

Stephen Rosenfeld, a foreign policy columnist for *The Washington Post,* at least tried to debate the issue, devoting a confused column to my article. The ink not spent on abusing my person was spent quoting a Washington public health official about the crack experience. Rosenfeld was so excited that he never noticed the official's description of the crack experience in no way contradicted my own. The damaging effects of addiction to drug war rhetoric were evident. Rosenfeld asserted that crack "withers the mothering instinct" among female users. Exactly how the drug does this, biologically and chemically, he was unable to explain.

The following Monday morning, I went on C-Span, the public affairs cable channel, and exchanged pleasantries with Brian Lamb, a conservative gentleman and a soothing interlocutor. Wasn't I condoning the use of crack? Lamb inquired. If anything, I was discouraging it, I said. The curious could learn about the drug from my article. If they took it seriously, they would learn that in one man's very limited experience, crack's pleasure quickly gave way to its side effects, combining "the worst of marijuana and cocaine" and inducing both stupefaction and paranoia. "Let's go to the phones," Lamb said, eyes twinkling. He was enjoying the prospect of my imminent pasting by the *vox populi.*

Thirteen of the next 15 callers approved of my article, several of them using the same phrase, "I'm with you 100 percent." What came through most consistently in the comments was a sense of relief at hearing someone in the media say something — anything outside the rhetorical consensus of just-say-no and zero-tolerance.

I went on radio talk shows in Washington, Milwaukee, Detroit and Boston. "What's crack like?" my interviewers inevitably wanted to know. Or did they? Crack has been around for six years and smoked by millions of Americans. I asked several of these media representatives if they had ever posed the questions to the many available crack users in their home towns. Most had not. They were such loyal soldiers in the drug war that they had forgotten to do their jobs. Others said that they regarded local crack smokers as less reliable and less interesting than me. "You're a real person," one TV reporter said in a revealing slip. "I mean, you're a real articulate person."

The inevitable second question was, "They say you smoke crack once and you're addicted. Are you addicted?" The answer was no. I often replied by asking why they believed that one-time crack use leads to addictions. "That's what everybody says," answered Mark Belling, a talk show host in Milwaukee. Had he ever conducted a survey of crack users in his city to answer the question himself? Neither he nor any other journalist critical of my article had ever attempted such reporting. (In fact, *Harpers's* magazine reported in November that 6 out of 10 crack users eventually become addicted, compared with 9 out of 10 cigarette users.)

My mother liked the article; my father hated it. He called to tell me I'd made a "big mistake." He said that I was an elitist wise-ass in the worst *New Republic* tradition who had trivialized a terrible problem by drawing attention to myself and not to the real issues involved. This criticism left me depressed for a week. Like the Sunday morning gasbags, my father is a Reaganite. Unlike them, he know's what he's talking about. He's a journalist who knows and works with neighborhood activists who are trying to extirpate the crack economy block by block in Minneapolis and St. Paul.

When I attempted to say something about challenging the Bennett propaganda barrage, he cut me off. "What's Bill Bennett got to do with the crack problem?" he demanded. A good question. I admit that I couldn't dismiss entirely his argument that even to join this spurious Washington debate, especially in the provocative way that I did, was "counterproductive."

The personal letters I received were supportive by a margin of about ten to one. "The criticism that you lacked sufficient reverence for the drug problem seems to me symptomatic of the very hysteria that you pointed out," wrote Dave Hage, a newspaper reporter from the Twin Cities. "I may take an even stronger position than you — that this drug hysteria is a grotesque deception and a classic case of inventing a problem we'd like to solve so we can ignore problems we don't want to solve." The letters to *The New Republic*, on the other hand, were critical by a margin of 15 to 8. The charge of irresponsibility recurred, most compellingly from people with firsthand experience in the drug problem. Michael Kellogg, a former prosecutor from the Bronx now living in Washington, said, "I felt nothing but sorrow for the kids who used and sold crack as a means of escaping their already blighted lives. I feel nothing but contempt for a twit like Morley who uses the drug to spice up his otherwise unimaginative writing."

Cynthia Malenfant of Newburyport, Massachusetts, said, "What gives him [Morley] the right to break the law?" Nothing, I had to concede. I'm in the same position as the journalist who wrote about

> "*I may take an even stronger position than you — that this drug hysteria is a grotesque deception and a classic case of inventing a problem we'd like to solve so we can ignore problems we don't want to solve.*"

Crack: A Disaster of Historic Dimensions?

his experiences in a speak-easy in the 1920s. I harmed no one and hardly tried to evade the consequences of my actions. I was (and am) prepared for drug enforcement agents knocking on my door, and I'm willing to go to court to testify about my actions. If the drug warriors want to get tough on that contemporary beast, "the casual user," then I am their man. But the knock never came, and I'm confident it never will. I have access to expert legal counsel and to the media. The drug warriors prefer to go after casual users who have fewer defenses.

The most original point was made by Kenneth Anderson of New York City, who said my article was "a print version of that *other* much-publicized, equally exploitative Washington drug buy." Anderson, of course, was referring to the drug enforcement agents' buy of three ounces of crack in Lafayette Park prior to President Bush's nationally televised address on drugs in early September. Anderson's analogy was apt, but I would add that Bush "used" crack to make a point that was frankly dishonest — despite what millions of Americans have been told by the president, you can't buy crack in Lafayette Park. I used crack to make points that were at least debatable.

I could tell the controversy was dying out when Abe Rosenthal, senior columnist for *The New York Times,* called. "Very interesting, very interesting," he said. Could I spare a few moments to answer some questions? I understood these sonorities to mean that he was preparing a vicious hatchet job on me.

"Ask away," I replied nervously.

How many times had I used cocaine in my life?

"Well, I'll put it this way, Mr. Rosenthal," I said. "I've used cocaine fewer times than Fawn Hall." *(The Washington Post* reported last summer that Hall had told drug enforcement agents investigating a local cocaine dealer that she had used cocaine some forty times while working for Oliver North.)

"And how many times have you used marijuana?"

I thought: Is this news that's fit to print? I said: "My favorite recreational drug is Miller Lite."

"Miller Lite," he murmured, as if I had uttered a pleasantry in Swedish, and he had to pretend, out of sheer politeness, to comprehend the meaning of such a strange expression. "Millerlite. Millerlite." End of interview. Rosenthal wisely decided not to write about me.

Since then, I've been receiving many more calls asking about my *Nation* article on the cocaine economy. I spent an hour on the phone lines on "The Mike Cuthbert Show" on WAMU here in Washington, and every caller save one was dissatisfied with the national drug debate. Jay Marvin, a talk show host on WTKN in Tampa, wanted to hear about banks in Florida that launder drug money. Jean (Queen) Steinberg, a talk show host on WQBH, a black community station in Detroit, was hoping for a wide-ranging discussion with her listeners. And "Addiction-Free Radio" (then KJIM, now KERR) in Boulder, Colorado, was especially receptive to alternative views on the drug war.

The new drug debate is hindered by the realities of our political culture. Representative Charles Rangel, appearing with me on "Larry King Live," said that the repeal of Prohibition in 1933 was a mistake. Rangel, of course, doesn't really want to ban alcohol. As a career politician, he just can't imagine entrusting the American people with the task of controlling antisocial behavior. Then again, he is a congressman from Harlem, a devastated community that has little reason to entrust its fate to the American sense of social responsibility. If we were all more civic-minded, Rangel's constituents would not be in such bad shape. Rangel's lack of faith in the collective social responsibility required to make drug reform succeed is understandable, if self-defeating.

"So what's your answer?" Rangel, a drug prohibitionist at wit's end, said to me, "Legalize?"

Well, yes. But legalization is only the beginning. The so-called war on drugs is no substitute for social policy — despite what the Bush administration pretends. And neither is drug legalization. The drug crisis in the United States is really two crises: a crisis of public health that has created millions of untreated drug addicts and a crisis of economic opportunity that has created millions of unregulated and untaxed drug entrepreneurs.

Current government policy is to eliminate these problems by coercively discouraging the desire, exhibited in the actions of as many as 50 million Americans, to use marijuana and cocaine. Few believe this experiment in social engineering will succeed. Bennett's aides routinely tell reporters that they don't expect to "win" the war on drugs for a generation; as much as 80 percent of the public say that they don't expect current policies to solve the problem. Yet in public debate most elected officials feel obliged to pledge allegiance to the government's fantasy. And many journalists feel it's not their job to question the officials who are promoting it.

Other journalists and citizens believe the public health problems related to crack are so severe that any discussion of pleasurable casual crack use in the media is irresponsible, even (especially) if it is accurate. Their intentions — to try to prevent crack from taking over any more lives — are unimpeachable, but I think they are also reinforcing the unreal drug debate. In fact, the drug experience is governed not just by the drug, but also by the person who uses it and the social setting in which he or she uses it. If I could rewrite my article, I would say even more explicitly that I was reporting on my own unique crack experience, which has no necessary implications for how anyone else would experience the drug.

Then why write about it? Because writing about my drug use did have one implication for other people: that it could be informative and useful to discuss drugs in ways that are considered unacceptable by the moral custodians of the current drug debate. That spurious debate, as even my sober Reaganite father knows, promises virtually nothing for the pathetic people whose only solace is crack. It trifles with the safety of policemen on the beat, who are asked to risk their lives to do the impossible, and it compromises our civil liberties in pursuit of the illusory (and undesirable) vision of a drug-free America.

Taken together, my *Nation* and *New Republic* articles suggest that our unreal drug debate ghettoizes the social problems generated by the drug economy. In the process, it removes from public debate the rewards of the drug economy: the political and financial opportunities now enjoyed by drug bankers and testers, by ambitious bureaucrats and sycophantic journalists and, most of all, by politicians who prefer to ignore the country's sad crises. I think a lot of people intuitively understand this, which is why interest is beginning to shift from what crack is like to the contradictions of cocaine capitalism.

Chapter 5

The Denial of Medical Marijuana to Sick People

The ultimate irony of the drug prohibition is that it fails to restrain social drug use and succeeds in depriving the desperately ill of adequate medical care.

—Robert Randall

Within a very short time, I became known as the Michigan "Green Cross," and I was nicknamed "Grandma Marijuana." Doctors in several surrounding countries began sending patients to me for help.

—Mae Nutt

NORML and ACT have attempted to perpetrate a dangerous and cruel hoax on the American public by claiming marijuana has currently accepted medical uses.

—John Lawn

Introduction

Marijuana, a medicine that has relieved the suffering of millions of people for thousands of years, is prohibited for medical use throughout most of the world. Doctors who would ordinarily prescribe natural marijuana to patients suffering from debilitating diseases including cancer, multiple sclerosis, glaucoma, and AIDS, are unable to do so for fear of criminal prosecution. Subsequently, many doctors quietly suggest that their patients obtain their medicine on the street. Thus, today, thousands of decent doctors are being forced to engage in a quiet conspiracy with their patients to violate the law.

As a result of the doctor-patient conspiracy, the National Organization for the Reform of Marijuana Laws pioneered a broad campaign to medicalize marijuana. In recent years, that campaign, which has involved the extensive use of legal action, has been spearheaded by the Alliance for Cannabis Therapeutics. The Drug Policy Foundation, founded in 1987, also became a strong supporter of this compassionate effort to ease the suffering of millions of seriously ill Americans. (In fact, both editors have served as counsel in recent action to once again medicalize marijuana).

The medical marijuana suit, active throughout 1987-88, involved extensive hearings before the chief administrative law judge of the Drug Enforcement Administration. Never before has the nature and safety of a drug been subjected to a more searching judicial inquiry replete with cross-examination. In September of 1988, DEA Judge Young's decision vindicated almost every important point made by the petitioners for the change of medical marijuana laws.

While not binding on President Reagan or DEA Administrator John Lawn, Francis L. Young's carefully reasoned decision provided an historic opportunity for a touch of compromise and compassion in the drug war. Perhaps President Reagan could have said as he left office in January 1989 that while the decision made him uncomfortable, the judge's ruling was based on an impartial hearing and should therefore be upheld by the U.S. government. However, the Reagan administration ignored the Young decision and the opportunity to make an exception that would help many ill people, especially elderly citizens so far removed from the drug trade.

In December of 1989, shortly before his retirement, DEA Administrator John Lawn overruled Francis Youngs's petition to make natural marijuana a medicine. The order could have simply explained in civilized terms why the U.S. government had decided to come down on the other side of the argument. Instead, John Lawn issued a statement that rates as the most uncivilized judicial or quasi-judicial decision we have encountered in our combined 55 years of legal experience.

A Harvard Medical School Professor Tells About His Son Who Suffered From Cancer[*]

I, Lester Grinspoon, being first duly sworn, states as follows:

1. My name is Lester Grinspoon. I am a medical doctor and an Associate Professor of Psychiatry at Harvard Medical School. I practice, teach and do research at the Massachusetts Mental Health Center in Boston, Mass.

2. I began to study cannabis in 1967, and by the time I published my book in 1971, I had learned that much of what I thought I knew about it had been wrong. In fact, that is the reason I gave my book the title *Marihuana Reconsidered* (Harvard University Press, 1971, Second Edition, 1978). Among other things, I learned that cannabis was used extensively in medicine from the mid-19th century until the passage of the Marijuana Tax Act in 1937. Nineteenth century physicians understood the many medical uses of cannabis and had no doubt about its safety. But at the time my book was published, I could not have anticipated that I would have a personal encounter with cannabis as a medicine.

---

[*] Affidavit of Lester Grinspoon, M.D., "In the Matter of Marijuana Rescheduling Petition," Dkt. 86-22 (U.S. Department of Justice, Drug Enforcement Administration, September 1987).

3. Early in 1972, after the death of Dr. Sidney Farber, the Harvard child oncologist for whom the Sidney Farber Cancer Research Center was named, my wife and I were invited to dinner at the home of a fellow Harvard Medical School faculty member who was eager to have me meet Dr. Emil Frei. Dr. Frei had recently arrived from Houston, Texas, to serve as Dr. Farber's successor. At dinner he told me the following story: an 18-year-old Houston man suffering from leukemia had become more and more resistant to cancer chemotherapy because he could no longer tolerate the nausea and vomiting. It was becoming increasingly difficult for his doctors and his family to persuade him to take the drug on which his life depended. One day, to Dr. Frei's surprise, he willingly agreed to take the drug, and from then on offered no resistance to chemotherapy. It was some time before Dr. Frei could get the young man to explain that he had started smoking marijuana about 20 minutes before each chemotherapy session. The marijuana seemed to prevent all vomiting and even the slightest hint of nausea. Knowing of my work, Dr. Frei asked me if the 19th century medical literature on cannabis supported such a possibility. I told him that it did.

4. On the way home, my wife Betsy, who had listened intently to the discussion, suggested that we obtain some cannabis for our son, Daniel. Daniel was first diagnosed as having acute lymphatic leukemia in July of 1967. For the first few years he was quite good-natured about his trips to the Jimmy Fund Building of the Children's Hospital in Boston for his treatments, and even about the occasional need to be hospitalized. But in 1971, he started taking the first of the chemotherapy agents that cause severe nausea and vomiting.

Afterward, he did not become nauseated and again asked for a submarine sandwich. From then on, he used marijuana before every treatment, and we were all much more comfortable during the remaining year of his life.

5. For many patients, including Daniel, the nausea and vomiting are uncontrollable and not sufficiently alleviated by standard antiemetics. He would start to vomit shortly after treatment and continue vomiting and later retching for up to eight hours. He vomited in the car on the way home. Once he arrived home he had to lie in bed with his head over a bucket on the floor.

6. These were awful, demoralizing experiences for all of us. In 1972, Daniel, who had been so courageous about his illness and its treatment, began to resist taking chemotherapy. He begged us not to insist on any more treatments.

7. It was our practice for my wife to drive Daniel in from Wellesley and meet me at the Jimmy Fund Building. I dreaded those pretreatment sessions.

8. I was shocked when Betsy suggested that we acquire some cannabis for Daniel. I objected strenuously, because it was against the law and might embarrass the staff at the Farber Cancer Research Institute, who had been so remarkable in

their commitment to Daniel's care. I dismissed the idea that night.

9. Daniel's next treatment was about two weeks later. When I arrived, Betsy and Daniel were already in the treatment room. I shall never forget my surprise when I walked in. Previously, I had been able to see the tension on their faces. This time they were both completely relaxed, and what is more, seemed almost to be playing some sort of joke on me. I was delighted and puzzled. Finally, they let me in on the secret. On the way to the clinic that morning, they had stopped near Wellesley High School. Betsy asked Daniel's friend Mark to get her some marijuana. Mark, once he recovered from his disbelief, ran off and reappeared a few minutes later with a small amount of marijuana in his hand. Betsy drove to the hospital, and she and Daniel smoked marijuana in the parking lot just before they went into the clinic. I was shocked, but at the same time relieved that Daniel seemed so comfortable. Daniel was not at all convinced that marijuana would solve his problem, but he did not protest as he was given the medicine. He was as surprised and pleased as we were when there was no nausea or vomiting afterward. In fact, he asked Betsy if he could stop for a submarine sandwich on the way home, and when he arrived at home he did not take to his bed but went right to his usual activities. We could scarcely believe it.

10. The next day, I called Dr. Norman Jaffe, the physician at the Jimmy Fund who was in charge of Daniel's care. I explained what had happened and told him that, although I did not want to embarrass him or the rest of the medical staff, I could not forbid Daniel to smoke marijuana before his next treatment. Dr. Jaffe was very interested in my story and suggested that Daniel smoke marijuana in his presence in the treatment room. Daniel did that the next time. When the chemotherapeutic was given to him, Dr. Jaffe observed for himself that Daniel was completely relaxed and did not protest at all. Afterward, he did not become nauseated and again asked for a submarine sandwich. From then on, he used marijuana before every treatment, and we were all much more comfortable during the remaining year of his life.

11. Dr. Jaffe asked me to join him in reporting our observations to Dr. Frei, who was sufficiently interested to do the first clinical experiment on the use of cannabis in cancer chemotherapy.

12. It saddens me that 15 years later it is still not legally possible to use cannabis in this way, although surreptitious illegal use is widespread, at least among adults with cancer. Oral tetrahydrocannabinol [now marketed as Marinol] is clearly less effective than smoked cannabis, which, shamefully, has not yet achieved its rightful place in the oncological armamentarium.

A Michigan Mother Tells About Her Two Sons Who Suffered From Cancer*

Mae Nutt, being first duly sworn, states as follows:

1. My name is Mae Nutt. I was born June 28, 1921. My husband is Arnold Nutt, who was born Dec. 21, 1919. We reside in Beaverton, Mich.

2. We were married on June 13, 1953. We had three children: Keith Earl, who was born Dec. 21, 1955; Dana, who was born June 4, 1958; and Marc, who was born Oct. 3, 1959.

3. In July, 1963, shortly after his fifth birthday, Dana complained he couldn't breathe, and then he passed out. He was rushed to our local hospital,

---

* Affidavit of Mae Nutt, "In the Matter of Marijuana Rescheduling Petition," Dkt. 86-22 (U.S. Department of Justice, Drug Enforcement Administration, May 13, 1987).

then taken to the Henry Ford Hospital in Detroit.

4. My husband and I were told Dana had Ewings Sarcoma. Emergency surgery was performed the following day, July 3, 1963. During the surgery, doctors removed a 1-pound tumor which was attached to one of Dana's ribs. The rib was also removed.

5. Dana remained hospitalized for nearly a month. Then he came home. For the next three years, Dana received chemotherapy and radiation treatments. He was often hospitalized at the Henry Ford Hospital for additional treatments.

6. The chemotherapy treatments made Dana very ill. When the cancer spread to his brain, he began receiving radiation treatments. These made him violently angry and difficult to manage. The therapy also made Dana listless and destroyed his appetite and, eventually, his personality.

7. Despite the powerful therapies which caused these severe adverse effects, the cancer continued to spread and began affecting other organs. In July, and in December 1964, additional surgical procedures were performed on Dana. During these procedures, portions of his lungs were removed.

8. For the remainder of Dana's life, he remained seriously ill.

9. Dana died Jan. 5, 1967.

10. Dana's protracted illness drained our financial resources. The emotional strain was extremely difficult on us and our other children.

11. In the spring of 1978, our eldest son Keith, who was living in Columbus, Ohio, phoned home to tell us that he had testicular cancer.

12. On April 19, 1978, we were in Columbus during Keith's first operation. During the operation, the diseased testicle was removed. After a biopsy, which found the tissue to be malignant, the surgeons removed a large number of lymph nodes between Keith's pelvic bone and breast bone in an effort to remove all of the cancer.

13. Keith was a very independent young man and he decided to remain in Columbus following his recovery from surgery. He made a determined effort to resume a normal life. He also discussed possible anti-cancer therapies with his physicians in Columbus. The doctors felt they had removed all of the cancer and thought no extensive chemotherapy or radiation treatments were warranted. However, Keith was unable to maintain his energy and in the fall of 1978, he returned home to live with us.

14. After returning home, Keith made a determined effort to remain active and vital. He quickly found a new job and started working. All appeared to be going well.

15. On the evening of Jan. 1, 1979, after a wonderful holiday season, Keith told us that his other testicle was hard and enlarged. He thought it might be cancerous.

16. The next morning we accompanied Keith to a urologist in Midland, the nearest large community.

17. After a brief examination, the doctor told us Keith's condition was serious and he needed another operation immediately. Keith was hospitalized later that day.

18. During the operation, surgeons removed Keith's remaining testicle.

19. Following the operation, our son was seen by an internist. He explained the cancer was spreading and told us Keith would require extensive chemotherapy treatments.

20. As soon as his surgical wounds healed, Keith was placed on a new, highly toxic form of chemotherapy called Cisplatin.

21. Keith's chemotherapy began in February 1979. The treatments made him extremely ill. After receiving his injections, he would vomit violently for 8-10 hours. Then he would become profoundly nauseated to the point he could neither bear to look at nor smell food.

22. In an attempt to curb Keith's nausea and vomiting, Compazine and other anti-emetic drugs were prescribed. These drugs did not provide any noticeable relief.

23. This combination of intense vomiting and debilitating nausea quickly took a toll on our son. Unable to eat or to keep down any food he managed to swallow, Keith rapidly began to lose weight. In less than two months, our son lost at least 30 pounds.

24. Keith's vomiting was so violent it became a heaving retch. Because he could not eat, he began to vomit bile. When there was nothing to vomit, he would simply retch and convulse. It was horrible for us to watch our child suffer such anguish.

25. My husband and I were alarmed by the intensity of Keith's vomiting and by his sudden, dramatic loss of weight. We felt Keith's weight loss to be an indication of just how rapidly he was being overwhelmed by his cancer and by the chemotherapy he was receiving to combat it. Together, the disease and treatment were a deadly combination.

26. Keith was suffering terribly. His treatments were wearing him down. At one point, he approached me and said he did not want to become like his deceased brother, Dana — so sick he could not take care of himself, completely incapacitated and a burden on the rest of the family. He told me when things got that bad, he wanted to be able kill himself, in order to escape his misery. Then Keith made me promise when there was no more hope, I would help him end his life.

27. One evening, while reading the newspaper, I read an article about a cancer patient who had received a brown bag of marijuana on his doorstep. The article noted there was medical evidence which showed smoking marijuana helped to reduce the severe nausea and vomiting caused by many anti-cancer therapies.

28. At first I laughed at the story. It seemed unlikely that marijuana would just suddenly appear on someone's doorstep. The idea marijuana had medical benefit was a new one to my husband and me. Later, however, we told Keith what we had read. We were desperate.

29. Keith told us that while he was in the hospital in Columbus he had met other cancer patients who were receiving chemotherapy. These patients told him about smoking marijuana to reduce the side effects of chemotherapy. According to Keith, these other cancer patients said marijuana really helped reduce the vomiting.

30. As a parent, I was strongly opposed to marijuana and other illegal drugs. My husband and I made sure our sons knew exactly how we felt. We told them we never wanted them to use such drugs for any reason. We do not doubt our sons may have tried smoking marijuana at one time or another while growing up, but we are also sure our sons had no drug problems and no illusions about our stern opposition to drug use.

31. It was hard to believe an illegal drug could be of any help. We thought the government would know if marijuana had medical value and, if so, would make it legally available to patients by pre-

scription. We made a few calls. One of the people we contacted was our State Representative, Robert Young. We asked Representative Young if there was any way we could legally obtain marijuana so our son Keith could try it and see if it helped.

32. I was surprised when Representative Young told me a bill to legalize marijuana for the treatment of glaucoma and cancer was scheduled to come before the Michigan legislature. Representative Young also gave me the name and phone number of Mr. Roger Winthrop, a man who was working with a number of Representatives and Senators to help enact the Michigan "Marijuana as Medicine" legislation.

33. I then contacted Mr. Winthrop. He provided my husband and I with information on marijuana and on the drug's medical use, including its anti-emetic effects relative to cancer chemotherapy treatments. We learned physicians and patients in a number of states had already succeeded in passing state laws to make marijuana available to seriously ill patients like Keith.

34. Shortly after my husband and I read these materials, Keith had to be hospitalized for another round of chemotherapy and observation. As always, the chemotherapy made him dreadfully sick.

35. We could not stand by and watch our son suffer. After a short discussion, we decided we had to get some marijuana for Keith. My husband and I are an older couple and we did not have the slightest idea where to find marijuana. In desperation, we contacted a close friend, an ordained Presbyterian minister. He worked with a number of local youth groups and we thought he might have some contacts. He listened quietly while we explained our problem and asked for his help.

36. Several days later, at 10:30 p.m., this minister showed up at our door. He told us he had managed to obtain some marijuana. It was the first time we had ever seen marijuana.

37. The next day we took the marijuana to Keith in the hospital. After Keith smoked the marijuana, there was a dramatic improvement in his nausea.

38. Before smoking marijuana, Keith would vomit and retch for at least eight hours following his chemotherapy injection. Then he would vomit less frequently but would become overwhelmingly nauseated and unable to eat. This inability to eat would continue until the beginning of his next chemotherapy session, when he again would start to vomit. The process would repeat itself.

39. Marijuana broke this cycle. After Keith smoked marijuana, his vomiting abruptly stopped. It was amazing to see. None of the anti-emetic drugs prescribed by the doctors had been effective. Now,

> *Marijuana also put an end to Keith's nausea. When he smoked marijuana, he was constantly hungry and could eat. He actually began to put on weight. His mental outlook also underwent a startling improvement.*

with just a few puffs of marijuana, Keith was no longer vomiting. It was a sudden, abrupt change.

40. Marijuana also put an end to Keith's nausea. When he smoked marijuana, he was constantly hungry and could eat. He actually began to put on weight. His mental outlook also underwent a startling improvement.

41. Prior to smoking marijuana, Keith would go to his chemotherapy, come home and rush upstairs. He would shut himself in his bedroom and stuff towels under the door to keep out the smell of dinner cooking. He would not join us for dinner and would remain in his room or the bathroom vomiting for the rest of the evening. The cancer and chemotherapy made Keith act like a wounded animal — timid and retiring. He would stay in his room and vomit. He would have intense hot and cold flashes, his joints became swollen and painful, his hair fell out and he felt sick all over. The anti-cancer drugs were so toxic Keith could pull off large pieces of skin where the chemotherapy injections had been given.

42. Smoking marijuana dramatically changed all of this. Immediately before chemotherapy Keith would smoke one marijuana cigarette. Following chemotherapy he would smoke all or part of a second marijuana cigarette if he felt queasy. On good days Keith didn't have to remain in the hospital after his chemotherapy treatments. When we got home, Keith would stay in the living room and talk with his brother and father. He would join the family for dinner, where he would eat more than his share. He became outgoing and talkative. Keith became part of our family again because marijuana controlled the debilitating symptoms of his chemotherapy.

43. Once my husband and I saw the dramatic improvement in Keith's condition, we made certain all of his doctors and nurses were aware of the situation. None objected, and some clearly approved.

44. We made arrangements with the hospital for Keith to smoke marijuana in his hospital room. This would save him from having to smoke in the parking lot before chemotherapy and allow him to smoke in his room after chemotherapy.

45. Even though use of marijuana is illegal, many people at the hospital supported Keith's marijuana therapy. No one at the hospital doubted marijuana was helpful and no one discouraged Keith from smoking marijuana to control the adverse effects of his anti-cancer therapies. In effect, reasonable people apparently decided the law did not match the reality of Keith's — and other patients' — needs.

46. My husband and I came to resent the fact Keith's marijuana therapy was illegal. We felt like criminals. We are honest, simple people and we hated having to sneak around. I was uncomfortable with our closest friends, our minister, and our other son, Marc, having to risk arrest in order to provide Keith with the marijuana he so obviously needed. I also wondered about other parents who might have a child suffering from chemotherapy who might not know marijuana could help end their child's misery, or who did not know how to obtain marijuana.

47. My husband and I approached Keith and asked him if we could tell his story to the newspaper. I told him it might help other cancer patients. He agreed, on one condition: that we not give the newspaper details about the nature of his cancer or of the surgical procedures which resulted in the removal of his testes. As a young man in his twenties, Keith wanted at least this much of his life to remain private. We quickly agreed to this condition.

48. A reporter for the local paper (*The Bay City Times*) came to our house, listened to our story and wrote an article which appeared on March 11, 1979. The story began:

"Keith Nutt of Beaverton doesn't care who knows he uses marijuana. It is the only thing that relieves the terrible nausea that follows chemotherapy treatments for cancer, says the 23-year-old man. Right now, Keith is still able to drive to his sources of marijuana. If the time comes when Keith can't get out of the house to buy the illegal drug, his mother, Mae Nutt, 58, says, 'that's where I come in! But it shouldn't be necessary to break the law to get help for a child who is very, very ill.'"

49. On the same day this article appeared, we went to Lansing to testify before the Michigan Senate Judiciary Committee. The hearings were on a bill to legalize marijuana's medical use by Michigan glaucoma, cancer, and multiple sclerosis (MS) patients.

50. During our testimony, one senator asked Keith if his doctors knew he was smoking marijuana. Keith, in an effort to protect his doctors and the hospital, said his doctors did not know he was smoking marijuana.

51. Doctor Barnett Rosenberg, the inventor of the new chemotherapeutic drug Cisplatin, which Keith was taking, also testified at the hearings and spoke in favor of the legislation.

52. Following the hearings, we spoke privately with Dr. Rosenberg. He was strongly supportive and encouraged Keith to keep smoking so he could continue with his chemotherapy treatments. Dr. Rosenberg told us many of the cancer patients in his test programs smoked marijuana while receiving chemotherapy.

53. Several reporters also spoke with Dr. Rosenberg. One story, which appeared after the hearings in a local newspaper, *The Gladwin County Record*, quoted Dr. Rosenberg at length. A portion of the story notes:

The Nutt family was backed up by Dr. Barnett Rosenberg, a Michigan State University biophysicist, credited with the discovery of a new platinum-based cancer treatment. Rosenberg told the committee cancer treatment drugs and radiation therapy induce intense vomiting and nausea. Although the research isn't complete yet, Rosenberg said it appears marijuana is the most effective drug for eliminating the painful side effects of cancer treatments. Rosenberg said doctors can now treat cancer patients with marijuana if they get federal Food and Drug Administration approval. But the process is time consuming and requires extensive research and study of each patient involved. Because of federal restrictions the Michigan bill may not make it easier for doctors to obtain marijuana for cancer patients, he noted. [Rosenberg] said he testified to increase public awareness of marijuana's potential [benefits] for cancer patients.

> *We also received more marijuana in the mail from people trying to help Keith. Keith continued to distribute the marijuana he could not use to other cancer patients.*

54. Following the Senate hearings, there was considerable publicity about Keith. We began receiving phone calls from other cancer patients in Michigan and throughout the United States. Many were seeking help. Keith often spoke with these patients late into the night, sharing information and trying to help.

55. Cancer patients and their relatives who lived close to us called and asked Keith for help and advice regarding how to smoke properly, how much to use, and how often. On several occasions Keith went on "house calls" to teach patients how to roll the cigarettes or properly inhale the smoke. This involvement with other seriously ill patients gave Keith great joy. He loved being able to help his fellow patients escape the dreadful side effects of their anti-cancer treatments.

56. One day, shortly after the hearings, we found a small brown bag of marijuana in our mailbox. There was no note, no identification, just an ounce or so of marijuana. Soon we received more marijuana in the mail. An Episcopal priest brought marijuana to our house. He told us he wanted to put it to good use and felt we would know who might benefit from it.

57. Most of the people who sent marijuana to us did not identify themselves. As news spread through the grapevine, however, we heard from some familiar folks. For example, we received a call one day from a woman who had attended elementary school with Arnold. She asked us to her home. When we arrived, she told us she had something for us and produced a cigar box filled with marijuana. She explained that her husband, recently deceased, had smoked marijuana to help control his pain. She had no use for the marijuana but did not want to throw it away.

58. It seemed to me many cancer patients were smoking marijuana. In my experience, most patients made an effort to inform their doctors. Most physicians, wanting to avoid the pitfalls of "a political issue," knew their patients were smoking marijuana and approved. Like Dr. Rosenberg, these physicians accepted that marijuana was therapeutically helpful in reducing nausea and vomiting. Unlike Dr. Rosenberg, most doctors were not willing to say in public what they told their patients in their offices: "Get some marijuana."

59. Throughout the spring and summer of 1979, Keith continued his chemotherapy treatments and smoking marijuana. He continued to assist other patients.

60. In early October 1979, my husband and I returned to Lansing, Mich., for additional hearings before the House Committee on Public Health. Keith was not with us. He was back in the hospital. Despite his continuing chemotherapy treatments his cancer was spreading and growing worse.

61. We testified again. On this occasion we were joined by another family, the Negens, from Grand Rapids, Mich. The Negen family had testified at the earlier hearings before the Senate, but had not given their names. At the time of the Senate hearings their daughter, Deborah, then 21, was in remission from her leukemia. At the second hearing, however, her leukemia was no longer in remission and she was receiving chemotherapy treatments again.

62. The Reverend Negen is pastor of the very conservative Dutch Christian Reform Church in Grand Rapids. He spoke of how he had prayed for guidance and had come to realize if getting marijuana to help his daughter through the terrors of chemotherapy offended his congregation he would leave his church. He knew he was breaking

the law. But his daughter was suffering. He spoke movingly about having to send his own young sons into the streets of Grand Rapids to purchase marijuana for his daughter's use. Marijuana was, he emphasized to the committee, the only drug that provided his daughter with any relief from the debilitating side effects of her chemotherapy treatments. It was easy for us to identify with Reverend Negen's obvious distress. He was being forced to break the law in order to provide for his daughter's medical needs. In the same way, we had to break the law to meet Keith's medical needs.

63. Deborah Negen was even more eloquent as she testified about how marijuana helped her cope with the vomiting and nausea caused by her chemotherapy treatments. She pleaded with the committee for help and asked them to consider that other seriously ill people were needlessly suffering. We were deeply moved by this family's anguished testimony. The story was so familiar, so close to home. We knew exactly how Reverend Negen felt about having to break the law. It is not something we did lightly, but something we were compelled to do by circumstances beyond our control.

64. Following the hearings in the House, my family received even more calls from newspapers, television and radio stations asking for more information. Cancer patients continued to call us seeking help or asking how they could help get the legislation enacted. We also received more marijuana in the mail from people trying to help Keith. Keith continued to distribute the marijuana he could not use to other cancer patients. He also continued to speak with patients who called for help, but he was very weak.

65. A week later, on Oct. 10, 1979, the Michigan House voted 100-0 in favor of making marijuana available to patients like Keith who suffered from life-or sense-threatening diseases like cancer and glaucoma.

66. On Oct. 15, 1979, the Michigan Senate concurred with the House and voted 33-1 in favor of making marijuana medically available to Michigan cancer and glaucoma patients for use under medical supervision. The following day *The Detroit Free Press'* Lansing Bureau Chief, Hugh McDiarmid, wrote, "Compassion Wins In Marijuana Vote."

67. On the evening of Sunday, Oct. 21, 1979, my husband went to say goodnight to Keith. We told Keith the Michigan Marijuana-as-Medicine bill would be signed into law the next day. Keith was happy his effort had made a difference. He smiled and said goodnight.

68. Early on the morning of Oct. 22, 1979, Keith died. Later that day Michigan's Lieutenant Governor, James Brickley, signed the Michigan Controlled Substances Therapeutic Research Program into law.

69. During the time Keith smoked marijuana to alleviate the adverse side effects of his chemotherapy treatments he never once experienced an adverse effect from marijuana. It was clear to us marijuana was the safest, most benign drug he received during the course of his battle against cancer. Certainly marijuana was immeasurably safer than the lethal chemotherapeutic agents which were supposed to prolong our son's life.

70. Following Keith's death, there was a tremendous outpouring of comment. People we did not know and had never met sent us touching cards and letters praising Keith's efforts to help others. We continued to receive calls from newspapers and other media sources asking about Keith. It was clear to me Keith had deeply touched many people throughout the country. Despite my grief, I felt

extremely proud of Keith for having had the courage to publicly discuss his disease and to fight to legalize medical access to marijuana so other patients could benefit.

71. In recognition of Keith's efforts, the Michigan legislature passed a Joint Resolution declaring in part: "Be it resolved by the Senate that our sincerest tribute be accorded in memory of Keith Nutt."

72. Several months after Keith's death, I went to see the oncologist who had helped treat Keith. I asked if he needed any volunteer help. He accepted the offer, and I helped to care for other cancer patients.

73. A short time after I began work, the doctor sent a patient to see me. The patient was suffering from debilitating nausea and vomiting and had threatened to stop taking her chemotherapy because of the adverse side effects.

74. I remembered how my son had reached out to other patients. We still continued to receive marijuana in the mail, though not as much as before Keith's death. The Michigan legislature had authorized marijuana's medical use, but acknowledged it would be at least 90 days before the state could begin to distribute federally approved supplies.

75. After some soul searching, my husband and I decided to use the marijuana Keith left behind for the benefit of other cancer patients. The doctor and his staff quickly learned if a patient was having a bad time they could send the patient to us for help. We would provide the patient with marijuana.

76. Before long we had a booming clinic. As more people became aware of what we were doing, we began receiving more marijuana in the mail or we would find a bag of it on our porch. The more marijuana we collected the more patients we could supply.

Physicians and patients decided it was easier to get marijuana on the streets than to deal with the complex paperwork and reporting requirements.

77. Within a very short time, I became known as the Michigan "Green Cross," and I was nicknamed "Grandma Marijuana." Doctors in several surrounding counties began sending patients to me for help. On occasion, patients who tried to get into the state program, which was not yet operational, were referred to me. I never asked these patients who in the State Department of Public Health was referring them to me. I simply did what I could to help anyone who had a legitimate medical need for marijuana. I never ran into any jokers; it is hard to fake cancer.

78. Most of the time patients quickly understood how to smoke marijuana. On some occasions, however, we had to provide them with help. I do not smoke. I found a woman in her mid-40s who had smoked marijuana at one time. Together we would make house calls to teach uninitiated patients the basics of marijuana therapy.

79. The "Green Cross" continued throughout the spring and summer of 1980. On several occasions I received calls from patients in the southern part of Michigan or from out-of-state. I occasionally

mailed marijuana to such patients.

80. I also tried to adapt marijuana so patients who could not or would not smoke marijuana could also benefit from the drug's medicinal properties. I soon learned I could boil marijuana and butter in a kettle of water for several hours, then let the mixture cool and use the butter which floated to the top.

81. Patients could either eat the butter on bread or bake it into cookies or brownies. However, dosage problems led me to start putting the butter into capsules.

82. I obtained the capsules from a hospital pharmacy. The pharmacy knew what we were doing and did not object in any way. The capsules made it simpler for those patients who did not want to smoke and who could not stand the smell or taste of food to get relief.

83. On one occasion a mother called. Her young daughter, around five, was undergoing chemotherapy treatments. The little girl could not smoke. Her mother had made brownies and these worked. But, on occasion, the little girl had fallen asleep after getting her chemotherapy and eating a brownie. Her parents did not wake her up to take another brownie. As a result, when the little girl did wake up, she began retching and vomiting. The mother wanted to know if there was some other way to use marijuana other than smoking or eating.

84. After speaking to some doctors and nurses, we decided to put pinholes in the capsules so they could be used as suppositories. We quickly discovered that this proved to be a highly effective alternative. While the relief was not as fast or as predictable when marijuana butter was used in this manner, patients did get relief from nausea and vomiting. Interestingly, we learned several years later federal drug agencies had attempted to develop a THC suppository and failed.

85. Despite promises from the Michigan Department of Public Health, the state marijuana program took far longer to develop than expected. Legislators, patients, physicians, researchers, and others throughout the state were pressing for action.

86. It seemed federal agencies were undermining the intent of the Michigan law. Instead of a compassionate program of patient care, research, and treatment, the federal agencies wanted to create a highly structured, very limited program of pure research. Instead of allowing physicians to treat patients and reach their own judgments, the FDA demanded detailed, complex, and standardized physician reporting procedures.

87. FDA and the Michigan Department of Public Health took nearly one year to implement the Michigan program.

88. The program that emerged from this constant bureaucratic friction was an administrative nightmare for doctors and patients alike. Instead of providing seriously ill patients with compassionate, legal access to quality controlled supplies of marijuana, the program became a research project in the hands of a limited number of physicians at the larger cancer centers. The welfare of patients did not seem to be a criteria under the federal government's procedures.

89. I realized the program my son, Keith, had worked so hard to enact was in serious trouble when the doctor who treated Keith, who knew about marijuana's medical benefits, and who was anxiously awaiting his chance to sign up, decided to drop out. I was furious. He, of all people, was abandoning the state program.

90. He explained he was practicing medicine. The

conditions, regulations, reporting, and other requirements of the state program had grown so dense and restrictive he felt they would intrude on his practice of medicine. He said he simply did not have the administrative staff or the time necessary to handle all of the paperwork involved.

91. In 1982, after two years of conflict between the Michigan Department of Public Health and FDA, the program continued to have problems. Patients and physicians throughout the state informally boycotted the program. Physicians and patients decided it was easier to get marijuana on the streets than to deal with the complex paperwork and reporting requirements.

92. In an effort to maintain marijuana's Schedule I classification, federal agencies have failed to aggressively pursue information on marijuana's medicinal properties and have blocked state efforts to make the drug available for medical applications.

93. In response to the conduct of federal agencies, the Michigan legislature enacted a Resolution detailing these concerns. In part, this Resolution of the Michigan legislature declares:

Federal agencies have...through regulatory ploys and obscure bureaucratic devices, resisted and obstructed the intent of the Michigan legislature.... Glaucoma and cancer patients, promised medical access to marijuana under the laws of Michigan, are being deprived of such access by federal agencies.

94. After outlining a series of complaints, the Resolution then calls on the president and the Congress to seek appropriate legislative or administrative remedies. In part, the Michigan Resolution calls for systemic reform. The Resolution reads:

That the Congress of the United States be urged to seek to remedy federal policies which prevent the several States from acquiring, inhibit physicians from prescribing, and prevent patients from obtaining marijuana for legitimate medical applications, by ending federal prohibitions against the legitimate and appropriate use of marijuana in medical treatments.

95. As the Michigan program became more and more bureaucratic, there were fewer and fewer physicians or patients willing to tolerate the regulatory excesses federal agencies demanded. After several years of work, and despite the efforts of many individuals, we realized there was little more we could do. We lost interest in the Michigan state program. I think it has become virtually useless to the doctors and patients that I set out to help.

96. It has been seven years since Michigan enacted a law to make marijuana legally available to patients with glaucoma and cancer. I still work occasionally at the doctor's office and for the last five years I have also worked in a local hospital's cancer ward. Doctors are still telling violently ill patients to smoke marijuana to relieve their nausea and vomiting and the patients are still getting marijuana off the streets. People who work closely with cancer patients know patients are smoking marijuana.

97. Marijuana is being used medically, but not legally. I know many doctors who quietly support marijuana's medical use. Yet, I do not know one doctor who is actively participating in the Michigan Marijuana Therapeutic Research Program. In fact, I have yet to meet a single Michigan cancer patient who ever obtained marijuana legally, through a doctor.

98. Despite its problems, it appears that Michigan fared better than most states in dealing with marijuana's inappropriate Schedule I classification. The doctors in Michigan who did participate in

the limited programs that were developed reported great success. It is my understanding nearly 300 cancer patients in Michigan received marijuana during their chemotherapy treatments. Marijuana successfully reduced nausea and vomiting for the vast majority of these patients. Equally significant, there were almost no adverse effects reported.

99. I am saddened the compassionate intent of the law my son helped enact has not been realized because of federal policies. However, I know that Keith, through his efforts, helped hundreds of desperately ill cancer patients in Michigan and throughout the country to become aware of marijuana's medical benefits.

100. The available studies show marijuana is medically safe for therapeutic use.

101. Michigan and more than 30 other states have legislatively recognized marijuana's medical utility. Hundreds of physicians throughout the country are telling their patients to smoke marijuana. Thousands, if not tens of thousands, of patients with glaucoma, cancer, multiple sclerosis and other disorders are gaining relief from smoking marijuana. As a parent, I once had to confront a stark choice — obey the law and let my son suffer or break the law and provide my son with genuine relief from chemotherapeutically induced misery. I chose to help my son. Faced with the same choice again, my husband and I would help our son again. We are confident any parents confronting such circumstances would make the same decision.

Their Government Tells Them All To Get Lost[*]

This is a final order of the Administrator of the Drug Enforcement Administration denying the petition of the National Organization for Reform of Marijuana Laws to reschedule the plant material marijuana from Schedule I to Schedule II of the Controlled Substances Act....

The two issues involved in a determination of whether marijuana should be rescheduled from Schedule I to Schedule II are whether marijuana plant material has a currently accepted medical use in treatment in the United States, or a currently accepted medical use with severe restrictions; and whether there is a lack of accepted safety for use of marijuana plant material under medical supervision. After a thorough review of the record in this matter, the Administrator rejects the recommendation of the administrative law judge to reschedule marijuana into Schedule II and finds that the evidence in the record mandates a finding that the marijuana plant material remain in Schedule I of the Controlled Substances Act.

The pro-marijuana parties advocate the placement of marijuana plant material into Schedule II for medical use in the treatment of a wide variety of ailments, including nausea and vomiting associated with chemotherapy, glaucoma, spasticity in amputees and those with multiple sclerosis, epilepsy, poor appetite, addiction to drugs and alcohol, pain, and asthma. The evidence presented by the pro-marijuana parties includes outdated and limited scientific studies; chronicles of individuals, their families and friends who have used marijuana; opinions from over a dozen psychiatrists and physicians; court opinions involving medical necessity as a defense to criminal charges for illegal possession of marijuana; state statutes which made marijuana available for research; newspaper articles; and the opinions of laypersons, including lawyers and associations of lawyers. The Administrator does not find such evidence convincing in light of the lack of reliable, credible, and relevant scientific

---

[*] John C. Lawn, *Federal Register*, Vol. 44, No. 249, p. 53767, (Dec. 29, 1989).

studies documenting marijuana's medical utility; the opinions of highly respected, credentialed experts that marijuana does not have an accepted medical use; and statements from the American Medical Association the American Cancer Society, the American Academy of Ophthalmology, the National Multiple Sclerosis Society, and the Federal Food and Drug Administration that marijuana has not been demonstrated as suitable for use as a medicine.

The record contains many research studies which have been published in scientific journals and many unpublished studies conducted by individual states....

...Both the published and unpublished research studies submitted by the pro-marijuana parties in this proceeding to support marijuana's medical use suffer from many deficiencies. They are, in essence, preliminary studies. None of these studies has risen to the level of demonstrating that marijuana has an accepted medical use for treatment of any medical condition....

Nausea and Vomiting

Five studies were presented by the pro-marijuana parties to support the medical use of marijuana as an antiemetic....

The research studies presented by the pro-marijuana parties in this proceeding do not support a conclusion that marijuana has a therapeutic use for treatment of nausea and vomiting associated with chemotherapy.

The pro-marijuana parties presented many testimonials from cancer patients, their families, and friends about the use of marijuana to alleviate nausea and vomiting associated with chemotherapy. These stories of individuals who treat themselves with a mind-altering drug, such as marijuana, must be viewed with great skepticism. There is no scientific merit to any of these accounts.... The accounts of these individuals' suffering and illnesses are very moving and tragic; they are not, however, reliable scientific evidence, nor do they provide a basis to conclude that marijuana has an accepted medical use as an antiemetic.

There were many physicians and other medical experts who testified in this proceeding. In reviewing the weight to be given to an expert's opinion, the facts relied upon to reach that opinion and the credentials and experience of the expert must be carefully examined. The experts presented by the pro-marijuana parties were unable to provide a strong scientific or factual basis to support their opinions. In addition, many of the experts presented by the pro-marijuana parties did not have any expertise in the area of research in the specific medical area being addressed. The pro-marijuana parties presented the testimony of five psychiatrists to support the use of marijuana as an an antiemetic. None of these invividuals is an oncologist, nor have they treated cancer patients. Three of the psychiatrists, Drs. Grinspoon, Ungerlieder and Zinberg are current or former board members of NORML or ACT....

Two pharmacologists, Drs. Morgan and Jobes, presented testimony on behalf of the pro-marijuana parties. Dr. Morgan is a professor at the City College of New York. He does not treat patients, nor is he an oncologist. His opinions are based upon a review of scientific studies and stories told to him by others. He has ties to NORML and is in favor of legalizing marijuana. Dr. Jobe is a pharmacologist and psychiatrist. He testified that his knowledge of marijuana's effects as a drug are based upon a review of the literature and stories from individuals undergoing chemotherapy....

Two general practionors, Drs. Weil and Kaufman, also provided testimony on behalf of the pro-marijuana parties, neither are oncologists, nor do they treat cancer patients. Dr. Weil is a wellness counselor at a health spa, and Dr. Kaufman is an officer of a company that audits hospital quality control programs....

Four oncologists presented testimony on behalf of the pro-marijuana parties. They were Drs. Goldberg, Silverberg, Bickers, and Stephens. Dr. Goldberg is a board certified oncologist, but practices primarily internal medicine. She only administers chemotherapy to one or two patients a year. In her career, she has administered chemotherapy to no more than 10 patients whom she believed to be using marijuana. On cross-examination, she could not recall any studies regarding marijuana. Dr. Goldberg was a member and financial contributor to NORML. Dr. Silverberg has practiced oncology for 20 years. He is a Professor of Clinical Oncology at the University of California at San Francisco, but is not a board certified oncologist....

...Although Dr. Silverberg has advised patients to use marijuana to control nausea and vomiting associated with chemotherapy, he has never been involved in any research nor has he documented any of his observations. Dr. Bickers is an ocologist in New Orleans and is a Professor of Medicine at the Louisiana University School of Medicine. Although Dr. Bickers claims that young patients have better control over nausea and vomiting after using marijuana, he has never documented this claim. Dr. Stephens, an ocologist professor of Medicine and Director of Clinical Oncology at the University of Kansas, characterized marijuana as a "highly effective, and in some cases, critical drug in the reduction of chemotherapeutically-induced emesis." During cross-examination, Dr. Stephens stated that he was unaware of any scientific studies which had been done with marijuana, and that he had never done research or treated patients with marijuana. He indicated that he received his information about the patient's use of marijuana from the nursing staff or the patient's family....

The pro-marijuana parties presented cases in which courts did not convict individuals of a crime associated with possession and use of marijuana based upon a legal defense of "medical necessity." These cases have no relevance to this proceeding which relates to marijuana's possible medical use. The courts found only that these individuals, who were seriously ill and believed that marijuana would help them, did not have criminal intent in possessing or using marijuana....

The pro-marijuana parties also presented evidence that 34 states passed laws permitting marijuana's use for medical purposes in those states. These laws provided that marijuana should be available for medical research. The term "research" is essential to a reading of these statutes. These laws made marijuana available for research and, in some states, set up research programs to study marijuana's safety and effectiveness as a medicine. These statutes are read for what they are, encouraging research involving marijuana. They are not an endorsement by state legislatures that marijuana has an accepted medical use in treatment.

The numerous testimonials and opinions of lay persons which were presented in this proceeding by the pro-marijuana parties are not useful in determining whether marijuana has a medical use. While experiences of individuals with medical conditions who use marijuana may provide a basis for research, they cannot be substituted for reliable scientific evidence. For the many reasons stated in the previous discussion of scientific evidence, these statements can be given little weight. Similarly, endorsements by such organizations as the National Association of Attorneys General, that marijuana has medical use as an antiemetic are of little persuasive value when compared with statements from the American Cancer Society and the American Medical Association.

Glaucoma

The pro-marijuana parties presented several studies to support their contention that marijuana has a medical use for treatment of glaucoma. In order for a drug to be effective in treating glaucoma it must lower the pressure within the eye for prolonged periods of time and actually preserve sight or visual fields. The studies relied upon by the pro-marijuana parties do not scientifically support a finding that marijuana has a medicinal use for treatment of glaucoma. Five of the studies presented by the pro-marijuana parties are pure THC studies. As previously noted, THC is only one constituent among hundreds found in marijuana. Therefore, the consequences of an individual ingesting pure THC as compared to smoking marijuana are vastly different. A few of the studies presented do document that heavy doses of marijuana over a short time period reduce eye pressure in most individuals. However, there are no studies which document that marijuana can sustain reduced eye pressure for extended time periods. The acute, or short-term, studies also show various side effects from marijuana use....

The pro-marijuana parties presented testimonials of individuals who suffer from glaucoma and believe their condition has benefited from the use of marijuana. Most of these individuals used marijuana recreationally prior to discovery of their illness. Chief among the individuals presenting statements was Robert Randall. Mr. Randall is president of ACT, and has been on NORML's Board of Directors since 1976. He has been a strong advocate for medical use of marijuana. Mr. Randall also has glaucoma. Mr. Randall began smoking marijuana as a college student in 1966, long before he was diagnosed in 1972 as having glaucoma. At that time Mr. Randall was treated with standard glaucoma medications. In the mid-1970s Mr. Randall was involved in a preliminary research study conducted by Dr. Robert Hepler. Dr. Hepler conducted some of the first published short-term marijuana studies relating to glaucoma. Dr. Hepler told Mr. Randall that he believed that marijuana in combination with other standard glaucoma medications would be helpful in reducing his eye pressure. In 1975, Mr. Randall was arrested for growing and possessing marijuana. His defense was medical necessity. Subsequently, he began receiving marijuana under an Investigational New Drug (IND) protocol sponsored by his physician. He also continued to receive standard glaucoma medications. Since 1976, Mr. Randall has been treated by Dr. North. Mr. Randall receives marijuana from

> *The pro-marijuana parties presented testimonials of individuals who suffer from glaucoma and believe their condition has benefited from the use of marijuana. Most of these individuals used marijuana recreationally prior to discovery of their illness.*

the federal government and continues to take standard glaucoma medications. Two physicians who treated Mr. Randall, including Dr. North, testified that Mr. Randall's eye pressure appears to have been controlled and his vision kept stable for the last several years.

Mr. Randall smokes approximately 8-10 marijuana cigarettes a day. Since Mr. Randall continues to take other glaucoma medication, his controlled eye pressure cannot be attributable solely to marijuana use. In fact, Dr. North testified that Mr. Randall needs the standard medications as well as marijuana, and that the marijuana itself is not totally effective in decreasing Mr. Randall's eye pressure. Mr. Randall's experience with marijuana, although utilized under a physician's directions, is not scientific evidence that marijuana has an accepted medical use in treatment of glaucoma. Dr. Merritt, one of Mr. Randall's physicians, responded to the question of why he did not publish the results of Mr. Randall's treatment by saying, "A single isolated incident of one person smoking marijuana is not evidence for other ophthalmologists who may want to use the drug."

...The pro-marijuana parties rely primarily on the opinions of two of Mr. Randall's physicians, Drs. North and Merritt, in supporting their contention that marijuana has a medical use in treatment of glaucoma. Dr. North indicated that his conclusion that marijuana has a medical use in treatment of glaucoma is based solely on his observations of Mr. Randall. Dr. Merritt is a board-certified opthalmologist and researcher who has authored many articles on the use marijuana and cannabinoids to reduce eye pressure. Dr. Merritt based his opinion that marijuana has a medical use in treatment of glaucoma on published scientific studies, treatment of Mr. Randall, and treatment of other glaucoma patients. As previously stated all the available studies concern high doses of marijuana taken over short periods of time. Even Dr. Merritt admitted that there are no studies to show that marijuana repeatedly lowers eye pressure over long time periods. The maintenance of lowered eye pressure is crucial in treating individuals with glaucoma....

Spasticity

In support of their contention that marijuana has a medical use in treatment of spasticity in amputees and those with multiple sclerosis, the pro-marijuana parties presented three studies involving THC, testimonials of individuals with spasticity who use marijuana, medical opinions, and state court decisions on the medical necessity defense. The three studies presented by the pro-marijuana parties were very small studies. All three totaled 17 patients, and used THC, not marijuana, to treat spasticity. There are no studies using marijuana to treat spasticity....

With regard to marijuana's safety for use under medical supervision, the administrator must again rely on the scientific evidence. While the pro-marijuana parties argue that no one has died from marijuana use, and individuals who use it have testified that they have not experienced adverse effects, there is little or no scientific evidence to support their claims. For example, while Robert Randall claims marijuana smoking has had no adverse effect on his health or respiratory system, he has not had a physical examination or pulmonary function in over 10 years.

In order to be effective, a drug's therapeutic benefits must be balanced against and outweigh its negative or adverse effects. This has not been established with marijuana. As the previously discussed evidence has demonstrated, there is as yet no reliable scientific evidence to support marijuana's therapeutic benefit. It is therefore, impossible to balance the benefit against the negative effects. The negative effects of marijuana use are well-documented in the record. Marijuana smoking, the route of administration advocated by many witnesses presented by the pro-marijuana parties, causes many well-known and scientifically documented side effects. These include decreased blood pressure, rapid heart rate, drowsiness, euphoria, disphoria and impairment of motor function, not to mention various negative effects on the respiratory and pulmonary systems. Therefore, the only conclusion is that marijuana is not safe for use under medical supervision, because its safety has not been established by reliable scientific evidence.

In summary, the Administrator finds that there is insufficient and in many instances no, reliable, credible, scientific evidence, supported by properly conducted scientific research, to support a conclusion that marijuana is safe for use under medical supervision. This agency, and the government as a whole, would be doing the public a disservice by concluding that this complex psychoactive drug with serious adverse effects has a medical use based upon anecdotal and unreliable evidence....

Conclusion

The Administrator finds that the administrative law judge failed to act as an impartial judge in this matter. He appears to have ignored the scientific evidence, ignored the testimony of highly credible and recognized medical experts and, instead, relied on the testimony of pyschiatrists and individuals who use marijuana. The administrative law judge relied heavily on anecdotal accounts of marijuana use by both physicians and seriously ill persons. The administrative law judge's findings of fact ignored any evidence presented by the government.

For example, in his findings regarding marijuana and nausea and vomiting associated with chemotherapy, Judge Young cites many of the physicians presented by the pro-marijuana parties by name as accepting marijuana as "medically useful." Not once in his findings or discussion does the judge acknowledge or mention the government's experts. Not once does the judge mention why he chose to find the pro-marijuana parties evidence more credible....

The Administrator rejects the administrative law judge's findings and conclusion. They were erroneous; they were not based upon credible evidence; nor were they based upon evidence in the record as a whole. Therefore, in this case, they carry no weight and do not represent the position of the agency or its Administrator. The inadequacy of Judge Young's analysis of the case is duly noted and so are the irrational statements propounded by the pro-marijuana parties. Such statements include the following: "marijuana is far safer than many of the foods we commonly consume. For example, eating ten raw potatoes can result in a toxic response. By comparison, it is physically impossible to eat enough marijuana to induce death." That such a statement would come from the proponents of marijuana is understandable. To give it the weight of an administrative law judge's finding is appalling....

As a final note, the administrator expresses his displeasure at the misleading accusations and conclusions leveled at the Government and communicated to the public by the pro-marijuana parties, specifically NORML and ACT. These two organizations have falsely raised the expectations of many seriously ill persons by claiming that marijuana has medical usefulness in treating glaucoma, spasticity and other illnesses. Their statements have probably caused many people with serious diseases to experiment with marijuana to the detriment of their own health, without proper medical supervision, and without knowing about the serious side effects which smoking or ingesting marijuana may cause. These are not the Dark Ages. The Congress, as well as the medical community, has accepted that drugs should not be available to the public unless they are found by scientific studies to be effective and safe. To do otherwise is to jeopardize the American public, and take advantage of desperately ill people who will try anything to alleviate their suffering. The Administrator strongly urges the American public not to experiment with potentially dangerous, mind-altering drugs such as marijuana in an attempt to treat a serious illness or condition.... NORML and ACT have attempted to perpetrate a dangerous and cruel hoax on the American public by claiming marijuana has currently accepted medical uses.

Politics Is The Real Issue*

As a cancer survivor, I find it discouraging and disappointing that the Drug Enforcement Administration has rejected the recommendation of its own chief administrative law judge that marijuana be reclassified to allow doctors to prescribe it. The judge, Francis L. Young, described it as "one of the safest therapeutically active substances known to man."

The anti-nausea properties of marijuana had only recently come to light when I was being treated for throat cancer in 1976. I had just turned 17 when my cobalt treatments began....

When I became nauseous, I was given injections of some drug (I was never told the name) that had no perceptible effect on my vomiting. I was also given barbituate suppositories, which were slow to take effect and didn't seem to help much either.

---

*Jim Hankins, "Casualties of the Drug War," *The New York Times*, Jan. 31, 1989, p. A27.

For the most part, though, I had to put up with the vomiting without any medicine to relieve it. Vomiting through a throat, nose and mouth that had been scorched by radiation is torture. So are dry heaves — bending over a toilet and trying to vomit with an empty stomach.

Needless to say, I lost weight. There was little incentive to eat after radiation had disabled my taste buds. I was 6 foot 1, and had dipped below 120 pounds. I was able to get marijuana, sporadically, after my family moved into a San Antonio neighborhood. I have no recollection of ever throwing up while under the influence of marijuana, which is more than I can say for the legally prescribed drugs I was given.

Once, my father announced he had dug up and thrown away marijuana seedlings found growing wild in the backyard, apparently sprouted from seeds dropped by neighborhood teenagers. I fished the plants out of the garbage and dried the leaves over a lamp in my room. There was barely enough for one thin cigarette, which I smoked. I felt better than I had in weeks, forgot about my nausea and was actually able to eat without forcing myself. I didn't mind that I could not taste the food, because the "munchies" (the desire for any food, especially sweets) caused by marijuana was overpowering.

A couple of times, I was able to smoke marijuana (obtained from new friends in the neighborhood) before I went to the hospital for outpatient cobalt treatments. This was a big help because the radiation, when directed at my throat from certain angles, would momentarily create ozone in my throat and nose. The smell of the ozone was sickening, and I had to learn to hold my breath and exhale sharply through my nose at the exact moment the machine clicked on to keep from being overwhelmed and vomiting. The marijuana made this experience much more tolerable, because it suppressed the nausea.

The combined effects of the cancer and radiation severely damaged my ears. I had to go to the hospital every other week to have my ear canals cleared of dried blood, wax and other discharges. It often caused a great deal of physical discomfort and anxiety, like an especially harrowing dental procedure.

One time, when I had smoked marijuana before hand, the doctor was surprised when I started giggling. Instead of suffering, I felt as if I were being tickled.

So it is ironic that the DEA Administrator, John C. Lawn, cites doubts about safety as one of the reasons for reclassifying marijuana so that, while it would be unavailable to the general public, it could still be prescribed.

Many cancer chemotherapy drugs have such onerous side effects that they can only be justified as a desperate measure against a relentless killer. We trust doctors to judiciously prescribe some of the deadliest substances known to man, yet we balk at a relatively innocuous drug like marijuana.

Obviously, safety is not the real issue. Politics is the issue. To permit marijuana would be a blow to President Bush's war on drugs. Patients would be able to use it openly and to discuss its effects — good, bad, indifferent — without fear of being labeled lawbreakers. If everybody had a cousin, grandmother or neighbor who had used marijuana, found it harmless and said so, it could greatly shake the public's confidence in the antidrug zealots.

How Cancer And AIDS Patients Suffer At The Hands Of The DEA*

Civility, reason and compassion are the inevitable casualties of any war. And in war even victories come with body counts and consequences.

The ultimate irony of the drug prohibition is that it fails to restrain social drug use and succeeds in depriving the desperately ill of adequate medical care. It is the lame, the near-blind, the dying who are most victimized by the brutality and banality of the political Punch 'n Judy act we so politely call drug control.

In the "war on drugs" there is a chemical, catechism, or cliche to suit every taste. And there is a large, familiar cast.

Zero tolerance is more than a mere phrase. It is a creed; a quest for social conformity which contrives to make us less secure while stretching the reach of agencies of enforcement.

We who are seriously ill have become lost souls, unwilling participants in this macabre charade. Non-combatants we are, as civilians, trapped between enraged armies battling over bitter spoils.

For more than a decade seriously ill patients have won many victories. It is patients who have spearheaded efforts to abolish the medical prohibition of marijuana. It is patients who persuaded 34 state legislatures to recognize marijuana's important medical value. It is patients who convinced the courts marijuana can be a drug of "medical necessity."

Legal organizations as diverse in outlook as the National Association of Criminal Defense Lawyers and the National Association of Attorneys General have recognized the needs of patients and called

---
* Robert Randall, President, Alliance for Cannabis Therapeutics.

on the U.S. government to end medical prohibitions against marijuana's therapeutic use.

In 1988, after two years of hearings and testimony from more than sixty witnesses, the U.S. Drug Enforcement Administration's own adminstrative law judge concluded that marijuana has important medical uses in the treatment of life- and sense-threatening diseases. After hearing the evidence Judge Young ruled the DEA-enforced medical prohibition is "unreasonable, arbitrary and capricious."

The DEA rejected the judge's historic verdict and refused to acknowledge marijuana's therapeutic utility or move to make the drug available to physicians for prescriptive medical use. The case is now before the U.S. Court of Appeals for the District of Columbia Circuit.

Even as political, judicial, legislative, medical and popular support for the DEA-enforced prohibition rapidly recedes, the population of patients with marijuana responsive diseases is expanding.

In 1990, AIDS was decisively added to the growing list of marijuana-responsive diseases. AIDS patients around the world may benefit from this action. They can thank Steve.

AIDS patients have been smoking marijuana for years to reduce the debilitating nausea and vomiting caused by HIV-infection and AZT-induced emesis. Which is to say AIDS patients smoke marijuana for the same reasons cancer patients smoke: to ease nausea and vomiting and to enhance the appetite.

But, AIDS patients, like cancer patients, seldom have the energy, or time — quite literally — to fight for legal access. Reform is for the living. The terminally ill have more pressing and immediate concerns. Particularly when they can more easily and readily purchase high quality marijuana off the streets.

Steve, sick and under arrest for smoking marijuana, was the first AIDS patient who asked the Alliance for help. Steve welcomed this contest. Against the odds he outlasted bureaucratic stonewalling and lived long enough to gain legal access to marijuana. Once he achieved this goal, and sent this signal to other AIDS patients, Steve died.

Victories and body counts.

News of Steve's success rippled outward. Persons with AIDS responded by demanding similar consideration. Physicians who treat AIDS patients, keenly aware of the limits of modern pharmaceuticals, do not cower when confronted by a politically objectionable drug which has important therapeutic implications for their patients. Instead, they demand prescriptive access.

This trend will accelerate.

This is written in high summer. My thoughts are with a young couple in Florida — Kenny and Barbra Jenks. Kenny, who is 28, has hemophilia. At some point in the mid-1980s, he received a transfusion of HIV-tainted blood. Now, Kenny and his wife Barbra have AIDS.

Barbra, who is 23, once weighed 155 pounds. Then, between Thanksgiving and Christmas, 1988, her weight collapsed to 112 pounds. She developed pneumonia, went into a coma.

Barbra recovered from these calamities, but she and Kenny continued to experience problems with nausea, vomiting, and diminishing weight. Other AIDS patients told the couple smoking marijuana helped to control AZT-induced nausea and vomiting and, as we all know, marijuana makes you want to eat.

For the next year Kenny and Barbra smoked marijuana, ate dinner, gained weight and stayed out of the hospital. Marijuana not only calmed their digestive upset, it permitted them to live fairly normal lives.

Normal lives. This comment, that smoking marijuana produces a discrete, vital alteration in perception, is consistently mentioned by the dozens of AIDS patients to whom I have spoken since Steve's death. They say marijuana makes AIDS a "tolerable" disease. What is it about marijuana that it makes terminality tolerable?

First, marijuana lacks the powerfully disorienting psychological and biochemical effects produced by most commercially prescribed tranquilizers, painkillers and mood elevators. With marijuana, AIDS patients can avoid or significantly reduce their use of highly toxic synthetic drugs. So, instead of feeling "doped-up," "sedated," "like a Zombie," marijuana permits AIDS patients to feel mildly euphoric — "relaxed."

To be dying and feel "relaxed" and, more specifically, to feel "relaxed" contemplating one's personal demise — this is not an immodest benefit.

Which is to say marijuana provides AIDS patients with a sense of perspective. As Steve so carefully phrased it, "When I smoke marijuana I'm living with AIDS. When I don't smoke marijuana I'm dying of AIDS."

Second, marijuana suppresses emesis and improves appetite. Sitting down with one's family to eat dinner without gagging on your own vomit cannot help but improve one's mental outlook and sense of physical welfare.

Kenny and Barbra Jenks were sitting down to dinner the night ten vice squad agents from the Bay County Narcotics Strike Force busted down their front door and held a gun to Barbra's head. This daring raid resulted in the seizure of two small marijuana plants. Kenny and Barbra were charged with felony cultivation with intent to distribute and are facing five years in prison.

Two days following their arrest, Kenny read an article I had written about Steve. What Steve desired most — that his efforts should help other AIDS patients — crystallized.

It must be very odd indeed to be on trial for possessing the one drug which helps you cope with a fatal disease. Considering the circumstances, there is reason to doubt threats of criminalization and long prison sentences will discourage Kenny and Barbra — or tens of thousands of other AIDS patients — from obtaining the marijuana they medically need.

DEA demands these patients get marijuana illegally, off the streets. Patients, however, prefer to get medicines from physicians. AIDS and HIV-positive patients join cancer, glaucoma, multiple sclerosis patients and others in working to make this possibility a reality.

Barbra and Kenny are under tremendous stress but, like Steve, they have decided to stand and fight. They have realized they can help other people with AIDS — just as Steve helped them. Through their trial other AIDS patients will learn marijuana can be helpful. They are, in short, beginning to sense their place — and power — in the ever screwy scheme of things.

When arrest and trial are transformed from pits of personal intimidation into platforms for issue pollination, the prohibition itself becomes untenable. In this light Kenny and Barbra cannot lose. Regardless of the legal outcome arrived at in a Florida courtroom, the general result is certain: AIDS patients in ever increasing numbers will learn of marijuana's potential benefits, obtain the drug and gain medical relief. Whether the marijuana they employ is legal or illegal, sanctioned or condemned is nearly irrelevant. Steve, in effect, started a social chain-letter. Kenny and Barbra are continuing the process.

Under the pressure of a geometrically expanding opposition the medical prohibition is doomed.

In essence, I felt that we in the medical profession had pronounced his death sentence. If he had any chance of living we took it away.

—*Seymour Rubin*

If he had more support and understanding from his doctors and from society perhaps his life and mine would have been different and perhaps in living differently he would still be alive today.

—*Lisa Polansky*

Before long Barbra will be beaten or raped or found dead: count on it. Another victory in the great American drug war.

—*D. Keith Mano*

Chapter 6

Why Make Narcotic Addicts Suffer?

Introduction

For many decades, the dominant expert answers to the question in the title have been that (1) only through Calvinistic suffering brought on by drug withdrawal will each addict improve in personal health; (2) addicts cannot function while taking drugs; and (3) if we give in to addicts and their base desires, more addicts will be recruited and the entire society infected and ruined. Thus, even though addicts may be suffering from a disease, as a general rule doctors should not be allowed to prescribe the drugs of their addiction to them in the form of medicine.

For some addicts these approaches have proven to be helpful. For many, perhaps most, disastrous.

Because of the suffering of so many narcotic addicts, many nations allow some exceptions to these rigid rules. The United Kingdom allows doctors to prescribe a wide array of drugs for the purpose of maintenance of addiction and the prevention of suffering. In some cases, the medicinal drugs include injectable and smokable methadone and heroin. The United States allows oral methadone, but no other medicines.

Regardless of a particular country's prescribing rules, many of the people of every nation treat addicts with suspicion and fear. According to the late Rev. Terence E. Tanner of London, this is "because addicts are the scapegoats of our age." Writing in 1979, this Catholic priest who ministered to street addicts explained that in ancient times a priest of the tribe chose a goat upon whom all the people's sins were recited. The goat was then set free to wander away into the forest and to thus take away those sins. "If anyone fed or touched him, he was contaminated and the sins the goat carried were transferred to him." And as for today, Rev. Tanner continued, "It is an apt description of what society does to the addict and to anyone who pleads the addict's cause."

Terence Tanner believed, in opposition to dominant social and medical thinking, that properly maintained addicts could be educated and assisted to lead relatively normal lives. So do many other experts involved in the addiction scene in the United Kingdom and across the waters. At the present time, the United Kingdom, Holland, and several other countries are moving toward ever greater reliance on narcotic maintenance as an important method of treatment. They are also showing greater kindness and understanding toward injecting addicts. In general, this is not the case in the United States.

Milton Polansky: We Pronounced His Death Sentence*

"A mature addict with a legal supply of clean drugs may well be a nice neighbor," was a thought I had put in a column that appeared in *The Washington Post* early in 1984. It had been written partly with Milton Polansky in mind, but I was also thinking of other drug addicts I had met since the early 70s, many of whom were decent people. Drugs, I had found, were morally irrelevant. Some people who take narcotic drugs behave immorally in other ways but not because of the drugs. Some people who are absolutely drug free are also free of any morals. The truly important issues for me have become not so much whether people take drugs but rather how they treat those to whom they should be showing love and care. All of those thoughts were behind that sentence....

Milton thought of himself as a heroin addict, nothing to hide, chin out, them's the conditions that prevail. "Who am I hurting?" he asked me defiantly one day over lunch. We both knew that, despite the views of many drug abuse experts, there was no scientific evidence that the narcotics caused any significant organic harm to his body. Yet there was sound medical research documenting the harm caused by persistent injecting of the skin, including abscesses and the many diseases that may be transmitted by dirty needles, such as hepatitis. Accordingly, I asked him if he was not hurting himself by the constant injections since 1940 when he started using heroin as a soldier. The look of disbelief that came over his face suggested that he viewed any person who did not use proper procedures in injecting as a fool. Once, during "the war" in about 1943, "I was at a long party with a jazz

* Arnold S. Trebach, *The Great Drug War*, p. 271.

band and we shared a needle, in New Orleans, and I ended up in the hospital with hepatitis for a while," but that was the last time he remembered suffering from injections.

However, it would be misleading to portray Milton Polansky as simply a sweet old grandfather, a helpless victim of the drug laws, although that is how he appeared at the tragic end. He was also part devil, a scheming and successful manipulator of doctors and the drug laws and the prescription system. One of his fellow addicts, with long years of experience, told me that Milton was virtually without peer in his ability to "make" doctors, to convince them to "write" for him. In some cases, this was accomplished by pitiful appeals to the doctor's sympathetic nature; in others, by appeals to the physician's pocketbook. Milton would then fill these prescriptions, using some of the drugs and selling the rest to a small circle of fellow addicts. During recent years, it is likely that he took in tens of thousands of dollars every year in drug sales. Of course, when his supply ran low, he would spend roughly the same amounts to buy drugs for himself, often from within that same small circle of addicts. On some occasions, however, this would require venturing onto the mean streets of Baltimore, into rough neighborhoods such as one notorious area known as "the block." Unlike the multitude of innocent organically ill people who need analgesic medicines every year in America and in many other countries, Milton Polansky, doting father and grandfather, was a criminal narcotic addict.

It is important that his status as a criminal be recognized because that status puts him in the same category, speaking in broad terms, as some of the most destructive inhabitants of America. The manner in which we react to people who are both addicts and criminals is important. They are a challenge to our sense of ethics. Each of them presents unique problems and opportunities. If we can understand how we threw away the human opportunity in this case, if we can see the cruelty that we as a nation imposed on this one "criminal" addict, Milton Polansky, late of Baltimore, Maryland, there is some hope that we can commence evolving a more humane and effective approach to all of our unfortunate neighbors whom personal stupidity, fate, biology, or bad luck, separately or together, have pulled into addiction and some degree of related crime.

Milton's behavior as a criminal addict did not preclude his functioning in many ways as a decent human being. As far as can be discovered, he never committed a violent act or a burglary or a theft to obtain his drugs, which were not difficult for him to obtain for most of his addicted years. He was virtually unknown to police blotters, at least for serious offenses; the man did seem to get stopped often by the police for driving without a license. During much of his life, which commenced on Nov. 19, 1918, Mr. Polansky was a successful Baltimore businessman, engaged in such fields as building renovation and real estate. He was a regular contributor to many charities. While he was not greatly successful in his marriages, he adored his children and grandchildren and I am told that they felt the same way about him. In most respects, he was a nice neighbor.

As the years passed, Milton Polansky developed a number of serious organic and painful diseases. None of them, to my knowledge, were attributable to his use of narcotics. Thus, like many addicts I have encountered, he was soon taking powerful narcotics as a form of self-medication to deal both with his addiction and his organic diseases. Also in line with the patterns of many of these dependent users, there were drugs he preferred and then there were those he found acceptable. In Milton's case, as with many addicts, his drug of choice was heroin and the acceptable substitute was Dilaudid, that legal synthetic opiate which may be several times more potent, dose for dose, even than heroin. He took methadone as a last resort but in general looked with disdain on the favorite drug of the addiction treatment experts of America. There you have him, warts and all, a far from perfect being.

That flawed human package walked into the office of Seymour H. Rubin, M.D., in a Jewish neighborhood in the north of Baltimore, on Oct. 20, 1982. Dr. Rubin knew a great deal about Milton and his family, having treated his brother who had died 17 years previously from diabetes and heart disease. He had not seen Milton since those days, and wrote in his notes, "I am shocked by his horrible and changed appearance. He looks 30 years older than his stated age." The patient, then aged 62, shuffled along haltingly and needed a cane. A medical examination revealed an even more shocking list of organic ailments. Dr. Rubin was especially concerned about the impending gangrene of both legs. Other serious conditions of the patient included diabetes, kidney failure, recurrent transient strokes, heart disease, and high blood pressure with congestive heart failure. Any one of these conditions, along with allied complications, could have rapidly fatal results, Dr. Rubin knew, especially if they were not treated properly. And, of course, those potentially terminal organic illnesses were being ignored by the patient because he was finding it increasingly difficult to find a steady source, legal or illegal, of medicines to treat his diseases — and thus his energies focused on an obsessive search for drugs to feed his addiction.

Seymour Rubin, a native of Baltimore and five years younger than Milton, is a graduate of the University of Maryland Medical School and board certified in internal medicine. He has little experience, expertise, or interest in treating drug addicts. Yet, through a series of unrelated events, he has come to strongly disagree with the current medical-legal approach to them. While a frontline infantryman in World War II, he saw at a newly liberated concentration camp how harsh deprivation of basic needs can reduce decent, proud human beings to sniveling, conniving beggars. Later, at medical school in the late 40s, he heard Harry Anslinger of the old FBN tell the students in a guest lecture how to think about addicts: they are basically evil people; they'll do anything to get drugs; if they don't commit themselves to the Lexington Hospital for detoxification, they should be put in jail and the key should be thrown away. "I feel that our medical profession is still guided by that attitude," Dr. Rubin now declares. "And yet I have found out that drug addicts are not all evil people. Many of them are pathetic people who have to be helped, to be led.... If, though, we treat any group of people badly enough, like what I saw at Dachau, we can turn them into whining puppy dogs.... If you just kick them out of the door, you may be protecting yourself as a doctor but you are not doing anything for the patient.... You're being a rotten doctor."

To avoid the common failing of being a rotten doctor in regard to a known drug addict, Dr. Rubin

> *Milton's behavior as a criminal addict did not preclude his functioning in many ways as a decent human being.*

wanted to act rationally on his objective clinical assessment of Milton Polansky. That extensive evaluation concluded that the major threats to his health, indeed to his life, came from his multiple organic medical ailments and not from his incidental though "very repugnant" problem of drug addiction. He decided to provide periodic prescriptions of Dialudid and then to seek to persuade his patient to go into a local hospital for treatment of his other major medical conditions. Milton refused to go into the hospital because he feared that the doctors there would attempt to detoxify him from Dilaudid and also perhaps put him on methadone, "which would tear me apart." He had been through 15 to 20 drug treatment programs within the previous quarter century and none had worked for him; he did not want to risk another attempt even if it was a prelude to easing his organic conditions. "I'll die of withdrawal!" he cried.

Seymour Rubin knew that every prescription of Diluadid he wrote for this known addict put his entire career at risk, and he knew also that the risk would continue even if his patient were to be hospitalized. It was all very chancy though. Very often, doctors were not bothered by the medical or legal authorities; in other cases, they were and their careers destroyed. He called a leading state drug enforcement official who said he believed Mr. Polansky should be prescribed narcotic drugs, as had other law enforcement officials over the years, according to Milton. But the physician was worried about his medical colleagues. Dr. Rubin told me that he wanted to be able to say, "Milton, I don't want any bullshit from you! You'll get Dilaudid but you must cooperate in this program of treatment." At that point, the doctor would have practically dragged his patient into a treatment slot he had ready at Baltimore's Sinai Hospital, especially for his limbs which were becoming gangrenous. But Dr. Rubin knew that he could not assure his patient of a steady supply of Dilaudid, which he was then taking in dosages of about 40 milligrams per day (down from a high in the past of 240 mgs.) After several months of treating this difficult patient and agonizing over the case, Dr. Rubin finally concluded that he had to protect himself somewhat, and he called the head of the medical committee that polices doctors for the state medical society: Stephen A. Hirsch, M.D., Chairman, Committee on Drugs, Medical and Chirurgical Faculty of the State of Maryland.

Dr. Rubin's case notes for December 28, 1982 relate that in response to his call, Dr. Hirsch had emphatically declared "that Milton is well-known to his committee, that he has manipulated many physicians, and that I should not prescribe Dilaudid for him. I will comply with his wishes." Those wishes were communicated in writing a few days later, along with barely concealed threats: "Our very strong advice to you is that you not prescribe any controlled substances for Mr. Polansky, although you of course may treat him for conditions other than his addiction.... Mr. Polansky has been advised of the availability of drug treatment programs in the community and that he should obtain treatment there for his addiction. Again, we appreciate your timely call. You have probably avoided much future difficulty."

Seymour Rubin was indeed out of difficulty with the medical powers who could obliterate his right to practice his profession but not with his own conscience. He could not sleep well for weeks because he felt so ashamed at his weak compliance with the inhumane and ignorant decisions of the appointed state medical drug experts. There was no way to separate Milton's organic diseases from his addiction — and certainly no drug treatment program of Dr. Rubin's knowledge that could cure his addiction. It was at about this time I called Dr. Rubin at Milton's urging, and while he agreed to talk with me, he asked that his name not be used because of his personal sense of shame. Since then, his sense of outrage has taken over.

"Even though I will prescribe no more Dilaudid, there is considerable conflict with what I consider the reasoned and compassionate practice of medicine," Dr. Rubin's notes stated. "Has Milton manipulated doctors, perhaps including me, because he is basically an evil person? No, he has done so because that is the only way available to him to obtain relief from his pains and agonies. Yes, he is at fault for having started his atrocious habit many years ago but do we treat chronic smokers and alcoholics in the same manner?... He is incurably addicted and more Dilaudid pills will do him no harm.... If we can take care of his other problems, his significant renal disease, his uncontrolled diabetes, etc., then we might make an attempt at treating his addiction. He is in far greater danger of the former than the latter, and is more likely to die of them." Operating on his own sense of medical science and ethics, Seymour Rubin had arrived at roughly the same humane point as had the Rolleston Committee some 56 years previously. Yet, he found himself unable to act on his convictions.

Dr. Rubin periodically responded to crisis visits and calls from his patient, to whom he would prescribe no more narcotics. He saw him deteriorate further before his eyes. On March 13, 1984, Milton showed up without an appointment at the doctor's office in a state of collapse. Dr. Rubin pleaded with him to enter the hospital immediately for treatment of all his conditions. Milton refused for all of his usual reasons. He was in enormous pain and shouted that he would lie on the examining table until Dr. Rubin gave him a prescription for Dilaudid. Even though he could barely walk because of the impending gangrene, he threatened to go out and rob a drug store if the doctor did not relent. The doctor did not. The elderly grandfather cursed and shouted and raved that Seymour Rubin was "just like the rest of the fucking asshole doctors."

After that incident, Dr. Rubin lost touch with Mr. Polansky. "I had heard rumors that these were agonizing times for him," Dr. Rubin told me. Almost a year passed. Milton somehow carried on although his doctor later observed, "It was a surprise he lasted as long as he did."

Milton Polansky, heroin addict, was pronounced dead by the medical examiner on March 8, 1985, at 3:50 p.m. Apparently, the old man died alone, perhaps in pain. His body laid undiscovered on the floor of his apartment for some time — since the medical examiner estimated on the death certificate that the date of death was March 3. The immediate cause of death was listed as "Arteriosclerotic Cardiovascular Disease." A contributing condition was listed as "Diabetes Mellitus." There was no mention of narcotic use or overdose.

Dr. Seymour Rubin shot off an angry letter to Dr. Stephen Hirsch and the state drug committee containing rare words of professional condemnation: "Your committee's concern with his drug addiction...was disproportionate and tangential. I thought it was more derived from sanctified dogma and bogus fears rather than from any true feelings about the quality of life or even the life itself."

Sitting in his office, alone with me on a quiet day during the holiday season at the end of 1985, Dr. Rubin was still ashamed and bitter: "In essence, I felt that we in the medical profession had pronounced his death sentence. If he had any chance of living, we took it away."

My Father's Life Was Redeemed In This Writing

November 29, 1989

Dear Mr. Trebach,

I received your book today and would like to thank you for sending it so quickly and for the inscription. I don't know what I could add or if I would change anything. I think that you were very honest in your portrayal of my Dad. It was painful to read but overall I'd say my father's life was redeemed in this writing.

I have been trying to write a book myself but it's about my mother and my father. I don't know what will ever come of my writings, but I did contact the director of the film *Tin Men* because you see, my father brought the aluminum siding business to Baltimore. "Breeze," my name for my Dad, is a larger-than-life character. When I was four or five years old my father was married to his third wife, not my mother. She was a drug addict and so was he. They smoked pot by putting tin foil on a glass to make a pipe. One of the earliest pictures I have was that "the silver foil on the glass is evil" I didn't know what pot was and I didn't know what heroin was but I have a repulsion and aversion to needles. Even today, at the age of 36, I am petrified of having a blood test. I would say that nevertheless I adored, practically worshipped my father, and he worshipped and adored me.

I went through many changes over his drug addictions. When I was about seven or eight I would throw a temper tantrum and storm out of the room if I happened in on my Dad while he was smoking, but by the age of 13, the Beatles were singing everybody smokes pot, and we became partners in the habit. As a child of the 60s I have tried every drug there is but I have never used a needle. I have been drug-free except for caffeine for the past two years. So over the years I have shared certain drug experiences, but have always been horrified at the sight of my father shooting up. My Dad always told us he was a "medical addict." He has not only been sick, but dying since I was born. The fact that he has real medical problems mixed with the fact that he has been a serious drug addict for years has caused great pain, embarrassment mixed with tenderness and love. It is difficult to explain.

Everyone eventually rejected my father. In 1984 he had a heart attack due to the fact that he had tried to get off drugs for his grandchildren. I flew in from Santa Cruz, Ca., to see my father. The first night he looked horrible and near death, very old. The next day he jumped up out of bed proclaiming that I was to drive him back to Baltimore. You see my father had miraculous regenerative powers. I can flash back on literally dozens of scenes in my life when my father was "dying" but then he'd be up and out the door before you could blink an eye. It was perplexing. Well, I drove him back to Baltimore. First we stopped at a hospital in York, Pa., if I remember correctly. My father was carrying on trying to get a prescription filled. I could never tell when he was serious. You see he was the most incredible salesman/con-artist that ever lived, or you could say he was very charming.... Anyway when we got to Baltimore he checked in to a hotel. I was in an adjoining room, and there he set up a shooting gallery. All the guys came around and hung out with my Dad because he was the one who had the supply and, yes, he made a fortune supposedly in the sale of drugs. I stayed for another couple of weeks and then flew home sick and devastated.

On Easter Sunday 1984 my mother died. After the funeral I went to Baltimore and spent what was to be the last summer with my precious father. I tried to take care of him. I thought, "oh, I'll cook and clean for him; I'll try to stabilize his life...."

Yeah I would cook meals but all that man ever craved was sweets. His diabetes was completely out of control and he spent many hours hunched over his arms at the kitchen table, trying in vain to find a vein but he was shooting all kinds of drugs, cocaine and heroin. I was in a state of shock from having just buried my mother. She was only 55 years old. I was going through my own traumas. I began to put on weight. I had always been slender, a perfect dancer body, and suddenly I was 20 pounds heavier. I have since gained an additional 40 pounds.

So many things happened in 1985. I left my father in August. I vaguely recall a Doctor coming to see him, I think it was Dr. Rubin. I returned home from my mother's funeral, and the summer with my Dad with an addiction of my own: Alcohol!

I spent the next six months drinking and going crazy in Santa Cruz. I am a jazz pianist. And I used the inheritance from my mother's estate to live on for a year. I was studying music and I was also drinking and carrying on. In March of 1985, I called my Dad. I was very thrilled to have joined a health club. I was starting to get my life together. He was happy for me. But he also told me that the doctors wanted to remove his legs. I have always felt guilty for not flying back to be with him. He died about a week after our conversation.

His death was very peculiar. Or at least I should say the events that led to his death were very strange. My father was in the hospital for his legs that were gangrened. Supposedly he got into an argument with a nurse. He called some friends to come pick him up but when they arrived he had already left in a cab. Typical! On Friday the week before he died he renewed his lease for his apartment. I have no idea how he was getting around in his condition. My aunt claims that she came to his apartment on Monday the following week. She claims Milton was not there but describes an eerie feeling and that there were newspapers piled in front of his bedroom door. My aunt is very ill and suffering with diabetes and depression so I have always wondered if she looked in the bedroom but I've never been able to ask. Supposedly she called a cousin of mine who lives in Westminster to look in on my Dad. He didn't get into the city until Friday when he called me and told me the news of my father's death. I spoke to the police and firemen who claimed the building was about to explode with heat. My father had the burners on the stove turned up. He was in the bedroom, partially dressed laying behind a dresser that was pulled away from the wall. I don't know what was going on in my father's apartment but thousands of dollars that he showed me six months earlier were nowhere to be found. I have turned this scene over and over in my mind. I have some suspicions about what really happened but no proof.

I returned to California where I have lived for the past 20 years. I did not become destructive after my father's death. In fact, except for a few minor problems, my life just keeps getting better. This year I tried once again to probe the finding and details surrounding my father's death. I have a pretty good idea about what happened to all the money, but there is nothing I can do.

You asked if I would change anything in your book. The only thing I wonder is "Would my father *still* be alive if he had more help from his doctors?" I doubt it. But if he had more support and understanding from his doctors and from society perhaps his life and mine would have been different, and perhaps in living differently he would still be alive today. Does that make any sense?

You should understand my father was smoking pot at age 13. That was 1931! I heard that he had a kidney removed while he was in the service and this is what caused his addiction originally to morphine. Yes, he had tried to withdraw many times and I believe it just made him sicker. Yes, he had many other illnesses: high blood pressure, diabetes, one kidney, cardiovascular problems, the list goes on... but he also had a decadent lifestyle....

It is impossible. There are a lot of men in Baltimore who are addicted. I've known them for many, many years, but in all of my life I have never met a junkie except for in Baltimore. They scare me, they disgust me, and on the other hand I have a deep feeling of wanting to help.

I was always thinking I could save my father. Did he tell you I had a step-brother who died of a drug overdose at the tender age of 20? Drugs have been the root of all the evil and sadness of my life. I don't have any answers. I hope this letter helps; actually it was just a great catharsis for me. In the last year I rejected my father because of all the scenes I witnessed in his apartment. I usually acted with great compassion but that was with three thousand miles in between. He was a genius; some say he was a legend in Baltimore for good things and for bad things. He was humanitarian in his beliefs. A brilliant mind and ability to achieve *whatever* he set out to do. He has had successful businesses all over this country but he has walked away from everything. He has made fortunes in the stock market, but just as quickly gambled it away or bought drugs with it....

I don't know what else to say but I thank you from the bottom of my heart for writing such an inspirational story about "The Breeze." You know this all came to me the week of his birthday. For me it was a magical message from him to me. The man of my soul! It cannot be denied, my father was an inspiration and I appreciate and will always cherish what you wrote about him. I think it was positive!

With love and appreciation from,
Lisa

I Feel that I am a Responsible Person

July 7, 1990

Dear Mr. Trebach:

My wife and I are having a terrible time obtaining methadone from the state of Vermont, even the neighboring states. We have recently asked nine Vermont physicians if they would apply for a license to dispense methadone to my wife and I. They all seem to be discouraged by the legislation and regulations associated with it.

At the present time we are being forced to drive into Harlem, New York every week to buy our medicine on the street. We are spending 50 cents on the dollar just to keep from being sick. Last week we bought some methadone not realizing it had been cut with clonidine and darvocet-n 100 because the color matches the disks when they are dissolved.

After nine years of reporting to methadone clinics for my daily medicine, I decided to try my hand at detoxification. So five months ago I checked into the well known McLean Hospital in Boston, Mass. I was shocked when I found out that a famous drug hospital like McLean was unable to locate another person who was on methadone maintenance for a few years, who was able to successfully detoxify (being clean for at least three years). In 30 days, my insurance ran out, so I came home from the hospital unable to eat, sleep, work, etc., etc. The physiological pain was so severe, and the treatment so ineffective for this drug, that I have been buying narcotics on the street ever since.

My inability to obtain our medicine legally has been conscience-shocking. Never in my wildest dreams did I think that sick people in America would be so inhumanely treated, forced to buy medicine on street corners.

Lastly, we are enclosing copies of some letters that began when we wrote to Dr. Ian McDonald, assistant to President Reagan. We would be very grateful if you could write something in the next *Drug Policy Letter* about this problem. Also would you or the Foundation know of an associate in the Vermont area that would consider treating my wife and I?

Thank you very kindly,
Lawrence K. Cushing

August 8, 1988
Dr. Ian McDonald
The White House

Dear Dr. Ian McDonald:

I am writing this letter to you in an effort to seek medical relief. I have exhausted every local, state, and federal agency in an attempt to purchase medicine for myself, and my fiancee without success.

I have been chemically dependent on methadone hydrochloride for the past 7-8 years. I have never missed a day without taking my medicine. We are originally from the state of Massachusetts where our treatment on methadone started. However, we now live in the state of Vermont, and there are no doctors in the state licensed to treat people with a methadone dependency. As a result of this we are forced to drive from central Vermont to Manhattan, N.Y., every week to purchase our medicine from a private clinic at a cost of $150 a week. The trip is a 630-mile drive, so that means another $50 for gasoline and tolls. However, the doctor has been kind enough to let us drink one dose there and take six days' supply home with us.

Nevertheless, it's just not enough. We have been making this trip for about a year now, and as a result of the distance we have to drive every week, and the loss of time on my job I am financially, mentally and physically drained.

I feel that I am a responsible person. I am 39 years old with two teenage daughters. And my fiancee is 35 years of age with two teenage children of which we do our best to support. I have worked as a welder, building power plants for the past 20 years. However, we are dependent on this medicine every day of our life.

To charge this kind of money for a few dollars worth of medicine is clearly taking advantage of the law. This doctor knows that there are no doctors in Vermont that we can turn to. At the writing of this letter, we have fallen behind on all our bills, including our payment to the doctor in New York. He told us if we can't afford his fee, he can't treat us.

We would appreciate anything you could do in assisting us to obtain our medicine more locally.

Thank you for your anticipated help with this medical problem.

Very Truly Yours,
Lawrence K. Cushing

Alcohol, Drug Abuse and Mental Health Administration
Rockville, Maryland 20857
September 19, 1988

Dear Mr. Cushing:

I am responding to your letter, dated Aug. 8, 1988, to Dr. Donald Ian MacDonald, Deputy Assistant to the President and Director, Drug Abuse Policy Office. I apologize for the delay in responding.

I sympathize with the difficulties you are having as a result of traveling 630 miles a week in order to get the methadone you apparently need. Nevertheless, I think it is clear that the federal government is constrained by Federal regulations at 21 C.F.R. Part 291 from granting you relief at this time.

As you know, the Food and Drug Administration is responsible under those regulations for overseeing methadone treatment to assure its appropriateness. The regulations stipulate that any federally-approved methadone treatment program must meet all state requirements. That stipulation is consistent with long-standing federal policy to leave the practice of medicine to states and professional societies.

I understand that Mr. Gerald R. Hajarian of the Food and Drug Administration has indicated to you that his agency would consider any request from a physician for approval to administer you methadone, including a request that would reduce the number of visits you needed to make to the physician's office.

As you may know, Massachusetts, unlike Vermont and other neighboring states, does have federally approved methadone programs available to out-of-staters. Mr. Lennie Kepsc, President, Habit Management, 648 Beacon St., Third Floor, Boston, Mass., 02215 has clinics that may permit you to take home a week's supply or more of methadone. One of those clinics is in Lowell, another is scheduled to open soon in Springfield. In order to explore those options, please call Mr. Kupsc at (617) 267-3488.

If you want to explore other options in Massachusetts, please contact Mr. Paul J. Tierney, Manager, Licensing and Regulations, Division of Drug Rehabilitation, Commonwealth of Massachusetts, 150 Tremont St., Boston, Mass., 02111. Mr. Tierney also can be reached at (617) 727-1960.

Finally, please understand that federal regulations, including those at 21 C.F.R. Part 291, generally are published only after review of public comment on proposed rules. Thus, they cannot be changed without a lengthy formal process involving further public comment.

Sincerely yours,

Frederick K. Goodwin, M.D.
Administrator

February 4, 1989
Frederick K. Goodwin, M.D.
Department of Health and Human Services
Rockville, Maryland 20857

Dear Dr. Goodwin:

I am writing this letter in reference to your letter dated Sept. 19, 1989, regarding federal regulations that control methadone prescribing for the treatment of narcotic addiction. I apologize for my delay in responding, However, when I received your letter I was very pleased to find that someone in government is knowledgeable with this subject matter.

You state in your letter that the federal government is constrained by federal regulations at 21 C.F.R. part 291 from granting me relief at this time. I think it is clear for you to say that I am constrained from obtaining medial relief as a result of federal regulations that seem to be experimental in nature.

I am now into my ninth year of reporting to a doctor's office every day, seven days a week, for the first six years so that a nurse can put a pill into a plastic cup, and mix a little bit of hot water to it in order to dissolve the pill, and then allowing me to drink my medicine as if I were a five-year-old child. For this service, a doctor charges me $75 a week. The best part is if I don't have the money, I don't get my medicine.

I realize that these regulations create thousands of jobs for people that would probably have trouble obtaining a real job. These regulations turn the patient into a slave for the doctor that owns the clinic, and enslaves the patients to his entire staff.

If you read my previous letter you know that I am 39 years old, I have two daughters, the oldest being 19 years of age, and the younger is 14. I have always played a responsible role in society. When I lived in Massachusetts I worked as a real estate broker for 10 years selling and building hundreds of homes to many happy families. In addition to this I am an engineer. I am presently working in the Vermont Atomic Nuclear power plant as a machinery engineer with *top security clearance* allowing me to work on equipment as sensitive as a nuclear reactor. I am adding this in order to give you some knowledge of my employment background.

These regulations were put into effect back in 1971. Keep in mind, we had no AIDS problem at that time. Prior to this, a local physician was able to prescribe this medicine to anyone in need of treatment. However, these federal regulations controlling the distribution of methadone have complicated treatment so much that it is almost impossible to obtain, unless you live and work next door to a clinic.

You say in your letter that Mr. Lennie Kupsc may *permit me* to take home a week's supply of medicine. Do you realize that 20 years ago when a drug addict robbed a drug store, they would flush the methadone down the toilet, because it destroys the effect of a real narcotic? Now, because it is so difficult to obtain, it is being sold for more money than heroin on the street. The federal government has turned the one chemical that truly works for opiate addiction into another valuable substance by simply implementing 21 C.F.R. part 291.

When these regulations were put into effect in 1971, they never took into consideration that a patient may need this drug for 10, 20 or 30 years or maybe forever. These regulations are clearly experimental in nature. From most patients' point of view, these rules are cruel and unusual medical treatment.

Lastly, I can only request that you would be kind enough to furnish me with the name of the legislators responsible for constructing these rules so that I could write to them. Or the government branch that I could appeal to for exemption for these regulations. If I need to appeal to the Department of Justice would you give me some guidance in this direction. Also, how does one obtain a review of public comment on these rules, because I for one would want to be present at these formal hearings.

This is not a problem of drug abuse; I suffer from a chemical imbalance of which the only relief I get involves being dependent on dolophine hydrochloride. Without this medicine I suffer from chronic pain and depression.

Thank you for your anticipated cooperation,

Lawrence Cushing

Office of the Administrator
Alcohol, Drug Abuse and Mental Health
AdministrationRockville, Maryland 20857
March 21, 1989

Dear Mr. Cushing:

Thank you for your letter dated Feb. 4, 1989. I apologize for the delay in responding.

I understand that after I wrote you on Sept. 19, 1988, you received a letter from Ms. Betty Jones of the Food and Drug Administration indicating that FDA has already provided you the assistance it can under methadone regulations published jointly by FDA and this Agency's National Institute on Drug Abuse (NIDA).

I regret that I cannot offer you any assistance beyond that which I have already offered regarding your specific problem with availability of methadone at a convenient location. If you have not already done so, you may want to take up the suggestion in my previous letter that you contact Mr. Lennie Kupsc in Boston. Mr. Kupsc had indicated a willingness to provide you methadone at various sites in Massachusetts that are closer to home than the one you indicated you are using.

As you may know, federal methadone regulations were published pursuant to the comprehensive Drug Abuse Prevention and Control Act of 1970 and the Narcotic Addict Treatment Act of 1974. An objective of these laws was to improve the quality of treatment by encouraging private physicians to treat narcotic addicts and to do so in an appropriate manner. Prior to 1970, there were relatively few physicians in the United States treating narcotic addicts because of confusion over the legality of dispensing addictive and potentially dangerous drugs. After 1970, diversion of methadone and other abuses prompted passage of the 1974 legislation. Thus, these two laws and implementing regulations were designed to provide a safe environment for the treatment of narcotic addicts.

Contrary to your assertion, these regulations are not experimental. Working closely with FDA, NIDA had established sound standards for treatment of narcotic addicts with methadone under the regulations.

FDA and NIDA may, from time to time, jointly publish revisions to the regulations. In fact, on March 2, 1989, they published in the *Federal Register* such a revision, extending from 21 to 128 days the maximum permitted detoxification period. However, the regulations continue to stipulate that narcotic treatment programs must meet all state requirements. Consistent with this stipulation, it is and always has been our policy to avoid interfering in the practice of medicine. Thus, FDA, which is responsible for compliance monitoring, would consider a request from a physician to reduce the frequency of visits you need to make in order to obtain methadone. We see no cause, however, for attempting to mandate that your state or any other state provide methadone treatment, or for dictating unnecessary operational details of such treatment.

I continue to believe the regulations are fair and workable. You indicate that methadone treatment you have received under these regulations has enabled you to avoid chronic pain and depression. You further indicate that you are holding down an important and responsible job. I trust and hope that our regulations may have provided you some small assistance in what you have accomplished and that you continue to function successfully.

In response to your request on how to seek changes to the regulations, you may want to contact your local representatives in Congress. Finally, in response to your question on review of public comment on any regulatory change that is proposed, such comments are available for public inspection. In order to review comments on past or future NIDA/FDA methadone regulations, please contact Docket Management Branch HFA-305, Food and Drug Administration, Room 4-62, 5600 Fishers Lane, Rockville, Maryland 20857. In addition, you and other members of the public are free to comment on any proposed regulations. Proposed regulations are published daily in the *Federal Register*.

Sincerely yours,
Frederick K. Goodwin, M.D.
Administrator

April 8, 1989

Dear Dr. Goodwin:

This letter is in response to your March 21, 1989, letter concerning methadone maintenance treatment.

Firstly, I want to say that the FDA has not provided any assistance to us whatsoever, other than the location of clinics that we are already aware of and have been for nine years.

Secondly, as for Mr. Lennie Kupsc, I was thrown off his clinic in Boston in 1987 without even the benefit of a detox. All because I asked the clinic if they would give me a one-week, take-home supply of medicine, so I could visit my family in Vermont. They refused after I had been in treatment for six years without any problems. Then, the director had the nerve to ask me how I felt about it? I was paying this clinic $80 a week, for $2 worth of pills.

Fortunately, a doctor took me in for treatment the very next day, in New York. Otherwise, I would be back out on the street.

Thirdly, as for holding down a responsible job, you have very much misrepresented my previous letter. I am forced to seek new employment every 60 days as a result of your strict methadone rules.

Fourthly, you state in your letter that it has always been your policy not to interfere in the practice of medicine. However, we both know that you would waste no time interfering if a doctor tried to truly help me by providing our family with a simple 30-day supply of medicine, would you not?

You also state in your letter that the methadone treatment I have received has enabled me to avoid chronic pain. Honestly, the underworld offers a more realistic treatment plan for less money.

As for this treatment being experimental, never in American history have we had a drug problem like we do under current federal policy. So let's just let nature take its course on the question of controls for desperately needed medicine. The only reason methadone patients are not flooding your office with letters is because 90 percent of them are forced to break the law to survive the bureaucracy.

Obviously all my efforts of writing to your office for help have been a total waste. Either you lack the desire, or you haven't the ability to pick up the phone and ask a Vermont physician to help me and my wife with methadone treatment, as it could only be achieved with the influence of your office.

I sincerely regret ever asking for help,
Lawrence Cushing

Barbra: I Don't Understand. Why Do I Have To Do This?*

Let me introduce Barbra: 22, pretty, Jewish, sweet. I got to know her last autumn while researching my novel, *Topless*. Barbra is a go-go dancer. She can earn $1,000 a week, tax free. (Some industrious dancers triple that figure.) With Barbra as my chaperone, I traveled the New Jersey and upstate New York topless circuit — areas that were then unknown to me. In payment for her guide service, I supplied transportation, a good tip, and breakfast at 5 a.m. Barbra was living with this guy, Joe. She always insisted we bring him a cheeseburger. I didn't think much about it. I liked Barbra. She was affable, unassuming and street wise. She did sleep a lot in the car, though.

Then, one Sunday afternoon, Barbra phoned me at home. The police were in her apartment. Joe had just threatened to kill her. Would I, she said, take care of her kitten for a while? She had

---
* D. Keith Mano, "Legalize Drugs," May 28, 1990, *National Review*, Inc., 150 East 35th Street, New York, NY 10016. Reprinted by permission.

to... go away. I said, Yes. Barbra came through my front door looking anxious and hyper. Everything distracted her. Where was she going away to? Well, Barbra said, she had a little problem... So tell me, I said. Well, her little problem was with...heroin.

You coulda fooled me. I had no idea. I mean, heroin is such an unstylish drug, so 1950s. (Barbra snorted it, she didn't skin-pop.) And, frankly she got along pretty well. She *functioned*. I thought: Well, at least she'll be rid of Joe, that's good — Joe had first given Barbra heroin when she was 19 — he wanted to make her dependent on him. (He told Barbra it was some cocaine variant.) On Monday she took out an order of protection against Joe and went into the neighborhood methadone program.

That was November. Barbra hasn't kicked heroin yet. It isn't so easy to do, my friends. And, given that circumstance, I was wrong. Dumping Joe hasn't been such a good thing at all. Now, you realize, Barbra will have to score her own heroin. Last time I saw her — fragile, vulnerable, very white, afraid — she was headed to Harlem. One week before, her money had been stolen there. As Barbra went down the subway staircase, she said: "I don't understand. Why do I have to do this? Why won't they let me have any junk?"

"Because," I said, "you live in a stupid country with stupid laws."

Before long Barbra will be beaten or raped or found dead: count on it. Another victory in the great American drug war.

Drugs are bad. But easily the worst thing about them is —they're illegal and (hence) they cost too much. A black addict father with three children, say, doesn't go bankrupt or take up chain-snatching because of heroin or cocaine. It is the grim *financial* hemorrhage that demoralizes an addict. In this sense our anti-drug stance has callously discriminated against poor people. If I were a liberal,

I could make an appealing case for legalization and government support. Rich folk in capitalist America can afford the cost of addiction, I'd say. Liberal Me might even propose Drug Stamps. Addicts, remember, are made desperate and dangerous because the substance they crave is illegal, unavailable and expensive.

Addiction of that sort can deplete a culture. Not only has the user been maimed by his chemical dependency, he also is made to feel outlaw and inferior — instead of ill. We guarantee our addict population (people who are victims, really) a felon status by compelling it to purchase illicit material every single day. That doesn't build character. If drugs were were legal, maybe the dude who mugged my son at knifepoint last October would never have left home. I put forward this heretical proposition: drug addicts might function well enough (not as pilot or bus driver, obviously), and contribute something to our culture in the way of work done and children loved, if their drugs were available at cost or below. Barbra, I know, would have been better off. As for the long-term effects — I agree, they are significant, at least as significant as the long-term effects of cigarette smoking or alcohol. (Joe, almost fifty, has been on heroin since 1960, more than one-quarter century, with only heart inflammation to indicate it. That and complete financial destitution). Societies which tolerate drug addiction may sound slack and unattractive. Let me instead call them societies which have considerably reduced murder, theft, and catastrophic public expense — while treating their addict segment with kindness, not hostility. That has a better sound....

Drug commerce between one consenting adult and another is nobody else's business. And a free-market mechanism should obtain. Instead, our welfare socialist approach has given monopoly privilege to organized crime by default. Let Squibb and Pfizer manufacture crack: that would be cheaper, safer, and more humane. I think there is a tremendous potential constituency for legalization in America — but it is a constituency much intimidated by anti-drug passion and propaganda. Give us one candidate with vision and courage enough to challenge Drug Prohibition. I promise him or her at least a long footnote's worth of immortality.

Meanwhile the addict is persecuted. Ernest van den Haag would've put Barbra in a POW camp. Policemen have their heads blown away. Castro and the mob get richer. Law-observing people are mugged and murdered as urban inner-America slouches toward chaos. Enough: let us confess that Drug Prohibition has been a witless and pathetic misadventure. For God's sake, end it soon.

Repeal of the needle laws will also be an act of conscience, a recognition that addicts are human beings. Defying that moral precept has already cost us dearly.

—Edward M Brecher

Mayor Dinkins declared when he closed the pilot program, "Providing needles to addicts is to surrender to drug abuse."

—Cherni Gillman

We all have a belly button, and we can all get AIDS.

—Dulcey Consuelo Davidson

Chapter 7

Forcing People to Face Death from AIDS

Introduction

It is just possible that the greatest threat to the survivial of humankind on this small planet may not be nuclear war or any of a thousand other possible threats but rather a disease virtually unknown a few years ago — acquired immune deficiency syndrome. There is a strong connection between drug abuse and AIDS since in the United States and many other western countries the major source for the transmission of this fatal disease is the injecting addict, not the active homosexual.

Many of these countries, led by the United Kingdom and The Netherlands, have taken the position that the prevention of AIDS is more important than the prevention of drug abuse. As a result in England, Holland, Australia and Canada, to name a few examples, there are many programs that seek to keep drug users alive and healthy even though they are using drugs. In such countries, the governments have started to encourage the medical profession to provide a wide range of assistance, which in some cases may include pure medicinal drugs, clean needles, condoms, advice on safe injecting, and advice on safe sex.

Such programs operate in scattered parts of the United States often in violation of various federal, state, and local laws. They also operate in fear of discovery and exposure from federal officials, especially U.S. Sen. Jesse Helms (R-N.C.) who is known to violently oppose such programs. Accordingly, AIDS barely figures in the drug strategy documents of President Bush and Drug Czar Bennett.

As AIDS spreads dramatically around the world, America's friends in other countries look at us and wonder why extremism is able to dominate the drug and AIDS control policy of the great American democracy. In their eyes, the United States is committing national suicide.

Needles And The Conscience Of A Nation*

Public health authorities established more than a century ago a scientific rule that is also a moral precept: don't try to protect some people from a contagious disease and leave others unprotected. Don't protect only the rich and the middle classes, or only the law-abiding; for the infection will sooner or later spread from the unprotected to the protected. Even those who detest prostitution, for example, must realize that protecting prostitutes

* Edward M. Brecher, "Needles and the Conscience of a Nation," *The Drug Policy Letter,* March/April 1989, p.5.

from syphilis is a necessary step toward protecting the public at large.

But the United States has tolerated one distressing exception to this principle — and we are currently paying a catastrophic price for our scientific and moral lapse. Here's the story:

One subzero winter night half a century ago, while a blizzard raged, two interns at the University of Nebraska College of Medicine puzzled over a very sick patient who suffered at times from very high fever, alternating with bone-shaking chills.

"Malaria," said one intern.

"You're crazy," said the other. "There isn't a live mosquito within a thousand miles."

That winter and the next, midwinter malaria was similarly reported in Chicago, St. Paul, San Francisco and New York City — where the mystery was solved in 1940. Some addicts were sharing the needles and syringes they used to inject heroin. If one of them was infected with malaria parasites, others who subsequently used the same needle without sterilizing it might acquire the infection, summer or winter. Thus, as early as 1940, the country was put on notice that infectious diseases can be spread via needle-sharing.

I retold the story in the February 1941 issue of *Readers' Digest*. I called it "The Case of the Missing Mosquitoes," and I warned in particular that in the summer of 1941, when mosquitoes returned, we could expect some of them to bite malaria-infected needle-sharers and then transmit the malaria parasites to other women, men and children.

I failed to add, however, what should have been obvious to everybody — that far worse diseases than malaria might spread in the same way among needle-sharers, and from them to the rest of us.

The U.S. heroin industry, not public health officials, saved us from a needle-borne malaria epidemic. Heroin dealers don't like their customers to fall ill; it gives their product a bad reputation.

And if a customer dies, it is a loss to the heroin trade. So dealers added quinine to the heroin "bag" to kill the malaria parasites. Indeed they used up so much quinine that they exacerbated a world shortage.

But the quinine protected only against malaria. Other blood-borne disease organisms remained free to spread among U.S. needle-sharers, and from them to others. *Ever since 1940, needle-sharing has been a disaster waiting to happen.*

Instead of seeking to avert such a disaster, U.S. drug law enforcement officials lobbied for measures that actually encouraged needle-sharing. They persuaded 33 state legislatures to pass "needle laws" making it a crime to possess syringes and needles unless prescribed by a physician; and some states also made it a crime for a physician to prescribe sterile injection paraphernalia for addicts.

These needle laws failed to discourage needle injecting; for anyone enterprising enough to secure a heroin "fix" can also borrow the paraphernalia needed to inject it. What the needle laws did accomplish was to teach drug injectors not to risk arrest by walking around with syringes and needles in their possession. Instead, they shared needles, and still do.

Heroin dealers also fear arrest under the needle laws. They may want to protect the reputation of their product and the lives of their customers by supplying sterile, disposable needles free or at a low cost, just as they add quinine to the heroin bag. Syringe-and-needle combinations designed for one-time use cost only 20 cents or so at the corner drug store if you have a prescription; no doubt the heroin industry could buy them much cheaper at wholesale. But the law stands in the way.

After quinine in the heroin bag had aborted the midwinter malaria epidemic, U.S. needle-sharers began to fall ill with other needle-borne infections. One was *bacterial endocarditis*, a devastating, often fatal infection of the heart valves that can be transmitted both by needle-sharing and by blood transfusion. By rare good luck, penicillin was discovered just in time to prevent bacterial endocarditis from killing countless blood transfusion recipients as well as needle-sharers.

Syphilis is another infectious disease that can be transmitted through needle-sharing — and through blood transfusion. No one knows how much syphilis has been spread along this route.

Hepatitis B is a debilitating, sometimes fatal blood-borne infection of the liver, and is thought to be a precursor of liver cancer. Following World War II, it was primarily a disease of needle-sharing heroin addicts. But after a while the hepatitis B virus got into the U.S. blood supply, and hepatitis became a frequent sequel to blood transfusions. Many died, needle-sharers and others alike. Then, at long last, the U.S. public health establishment took notice and adopted emergency safeguards.

Common sources of infected blood for transfusions in those days were the commercial blood donor centers occupying store fronts along our urban skid rows and tenderloins. The easiest way for an addict down on his luck to raise money for his next fix was to sell a pint or two of blood at one of those drop-in centers. The centers were closed down when their role in the spread of hepatitis was discovered — but that was locking the barn after the horse was stolen. The hepatitis B virus had already been spread by blood transfusions far beyond the boundaries of the drug-injecting community. It remains endemic in this country today.

In the beginning, no test was available to screen blood for hepatitis B viruses; so a crash program was launched to develop a screening test. The American Red Cross and other non-profit organizations established today's nationwide system blood banks through which blood screened for hepatitis viruses and for syphilis bacilli is made available for transfusion.

But that basic public health principle was violated. The precautions taken were designed to protect blood transfusion recipients *without protecting heroin addicts*. No state legislature adopted the most obvious public health safeguard: repeal of the needle laws. As a result, our country remained vulnerable to the possibility that some *additional* blood-borne infectious disease, more terrible even than hepatitis B, might spread like wildfire among needle-sharers, and then on to the rest of us.

Having thus sown the wind, the United States is today reaping the whirlwind. The AIDS epidemic among needle-sharers has spread on schedule, just like hepatitis B, from them to the outside community.

Once again, we have hurriedly taken emergency measures. A crash research program has developed effective screening tests to safeguard our blood supply against the AIDS virus.

But, once again, lobbying by drug law enforcement officials has blocked repeal of the state needle laws. As a result, we remain in peril that some future devastating infection — perhaps one as incurable as AIDS, perhaps one even more disastrous — will spread like malaria, bacterial endocarditis, syphilis, hepatitis B and AIDS.

Would repeal of the needle laws safeguard the public's health? Decisive evidence comes from Minnesota, where the state legislature has stubbornly refused to be stampeded by drug law enforcement officials into mandating that proof of a prescription is required in order to purchase syringes. The results of this stubbornness were reported recently by two University of Minnesota Medical School professors, Dr. James A. Halikas and Dr. Joseph Westermeyer.

In Minnesota, they point out, intravenous drug users "have always been able to buy clean needles and syringes over the counter." (Pharmacists are not actually allowed to sell syringes for illicit use, but the law does not require them to ask for proof of a prescription, and the state rarely prosecutes addicts for possessing clean needles and syringes.) Blood tests of heterosexual Minnesota drug injectors have turned up very few AIDS-virus infections; and most of those infected, Drs. Halikas and Westermeyer explain, "lived for significant periods outside the Twin Cities region, in New York City or other major cities, and are thought to have become infected through sharing drug paraphernalia there.

"We have treated hundreds of other patients at high risk [for AIDS]...and have yet to find a heterosexual drug user who is positive for the AIDS virus as a result of intravenous drug use." The doctors attributed this to the unwritten Minnesota policy of not criminalizing people who buy syringes without a prescription.

The data from the state of Oregon, Canada, Britain and Holland point in the same direction.

Repeal of the needle laws by all 33 states that have them would achieve only a modest effect on the AIDS epidemic; it is already several years too late. But repeal may profoundly affect the next blood-borne infection to threaten the public's health. If we wait until the next needle-borne health disaster surfaces, however, it will once again be too late.

Repeal of the needle laws will also be an act of conscience, a recognition that addicts are human beings. Defying that moral precept has already cost us dearly.

AIDS: We Have No Strategy. No Program. No Policy.*

My reading of history is that our country's political system is driven by the values of religious fundamentalism. The first white settlers came as individuals fleeing religious persecution. These Puritans regarded their fellow humans as morally frail creatures constantly tempted by the Devil and sin. Redemption could be procured only by strict adherence to the God-fearing ways they advocated.

Transgressors were dealt with harshly by the Puritans. So-called sinners could be banished from the community, as with the "adultress" in the novel, *The Scarlet Letter*, or even, as in the Salem Witch trials, publicly executed.

It is my opinion that this rigid doctrine polarized fellow humans into "us" versus "them," dividing those who appeared to conform to prevailing values against those who did not.

Why have I started with a not-so-original interpretation of cultural history?

Because two epidemics characterize our time. Drugs and AIDS.

And historically, bifurcating the community into "us" against "them" explains how policy regarding drug use and the transmission of AIDS is formulated.

Our political heritage of rigid fundamentalism affects how science is used to form public policy.

Indeed, fundamentalism affected whether science, the theory of evolution, was allowed to be taught in U.S. schools.

I will offer some disquieting observations about how science is used to form, in this case, health policy.

It is conservatively estimated that 50 percent of New York city's 200,000 intravenous drug users (IVDUs) are infected with the virus that causes AIDS.

But the response to the AIDS epidemic has not been based on epidemiological strategies. Instead, the response is based on politics. Politics has turned the issue into a choice between combating AIDS or addiction.

In the United States, dominant public opinion remains entrenched between those who regard addiction as a crime and those who view it as a disease. Proponents of a moral/legal perspective are the dominant group. They believe that drug use indicates moral weakness (Nancy Reagan's famous "Just Say No"), and that laws should punish addicts as criminals. Advocates of the disease model see addicts as individuals with a biochemical problem that requires physiological treatment. Nonetheless, adherents of both models disapprove of addiction and agree that it must be stopped — even though fewer than 40,000 drug treatment slots exist for the City's 200,000 IV drug users.

I argue that the impasse on preventing AIDS among injecting drug users, their sex partners, and children, is ideological. The division in the power structure that impedes responding to AIDS among IV drug users reflects irreconcilable attitudes that are held by the American public. Typically, the American public regards drug users as criminals. However, when surveyed, approximately half of adult Americans favored giving needles in order to prevent or slow down the spread of AIDS.

Given the different priorities of the medical and criminal ideologies, I contend that the power structure (of elected officials, the law enforcement community, and the medical establishment) is aligned in such a way that an external individual or agent is necessary for initiating change warranted by the AIDS epidemic. When a political system is unable to respond to a health crisis, public policy

---

* Cherni Gillman, Ph.D., Narcotic and Drug Research, Inc., New York, N.Y.

can be influenced by an individual or organization that represents a competing ideology.

The New York Experience

In New York, Health Department officials were prodded by ADAPT, an advocacy group for the rights of injection users, to establish a government program for the plight of users because of AIDS.

Treating AIDS and drug use as public health problems instead of legal or medical issues was not easily achieved. (Nor was it retained). The city's narcotics prosecutor delayed the start of the needle exchange for six months with legal objections. "The Health Commissioner can designate whoever he wants to have needles, but you cannot take a legal instrument and use it for an illegal purpose," the prosecutor asserted. Making a pun, he noted with satisfaction, "I think that's stopped them in their tracks." The Commissioner was then forced to concede, "Without the cooperation of law enforcement officials so that addicts are not arrested the moment they walk out the program's door, the plan cannot work."

Before it had operated even a month, the City Council voted to end the needle exchange program. The vote was 30-0. However, the vote was non-binding and therefore only symbolic. Then-Mayor Koch chose to invoke the moral authority of science by having a representative retort, "We're glad it's non-binding because we need to follow the advice of the medical community and try this plan."

What happened at the needle exchange during the one year the city tried this plan?

Very briefly: 318 drug injectors enrolled. Half of them tested positive for HIV. Nearly 80 percent accepted referral to drug treatment programs.

What did we learn from this experiment?

To begin, we learned that, yes, it is possible to operate a needle exchange — even located in the worst place. Outside the needle exchange office is probably the largest concentration of narcotics detectives in the Western world. Also located in the same area there is the Criminal Court, Civil Court, Family Court, and the Supreme Court. Not to forget the Tombs, a prison where all arrested drug users are put in handcuffs.

In short, the city placed the needle exchange in the heart of the drug war.

> *The moral of this short list of events is that: Intravenous drug use is as American as apple pie.*

Getting clients to come to the needle exchange was a daunting task. But the program surpassed its quota of 200 participants — 318 intravenous drug users came. Charles ("Chuck") Eaton, the project's director, explained, "You learn to become a lawyer in this business. We decided that 200 meant 200 active participants." (Clients left active status when they entered drug treatment or were out of contact with the program for more than 10 working days.)

The needle exchange got participants to come by chauffeuring them in the Commissioner's car and literally walking them through the building. Otherwise, Eaton said, the project would not have had participants. If they were ferried by car, 1 out of 2 clients (versus 1 out of 12) would appear. It cost the project four and a half cents per needle. "Our gasoline bill for driving clients to the project was higher than our needle budget," said Eaton.

Eaton, who still directs the "Bridge to Treatment" that the exchange has become, says, "I don't like military metaphors. What I learned is that fighting in this war does not mean marching in a parade with with the sun gleaming off your rifle barrel. Instead, it's sneaking around the barn and finding your way through the woods."

What else was learned from the needle exchange experiment?

We found out that drug injectors would enroll even though they were limited to receiving ONE sterile needle per visit. "If time is money," Eaton observed, "these were the most expensive needles in the world."

Usually, the program had two contacts with clients: one for needle exchange, and the other to get clients placed in the drug modality they chose. Demonstrating that it could function as a supportive "bridge" to treatment became a primary objective. Since placement into drug treatment often took place in a single visit, the project was in direct contact with clients for an average of one to three days. Out of a sample of 250 clients, 78 percent accepted referral to a drug treatment program.

It is quite likely that intravenous drug users attended the program because the staff could be helpful and deliver services. The new Bridge to Treatment program is still able to retain clients because it provides them with primary health care.

Who came to the needle exchange?

Again, out of a sample of 250 clients, two-thirds were male. One-third were homeless. At intake, 11 percent had infectious syphilis. Their mean age was 33. (Our clients are curious and adventurous people," commented Eaton. "Who else would go through all this hassle for one free needle?")

Lastly, the needle exchange demonstrated that most users are willing to enter treatment. And that teaching needle hygiene is a difficult task which requires a context.

Now let's examine the objectives of the needle exchange experiment.

When we look at the Department of Health's official report we find something unexpected:

There are none.

There were never measurable, observable criteria for evaluating the needle exchange program. Agreement never existed among the community, the political structure, and the people running the program on ANYTHING.

The needle exchange program was established as a scientific experiment.

But for experiments to qualify as science, experts must share standards for measuring methodology and outcomes. That's why we have peer review.

What occurred at the needle exchange was that an experiment was implemented. Over 300 addicts enrolled. And NO ONE ELSE paid attention.

Success or failure of the program could not be determined because politicians never bothered to consider what it would have to accomplish to prove its value.

Intravenous Drug Use in the U.S.

Well, how did we get here? Here's a different history from the one I opened with.

In the 1830s, morphine was isolated.

In the 1840s, the hypodermic syringe was invented.

In the 1860s, the first major war where the new discovery of injectible morphine was applied occurred in the U.S. Civil War.

Set in the 1870s, a play featured a cowboy who was a morphine addict.

The moral of this short list of events is that: Intravenous drug use is as American as apple pie.

Jumping to the present, there are two popular ways that people ideologically view the AIDS epidemic. Let me warn you that I'll ask you to think over how you would apply these explanatory schemes to drug use.

The dominant group regards AIDS as punishment for sin. The sin of homosexuality or the sin of drug use. These people do not believe that treatment or therapy is needed because "Voila!" the problem solves itself. Sinners live short lives.

Those holding a medical view see AIDS as caused by a retrovirus which is not transmitted by casual contact and is hard to contract. Supportive therapies can have an impact, but they cannot eradicate the virus. Prevention is through education.

I would like to ask you to consider: Where are the parallels to drug use? How do you think people who believe that AIDS is caused by selfish, sinful behavior, regard drug use?

At least in the United States, the dominant view is that drug use is pleasure-seeking behavior engaged in by people of weak character. Marijuana, heroin, crack: historically, each has been seen as easy to get addicted to, both seductive and insidious.

What's the treatment for this type of behavior? RELIGION.

Or at least, Reform.

People have to get their values and strength of character from somewhere.

And failing that, incarceration is deserved.

Now let's analyze the structure of the rhetoric used by the U.S. Secretary of Health when he commented on the viability of needle exchange programs. Here's Sullivan being quoted from an inner office memo:

"Getting into drugs is easy for young people. Take no action that will even remotely suggest that use of illegal drugs is acceptable. Solving the problem of HIV infection in these communities involves more than fighting a virus. We must take every reasonable step but we cannot in this battle lose sight that our war is against drug use in America. There is a danger that the controversy surrounding needle exchange will overshadow the greater issue of drug abuse in society. We cannot have a solution become part of the problem."

This position contrasts sharply with the Chief of Police in San Francisco. He says, "I don't arrest people who give out needles. I've got real crime to worry about. These people are part of the solution, not the problem."

Getting back to Sullivan it is important to recognize that he is the top official in the United States stating his perspective on the nature of drug use and how policy should be based for addressing the AIDS epidemic. To quote Sullivan again, "The greater issue is ZERO tolerance of drug use in society."

So, here we have the Party line.

Where does science fit in this?

Sterile needles are the most expedient agent that can stop the AIDS virus from being transmitted by injection.

But our government prohibits people from taking advantage of the best information and technology we have for slowing the AIDS epidemic.

I began by saying I would offer some disquieting observations about science and policy.

Mayor Dinkins declared when he closed the pilot program, "Providing needles to addicts is to surrender to drug abuse," and that the test project had not changed his mind. "I don't want to give people the [injection] paraphernalia," he announced.

So, where we are right now is that there are no criteria, no data, no findings that can influence our city policymakers. Although the rhetoric was given that we needed scientific data to demonstrate the effectiveness of needle exchange to inform public policy, we have every evidence that public policy does not respond to scientific data. Instead, another perspective dominates and is used to define the situation.

The aftermath of New York City's needle exchange experiment is that we cannot presume that science will inform public policy. "The outcome for our program will be politically determined," Eaton had predicted. "We interact with politicians, not scientists."

The real status after ending the needle exchange one year later is that the exchange was a feasibility study that was crippled at the start. It was never a public health measure.

What this exposes is that we are not at even the first step of seriously addressing the transmission of HIV. We have no strategy. No program. No policy.

Dead People Can't Get Into Drug Treatment*

Men and women, many of them under 30, come to see Dave Purchase.

For the most part, they are thin and gaunt, some with needle tracks and sores, their young bodies wasted from drug abuse and street life. Others step out of vehicles that have pulled up for a quick stop, or get off a bus with a bag of groceries in their arms — people you would never guess are intravenous drug users.

Purchase gives them free "rigs" or "outfits" — needles and syringes — in exchange for their used ones. He also dispenses alcohol wipes, small bottles of bleach, and condoms from a van parked on the street. But mostly, he gives them dignity.

He listens to their latest hassle — a squabble with a boyfriend, a run-in with the police — and some stop by to tell him they've kicked their drug habit.

"Stay alive, now" is his parting advice to all.

Purchase runs the needle exchange program in Tacoma, Wash. — one of the first of its kind in the nation. He founded the program in August 1988 as a private effort to prevent the spread of AIDS.

"Dead people can't get into drug treatment," he said of his visitors. "You can get over being stupid, but you can't get over being dead.

"The issue is AIDS. It's as simple as that."

Besides the AIDS preventive wares, Purchase also dispenses advice: how to use bleach to sterilize a used needle, the need for condoms, and the availability of drug treatment.

But beginning such a controversial — and perhaps illegal — enterprise as the needle exchange required the support of many community leaders, including the local health department, the police, and others.

The deadly link between drug abuse and AIDS posed new challenges for those working in drug treatment and public health: How to find a way to help curb the spread of AIDS, especially among IV drug users. For some in the public sector, the question seemed easily answered. If people stopped using drugs, their risk of exposure to the virus would be lessened. For those familiar with the harsh realities of drug abuse, this was an oversimplified answer which would doom many individuals to a painful and costly death. Set against the backdrop of the complexities of drug treatment, some health officials and drug treatment counselors realized that a successful AIDS prevention program for IV drug users would require potentially controversial steps.

---

* Dulcey Consuelo Davidson, Institute for Citizen Education in the Law, Puget Sound School of Law, Tacoma, WA.

"It's an issue of whether we are going to choose to protect the lives of all of us, or whether we are going to choose to have a public health system which is only available for those people we like or whose behavior we approve of," said Purchase.

As former Tacoma Mayor Doug Sutherland recalls, the issues surrounding AIDS had been known for some time. As a member of the Tacoma-Pierce County board of health, he had attended study sessions about the virus. Many people, he said, continued to think of AIDS as a disease limited to gays or to IV drug users.

"Many people had the tendency to downplay it and to say 'That's their problem,'" said Sutherland. "But it became obvious that this was a health issue that needed a substantial amount of public education, that it was not just their problem, that it was our problem. I, along with some others, had some educating to do.

"There was some real difficulty early on when we discussed ways to attack it. Dave Purchase had decided that our approach was taking far too long, that there were too many people being exposed (to AIDS) in the meantime. And he unilaterally decided to start the process of needle exchanging, that he would begin the distribution of free, clean needles."

Purchase contacted community leaders to inform them of his plan to begin the needle exchange, including Allen Sutherland, Terry Reid, a substance abuse section manager at the health department, and Ray Fjetland, Tacoma's chief of police. Others volunteered to assist Purchase on the streets, educating clients on safe sex practices, "bleach and teach," and methadone treatment.

"Dave called me up and said 'I want to start a needle exchange,'" said Reid, who has counseled IV drug users for years. "We'd worked as counselors together for many years and knew each other well. We talked about how a needle exchange might work in Tacoma."

After operating the needle exchange as a private enterprise for five months, Purchase approached the Tacoma-Pierce County board of health with a proposal to incorporate the program into the health department's AIDS prevention efforts. Both Purchase and health officials realized that public education about drug abuse and AIDS was a necessary step in building support for such a controversial measure.

"In some parts of the country, just recommending it is an invitation to dismissal or more problems than you care to deal with," said Dr. Al Allen, director of the Tacoma-Pierce County Health Department. "I didn't really think so much that I was putting my neck on the line, but I knew that it there was considerable risk potential."

"Most of us said, 'Oh my god. We need this like a hole in the head,'" said Sutherland. "We knew that it was going to be an enormous political problem. There were several conversations among members of the health board and it became apparent that there was a majority of the board in support of the program.

"Each of us had to wrestle with questions: Was this a health problem? By endorsing the program,

> *You can get over being stupid, but you can't get over being dead. The issue is AIDS. It's as simple as that.*

were we in fact endorsing the use of drugs? And were we really in violation of state and federal law?," he said. "Public hearings were held to find ways to mitigate the impact of the program, since it was not the kind of program that was going to be readily accepted. But we didn't have the luxury of taking a year's period of time to sell the program."

In January 1989, the board of health adopted the needle exchange, providing $43,000 in city and county funds for the program. Purchase is quick to credit local officials for their role in the successful implementation of the controversial project.

Allen recalled how education about AIDS played a significant role in making the needle exchange possible.

"One of our board members remarked how unusual it was for a board of health in the United States to consider this," said Allen. "She attributed the attitude of the board to the study sessions. So what was originally shocking over a period of time was no longer shocking — it was still controversial, but supportable by four out of five members of the board."

"Dave Purchase was also very amenable in trying to make the program work," said Sutherland. "We started a very concentrated and reactive media campaign because this was not only the first needle exchange in the nation where we had an opportunity not only to show how it works, but also to get statistics."

They decided that a van, supplied with outreach materials such as AIDS information, methadone treatment coupons, condoms, bleach, food, and clothing — as well as hypodermic equipment — would be located in a downtown area frequented by IV users. A second needle exchange was established at the health department's drug treatment section. But even though the board of health had been convinced of the need for the needle exchange, Purchase and others found themselves in the middle of a political hurricane.

With the number of AIDS cases rising among intravenous drug users and their sexual partners and children, many health officials believe that a needle exchange program is a prudent way to try to keep the virus and other diseases in check. But some politicians and business people claimed that the program would promote drug use, and its presence downtown would serve as a mecca for criminals, prostitutes, and junkies. They cited concern that such programs legitimize drug use by providing paraphernalia for the users at a time when drugs and drug-related crime were high profile issues.

Purchase feels that many opponents of the needle exchange program choose to disregard medical data that indicates such exchanges actually reduce drug use. Such attitudes, he says, stem from ignorance about drug cultures and social prejudice toward his clients.

"Look at who we're dealing with: hookers, junkies, and dope fiends. Just imagine what it would be like if AIDS was transmitted by the steering wheel of $30,000 cars. What would America have done about AIDS years ago?" charged Purchase. "And now there are over a million Americans infected."

The Tacoma-Pierce County Health department estimates that there are 3,000 intravenous drug users in the county. About two to five percent of them already have tested positive for exposure to the AIDS virus.

Studies of the program indicate that 80 percent of people using the exchange have changed their injecting practices. On average the number of times people inject with pre-used syringes has been reduced by half, and bleach use has increased substantially. In addition, 350 individuals have signed up for methadone treatment, using coupons that Purchase and other outreach workers dispense.

Also, the Tacoma Police department reports seeing fewer needles discarded on streets, in alleys, or parking lots where they may be picked up or stepped on.

"From a modest beginning, we developed a really first-rate program, and it wasn't long after that we won a national award for the best public health program at the local level for the AIDS prevention program," said Allen. "Part of what allowed me to support the needle exchange was that I felt there was a possibility of acceptance by our community. One of the indications of tolerance was our police chief, Ray Fjetland. He could have poisoned it publicly and on the streets through his officers. But he's very progressive."

Fjetland had been approached by Purchase about the needle exchange. Though under existing law, he could have used his authority to arrest individuals who distributed needles — a misdemeanor charge — he decided to wait and see what the effects of a needle exchange would be on the streets.

"We felt that AIDS was a bigger threat," said Fjetland. "We anticipated that community leaders would be divided over it, but we knew that the prosecutor's office wasn't going to prosecute. So we felt that the right thing to do was let Dave try his program.

"From our point of view, it was better for the users to be disposing of their needles safely, rather than leaving them on the streets," added Fjetland. "And in the course of getting their needles, these people would come into contact with health workers who can give them literature and advice about getting off drugs. So we saw it as an opportunity to actually reduce some of the problems associated with drug use."

But it will be 6-10 years before the success of the program can really be determined.

"That a long time, especially for a junkie, where a week is a dozen lifetimes," said Purchase.

Purchase is also dismayed by those who have criticized the needle exchange based on the congenial atmosphere created where he sets up shop. He feels that his clients, like those of any other service-oriented business, will be more likely to respond positively to his message if treated with some dignity.

When users arrive to trade in their rigs and pick up other AIDS-preventive wares, the outreach workers are friendly, chatty, and concerned. Much of the talk is about what's happening in the clients' lives, but in the language of the streets. After working on downtown street corners for almost two years, Purchase, Garcia, and others know most of the junkies by name.

Purchase's response to the notion that those people are not worth public concern is a cry of disbelief.

"Fascism is not a small current in 20th century history — and we're probably not over it yet," he said. "But it's real clear that we're all the same. We all have a bellybutton, and we can all get AIDS."

Tacoma's precedent-setting needle exchange program has been widely lauded as a national model. Its supporters include a host of national, state and local health officials.

Despite the support for such programs, some politicians continued to feel that the needle exchange tacitly endorsed drug use. In the spring of 1989, the Washington state legislature passed a comprehensive drug bill which outlawed needle exchanges. Though Governor Booth Gardner vetoed that portion of the bill, further clouding the issue were conflicting state laws. Some argued that the exchange was prohibited by an anti-drug measure adopted by the legislature years ago, while others contended that it was authorized by the AIDS Omnibus Bill of 1988 which allows health departments to use any necessary means to combat AIDS.

A conservative state legislator asked the Washington state attorney general to issue a legal opinion on the needle exchange. His opinion found the exchange to be illegal — specifically that an AIDS prevention bill passed by the legislature in 1988 did not preempt an earlier law that prohibited the sale of hypodermic needles for illicit purposes.

Purchase, who worked as a drug counselor for almost 20 years and who served on the Washington state substance abuse advisory board, found himself accused of promoting drug use. He calls the political wrangling about the issue "scary."

"This isn't the kind of question where the classic compromise in government tends to find some middle ground," he said. "This is life and death. There isn't room for political jostling.

"If the legislature, or any government body, were to specifically make needle exchange programs illegal, the direct result would be the death of people in this state. It's just that those people will not die the day after the law is passed, they'll die in 7-10 years."

Following the attorney general's opinion, Tacoma City Attorney Bill Barker advised city finance officials in September 1989 to withhold funds from the program until its legal status was more firmly established. The county, under its funding guidelines, also had to withhold its payment to the program. This left the health department with enough money to continue the needle exchange program in Tacoma until the end of the year.

The Tacoma-Pierce County Health Department filed suit against both the city and Pierce County to restore funding, which also put the question of legality in the hands of the court.

In Seattle, where the Seattle-King County Health Department operates a needle exchange, city attorneys also reviewed the legality of needle exchanges. Randy Gainer, assistant attorney for the City of Seattle said that under the AIDS Omnibus Bill, his department concluded the needle exchange is legal.

"Though it's not perfectly spelled out, there is sufficient latitude in the wording of the AIDS Omnibus Bill to argue in favor of the legality of the needle exchange. Tacoma's city attorneys had an arguable case," he said, "however, because of health implications, we advised the Seattle City Council to continue support of the needle exchange."

"It boiled down to a test of whether the attorney general's opinion was supportable," said Allen. "After a lot of jawboning, the decision was to arrange a friendly suit."

"I engineered the lawsuit using the issue of nonpayment," said Sutherland. "We got the parties together and set up a civil suit. The question of legality was dicey, but it had to be answered. So here again, we took a chance."

Though some argue that the legal maneuvering on the part of the city was unnecessary, the issue was later settled, at least temporarily, by the historic decision on April 9, 1990, by Superior Judge Robert H. Peterson that declared needle exchanges legal in Washington State. And in the meantime, the program earned more accolades in the medical community, including the 1989 national achievement award by the National Association of County Health Officers.

But the needle exchange has also drawn criticism from members of the Bush administration's anti-drug team.

In late September 1989, Reggie Walton, assistant to drug czar William Bennett, who was in Tacoma to address a conference of drug treatment program directors, criticized needle exchanges for sending a message that condones drug use.

Walton, who did not visit the site of the needle exchange where many people go to receive clean needles, said at a news conference later that he doubted that the needle exchange reduces needle-sharing. He postulated that most drug users will use any needle immediately available to them.

"I doubt that they are going to say 'I want to get high, so I will go down to the local distribution center, collect my needle, and then go back and shoot up drugs,'" he said.

But health department statistics confirm an earlier study that showed the needle exchange is effective in curtailing needle-sharing among drug users.

"Some days I come home and I'm just beat," said Purchase. "On those days, I say to myself 'Today, one. One person didn't get AIDS.'"

Bravery In Australia*

Chamberlain described Czechoslovakia at the time of the Munich Agreement as "that far away country about which we know so little." Australia often feels like that. Isolation has its advantages and disadvantages.

The strong links between the gay sister cities of San Francisco and Sydney inevitably resulted in the rapid spread of human immunodefiency virus infection to Sydney homosexual and bisexual males. As a result, 70 percent of Australia's AIDS cases are within the state of New South Wales and concentrated in Sydney, the largest metropolis in the state. Most of these cases have occurred in Sydney's eastern suburbs, which function as a gay ghetto. The same neighborhoods are also known to have a high density of injecting drug users, and it is therefore surprising that after a decade of HIV infection in the homosexual community HIV infection is still so infrequent among injecting drug users. This may in part be due to serendipity; it is also likely that the early and vigorous implementation of HIV prevention strategies for injecting drug users has contributed.

The experiment with needle and syringe exchange in the Netherlands in the early 80s became well known in Australia soon afterward. Many prominent scientific and medical authorities publicly advocated the rapid institution of similar policies in Australia. As recognition of the critical importance of this strategy increased, more and more official bodies and commentators began pressing for needle and syringe exchange in Australia by 1985.

However, the matter remained controversial and vigorous opposition to this notion soon developed. The fact that this strategy was also supported in the United Kingdom by Sir Gerard Vaughan, the former Conservative Health Minister under Margaret Thatcher, was also thought to be significant.

The government's senior medical and scientific advisory body on AIDS at the time — the National AIDS Task Force — had some reluctance about fully embracing the idea. The notion of "careful and scientific evaluation of pilot studies" developed. Several such pilot studies were devised and considered. Throughout 1985 and 1986, it was clear that the proposal to subject this strategy to research would inevitably delay the introduction of the policy. Some influential policy makers felt that Australian political leaders and the community were not ready for such an adventurous departure from existing drug policy. They preferred to choose policy options from among those thought to be more acceptable. The size, duration and extent of the evaluation was also discussed in some detail.

My involvement in this area had begun fairly early as I had provided gastroenterological diagnostic services to the first AIDS patients in the country who started appearing at my hospital in 1983. By 1984, we already had seen antibody

---

* Alex Wodak, M.D., "Bravery in Australia — Breaking the Impasse in the War on AIDS," *The Drug Policy Letter*, January/February 1990, p.3.

positive homosexual injecting drug users, and it became obvious that Australia would also inevitably succumb to this new, frightening complication of illicit drug use.

I had prepared several research proposals and was in the habit of regularly supplying material on the subject to the media, which commendably showed great interest in this subject.

I also briefed my local member of Parliament on the subject even though he was known to have distinctly conservative leanings. I provided him with the information that the right-wing of Thatcher's Conservative Party had sponsored a bill in the British House of Commons advocating needle and syringe exchanges.

As the months passed, more and more people concerned about the spread of HIV infection in Australia became convinced that this was an important initiative and needed to be started as soon as possible. However, committee after committee referred this matter to other subcommittees or called for more data. A colleague decided to do a Ph.D. on evaluation of the strategy of making needles and syringes available and several of us attempted to devise a project whereby conclusive proof could be obtained of the effectiveness of this strategy. It was readily apparent within a few hours that it was not possible to determine the effectiveness of this policy in reducing the spread of HIV infection among injecting drug users because of the multiplicity of factors involved in HIV transmission.

Setting Up a Needle Exchange

On returning from yet another committee meeting on the subject in November 1986, I decided that we could wait no longer and had to go ahead without requesting permission from anybody. Therefore, my staff and I decided to personally donate money for the establishment of our own pilot project, obtain the required sterile injection equipment and place notices on the doors of our building. The next day, Nov. 13, 1986, the "Darlinghurst Pilot Needle and Syringe Exchange Programme" had begun. It was the first needle and syringe exchange program in Australia. Some days later, I received an official invitation from the state Department of Health to discontinue the project. I pointed out innocently that the pilot needle and syringe exchange project was being undertaken by private individuals, funding the exercise out of their own pockets, and making up any time lost from their employment. The project was a voluntary one, and I was therefore not able to order my staff to stop the project.

Days later, while I was attending a regular Department of Health committee meeting, I was informed that the provision of injection equipment to drug addicts was in breach of the state Drugs Misuse and Trafficking Act. I replied that I was unaware of this breach of legislation but should the department wish to proceed with police action, the rationale of the exercise would need to be explained to waiting television cameras, and that, undoubtedly, this would not reflect well on the department. I was privately advised that no police action would be instigated.

A little while later, I was invited to meet the senior members of the New South Wales Drug Squad to explain my actions. I summarized to these police officers the existing global knowledge on HIV infection in injecting drug users and also summarized the experience thus far with needle and syringe exchange. I was advised that the meeting had been arranged to obtain information for the Minister for Police who would be advised that prosecution was unwise. It seemed perfectly evident at the time that if our action was in breach of the Drugs Misuse and Trafficking Act, the law would have to be revised or repealed. I made no secret of these views.

The government started its own scheme of sterile needle and syringe availability through retail pharmacists in the state of New South Wales just one month after our own pilot exchange program. However, the pharmacy scheme made little provision, if any, for the possibility of exchanging used equipment, and it was apparent that the dangers of a pure distribution scheme were considerable. Not only could this inadvertently increase the supply of used injection equipment and thus lead to increased sharing, but it could also lead to the discarding of used injection equipment in public places such as streets, parks or beaches.

The pilot needle and syringe exchange programs were emulated by a number of other colleagues throughout New South Wales and other parts of the country within a matter of weeks. It was clearly an idea whose time had come. Within a short period of time, it was apparent that the desire to increase the availability of sterile needles and syringes (and reduce the availability of used injection equipment) conflicted with the Drugs Misuse and Trafficking Act. In particular, sections on the supply, possession and self-administration were problematic. A decision was made to repeal the sections on supply and possession of injection equipment while keeping self-administration illegal. It was thought that the government could not move too far in advance of public opinion since the act was passed only two years earlier. However, the effect of retaining the section on self administration was that drug users were soon aware that responsible behavior involving the proper disposal of used injection equipment at needle and syringe exchanges carried the risk of apprehension and prosecution. That is, used injection equipment was defined as possible evidence of self-administration of illicit drugs under the law.

Drug users began to discard used injection equipment in the streets, parks and beaches rather than risk the possibility of apprehension. Predictably, this resulted in a public outcry at the fouling of the environment with potentially dangerous materials which threatened the survival, let alone expansion, of this important HIV prevention strategy. At the time of writing, this matter has still not been satisfactorily resolved.

Effect on Overall Drug Policy

One further matter of interest is the attitude of policy makers toward the possibility of liberalizing drug policy by repealing restrictions on supply and possession of injection equipment. In order to ensure that this change did not result in increased vulnerability of the government to criticism, a new piece of legislation was introduced to outlaw equipment used for the consumption of cannabis. This legislation made it an offense to be in possession of a "bong," despite the fact that legislators had particular difficulty in defining precisely what was entailed by a bong. Bongs can be constructed from a variety of ready-made materials, including a milk carton and two straws. No prosecutions have been initiated under this legislation.

There are many lessons from this particular saga. The specter of AIDS has highlighted a new approach to drug policy in many parts of the world and speeded up a process of change so that rapid changes of policy can occur in months rather than decades. Second, the development of policy in this area highlights the difficulties of medical and scientific policy advisors operating in fields of major political tension where advisors are often tempted to "second guess" their political masters. Clearly this is a temptation to be avoided at all costs.

Third, the initiation of this policy at a time when implementation was in breach of existing legislation, was in large part possible because the act was carried out by a physician. Quite possibly, prosecution would have followed if an identical action had been undertaken by other health professionals. This should not be construed as a defense of an inegalitarian hierarchy of professions, but rather as an opportunity for physicians in countries where needle and syringe exchange is still not available to consider direct action.

Fourth, the development of this policy evolution also demonstrates the real possibility for research to be used as a weapon against change and for scientifically minded health professionals to fall into a trap. Again, this is not to decry the value of meticulous scientific research, but to emphasize the importance of differentiating slow and careful for chronic and unchanging conditions as against the need for more qualitative and speedier evaluation at times of a public health crisis.

During the evolution of this debate, many supporters of needle and syringe exchange were criticized by their opponents for opening the door to provision of illicit substances. It was argued that if one provides the syringe and needle, one may as well provide the rest of the materials. In retrospect, this argument used by the opponents of change was correct. In Australia, as in many other countries, we now provide sterile needles and syringes, swabs, spoons, and sterile water. We also provide specially prepared paper with HIV prevention slogans printed on it knowing (and intending) that it be used for wrapping illicit drugs. There does seem little point in providing all of these materials and yet not providing, under carefully controlled conditions, a safer formulation of the same drugs that can be bought illegally around the corner with unknown contaminants and at unknown concentrations.

Compassion And Success In Liverpool — The Mersey Harm Reduction Model Today[*]

Introduction

The Mersey Drug Training and Information Centre was established in 1986 by Mersey Regional Health Authority with the aim of providing information and training to a wide variety of groups and organizations throughout the region. Initially the center's aim was solely to be an information resource and provide training service, but circumstances dictated that the service develop a wider role than its initial aim. The Center has been a central point in the development of the Mersey Harm Reduction Model. There are many others whose contribution to this strategy has been equal to, and in some cases, greater than my own. Any consideration of this agency must primarily recognize the contribution of Allan Parry who founded the agency and was responsible for many of the developments that have made the service what it is. Allan's radical initiatives and his tenacious advocacy have resulted in the establishment of a unique program that has made Mersey Region a model of radically sensible drug policy.

Establishing and Developing the Service

The Mersey Drug Training and Information Centre was established by people who understood drug users and their needs. Its establishment also coincided with that of Liverpool's first specialist Drug Dependency Clinic. The two units happened to be located next door to each other and so a close relationship between the two agencies was forged

[*] Pat O'Hare, Director, Mersey Drug Training and Information Centre, Liverpool, England.

and their policies evolved symbiotically.

It might be well to mention another important historical factor in the emergence of Merseyside's strategy for dealing with drug use. Although the new prescribing clinics that followed the second Brain report on dealing with drug use initially continued with the policy of maintaining users on injectables, this policy had begun to fall into disfavor and in most parts of the country. Drug Dependency Clinics no longer offered maintenance or injectable drugs. Liverpool, as a provincial backwater, had failed to move with the times and Consultant Psychiatrists, usually the doctor in charge of a clinic, were still maintaining addicts on injectable drugs. Experience had convinced many working in the field that although abstinence may be a desirable goal, it was not immediately attainable for many, but real, positive improvements in the lives of many drug users were attainable by the provision of a pure, legal, controlled dose of methadone or heroin.

It was during this period that the connection between HIV/AIDS and intravenous drug use first came to light. In an effort to combat this, Allan Parry, then manager of the agency, initiated one of the country's first syringe exchange schemes, based upon the low-threshold model of service delivery established in Amsterdam on the effort to combat the spread of Hepatitis B. Though established on a shoestring and run from a converted bathroom, the success of the scheme provided a lead and a model for syringe exchange schemes nationally.

HIV and AIDS were responsible for much of the agency's subsequent development. If the syringe exchange was to be successful, it was important to gain the cooperation of the local police force. If treatment policies had a role to play, it was necessary to educate local doctors. As a consequence, the agency began to play a role in training local police officers, doctors, medical students, drugs workers and other groups. The content of that training was harm-reduction, rather than abstinence-oriented. A result of this work was that a consensus slowly emerged around how we should deal with drug problems in the area.

Given the imperatives of HIV and AIDS however, training was a relatively slow method of transmitting information. The

AIDS In Europe*
Among IV Drug Users

Country	Number	Percent of all AIDS patients
Italy	3491	66
Spain	2910	63
France	1603	18
Germany, F.R.	506	12
Austria	104	28
United Kingdom	80	3
Netherlands	75	7

Source: World Health Organization, "AIDS Surveillance in Europe," December 31, 1989.

* The Centers for Disease Control estimated there were 99,936 total AIDS cases in the U.S. as of June 30, 1989; 27% were related to IV drug use.

Mersey Drugs Journal was established in order to educate and inform local workers of developments in the field. However, it was recognized by those responsible for the journal that treatment policies were constrained by other factors and so the journal began to look at drugs and drug use in a wider context.

As the syringe exchange scheme was highly successful, and new HIV/AIDS prevention initiatives such as outreach work with male and female prostitutes and injecting drug users began to take off, this side of the agency's work outgrew its origins and so became a separate agency, The Maryland Centre.

Mersey Drug Training and Information Centre Today

With the hiving off of the HIV/AIDS prevention aspects of the service, Mersey Drug Training and Information Centre has returned to its original role, the provision of training and dissemination of information on drugs and drug-related issues. The Mersey Harm Reduction Model is dependent upon the cooperation of a number of agencies: drug dependency clinics, local police, social services, syringe exchange schemes, and outreach workers. The agency continues to recognize the need to service these various bodies with accurate information and training at a local level. However, the demand for the services that we offer has grown, at both national and international levels.

Growing international interest in what was going on in the drugs field on Merseyside and in the views expressed in the Mersey Drugs Journal was eventually to lead to its rebirth as The International Journal on Drug Policy. The IJDP has become one of the major journals for the increasingly influential debate on drug policy, being committed to publishing articles in many fields, from treatment policies to governmental policy and international policy. While it publishes articles on both sides of the debate, it is firmly committed to looking at radical initiatives aimed at facilitating the emergence of rational and humane drug policies.

The agency also facilitates the transmission of information through the organization of conferences. One-day seminars have been run on matters such as Drug Education, Harm Reduction and Maintenance Prescribing. This year MDTIC established the First International Conference on the Reduction of Drug Related Harm. Held in Liverpool, it attracted many of the most prominent thinkers in this field from all over the world and was highly successful in drawing together like-minded people to share their knowledge and experience of harm reduction strategies. Many of the papers are to be published in book form next autumn. Subsequent conferences are curently being planned, to be held on an annual basis, the next scheduled for Barcelona in May 1991, and the third in Australia in 1992.

The Role of Information and Education in Harm Reduction

British criminologist Jock Young, in his book *The Drugtakers* (1971), spelled out 10 rules that inform the development of a path toward a sane and just drug policy. While all of these rules have a bearing upon the philosophy of the agency, two in particular inform the work that we do.

Young's first rule is to "Combat Absolutist Dogma." Those with a commitment to our existing drug policies have tended to present them as the only means by which we can deal with drug problems. Underlying presuppositions are taken for granted by advocates for the status quo or increasingly repressive drug laws. Furthermore, their arguments are bolstered by reference to somewhat "scientific" evidence. Rule eight identifies the need for "Positive Propoganda." As he points out, "The majority of information fed to the public as to the nature and effects of psychotropic drugs is misleading and inaccurate. This results in widespread scepticism." Young goes on to argue that information aimed at controlling drug use must take into account the life experiences of drug users and supplement and correct this by the use of authoritative outside sources.

Part of the success of the agency may result from the fact that it has always had close contact with, and taken account of, the views of active drug users. As a consequence, information about drugs has always been informed by the experience and cultural values of users. This does not necessarily imply information is presented in glowing terms. What we seek to offer is factual information, presented in non-judgmental fashion, on the matters that have real importance for drug users in their everyday lives. For example, the possibility that cannabis may affect the reproductive capacities of mice is of no consequence to committed smokers. Reports on whether the crop has been sprayed with paraquat is.

Drug Education for Young People

One area in which I believe the work in our area is not as effective as I would wish is in the provision of drug education for young people. In the United States, much drug education appears to be based upon a primary prevention model: explicit messages about the negative aspects of drug use aimed at deterring experimentation There are a number of difficulties associated with this model, not the least of which is that there appears to be no evidence that demonstrates its efficacy. In short, it doesn't work. Some young people will never take drugs. There is no evidence that indicates this is a result of drug education. Others go on to use drugs regardless of exposure to drugs education. Information may actually be inaccurate, deliberately so, as "prophylatic lies" are used to attempt to dissuade young people from using drugs, according to *The Great Drug War* by Arnold Trebach.

In the United Kingdom today, there is a consensus that education about drugs should be intergrated into a school program of personal and social education (PSE). I would contend that PSE is part of an educational philosophy aimed at empowering students and expanding their personal choice. This style of education does not sit easily with a "Just Say No" approach to drugs education. In fact, such courses devolve very little power to young people and it is paradoxical to attempt to empower or expand personal choice in an institution where only a very limited and prescribed range of attitudes and behaviors are acceptable.

Despite the intrinsic flaws in these models, I would like to see drug education for young people make far more use of secondary prevention and harm minimization models. Such approaches will attempt to offer both information on the relative harms associated with drug use, and specific skills such as first aid, counseling and helping skills. Such education should be offered to all young people, rather than targeting "at risk" individuals in order to avoid stigmatizing or bestowing status upon the recipients, and avoid a potential "self-fulfilling" prophecy. In the final analysis, young people need education about drugs as opposed to education against drugs.

Conclusions and Recommendations

While there was a degree of specificity about the emergence of this model on Merseyside, I believe that there are a number of levels at which education and information must be directed in order to create a coherent and cohesive harm reduction-oriented drug service.

It is essential to gain the cooperation of other services in the area. Such services are unlikely to cooperate willingly unless they understand the reasons for policy changes. Training and information must be directed at managers and staff of drug program, medical personnel, social workers, police officers and others working in the criminal justice system.

An important component of harm reduction strategy is an emphasis upon empowering drug users. The failure of previous education strategies has been due to their tendency to regard drug users and potential dug users as empty vessels, waiting to be filled with the wisdom of experts. Drug education must recognize the ways in which the drug using subculture transmits information, and the role that an individuals experience of drug use plays in shaping that information. Accurate and non-judgmental information must also be aimed at the people close to drug users, family, friends etc. The uninformed reactions of such people can make a situation far worse than it already is.

Harm reduction strategies do not occur in a vacuum. Their potential for success or failure is to some degree determined by the wider context. Policies that criminalize or socially marginalize drug users, rather that seeking their social intergration also serve to make the problem worse. Information must be aimed at the level of the policymakers if we are to maximize the potential success of a harm reduction strategy.

Outside the information and education field, I am aware of a number of initiatives that could usefully promote the value of our existing harm reduction model. In Liverpool, the police have a policy of non-prosecution of first-time offenders for possession of all drugs. Instead, users are cautioned, and referred to appropriate services. This has the effect of preventing use escalation as the sanction of a criminal record for drug use still exists.

It is also part of the Merseyside police policy not to devote a high proportion of their resources to pursuing individuals for possession of small quantities of any drug for personal use. However, such a policy is at the discretion of individual police forces and such an enlightened policy may not operate in other areas. I believe that there are insufficient reasons for maintaining criminal sanctions for possession of cannabis and they should be removed at the soonest opportunity. This would have the effect of removing the major problem associated with what is otherwise a relatively unproblematic form of drug use. As an experiment, it could also act as a pilot for reevaluating the existing legal controls over other forms of drug use.

Despite the large numbers of drug users receiving prescribed drugs in the region, there is still a sizeable demand for injectable maintenance and syringe exchange that is not being met. There are also parts of this country, and of many others, where such treatment options are unavailable. These areas often coincide with the areas where rates of HIV infection and AIDS are highest. I believe that there is a need for the expansion of programmes based upon the controlled availability of such drugs, not only locally and nationally, but also internationally.

Finally, as a society, we should recognize the ad-hoc, reactive nature of our existing drugs policies, and commit ourselves to a thorough reevaluation of policy upon rational and humane grounds. Before HIV and AIDS, such a reevaluation was necessary for the protection of our civil liberties and our human rights. Today, it is a matter for our moral consciences. How much longer can we afford to let people die because we disapprove of the substances they choose to put into their bodies? How much longer can we allow the toll of casualties to rise in this unending civil war?

When They Visit New York They Say They Want To Cry*

"Have you ever found a gun on any person you have arrested?" I asked the Liverpool police detective.

"In 13 years I have never had the honor," he replied with a wry smile.

We were in a small house in Toxteth, a predominantly black neighborhood scarred by riots during the early 80s. Now, it was July 1989, and the detective was taking a report on a burglary at the house. He and his partner (both unarmed, as are virtually all U.K. police) were convinced that heroin addicts had done this job as they had many others in the area.

Yes, Liverpool, that brawny, economically depressed seaport city on the great Mersey River, has an ample supply of ethnic conflict, drug addiction and crime. American officials are always fond of pointing to Liverpool and other British cities and saying, "See what happened to them when they legalized heroin!" After Margaret Thatcher became prime minister, the Americans bragged that our British cousins learned their lesson and now stand shoulder to shoulder with the United States in an international war on drugs.

Nothing could be further from the truth. The British talk tough on drugs but act with compassion. On the other hand, Americans talk drug war and act it. The perverted result is that a potentially moderate problem is aggravated into an international catastrophe. Now, American officials are in danger of assassination at the hands of drug barons, who would be powerless local hoodlums but for the bull market our drug policies helped create. American irresponsibility in the drug arena is compounded by macho, destructive policies regarding guns and crime control.

The British — and particularly the Dutch — practice "harm reduction" in regard to drug control and a whole series of social problems. Some of the best harm reduction programs operate in the Liverpool area.

Deviants Deserve Help

The harm reduction drug strategy declares that drug control should have a series of objectives, with abstinence or a drug-free society being the highest but not the only goal. Indeed, that goal is now viewed by leading British experts as being so impractical that its actual pursuit (as in America) would produce perverse and destructive results. In 1988, the leading British body on drug policy, the quasi-official Advisory Council on the Misuse of Drugs, declared flatly: "HIV is a greater danger to individual and public health than drug misuse." In light of current British and American history, that was a revolutionary statement. The British drug experts are acting as if it were a vital truth. The Americans, including the entire staff of Mr. Bennett's Office of National Drug Control Policy, are acting as if they were blissfuly ignorant of it. Such ignorance can, has and will kill.

Throughout the Mersey Regional Health Authority, which covers Liverpool and many other communities, there are a series of health services aimed at keeping injecting addicts, prostitutes, their sexual partners, and their families alive and functioning. (Casual users are barely mentioned.) I saw

---
* Arnold S. Trebach, "Compassion, Not Hatred, Makes the British System Work," *The Drug Policy Letter*, September/October 1989, p.12.

people walking in anonymously off the streets to AIDS prevention centers, being welcomed courteously, being offered health advice on safe injecting and safe sex, immediately being given condoms and clean needles, and being told how to use them. Injecting addicts were offered a variety of needles and barrels, depending on their preferences, their drug of dependence and their methods of injection. The staff explained the best injection sites so as to keep the addicts away from the worst ones. A staff worker said to me, "It is very difficult to rehabilitate a dead addict."

To participate in the needle exchange "scheme" or program the drug user need only give a set of initials or a pseudonym (Mickey Mouse will do) and a date of birth. A record may thus be kept on the number of needles taken and returned. Addicts are asked to return the used needles so that there is no temptation to share and so that they are not thrown into the streets where children might find them. The date of birth is helpful in the event the participant forgets the fake name. Secure boxes are provided to keep and return the old needles so that the addicts, their families and health staff reduce the risk of disease.

Some Doctors Still Prescribe Heroin

Despite distortions by American officials and journalists, British doctors still enjoy a majestic independence and virtual immunity from police control in regard to the prescription of hard drugs in medicine. Some Liverpool drug clinic physicians, like Dr. John Marks, believe that the prescription of a wide variety of drugs to addicts, including injectable heroin, removes the issue of obtaining drugs from the minds of their patients and allows them to get on with the business of relatively normal functioning, even though they are on drugs. Other physicians in the area believe that they obtain better results with only one drug, usually oral methadone. Others still believe in virtually no drug prescriptions. In the end, the doctors decide on prescriptions for addicts, not the police and not the politicians.

Securing a supply of clean drugs remains a problem for some addicts. Addicts who live in an area where the clinic doctors do not believe in maintenance thus are forced to move, to lie about their address, or to buy in the black market. While this system of doctor domination produces a mixed pattern of prescribing results, it does allow for a great deal of experimentation in drug maintenance methods. During three weeks in England this past summer, I met addicts with a surprising variety of prescribed drugs with which one doctor or another was experimenting. Dr. Marks has even convinced a pharmacist to produce heroin and methadone "reefers."

The pioneering physician prescribes the reefers to help wean some patients off injecting. While smoking certainly has its dangers, every action that reduces the likelihood of AIDS transmittal must be considered. The major engine for the transmittal of the virus is the heterosexual injecting addict. The message Dr. Marks gives is: use drugs if you must but in a less harmful manner.

Small Steps, Compassion Essence of Harm Reduction

As explained by Allan Parry, the doyen of Liverpool AIDS experts, Marks' message is the essence of harm reduction. Harm reduction takes small steps to reduce, even to a small degree, the harm caused by the use of drugs. If a person is injecting street heroin of unknown potency, harm reduction would consider it an advance if the addict were prescribed safe, legal heroin. A further advance if he stopped sharing needles. A further advance if he enrolled in a needle exchange scheme. A much further advance if he moved on to oral drugs or to smoked drugs. A further advance in harm reduction if he started using condoms and practicing safe sexual practices. A further advance if he took advantage of the general health services available to addicts. A wonderful victory if he kicked drugs, although total victory is not a requirement as it is in the United States.

Mr. Parry and other Liverpool health leaders give much of the credit for the harm reduction idea to venerable British traditions and also to recent Dutch innovations, particularly the notion that addicts and prostitutes are still valued human beings. Radio ads, posters and outreach workers saturate the community with that compassionate message. Hardy staff members go out into the mean streets and hand prostitutes condoms and pamphlets on safe sex, along with pleas that they ask their Johns to use condoms and that the working girls come into the center for a health checkup and perhaps for clean needles, in the event they also happen to be injecting addicts.

Police Support Harm Reduction

Harm reduction could not work in Liverpool without the support of the local police. Addicts and prostitutes often live in violation of the law or at its murky edges. For example, even though it is usually legal for U.K. addicts to have needles, the microscopic traces of drugs in the needles are illegal, unless they have a prescription for that drug, explained Derek O'Connell, the detective superintendent in charge of the Merseyside Drug Squad. O'Connell looks and acts like the model of a tough city cop, which is no surprise since Liverpool is a very tough town. He is also a smart police officer working in a police department that has an enlightened view of its role in society.

O'Connell and the Merseyside Police believe in the enforcement of the *law and in harm reduction*. The result is a series of rational compromises that serves the original, but often forgotten, goals of civilian law enforcement (which was established in 1829 in London). Those goals are keeping the peace and advancing the health of the people. Liverpool police avoid being on the streets near drug clinics and needle exchange schemes whenever possible. The police have discovered that even if they are in the neighborhood dealing with an accident, suddenly there are no customers for the clinics and the schemes. If an addict is caught with needles by the police, they will usually ignore the needles. However, if the police feel compelled to seize the needles, they will give the addict a written receipt so that he can go to the exchange and satisfy the requirement for returning needles. If a drug user is arrested for the first time, he is "cautioned" (released with a warning and no record) and then given detailed instructions by the police on the health services available.

By almost every standard, harm reduction in Liverpool has been a success. Crime has gone down since the new harm reduction programs came into operation three years ago. (Homicide has never been high, but it may be of some interest that in the Greater Liverpool area, 1.5 million souls, there were 13 murders last year, none in the drug trade.) In the entire Merseyside Health Region, which comprises 2.5 million people and many thousands of injecting addicts, authorities are aware of five addicts with AIDS and nine who tested positive for the HIV virus. Tests of approximately 3,000 other injecting addicts produced negative results.

Cry for America

When Allan Parry and other Liverpool treatment leaders visit America, they are appalled at the bar-

barity of American methods, at the inhumanity of the war on drugs. When more effective models are so readily available, they wonder why our leaders persist at harm expansion. When they visit New York City, they are shocked to see an armed citizenry at war with an armed police force, massive violent crime, and tens of thousands of addicts infected with AIDS. And when they are told of the death of friends they saw the previous year who would be alive if they lived in Liverpool, they say they want to cry.

Marijuana users should not be cast out of society because they prefer marijuana to scotch, gin or bourbon. They are people from all walks of life who have used marijuana and are none the worse because of it.

—*Marvin D. Miller*

Legal, political, and social pressures have made it almost impossible to acknowledge publicly its non-medical virtues. In my twenty years of lecturing and writing about cannabis, I have until now never felt free to speak about this matter.

—*Lester Grinspoon*

Chapter 8
Why Make Criminals Of Marijuana Users?

Introduction

According to the U.S. government, 61,940,000 Americans have used marijuana at least once in their lives. That is, one in four Americans have experimented with marijuana. During the past several decades this huge multitude of smokers has consumed tons of it. Yet, it is impossible to identify a single overdose death — whether due to accident or suicide — caused primarily by this intoxicant. Thousands of overdose deaths are attributable to cocaine and heroin every year and hundreds annually from the use of such common milder substances as Darvon, Valium, Tylenol and aspirin.

It was solid evidence such as this, amplified in scientific detail a thousandfold in the historic 1987-88 impartial hearings that convinced the chief Drug Enforcement Administration administrative law judge (and medical experts the world over) that marijuana is one of the safest therapeutically active substances that human beings imbibe. That solid evidence is ignored, however, by the U.S. government and other governments which make marijuana users the principal targets of their massive law enforcement wars against drugs.

Whenever we point out this fact — marijuana users are the main targets of the multi-billion-dollar drug war — many sympathetic listeners simply do not believe their ears. Yet, evidence of this fact is easily available. Such evidence is found, for example, in the Bush-Bennett war plans of 1989 and 1990 that stated flatly that functional recreational drug users, rather than bottomed-out addicts, would be the principle focus of attack. The great majority of recreational drug users are peaceful, otherwise noncriminal, marijuana smokers.

On the basis of a massive disinformation campaign, marijuana was made illegal as a recreational intoxicant in 1937. There was no basis in fact for that federal prohibition law then. Today, there is still no reason to make otherwise decent and peaceful marijuana smokers into criminals.

Let Us Not Punish The Millions Who Choose A Different Path*

Prohibition Failed: Drug Availability is Unchanged

Despite the "War on Drugs" and the recent tripling of the resources committed to it, drugs are still as available as ever. During the Dec. 8, 1987, hearings conducted by this Committee, the honorable chairman of this committee asked Mr. Francis A. Keating, II, Assistant Secretary of the Treasury (Enforcement), Acting Chairman, Drug Law Enforcement Coordinating Group, National Drug Policy Board, the following question:

...I am just asking; as a result of all these efforts in the increase of expertise, technology, and efforts put into this area, are you suggesting that there might be one ounce less of heroin, opium, cocaine, or marijuana on the street as a result of that?

Mr. Keating: No.

Mr. Keating was correct. Availability is unchanged by current policy.

The State Department reported a 25 percent increase in foreign marijuana production during 1987 and the Drug Enforcement Administration estimated a 50 percent increase in domestic production, after eradication, during the years 1986 to 1987. Mark Dion from the Department of State in earlier congressional testimony estimated that as much as 9,000 metric tons of marijuana were imported into the United States in 1986 alone.

There are indications that the government figures on the number of metric tons available in the United States, as high as they may seem, nonethe-

---

* Marvin D. Miller, Esq., Statement on Behalf of the National Organization for the Reform of Marijuana Laws Before the House Select Committee on Narcotics Abuse and Control, "Hearing on Proposals to Legalize Drugs," Sept. 29, 1988.

less, are underestimated. This is demonstrated by an observation of the President's Commission on Organized Crime (1986) which noted that in 1984, the Mexican police, in raids on only five farms, seized over 2,000 metric tons of marijuana. This was eight times more marijuana than Mexican and American authorities had previously claimed was being produced annually throughout all of Mexico.

Wesley Pomeroy, one of the first administrators of the Law Enforcement Assistance Administration and a former police chief, said in a recent issue of the *Drugs and Drug Abuse Education Newsletter* what many in law enforcement will admit, if they can speak off the record, that marijuana cannot be controlled. It is a weed that can be grown anywhere. One can grow it in her bathtub, in his flowerpot, their outside garden or anyplace else. The greatest amount of marijuana actually destroyed by eradication, as a practical matter, is that which is grown wild rather than that which is cultivated for consumption. Eradication will not stop people from smoking marijuana.

At present marijuana is part of an unregulated, untaxed underground market. If allowed to surface, marijuana could be better controlled and at the same time, turned into an asset to be used against other more harmful substances.

Prohibition Fuels the Underground Economy

Wharton Econometrics determined for the President's Commission on Organized Crime in 1986 that one half of organized crime's revenues were derived from illegal drugs. Prohibition has created an enormous underground economy which is totally untaxed and unregulated. Large sums float around the economy but do not contribute to it. These sums are not available for use in drug education and treatment. Taxation and regulated availability of marijuana would allow us to educate and treat those with hard drug problems.

It is estimated that the domestic marijuana crop is the most valuable cash crop, overall, in the United States. It has an estimated value of over $10 billion. Revenue from this large cash crop could be used to improve our economy. The tax revenues could fund treatment and education for those addicted to hard drugs.

It is clear that the unintended beneficiaries of our current drug prohibition include those whose profits have increased because prohibition causes higher prices. In the 1980s, like in the 1920s, Prohibition and the application of increased penalties increases the risk which, in turn, increases the price and the profit. Since the actual costs of production remains about the same the profit margin increases.

Interestingly, prohibition's inclusion of drugs such as marijuana with hard drugs such as crack/cocaine and heroin, has also contributed significantly to the prevalence of hard drugs in our underground markets and in our society. One can obviously smuggle a smaller amount of cocaine at a significantly greater value with less chance of detection than it would take to smuggle a larger amount of marijuana of comparable value. Smaller is easier. Drug Enforcement Administration reports indicate that the costs of bulk cocaine in Florida have gone down dramatically while the cost per unit on the street has remained the same. An obvious effect of this is to increase the margin of profit. It is also demonstrative of the increased volume. The underground market has an interest in turning people toward more harmful drugs since they are easier to handle and produce easier profits. Lumping marijuana with hard drugs is counterproductive and makes this underground market more harmful to our society....

Marijuana arrests for simple possession comprise the greatest bulk of all drug arrests. The funds spent on marijuana prohibition should be diverted to help the tens of thousands of people who would like to obtain treatment for hard drug problems but have no place to go. Making marijuana available through taxed, regulated control would release a lot of resources that could be put to better use. Rather than criminalize productive citizens who occasionally smoke marijuana, we should allocate these resources to treating and educating those with hard drug problems....

Too Little for Too Much

The largest portion of our budget is wasted. Well over 68 percent of all drug arrests are for simple possession. Of these arrests, the vast majority, by far, are for marijuana. Indeed, marijuana arrests comprise about 40 percent of the total of all drug arrests nationally. Simple marijuana possession accounts for 77 percent of these arrests. With marijuana possession cases accounting for the bulk of all state and federal drug arrests in this country, we are wasting significant resources that could be allotted to treatment and education for hard drugs.

It seems counterproductive to spend billions of dollars and tie up the vast majority of our time and effort going after marijuana possession when tens of thousands who are heroin and cocaine/crack addicts are left in the criminal milieu, unable to get treatment for their problems. It is not sensible to devote so much of our enforcement budget to suppression of a relatively benign substance such as marijuana which has no toxic dosage while letting those addicted to such severely debilitating drugs as crack/cocaine and heroin go untreated for a lack of resources.

Given the fact that we have a $20 billion national budget for state and federal efforts and that 40 percent of all drug arrests relate to marijuana,

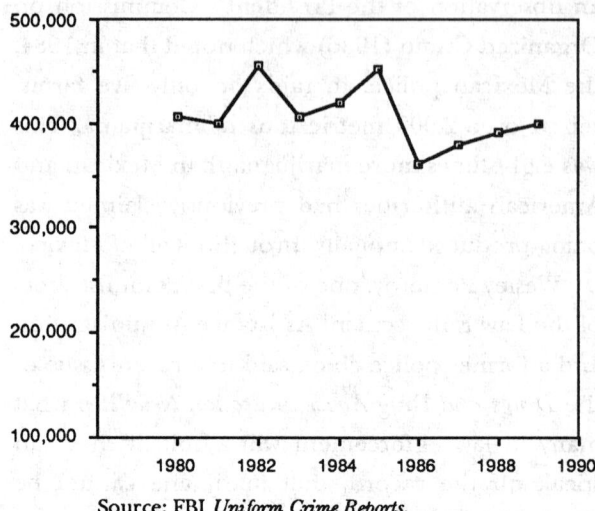

Drug Arrests for Marijuana in the 80's

Source: FBI *Uniform Crime Reports*.

removing marijuana from this prohibition effort would free enormous resources for more practical application.

In California, for example, a 1987 analysis of the fiscal savings attributed to the decriminalization of possession of an ounce or less of marijuana indicated that the total savings for the period of 1976 through 1985 was close to $1 billion. This policy generated additional revenue income in the neighborhood of $4 million.

Alaska has allowed marijuana to be available for personal use since 1975 with no deleterious consequences and at great savings. Indeed, it is better off than many other states because its policies are not fueling an underground market, nor are they criminalizing their citizens for a lifestyle choice. That state does not have the rampant increase in drug problems that many incorrectly claim happens when marijuana is made available.

In Texas, by comparison, they still prosecute all levels of marijuana possession. The lack of benefit compared to the enormous costs involved has given cause to some legislators to consider changing the law. In a report prepared for Texas State Senator

Craig Washington, it was estimated that the actual amount of revenue expended per year to punish those who possess minor amounts of marijuana might be as high as $50 million annually. That large amount resulted in punishing only 1 percent of the user population. The cost of the prohibition policy and punishment was considerable. Not only were taxpayer funds expended to little effect, but a lot of damage was done to the private lives of otherwise law abiding citizens. Many ordinary people from all walks of life were arrested and jailed on marijuana charges. They would not be criminals by any definition of the term other than by their act of possessing small amounts of marijuana. These people are being punished but there is little noticeable effect on the marijuana situation in Texas. It costs millions of dollars to the Texas taxpayers while having no effect on marijuana use.

This Texas report estimated that in the United States, as a whole, 1 in 10 people might possess small amounts of marijuana for personal use with as many as 1 in 4 having experimented with it or perhaps using it occasionally. That left approximately one and a half million Texans who regularly violated the law and over 3 1/2 million who occasionally violated the law. Cost benefit analysis indicated that there was, as has been shown in California, a misapplication of resources in the marijuana prohibition laws.

Applying the lessons to be learned from the Alaska, California, and Texas situations to the national marijuana prohibition policy teaches us that the current policy of marijuana prohibition is counter-productive to the overall policy of addressing our national drug problems. We spend twenty billion dollars annually from the coffers of the state and federal government on drug prohibition. We expend the largest portion of these resources on the simple possession of one single drug which is the most benign of them all, i.e., marijuana. We criminalize approximately one-quarter of our population, the 50 million marijuana users, because they smoke marijuana while ignoring the treatment needs of tens of thousand of people who want help for their hard drug problems. Treating all drugs the same is not cost effective. We are wasting our resources. In 1982, the National Academy of Sciences recognized after five years of study that regulated availability of marijuana ought to be allowed on a state-by-state basis. It is a matter of state's rights, not federal action.

Not All Drugs Are the Same

Lumping marijuana with crack/cocaine, heroin and other more severe substances is as impractical as it is inaccurate. Marijuana is not addictive, is not a gateway drug, does not lead to violence, and does not exact the costs to our society as do other drugs such as alcohol and tobacco.

Nearly all drugs and medications have toxic and potentially lethal dosages but this is not true for marijuana. There are no documented marijuana-user fatalities. As a DEA administrative law judge recently found, the consumption of ten raw potatoes can cause a toxic effect on an individual but it is not physically possible to eat enough marijuana to induce a toxic reaction. One would have to smoke 1,500 pounds in 15 minutes for a toxic overdose. There is no credible medical evidence that marijuana has caused a single death. Contrast this to aspirin which causes hundreds of deaths every year by overdose....

Marijuana users do not go about committing other crimes to support their recreational use. The millions of Americans who use marijuana are generally productive members of our society. Their only criminal association occurs because marijuana is a prohibited substance and its possession is a crime. They are forced to have contact with and fuel the underground market in order to obtain marijuana for their personal use.

They should not be cast out of society because they prefer marijuana to scotch, gin or bourbon. They are educated, skilled and dedicated men and women. They are people from all walks of life who have used marijuana and are none the worse for wear because of it. Making 50 million citizens criminals does more harm than good.

Removing Marijuana from Current Drug Prohibition Would Help Solve the Nation's Drug Problems

Marijuana is the most widely used of all drugs currently prohibited. It is the one which has the least potential for abuse. It has less toxic potential than alcohol or tobacco. It is not a gateway drug such as tobacco. Alcohol and tobacco combined contribute to five hundred thousand deaths each year in the United States. this is not true for marijuana. Alcohol contributes significantly to 54 percent of all violent crimes in the United States. This is not true for marijuana. Alcohol costs the country $100 billion in economic losses each year. This is not true for marijuana.

Prohibition of marijuana does, however, criminalize tens of millions of law abiding Americans who, except for their occasional use of marijuana, would not otherwise be the least bit involved in the criminal law system.

Removing marijuana from the current prohibition scheme and making it available through taxed, regulated access would also deprive the blackmarket economy of an enormous economic resource which it currently uses to fuel other criminal activity. It is estimated that organized crime derives one-half of its resources from drug profits.

Crop value estimates place the domestic marijuana crop at a value over $10 billion. It is believed by some to be the most valuable single cash crop in our country. Given the underground nature of the market, these are conservative estimates.

Taxed and regulated availability would not only liberate billions of dollars in law enforcement resources and allow them to be diverted toward education and training for drugs that present a greater problem to our society, but this policy change would also generate revenues in the neighborhood of $10 billion per year. It would no longer be necessary for tens of thousands of drug addicts to be compelled to remain in the criminal milieu because there is no treatment facility available for them. It would make it possible for the government to begin to use the most proven and reliable means known for changing societal behavior — education.

The regulated, taxed availability of marijuana would allow billions of dollars that are now channeled through law enforcement and the backways of illegal blackmarkets to be used to educate and treat those with hard drug problems.

This would not be a surrender to the dealers. It is a means to take them out of the black market. It is not an endorsement of use but recognizes that it is a matter of choice. When we tell young people about the harm of drugs, if we honestly admit that marijuana is not as harmful as other substances, then they will more likely listen to and believe us when we warn them about other drugs. If we tell young people lies about one thing, they will likely not believe us about anything else. To lump marijuana with hard drugs and treat all of them the same is to not tell the truth....

The issue of the use of psychoactive drugs as a moral issue is a red herring. Everyone alters their consciousness. Some do it through alcohol, others through caffeine or nicotine, while some use through fiction novels and fantasy movies. Others alter their consciousness through meditation and through religion. People should be allowed to choose their own means of altering their consciousness in the privacy of their own home without interfering with others or being subjected to interference from their government. Altering one's state of consciousness in one's own way should be a constitutionally protected right. Let us not punish the millions who now sit at home and choose a different path.

Marijuana is a mild consciousness-altering substance that is nonaddictive and comparatively nondeleterious when compared to alcohol and tobacco. Its regulated availability ought to be allowed.

Americans respond to honesty and education. Let us be honest and remove marijuana from its current prohibition. Let us not lump it together with other more harmful substances. It is different. Let us admit this truth. It is less harmful. Let us say so. Let us use the funds that we can save from this failed marijuana policy to educate and treat those who need it.

Education has led to an overall reduction in the consumption of tobacco, hard liquor, red meats and fatty foods. Americans are becoming healthy, not because it is a crime to be unhealthy, but because education is telling them it is the right thing to do. Let us take our dollars out of criminalizing tens of millions of our people for a choice of lifestyle and put that money into education so that the people can learn the truth about such substances as crack, heroin and PCP. Let those who wish it have available treatment. Let us give them someplace to turn other than a jail cell.

We can achieve all of this by making marijuana available in a controlled and regulated system. Let us be reasonable.

Marijuana Enhances The Lives of Some People*

I began to study marijuana in 1967. By the time I had completed the research which formed the basis for a book, I had become convinced that cannabis was considerably less harmful than tobacco and alcohol, the most commonly used legal drugs.

At that time I naively believed that once people understood that marijuana was much less harmful than drugs that were already legal, they would come to favor legalization. In 1971, I confidently predicted that cannabis would be legalized within the decade for people over 21. I had not yet learned that there is something very special about illicit drugs. If they don't always make the drug user behave irrationally, they certainly cause many nonusers to behave that way. Instead of making marijuana legally available to people 21 years of age or more, we have continued to criminalize many millions of Americans and to arrest approximately 400,000 (about the same number who die from the effects of tobacco) mostly young people on marijuana charges each year. What's more, the political climate has deteriorated, particularly over the past few years, to the point where it is difficult to discuss marijuana openly and freely. Surreptitious smokers of the 60s and early 70s who became more open toward the mid-70s had to go back into their closets during the Reagan years.

I will give two further pieces of evidence for this climate of psychopharmacological McCarthyism. The first is mandatory drug testing. Many of you will remember that one product of the McCarthyite climate of the 50s was the loyalty oath. Hardly anyone really believed that forced loyalty oaths would enhance national security, but people who refused to take such oaths neverthe-

---

* Lester Grinspoon, M.D., Harvard Medical School, Cambridge, MA.

less risked losing their jobs and reputations. Today we are witnessing the imposition of a kind of chemical loyalty oath. Mandatory, often random testing of urine samples for the presence of illicit drugs is increasingly demanded as a condition of employment. People who test positive may be fired, or if they want to keep their jobs, may be involuntarily assigned to drug counseling or "employee assistance" programs.

All this is of little use in preventing or treating drug abuse. In the case of cannabis, for example, the test requires analysis of the urine for a breakdown product or metabolite of tetrahydrocannabinol called 9-carboxy-THC. It is assumed that anyone with THC metabolites in his or her urine uses marijuana, and anyone without it doesn't. But clever or well-instructed marijuana users can easily defeat the test by chemically altering their urine or substituting someone else's urine. And even if the urine sample has not been altered, the available tests are far from perfect. Most programs start with immunoassays, which are cheap but inaccurate, missing THC metabolites that are there and finding them when they are not there. So urine that tests positive on immunoassays is now being subjected to more accurate and far more expensive techniques such as gas chromatography-mass spectroscopy (GC/MS). However, used in this sequence, GC/MS of course does nothing to detect false negatives. Furthermore, it is fallible because of laboratory error and passive exposure to marijuana smoke.

Even if there were an infallible test, it would be of little use in preventing or treating genuine drug abuse. The presence of cannabis metabolites in the urine bears no established relationship to drug effects on the brain. It tells us nothing about when the drug was used, how much was used, or what effects it had or has. Marijuana metabolites remain in the urine for days after a single exposure and weeks after a long-term user stops. Like loyalty oaths imposed on government employees, urine testing for marijuana is useless for its ostensible purpose. It is little more than shotgun harassment designed to impose an outward conformity to certain dominant social passions and prejudices.

Today we are witnessing the imposition of a kind of chemical loyalty oath.

My second example of psychopharmacological McCarthyism is the response to a publication in the May issue of the *American Psychologist*. Two psychologists at the University of California, Berkeley, followed 101 children from the age of 5 to 18, in a scientifically rigorous longitudinal study. They were interested in the relation between psychological characteristics and drug use. Their data demonstrated that adolescents who had engaged in some drug experimentation (primarily with marijuana) were the best adjusted in the group. Adolescents who used drugs frequently "were maladjusted, showing a distinct personality syndrome marked by interpersonal alienation, poor impulse control, and manifest emotional distress. Adolescents who had never experimented with any drug were relatively anxious, emotionally constricted, and lacking in social skills. Psychological differences between frequent drug users, experimenters, and abstainers could be traced to the earliest years of childhood and related to the quality of their parenting. The findings indicate that (a) problem drug use is a symptom, not a cause, of personal and social maladjustment, and (b) the meaning of drug use can be understood only in the context of an individual's personality structure and developmental history." The study suggests that current efforts at drug prevention are misguided to the extent that they focus on symptoms rather than on the psychological syndrome underlying drug abuse.

The hue and cry began immediately. The director of a San Francisco drug prevention program said that it was irresponsible for the researchers to report that "dabbling with drugs was 'not necessarily catastrophic' for some youths and may simply be a part of normal adolescent experimentation." A physician who directs the adolescent recovery center of a metropolitan hospital asked, "What does this do to the kids who made a commitment to be abstinent? Now they're being told they're a bunch of dorks and geeks. You can imagine how much more peer pressure is going to be put on them." An article in the *PRIDE Quarterly* Summer 1990 stated: "Based on the experiences of only 101 subjects, all living in San Francisco, the study drew national attention due to its outrageous conclusion." The article went on to say, "Unfortunately, the permissive thinking which surfaced in the California study will continue to exist in the United States until truly effective drug education reaches beyond the elementary classroom. However, too few educators themselves have seen the latest discoveries about the health consequences of drug use." I am reminded of Soviet party-line criticism of science which led to the phenomenon known as Lysenkoism.

Despite the hysteria, large numbers of Americans continue to use cannabis regularly. What was once considered primarily a youthful indulgence or an expression of youthful rebellion is now a common adult practice. Millions have smoked marijuana for years, and most of them will continue to smoke it for the rest of their lives. They are convinced that they are harming no one else and not harming themselves as much as cigarette smokers or alcohol drinkers. Many, if not most, believe that marijuana enhances their lives.

Like *Marihuana Reconsidered* itself, the public discussion of marijuana has focused almost exclusively on its potential harmfulness. In more than two decades of research, I have read and heard little about the *value* of cannabis. There has been some interest in its medical potential, but far less than there would be if any other drug had revealed a similar therapeutic promise. There are many reasons for this. One is that new drugs are developed and promoted by drug companies. The capital needed to take a drug from shelf chemical to pharmaceutical product is as much as $100 million. Needless to say, only substances which can be patented will attract this kind of investment. Cannabis and its cannabinol and cannabidiol derivatives cannot be patented because they are natural substances.

Furthermore, the government's intense antipathy has blocked medical use of cannabis for years. If legal, political, and social pressures have hindered the due recognition of the medical uses of cannabis, they have made it almost impossible to acknowledge publicly its non-medical virtues. In my twenty years of lecturing and writing about cannabis, I have until now never felt free to speak about this matter. It seems to be implicitly understood that that would be improper for an academic. To discuss what is good and useful about this substance is to risk being seen as the "Timothy Leary of pot." I have felt the disapproval and even censure of colleagues merely for arguing that marijuana is not as dangerous as alcohol and tobacco. On this subject attitudes in academia reflect the erroneous common wisdom.

The authorities who want to reduce the demand for cannabis have very little idea why that demand is so powerful and persistent. As Bob Dylan says to Mr. Jones in his famous song, "Something is happening here, but you don't know what it is." If they did know, they might be less concerned about diminishing the demand and less sanguine about the value of punitive legislation. Our society must make informed decisions based on the fact that tens of millions of its citizens use cannabis. It is important for us to know why those citizens not only like to use the substance, but in many cases believe that it has enhanced their lives.

The best way to learn about cannabis is to let users speak for themselves. In the last few months I have met two artists and a scientist who believe that the use of cannabis is important to their work. The first is a man in his mid-40s who consulted me because, as he said on the telephone, he had a "problem" concerning marijuana. He is a happily married man, the father of two children, who decided about 10 years ago that he was sufficiently successful as a painter to give up an ancillary job. He was able to make his living as a painter until eight months ago, when he was forced to give up the use of cannabis because of its illegality.* Before this, his successful painting routine had been as follows: he would take two tokes (puffs) of marijuana when he started to paint and another two tokes every two hours as long as he continued to work. He never took more than that. An ounce of cannabis would last him six or seven weeks. He describes the effect as follows: "With it, I get eager, motivated, even excited to paint. My mind focuses on one thing to accomplish at a time. I'm clear of negative thoughts and able to see instantly colors and shapes rather than a subject. I can now see the beauty in something I may have thought of as mundane or boring. My thoughts now seem to be of how precious time is and making the best use of every moment. This leads to greater accomplishments during the day which makes me feel content, satisfied, even happy; self-confidence grows and I want to go after something with a greater challenge."

Since being compelled to cease the use of marijuana, he finds that he sits "for hours before the canvas, unable to accomplish anything. I may look at one painting for an average of 200 hours, and I find myself full of self-doubt and lack of confidence. I may work for weeks on something, only to cover it up later. I waste time, I have no motivation, I get depressed." This man has not produced a saleable painting for eight months and his financial situation is desperate. All his technical skills are intact, but he cannot produce paintings of the same caliber that he sold so readily before.

> *Since being compelled to cease the use of marijuana, he finds that he sits "for hours before the canvas, unable to accomplish anything. I may look at one painting for an average of 200 hours, and I find myself full of self-doubt and lack of confidence."*

---

* I cannot provide more details because it would compromise his anonymity.

The second artist who finds cannabis important to his work writes as follows: "Marijuana has over the years served as a creative stimulant to my work as a performer and to my more occasional inspirations as a composer. For me, marijuana is a creative stimulant; almost all my finished choral pieces and songs have been composed partly or wholly under the influence: melodic and rhythmic ideas may just pop into my head during relaxed and happy moments, "points of creative release" one might say. The work of forming these seminal ideas into a whole composition, for me who am not prolific, then takes place over an ensuing period: a few days to a few years (in the latter extreme, intermittently, of course). As a performer, I have certainly gained insights into the inner meaning of the musical masterpieces which I play. Practicing new repertoire while intoxicated by marijuana is not a very good nor productive habit: the keen mental concentration of learning notes is not aided and abetted. But once a piece is fluently learned, my understanding of what it means as an entirety is often enhanced. A usual practice day for me is to work in the morning with a few cups of coffee in me. In the late afternoon I often have a little workout in the gym, and this renews me and gets the adrenalin flowing so I can come back to the piano, have a bit of marijuana, and practice very enjoyably and productively for one or two hours. I never try to perform in public when stoned, but as it is well known that marijuana can enhance the pleasure of listening to many kinds of music, I often listen after having smoked some marijuana. And so do many others who I know and have known over the years. WGBH-TV has produced a special on Satchmo, in which his lifelong affection for marijuana is not kept from the viewers. He found it both an inspiration for his music and a balm against life's trials. It seems to work the same way for me; it's one of my best friends, though, as I mentioned earlier, I wish for a better way to partake than by smoking it — pills, cookies, fudge, or whatever."

The scientist, like the two artists, has been using cannabis for years, and he too believes that it contributes to his work: "As a scientist I have spent literally years training the analytical side of my mind — to be suspicious of my data, to look for order of magnitude arguments to test the reasonableness of my results, to use lateral thinking to try to arrive at the same conclusions by alternative means. This has been an *active* process of mental discipline: idealizing physical situations, making assumptions to reduce the system to something solvable, and applying logic to determine the outcome.

"What has often been neglected in concentrating on only those things I have chosen to think about is an awareness of the wider perspective and significance of the work and the sense of personal wonder which led me into the field to begin with. There have also been many times when the answer to some question was right before me but I was unable to see the "forest for the trees." This is partly due to the same training which enables me to work through complicated analytical problems: in order to concentrate on those pertinent aspects which I have included in the model I will deliberately omit distractions which might perhaps hold the key. This is particularly true of working with computers, which have no tolerance for vague suggestions that perhaps something of importance has been left out of the equations, but will happily spit out results with an apparent accuracy of many decimal digits.

"If it were possible, say through yoga for example, for me to turn off the rational side of my mind and think creatively (and randomly) for short time periods, to reverse the training temporarily and see my work in a different light, then it would probably be as productive as getting high (although perhaps not as pleasant). Part of the neccesity for getting high is the human habit of going over old ground and seeing what you believe to be there rather than what actually exists (the same reason why it is almost impossible to proofread one's own writing).

"Obviously it is inefficient for me to try to pursue these new ideas while high, because I am too easily distracted and my analytical capabilities are unquestionably impaired; instead I enjoy the relaxation and keep notebooks recording my unchanneled thoughts in lists and outlines. I would state flatly that both aspects of getting high, namely relaxation and observation of subtle details of problems which I overlook at other times, have been valuable contributions to my work."

As you will have noticed, my informants do not identify themselves. How can we expect people to share these experiences openly in the present atmosphere? The government's newest legal assault includes a fine of up to $10,000 for possession of a single marijuana cigarette. Yet fear of the law is probably less important than fear of the consequences of being seen as irresponsible and deviant. When homosexuals started to come out of the closet a decade ago, many people were surprised to learn that they were not sick, antisocial, or in other ways "different" aside from their sexual orientation. It was an effective way to reduce this form of bigotry. So, too, cannabis users may eventually have to provide the public with an opportunity to test stereotypes against reality. They too are targets of bigotry and may have to adopt the same strategy in their struggle against it.

We, as parents of all nations, must say to our local law enforcement officer, "If my child, my loved one, or my friend breaks the law by using illicit drugs, please arrest him or her."

—Thomas J. Gleaton

In treatment like this, we're dealing with little animals. People forget that these kids are druggies. They cannot maintain any self-control. It's our job to get out their anger and remold their lives.

—Ann Petito

Chapter 9

Imprisoning Our Children to Save Them from Drugs

Introduction

Nancy Reagan, Ronald Reagan, and George Bush, among other American luminaries, are strong supporters of Straight, Inc., a hard-line drug treatment organization which has been known to imprison youth in order to save them from drugs. This may seem to be an extreme statement but the tactics of Straight have been documented time and time again in court proceedings.

What is even more remarkable is that there is so little sustained outrage over these illegal actions expressed in the press and media of America or of other democratic countries. So also is there virtual silence from professional organizations, such as medical or bar associations, who normally would be deeply concerned. Even when the destructive activities of Straight, and of similar cultish organizations, result in adverse court decisions, the definitive meaning of those verdicts is also generally ignored. For example, young Fred Collins won a $220,000 verdict from a federal court jury against Straight in 1983 because he was imprisoned illegally for 135 days.

Yet, in 1985 First Lady Nancy Reagan took Princess Diana on a regal visit to the very Straight facility in Springfield, Va., where this young American citizen had been held without cause for part of his illegal confinement. As she had done in the past, Mrs. Reagan pointed to Straight with pride as one of the best examples of American treatment practices, a model for the world. Not a single word appeared in the press regarding that visit about the documented abuses of Straight, many of which had propelled an outraged jury in an Alexandria federal court house a few miles away to hand down that large verdict.

This harsh treatment of children has its roots in the American Parents Movement which received enormous support from Mrs. Reagan and the Reagan administration. Members of that movement believe fervently, passionately, devoutly in a set of beliefs that are quite congruent with the notion of a holy war against drugs — and which lead to the ideology that supports forced institutionalization of young people to save their souls and bodies from drugs. Key elements of that ideology are:

1. This generation of American youth are out of control when it comes to drugs and sex. They have been corrupted by the legacy of the permissive 60s.

2. Even one marijuana cigarette or one beer will very probably spell destruction to most young people.

3. Through a harsh but necessary form of love, sometimes called Toughlove, youth must be sometimes subjected to a great deal of control and restraint.

4. Where necessary, that restraint may involve forced incarceration in treatment centers, or even arrest by the police, in order to save young people from the greater dangers of drugs.

5. In treatment centers, such as Straight, Inc., the young residents are taught that any use of drugs or any involvement in sexual activities is proof of addiction to chemicals. The idea of recreational drug use is a "do-drug message" being foisted on the youth of America by intellectuals in league with the drug dealers and organized crime.

6. Intellectuals who propose legalization of drugs or lessening the rigid enforcement of drug prohibition are being likewise irresponsible for they also are giving a "do-drug message" to the youth of the country and the world.

This extreme set of ideas lies at the heart of American drug policy. They have enormous grassroots support in the United States and in many other countries as reflected in the Bush-Bennett national strategy reports and in the growing attendance at PRIDE meetings from around the world. One of us attended the International Conference on Drugs presented by the Parents Resource Institute for Drug Education, Inc. in Atlanta during April of 1985 which attracted 2,000 people from 50 countries. PRIDE is the leading organization of the parents movement around the world.

Arrest (Even Lobotomize) My Child*

The April 1985 conference was actually two conferences, both supported heavily by federal funds, as have been similiar parent conferences before and after this one. The initial event in 1985 was entitled "The First Ladies Conference on Drug Abuse," which was scheduled for April 24 in the White House and April 25 in Atlanta. On April 24, Mrs. Reagan and the first ladies of seventeen other countries met in Washington to hear Dr. Carlton Turner of the White House explain national drug strategy, Joyce Nalepka, President of the National Federation of Parents for Drug-Free Youth, tell about the parents movement, and other adult leaders who laid out national policy directions....

The only young person on the program held at the White House, and the only one with an admitted drug problem, was 16-year-old Robin Page, listed as "Graduate of Straight, Inc., Drug Rehabilitation Center," who spoke on "Why I Used Drugs — Why I Stopped." While Ms. Page was apparently helped by the treatment she received at Straight, as other young people have been, no questions were raised about the dark side of the organization.

The second day of the First Ladies' conference merged with most of the events of the PRIDE meeting in Atlanta, at which only 15 of the other first ladies were present. I was able to attend it because it was touted as a meeting of private citizens that was open to any memeber of the public willing to pay the registration fee. However, when I sought to take one of the many vacant seats in the front rows of the huge ballroom, I was stopped by white paper signs on them saying "Reserved For DEA."

---
* Arnold S. Trebach, The Great Drug War, p. 123.

As on the day before in Washington, the first substantive speaker was Dr. Turner whose speech was entitled, "We Are Winning the War on Drugs...."

Thomas Gleaton: Arrest My Child

Several of the major ideological leaders of the parents crusade dominated the remainder of the day. Each talked in kindly terms about the need to save children around the world from drugs. Each seemed blissfully unaware that the programs proposed might have little impact on drug abuse but could well serve to repress many traditional democratic values and freedoms.

The Director of PRIDE and the Chairman of the conference, Thomas J. Gleaton, who holds a doctorate in education and is a professor of physical education at Georgia State University in Atlanta, explained how PRIDE was formed at the university in 1977 "to provide education and training for parents who wanted to fight back against the commercialized drug culture." Soon, Dr. Gleaton continued, the internationalization of the parents movement began. By 1983, representatives of 17 countries came to the PRIDE conference. By 1984, 34 countries attended. At this conference, over 50. "The internationalization of the parents movement has become a reality," Dr. Gleaton declared proudly. To that international audience, he repeated a powerful theme of the American parents crusade: "In nearly all cases, prevention fails when it does not address the gateway drug — *cannabis* — and instead concentrates on treatment of `end of the road' drugs — opiates and cocaine." As he uttered those words, I noted not a smile, not a questioning look, not a doubting comment around me. The huge audience was quiet, deadly serious, determined, seemingly united: fight marijuana and conquer the drug menace.

Unfortunately, Dr. Gleaton said, the worst mistakes of the American experience, especially decriminalization of marijuana, are being repeated in other countries, usually by the inaction of enforcement officials. "The result of this *de facto* legalization is a legal muddle that supports increasing drug use. If possession and use of an illegal drug is condoned or excused, the primary cause of the drug epidemic is ignored — the user." Having laid out this simplistic explanation for the rise in drug use, Dr. Gleaton then propounded one of the most repressive principles in the drug-free dogma: "We, as parents of all nations, must say to our local law enforcement officer, 'If my child, my loved one, or my friend breaks the law by using illicit drugs, please arrest him or her.'"

Thus, there was complete support for the logic of the law. Not a single person in the entire conference seemed capable of the venerable American exercise of raising questions about the simple horse sense of the laws. Not a single person seemed capable of asking if the classification of the drugs into legal and illegal was more an hysterical action from decades past than a matter of current objective science. Not a single person seemed to understand that the genius of America lay in periodically challenging irrational laws. All seemed to accept the extraordinary notion that we Americans should actually applaud the act of calling in the police to arrest our children and other loved ones if they so much as smoke a marijuana cigarette, which is, technically, still a crime in most of the United States. Not a single person pointed out that many experts find the gateway theory without factual foundation.

Not a single person raised questions, moreover, about the ideas put forth by the next speaker, Jean-Michel Cousteau, eldest son of the famous ocean explorer Jacques Cousteau. Jean-Michel narrated a film, "Snowstorm in the Jungle," produced by his famous father. The film dealt with cocaine trafficking in South America. To me it all seemed out of place in a conference on drug education for youth. Even more bizarre was the vivid showing of how some doctors in Peru were dealing with cocaine addiction among Peruvian youth: the equivalent of a brain lobotomy. Right there on the screen in Atlanta before 2,000 parents and young people was patient 29, aged 16, "deemed irrecoverable" and going under the knife as a last resort. And there was Jean Michel Cousteau clucking in a kindly voice as if to say how sad but to exorcise evil spirits one must do some cutting. My skin crawled and I tried to block out the images on the screen but everyone else there seemed to accept the idea of operations on the brains of addicted children as one of the exciting new technologies for the future. Sadly, Jean-Michel tells us, patient 29 relapsed a year later.

Straight Rides Over Kids Again...And Some Say They Love It[*]

Sixteen-year-old Chad Barnes found himself pinned face down on a cold tile floor, his arms and legs stretched out from his body. Four other boys were holding him pressing so hard that Chad screamed in anger. Just a few moments before, Chad had tried to start a fight in the gymnasium-sized meeting room of one of the toughest adolescent drug-treatment programs in the country: Straight, the program chosen by Republican gubernatorial nominee Clayton Williams to cure his own son.

Chad, a wiry boy with eyes the color of coffee, was furious over the way a veteran in the program, known as an oldcomer, had confronted him.

---

[*] Skip Hollandsworth, "Can Kids on Drugs Be Saved?" Excerpted with permission from the June 1990 issue of *Texas Monthly*. Copyright 1990 by Texas Monthly.

Imprisoning our Children to Save them from Drugs

"You're lying to us, Chad!" the older teenager had yelled. "You're not working the program! You're holding the rest of us back, Chad!" Chad had shouted an obscenity and shoved another kid next to him, and within seconds, other teenagers had thrown him down. Anyone who rebels at Straight is quickly restrained by oldcomers or by recent graduates working as counselors. Wild-eyed, like a trapped animal, Chad tried to shake loose. A "first phaser" like himself — someone in the first level — couldn't take one step anywhere in the building without an oldcomer holding on to one of his back belt loops. He couldn't even use the bathroom without someone watching him.

At Straight, kids who don't admit to having a drug-oriented lifestyle are yelled at by the other kids until their defenses are broken. Nearly 120 young people, ages 12-22 are in various stages of treatment, and spend almost the entire day in this windowless room in a brick office complex in the Dallas suburb of Irving. For nearly 12 hours each day, they must sit erect in blue plastic chairs, not speaking or standing or making eye contact with another person without permission. Those who misbehave are held back in their chairs or, like Chad, spread-eagled on the floor. The theory at Straight is that kids on drugs are more likely to accept therapy from peers who have been through the program than from adults who have not. A 14-year-old program with treatment centers in nine U.S. cities, Straight has been called the best program of its kind in the country. Clayton Williams was so impressed with Straight that he wants the state to spend at least $50 million for adolescent-treatment centers based on Straight principles.

But others are not so impressed. Acting on complaints from parents and teenagers who had been through the program, the Texas Commission on Alcohol and Drug Abuse launched an investigation last year to determine whether Straight abuses kids. The head of a rival treatment program calls Straight "fiercely controlling" and questions its long-range success. "It decides what a kid's identity is going to be and then does all the thinking for him," says Mike Townley of Bedford Meadows psychiatric hospital in Bedford, a dozen miles west of Straight. "By the time a kid gets out of the program, he really has trouble thinking for himself."

The controversy over Straight underscores a dirty little secret: Our vast drug-treatment system, with its armies of therapists, medical conferences, and marketing strategies, doesn't really know what it's doing. Even though hospitals and treatment centers bombard the public with haunting commercials about costly state-of-the-art treatment programs and claim that they have high success rates, one jarring statistic is always left out: According to the latest independent research, about 80 percent of the adolescents who complete such programs will, within a year, relapse and return to drugs, regardless of the program they attended.

Adolescent drug treatment is portrayed as a science, but in reality, it is a huge psychosocial laboratory where therapists attempt an array of experiments — from fierce behavior-modification techniques to ancient superstitious practices, from chemical aversion to spiritual conversion — just to see what it takes to keep the laboratory mice, our kids, from wanting to get high. Considering this is where the real war on drugs will eventually be fought — people must learn not to want drugs — the results so far haven't been exactly impressive. There is very little good scientific evidence that any of these programs really work.

By the time Chad Barnes arrived at Straight, he was already a savvy player in the drug treatment game. Having been to three treatment centers since the age of 12, Chad knew exactly what to say and how to act in order to make his counselors and his parents believe he was turning his life around. He could talk about life's pressures and family problems. He had mastered all of the Alcoholics Anonymous phrases. For him, like many of his peers, going to a treatment center was a rite of passage. Invariably, however, within days of his release from each facility, Chad would be back with his old friends, happily using a variety of drugs.

But Straight was unlike anything Chad Barnes had ever seen — a modern day *Lord of the Flies*, where teenagers control other teenagers. The other boys finally released Chad, only to slam him into his chair, and the group therapy continued. Another boy, Will, was asked to stand up, and an oldcomer began telling him that he wasn't being honest about his drug use. Will seemed to lose it. He leapt over his chair, screaming at the group to leave him alone, and then rushed toward the girls' side of the room, causing two girls to smash backward into one another and start fighting. Suddenly, Chad was up again, his jaws clenched, and he stepped toward another teenager, letting fly a hard right that would have knocked even a grown man off his feet. By then, a small riot was breaking out. Another boy took a swing at someone, and a couple of boys tried to escape out the back door. More counselors and other adults poured into the room, and Chad, gasping, his shirt torn across his chest, was dragged to a timeout room where he would remain for the rest of the day.

Ann Petito, who was Straight's Clinical director last October, at the time of the brawl, said that such a large fight was not entirely unexpected. "In treatment like this, we're dealing with little animals," she said. "People forget that these kids are druggies. They cannot maintain any self-control. It's our job to get out their anger and remold their lives."

But does treatment really remold their lives? Or are these programs ultimately better at teaching kids to remain sick rather than teaching them to be well? For nearly six months I followed Chad Barnes through Straight, and I also visited 10 other adolescent treatment centers. I watched a kind of contemporary morality play unfold, one in which hundreds of young people were asked to transform their lives and save themselves. The play itself, however, was often dwarfed by its own dark setting: a treatment industry that seems to be driven more by economics than by clinical research, that knows how to turn parents' deepest fears into profit margins, and that always has simplistic solutions for our kids — solutions that when analyzed, lead only to more questions....

The Last Hope

By August 1987, Chad Barnes had flunked the seventh and eighth grades, and his parents were wondering how much longer they could keep him in the house. He would wreck his bedroom, throw stuff at his parents, hide in his closet and do inhalants, sniff spray paint or whatever he could find.

Then Gail Barnes heard about a new program in Irving that had a Marine Corps approach to treatment. It turned out to be Straight. The program, which lasted at least a year, was not as expensive as the others had been — about $11,000. The Barneses were typical of many parents who come to Straight — they were at the breaking point, willing for anyone to do anything with their child as long as it got some results. For them, it was a relief to find a program that ignored all the psychiatric talk and got right down to berating the child for his behavior. Chad knew about Straight. He and his drug-using friends would trade stories about the different programs — which ones were the easiest, which ones had the best gyms, which ones were lax in checking your suitcase if you wanted to sneak drugs in. When his father came to

Imprisoning our Children to Save them from Drugs

tell him that he was headed for Straight, Chad stiffened.

"Anywhere, Dad, but there," he said. Donald begged Chad to at least give Straight a chance.

The kids do not come to Straight easily. Some are brought in by their parents under false pretenses — a father might ask his child to accompany him on an errand — and others literally have to be carried into the building. On Aug. 17, 1987, however, Chad Barnes was numb with shock as staff members escorted him away. "I heard about torture and beatings in there, stuff like that," says Chad. "I couldn't believe I was going into that place."

A mother whose son was already in the program cut Chad's shoulder-length hair. A staff member placed Chad in the front row on the boy's side of the large, stark meeting room. The other kids, about 60 boys and 40 girls in all (many inpatient treatment programs have only 20-30 adolescents at a time), were performing a peculiar arm-flapping routine called motivating — waving their arms wildly to get the attention of a group leader so they could be called on to speak. Some teenagers stood behind the chairs, watching closely, ready to catch anyone who might want to run.

The kids looked drab, almost pale under the fluorescent lights. Straight's rules for newcomers forbid makeup, jewelry, shirts with decals or writing, nylons, high heels, hair dryers, curling irons, and even mouthwash. There is also a huge sense of detachment from the rest of the world. Newcomers must temporarily drop out of school. They cannot use the telephone, speak to their parents, visit with friends, talk to a Straight member of the opposite sex, carry money, listen to the radio or record player, watch television, or read any books except AA literature or the Bible. If they need to walk in front of an adult, they must stick their arms out, fingers pointed in the direction they want to go, until the adult nods and waves them on. The kids are told to call themselves "druggies" and to refer to their pre-Straight friends as "druggie friends." Although Straight advertises itself as a drug-free program, it does allow physicians to prescribe drugs like Thorazine for youths in its care.

> *The kids are told to call themselves 'druggies' and to refer to their pre-Straight friends as 'druggie friends.'*

To graduate from Straight — the average duration is about a year and a half — a participant must make it through all five of the program's rigid phases, winning a little more freedom and responsibility with each promotion. First phase — which usually lasts from a month to a year, depending on the counselors' assessment — is the strictest. A first phaser must live in a "host home," a house belonging to a parent whose child is farther along in the program. Host homes have alarms on the windows and doors to prevent escape. An oldcomer must supervise a first phaser in the host home — if a kid just wants to pick up a pen, he has to ask permission from an oldcomer — and the kids must call the parents of the host home "Mom" and "Dad" as if they are part of a new family.

During second phase, which lasts about a month, the child can live in his own home, but he can't talk to anyone except his family. Parents, at their own weekly group meetings at Straight, are told to get back in charge of their families at this time. They are required to institute no-nonsense discipline, telling their child that they will keep him at Straight through the rest of his teenage years unless he follows the rules. A second phaser can't go outside the house, not even to the back yard.

In the third phase, which lasts a minimum of three weeks, the teenager can return to school or to work on weekdays, but he must come to the Straight program for the afternoon and evening. Third phasers have more responsibility at Straight — running errands, serving dinner, accompanying first phasers to the bathroom — but they still can't talk to Straight members of the opposite sex or go outside without permission. Fourth phasers come to the building 4 days a week for at least three months, and they can't go anywhere without their parents except to AA meetings. And fifth phasers spend three days a week at Straight for about two months. They can finally talk to members of the opposite sex, but they can't date them. After graduation, there is a 6 month aftercare program, in which kids come weekly for classes or raps.

With only one lapse, a kid either starts over or gets moved down to a lower phase. Kids have been dropped to lower phases for trying to escape, fighting, yelling at their parents, talking to a girl, or smoking. I met one young man, 20-year-old Brett Sharp, who had spent two years at Straight and had graduated in 1988. Earlier this year, walking by a neighbor's house, he was offered a beer and accepted. When he told his parents what he had done, he agreed to go back to Straight. "These are unmanageable, druggie kids," says his father, Colonel John Sharp, an Air Force doctor in San Antonio. "If you don't control their behavior right at the start, then you can count on them going out of control."

Boot Camp for Druggies

The controversy that has plagued Straight nearly since its inception centers on this very matter of control. Straight's goal is to force a kid to see how much damage his drug use has caused his family and himself, but in this authoritarian environment, casual counseling doesn't have much of a place. Group therapy usually turns into harsh encounters, conducted not by experienced, trained therapists but by other teenagers. Straight calls this "positive peer pressure."

"You're lying!" a higher-phased girl screams at a teary-eyed newcomer in one session. "You think you look nice, and you think you're making us believe you're improving, but you're lying! You hurt inside! You still want drugs!" The newcomer, looking frightened, tries to control the trembling of her lips. "Now you better tell us everything you're lying about," the older girl continues, "because lying is going to kill you, just like drugs are going to kill you!"

Even though the program has a staff of four young adult counselors, the higher-phased youths and the paraprofessional graduate counselors, mostly teenagers, do almost all of the daily work with the kids. "Adult therapists have lost the perspective on what counseling is," says Page Peary, Straight's national vice president. "Only peer counselors can say, 'Hey, I've been there.' They can share experiences on an emotional level, and they can also see right through you when you're lying." But the only training is a six-week course for the paraprofessionals. There's no such class for the higher-phased kids; all they have is their experience in the program.

What I observed were nit-picking confrontations that did nothing to encourage sharing and camaraderie within the group. "I heard you talking about playing with a Ouija board!" one girl yells at another. "You think that's going to help you become honest?" A boy confesses that he has been having thoughts about girls, a feeling that seems rather natural for an adolescent male. Immediately, an oldcomer leaps up. "Maybe you ought to look into those sexual thoughts," he yells, "because it shows you're not taking any pride in yourself!" When another boy is accused by an oldcomer of leafing through Playboy at school, he drops his head. The oldcomer presses him. "Why would you ever look at a magazine like that? Is your self-esteem that low? You don't want to help the group out. You just want to get out of here!"

At Straight, as in boot camp, everyone is forced to work toward a common goal; the group breaks a kid's selfishness. There is such constant talk about supporting and improving the group that Straight begins to resemble a teenage cult, with its own rituals and codes. The kids talk about "being aware," "copping out," "receiving attitudes from others," and "acting FOS" ("full of shit"). They are told never to speak to anyone who has dropped out of the program. They can't talk to outsiders about the treatment program. Parents aren't allowed to sit in on any of the daily raps. Sometimes, among the group, one can see kids who look as if they have barely a vestige of self-esteem left, too scared to talk in front of the others, their egos too devastated to try to make a conscious change in their own lives.

Straight Beliefs, a list of guidelines for the counselors, proposes, "Defiance is dealt with by the Group." Those kids who talk about straightening up are accepted; those who don't are confronted. "The reason you change is because you get tired of being confronted," says 15-year-old Marilee Kossack, a fifth phaser who's been in Straight for 15 months. "I knew if I didn't start acting better, I wouldn't be a part of the group."

Deaths To U.S. Children Due To Drug Overdoses Age 6-17

year	number
1980	43
1981	48
1982	36
1983	48
1984	49
1985	52
1986	57
1987	59
1988	88

Source: NIDA, Drug Abuse Warning Network

This is the key to sobriety at Straight: For months, a kid is relentlessly nagged and browbeaten until he breaks down and confesses. Through the group's guidance, he learns to regulate his behavior and express his feelings instead of avoiding them through drugs. He also finds new role models in the program's young leaders.

"There are a lot of professionals who think Straight is the best treatment program around. Its model for treatment is unmatched by any other program," says Dr. Ian Macdonald, the former director of the Drug Abuse Policy Office at the White House. "Its structure can deal with the most severe kids in our society, forcing them to change, giving them discipline."

But some parents and kids who have been through Straight feel otherwise. Stephen Combs, a six-foot-four-inch 16-year-old who was in the program from April 1989 until last February, when he ran away, says he was restrained the second day he was in the program. "Some guys were yelling at this little guy, and I got tired of it and said to stop yelling at him, and then five or six guys jumped on me, trying to push me back in my chair. I fought back, which made them hit me harder." Combs says he saw a boy thrown down so hard that he was knocked out; he also saw a girl get slugged in the face. "Heck, as soon as we got up in the higher phases," says Combs, who reached third phase before leaving, "we all wanted to restrain people. It was like they had done it to us, so let's do it to the new ones. On Feb. 1, the day before I left, some kid was singing to himself, which is against the rules, and when he wouldn't shut up, I stuck my hand in his face and pushed him on the ground." Combs chuckles. "That's what we called a restraint."

Dena Latham, from the East Texas town of Athens, entered the program in the spring of 1988, at the age of 13. "They found this lighter and razor blade in my pocket the day I came, and they accused me of doing cocaine," she recalls. "I had never, ever done cocaine. But they kept screaming at me about it and jumping on me. It was so humiliating. They kept it up every day. One time, I just couldn't take it and tried to get out of my chair, and these girls were on me in a second, four-pointing me to the floor. They took my knees and elbows and twisted them and pulled my hair."

Rob Stegall entered Straight in April 1988 and stayed six months, the entire time on first phase. "At first I was rebellious against the program," he says. "They said 'You're going to be sober and you're going to like it.' They did all the usual things — throwing me on the floor, pulling my legs apart like a wishbone — and one day I just stopped fighting it. I just remember going away someplace in my head, thinking that was the way to survive."

His mother, Lynne Armstrong, saw him only occasionally on Family Night. "I didn't know what was happening to him because they wouldn't let me talk to him," she remembers. "They called after 6 months and said I should come get him because he was acting depressed and they wanted to medicate him. When I came to get him, I could barely recognize him. The day I brought him home, he was incapable of completing a sentence. He went into his room and just stared at the books on his shelves for 10 minutes." Her voice breaks. "And then I asked him to come outside. It was such a beautiful day, the birds were chirping, and there I was, discussing the weather. It was so overwhelming for him that he had to go back into his room. He hadn't seen the outside in four months. My God, I couldn't stop crying. I felt like my son was a POW back from the war."

Today Rob has a job at a department store and goes to AA meetings to stay sober. He even credits Straight for informing him about AA. "I just don't think they needed to try to warp my brain to tell me drugs were bad," he says.

Carol Koenecke, the director of Straight in Irving, denies the existence of such violence, dismissing the talk simply as bitter allegations from those who failed the program. "You're dealing with highly dysfunctional kids and highly dysfunctional families who haven't come to terms with who they are," days Koenecke. "There are always going to be clients in a program like ours trying to rebel. And there are going to be times when we have to quickly stop them from hurting others or hurting themselves. We are not a violent program. Anyone who thinks this program should be a lot easier needs to educate himself about adolescent substance abuse."

Chad's Rebellion

Fifteen months after Chad was admitted to Straight, the program's administrators called his parents and said Chad wasn't making any progress. He would just sit through the day in his blue chair, doing nothing. A psychiatrist had given him anti-depressants, thinking that might raise his level of energy, but Chad didn't respond. Whenever someone confronted him, Chad would just shrug.

Donald and Gail Barnes thought that 15 months at Straight was a long time, especially when there was so little to show for it. "We thought maybe Chad had developed a clinical depression or an emotional problem or something," says Donald. "We didn't know. So we decided to withdraw him on a medical discharge."

Chad had been biding his time like a prisoner, knowing that if he just waited, his parents would finally give up. "I was so sick of all this drug treatment I just wanted to be left alone," Chad says.

In late 1988, the Barneses took Chad off the anti-depressant medicine, hoping he would feel better. He did feel a lot better. He began using drugs like crystal and cocaine. He hid his drug use from his parents until the spring of 1989, but when they finally discovered it, his mother, hysterical, said Chad could not live in the house any longer.

The family was falling apart. Chad and his father moved into an apartment in Plano, where Donald got another job with the Post Office. Gail remained in Corsicana with their two daughters. While Donald was at work during the day, Chad turned into a first-class juvenile delinquent. He got high. He got into fights. He stole his dad's car and drove it to Corsicana to buy drugs. He was taken into custody for vagrancy.

On June 29, 1989, Chad Barnes, 15 years old, woke up in his bedroom to find an off-duty police officer, several boys and fathers from Straight, and his own father standing around him.

"You're going back," said Donald.

They handcuffed him, tied him down in the car, and still he tried to run. He cussed and kicked, and when he got an arm free, he started swinging at anyone close to him. When they reached Straight, he went wild, screaming and kicking. As soon as he was put in the meeting room with the others, he fought with the nearest boy available and was immediately thrown to the ground. Sullenly, Chad returned to his chair. He told the counselors that he would never cooperate. He was prepared to sit there until he was 18 and could legally leave.

> *He hadn't seen the outside in four months. My God, I couldn't stop crying. I felt like my son was a POW back from the war.*

Though Straight will kick a kid out of the program if he is too violent or shows major psychiatric problems, the counselors decided that Chad, for all his rebelliousness, did not pose a major threat and allowed him to stay. But the Barneses also made a decision. "I realized I had been too passive with Chad," says Donald. "I had let him get the better of me because I wanted to believe in him so much." Now, no matter what Chad did at Straight, he wasn't leaving.

Upon Chad's return to Straight, Donald and Gail came to Family Night, a group meeting for kids and their families held every Friday night. The teenagers, sitting erectly on one side of the room, face their parents, who sit on the other. The children, their hands on their knees, do not smile. After an opening song and introduction, the newest members of the group are to stand and announce their first names, admit they are druggies, confess the number of drugs they used in the past, say how they have hurt their families, and then explain what their goals are. If they deviate from that spiel, a counselor loudly interrupts.

During the only moment of the week when a newcomer is allowed to see his family, he must stand alone and listen as his parents and siblings rise to face him — he is not allowed to make eye contact with them as they talk. In the parents' meetings held before the Family Night, the parents are pushed to express their anger and are criticized by other parents if they don't.

"You're not my daughter ever again until you finish this program!" one mother yelled at her weeping child. "What is the matter with you?"

"It feels so good to have a good night's sleep," a father cried out at his son, "knowing that you haven't sneaked out of the house to do your drugs!"

Another father, his face red with rage, bellowed at his son: "I am so furious with you! You stole my money, you pawned my watch for drugs. Don't you ever expect to walk into my house again unless you graduate from here!"

The child can answer his parents' comments only with the sentence "I love you."

When the time came for Chad's parents to speak, they described how he had made their home a living hell, how they knew he would die if he didn't get help.

When they finished, Chad raised his hand and stared at them for a moment. When a counselor asked what he had to say, Chad shouted as loudly as he could: "F— you!"

The Investigation

In July 1989, just after Chad had begun his second stay in Straight, David Tatum, an administrator at the Texas Commission on Alcohol and Drug Abuse, received a complaint from a parent whose child had been in Straight. The parent told Tatum that Straight counselors were mistreating kids....

Last year in Texas an Arlington woman named Tempie Worthy, whose daughter had been kicked out of Straight for insubordination after only a month, formed an organization called People Against Straight Treatment. Hoping to shut down Straight, Worthy engaged in letter-writing campaigns to the media, the police, and the Dallas district attorney's office. She wrote and called parents whose children were still in the program. She obtained materials from Straight's dumpster, looking for evidence of abuse. Worthy also picketed the Straight center, using a bullhorn to denounce the program for its brainwashing tactics. Last December, Straight won a court order against Worthy, preventing her from coming near the premises, contacting employees, or harassing clients.

Despite the criticism, Straight garners strong national support. President Bush has endorsed the organization. Nancy Reagan and Diana, Princess of Wales, praised the organization after touring the facilities in Washington, D.C. And in Texas there's Clayton Williams. "I like it," Williams told me, "because if you start going wrong, they four-point you to the ground until you're ready to do it the right way." Straight officials introduced me to several graduates of the program, all of whom said that Straight had whipped them into sobriety. The organization claims — without offering any statistical evidence — that 70 percent of its graduates remain drug-free.

David Tatum recognized the importance of "tough love" treatment programs for undisciplined drug-using youngsters, but he still wanted to know whether the ends justified Straight's means. Tatum launched a formal investigation in July, and by Oct. 20, he had received a total of 15 complaints against Straight — all of them from parents whose children did not complete the program. The state investigators looked into five incidents in which

Straight kids were restrained for such incidents as "failure to sit up properly," "failure to move," and "failure to attend to personal hygiene." One staff member allegedly tied a client with a nylon rope to prevent him from escaping from a vehicle, and other staff members did nothing while some kids scratched their arms with pieces of metal....

Last December Straight and the Texas Commission on Alcohol and Drug Abuse agreed that only trained staffers — the paraprofessionals and the adult counselors — would be allowed to restrain clients. Time-out rooms were banned, and host homes were required to provide better living arrangements. The state was to make inspections every 120 days through 1990. But Straight did not have to admit to any of the allegations of abuse....

But things at Straight didn't seem that different. In January, when I visited Straight again.... Straight still had that same feeling of potential explosiveness. There never seemed to be enough supervision; only two adult counselors and three paraprofessionals were in the room of 100 kids at one time. After two years at Straight, one counselor quit because she said she suffered from burnout. "It is impossible to care for such a huge group of people every day without feeling like you were neglecting some of them," the counselor told me.

The Moment of Change

But one thing at Straight did change. One January afternoon I walked into the meeting room and saw Chad Barnes, his shirt hanging limply from his hollow-chested body, standing up to address a newcomer in the group. I heard him say, "You have to say you want off these drugs." The newcomer was scowling. "I'm telling you," said Chad, "it works."

The military has good reason to resist this call to arms. Given how many countries produce drugs, including the U.S. itself, the chances of winning are small compared to the likelihood of tearing apart the social and political fabric of countries in which the military intervenes.

—Jonathan Marshall

No wonder that lawyers for the dictator charge that Operation Just Cause — the ludicrous code name for the Panama invasion — was "outrageous" and "the first time the United States has invaded a county and leveled it to arrest one man."

—Tom Wicker

Chapter 10

The Soldier's Bayonet and the Headsman's Axe

Introduction

As the cycle of frustration, anger, and violence spiraled upward on all sides of the drug conflict in the United States and other countries, anguished cries for resort to the military and the death penalty and other extreme measures were heard in the highest councils of government. To what extent should we override the traditional democratic Anglo-American prohibition on the use of the military (or military tactics) to enforce laws passed by civilian authorities, in this case, the drug laws?

To what extent should we apply the death penalty to those involved in the drug trade?

It Is Becoming A Real War[*]

The war on drugs, a phrase first used by President Richard Nixon in 1969, is quickly taking on the characteristics of a real war. At home it is as if martial law has been declared. Some of the same troops that invaded Panama are now being used against U.S. citizens in a militaristic marijuana eradication campaign. The National Guard is assisting in the drug war in 49 of the 50 states and SWAT teams routinely serve search warrants related to drug offenses. The police commonly search people on the streets of underclass neighborhoods, as well as travelers on the highways, in airports, train stations and bus terminals. Public housing projects have been subjected to house-to-house searches, neighborhoods have been roadblocked, and rural areas have been subjected to intensive helicopter surveillance by men in camouflaged uniforms.

The United States has sent its troops abroad to Latin America. Uncle Sam has invaded Panama, captured its leader and brought him to the United States for a drug war trial. In other countries the U.S. has set up military encampments, sent in Green Berets and provided military equipment, personnel and training. The U.S. government has threatened blockades, the U.S. courts have judged that the rules of our Constitution do not apply and the U.S. military has kidnapped foreign nationals to bring them to the United States to stand trial for drug war crimes. Countries that refuse to cooperate in our war on drugs are threatened with financial cut-offs. They must accept our battle plan or pay a heavy price.

[*] Kevin B. Zeese

Since the eight decades of trying to control people's choice in the use of various substances has failed, the U.S. government has moved toward a more militaristic drug policy at home and abroad. The more we try, and the more we fail, the more the spiral of violence and war escalates. As Nobel Laureate Milton Friedman said in a recent plea to drug czar William Bennett:

"Every friend of freedom, and I know you are one, must be as revolted as I am by the prospect of turning the United States into an armed camp, by the vision of jails filled with casual drug users and of an army of enforcers empowered to invade the liberty of citizens on slight evidence. A country in which shooting down unidentified planes 'on suspicion' can be seriously considered as a drug war tactic is not the kind of United States that either you or I want to hand on to future generations."

Unfortunately, the Bush administration has ignored the plea of Mr. Friedman and has since continued on an even more militaristic path. Across the seas U.S. armed forces are becoming engaged in a jungle quagmire. At home, U.S. police and the National Guard are becoming more militaristic and treating U.S. citizens as traitors in the war on drugs. Our government seems bent on enforcing its choices on its citizens at the point of a bayonet.

The History of Military Involvement in Law Enforcement

Distaste for military involvement in law enforcement is evident at the roots of the founding of our country. King George's use of troops to enforce laws in the colonies, laws which sometimes involved the use of the once-prohibited caffeine, was one of the causes of rebellion against England.

The First Continental Congress passed a series of resolutions in September 1774 that included a protest against "the keeping of a standing army in these colonies in times of peace." Two years later the Declaration of Independence declared that the "King of Great Britain" had established "an absolute tyranny over these states." As proof of that declaration our Founders stated that: "He has kept among us, in times of peace, standing armies, without the consent of our legislature. He has affected to render the military independent of, and superior to, the civil power."

The U.S. Constitution's provisions concerning the quartering of troops in private homes and the use of the military "against invasion" demonstrate the antipathy the founders had for standing armies. The Constitution nowhere expressly authorizes use of the army to execute laws. To place clearly into law the historical and constitutional antipathy toward military involvement in law enforcement the Congress passed the Posse Comitatus Act in 1878.

In proposing the Posse Comitatus Act, Representative William Kimmel of Maryland stated in 1878 that "This dread and detestation of standing armies appears on every page of their progress toward independence and the establishment of the Constitution in 1789." In an hour-long speech he quoted many of the Founding Fathers' views on this improper use of the military. Patrick Henry described standing armies as used "to execute the execrable demands of tyranny." George Mason stated such use would "make the people lose their liberty." Moreover, the Father of the Constitution, James Madison, saw such use of the military as "one of the greatest mischiefs."

Interestingly, much of the opposition to the act was around concern over the sheriff's inability to enforce whiskey laws in the mountains of Kentucky where moonshiners were supported by the local population. Enactment of the Posse Comitatus Act would put an end to the use of the army to raid illicit whiskey distilleries.

After passage of the act, court decisions acknowledged that the law was merely an extension of the Constitution and the intent of our founding fathers. In *United States v. Walden*, the court said:

"The policy that the military involvement in civilian law enforcement should be carefully restricted has deep roots in American history. Whether there should even be a standing army was a question fiercely debated among the framers of the Constitution. In the congressional debate on the Posse Comitatus Act several senators expressed the opinion that the Act was no more than an expression of constitutional limitations on the use of the military to enforce civil laws."

The Military Joins the Drug War

In 1981, in the name of the war on drugs, Congress began to violate the Founders' notion that the military had to be kept separate from civilian law enforcement: amendments to the Posse Comitatus Act that allowed the military to provide law enforcement with intelligence information, lend law enforcement authorities military equipment, and train and provide technical assistance for civilian drug enforcement authorities.

That was the beginning of a path that the drug warriors could not resist pursuing. Once again in 1985, Congress passed amendments to the act which gave the military authority to stop, search and arrest suspected smugglers anywhere on the world seas. The amendment's sponsor, U.S. Rep. Charles Bennett (D-Fla.), whose son died of an overdose of Valium in 1977, said he sponsored the amendment because "I don't want to waste my pain." He went on to describe the Posse Comitatus Act, as a "sinful, evil law."

Measures passed by the House in 1986 and by both the House and Senate in 1988 ordered the president to deploy enough military equipment and personnel to halt the penetration of U.S. borders by aircraft or vessels carrying narcotics, within 30 days. The bill gave DoD 45 days after deployment to "substantially halt" the drug flow.

Opposition to the military's involvement has come from a variety of sources. The most significant opponent to the amendment was Casper Weinberger, secretary of defense under President Ronald Reagan. Weinberger said in a letter to Congress the amendment would break down "the historic separation between military and civilian spheres of activity," which he described as "one of the most fundamental principles of American democracy." The defense secretary said, "We strongly oppose the extension of civilian police powers to our military forces."

Since the amendments to the Posse Comitatus Act, the military has played an increasingly important role in drug enforcement. In 1990, the military was allocated $1.2 billion for the drug war. The military has by law now been designated the lead agency in drug interdiction and eradication. It has loaned equipment to civilian authorities, used AWACS and E-2C radar planes for surveillance, and, during the 1985 marijuana harvest, Navy and Coast Guard vessels blockaded the Colombian coast. Even before the invasion of Panama, the United States had sent troops into Bolivia and Peru.

A secret directive, signed by President Reagan on April 8, 1986, and announced by then-Vice President George Bush on June 7, defined the drug trade as "a national security concern" and authorized expanded military support to the war on drugs. One month later, Operation Blast Furnace was announced and U.S. Army personnel and equipment entered foreign soil to fight the war on drugs. The operation also involved the deployment of 170 U.S. military personnel, six UH-60 Blackhawk helicopters and a Hercules C-130 cargo plane carrying trucks, jeeps, radio equipment and field gear to Bolivia's Chaparé region for a four-month mission. In addition the operation included raids on suspected cocaine laboratories by DEA agents and Bolivian anti-drug forces, known as "The Leopards." This major U.S. initiative produced a temporary decline in cocaine production but made no significant seizures of cocaine, supplies or suspects. As soon as the four-month operation ended, coca prices resumed their normal level.

In 1988, the military began Operation Snowcap, a long-term U.S. presence in the coca growing regions of the Andean mountains of Peru and Bolivia. The military provided support for U.S. helicopter strikes by DEA agents and local forces against drug laboratories. Hand-picked teams of U.S. Special Forces personnel provide training to local military and police forces in counterinsurgency and small-unit tactics.

Secretary of Defense Cheney has differed with his predecessors — Weinberger in particular — on the proper role of the military in the enforcement of drug laws. On Sept. 18, 1988, Cheney issued a directive to all U.S. military commanders, ordering them to develop plans for a major campaign in the drug war. He declared

Total Drug Arrests in the 80's

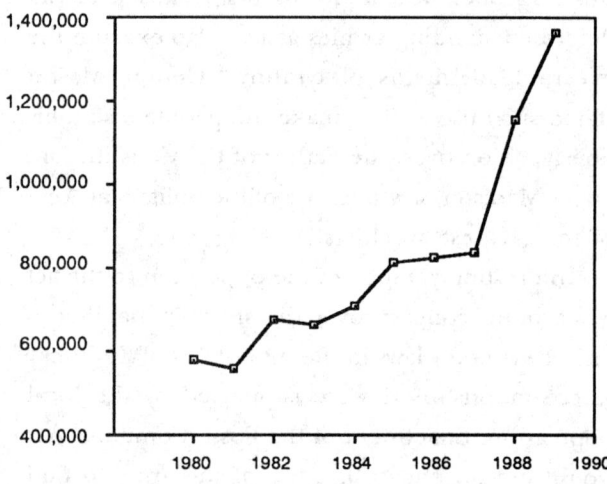

Source: FBI *Uniform Crime Reports*.

that the drug war was "a high priority" and that the Defense Department "will assist in the attack of illegal drugs at the source."

Under Cheney's administration the DoD has taken on a more aggressive role in drug enforcement. Among the activities that occurred under his administration are: the invasion of Panama justified by the need to bring Manuel Noriega to the United States to face drug charges; the sending of Army Special Forces to Bolivia and Peru, along with 100 civilians and at least 50 Green Berets working under "Operation Snowcap" in Peru and 60 to 100 military specialists in Colombia; the use of AWACS to monitor air traffic in the Andean Region; and the sending of a flotilla to the Colombian coast.

Vietnam Analogy

It is always dangerous to mention the Vietnam War in discussion of current policy because of the powerful emotions raised by that difficult period in American history. However, it is an analogy that is inescapable when the increasing involvement of the armed forces in the drug war is discussed. There are so many similarities that a comparison with the Vietnam experience must be considered.

U.S. troops are faced with a very complex situation. In September of 1989 Peruvian drug lords communicated a threat to U.S. personnel by sending 20 headless corpses floating down the Huallaga River past a U.S. Special Forces base in the heart of Peru's coca-growing territory. In early 1989 the United States had to suspend Operation Snowcap, a DEA and Green Beret military presence in the Upper Huallaga Valley of the Andean mountains, because safety of U.S. personnel could not be ensured. In April 1990, while Peruvians used M-60 machine guns, Huey Helicopter gunships were flown by U.S. pilots, in a fierce two-hour firefight with guerillas supporting the coca growers. The 30 American drug warriors and 500 Peruvians were defending the U.S. base at Santa Lucia in the Upper Huallaga Valley against the Shining Path guerillas.

Peruvian drug lords communicated a threat to U.S. personnel by sending 20 headless corpses floating down the Huallaga River past a U.S. Special Forces base.

By providing housing and sports facilities to the urban and rural poor, the drug traffickers have succeeded in gaining some level of popular support. Guerrilla forces, which are trying to overthrow their governments for cultural, political and economic reasons, are engaged in civil wars in both Peru and Colombia. At times, tenuous alliances, or "marriages of convenience," may take place between drug traffickers and guerillas, but the two are actually ideologically opposed. While the U.S. media portrays the Colombian conflict as one between drug traffickers and the government, the situation is much more complex. Indeed, presidential candidates, judges, police, prosecutors, reporters and civilians all have been assassinated. Since 1980 the death count in Colombia has reached over 17,000, and estimates in Peru were just as high. Yet the main agents of murder are not drug traffickers or guerrillas, but right-wing paramilitary death squads. These death squads are comprised, in part, of drug traffickers, in addition to other economic elites (e.g., large landowners) and members of the Colombian security (military and police) forces.

The countries in the Andean region are widely corrupted by drug money. Even before the war begins in earnest, local governments have been compromised by the so-called enemy. In addition, the governments are not trusted by their own people because the governments have historically abused the human rights of their citizens. Thus, the U.S. government is allying itself with governments that do not enjoy the safety of the hearts and minds of their people.

The drug war, like the Vietnam War, is being fought in difficult jungle terrain, making it impossible for normal military tactics to be successful. Opposition forces do not find it difficult to resist or evade attack. Moreover, the U.S. is entering into a jungle quagmire that could encompass much more land mass than Southeast Asia. Vietnam and Cambodia are 195,000 total square miles. The square miles of Bolivia, Colombia and Peru total over six times that: 1.3 million square miles. Now that cocaine production is spreading to Brazil, one can add 3.2 million square miles to that figure.

While the similarities with Vietnam are forboding, the differences may be even more important. Unlike Vietnam, this is a war being financed, on both sides, by American dollars. Drug consumers in the U.S. spend billions of dollars for drugs from the cartels. At the same time, the U.S. government gives hundreds of millions to the Colombian government to fight the cartels.

The War at Home

The National Guard has been involved in drug enforcement throughout the 1980s. The role initially was to work in marijuana aerial surveillance and eradication programs. But as the drug war has escalated the Guard has become involved in a variety of tasks including monitoring the Mexican border, assisting local police in processing and analyzing intelligence information and providing radar support in the Caribbean. The Guard is playing a growing role in many aspects of domestic drug enforcement.

Active duty federal troops were used for the first time in history during Operation Greensweep in northern California in July 1990 and Operation Ghost Dancer in Oregon in August 1990. Declarations made by people living in the areas under siege describe living in a war zone where rights are routinely violated. As a result of this activity the Drug Policy Foundation filed *Drug Policy Foundation v. William Bennett*, No. C-90-2278FMS (U.S. District Court for the Northern District of California). The lawsuit alleges a variety of constitutional and statutory violations.

Our local police have come to be more and more like armed forces. It is as if they are acting with martial law authority, even though martial law has not been declared. The Los Angeles police have used a tank to attack crack houses. In Northern California, the Campaign Against Marijuana Planting, has roadblocked entire towns, used helicopters to harass local residents and trespassed onto private lands without search warrants. In Chicago, police have locked the doors of housing projects and conducted house to house warrantless searches. In suburban Fairfax, Virginia, as in many parts of the United States, every drug search warrant is served by a SWAT team.

Unfortunately, the courts have allowed this increasing militarization. The U.S. Supreme Court has upheld warrantless helicopter searches for marijuana growing inside a greenhouse, allowed police to stop, detain, and question travelers who fit a broad set of characteristics resembling drug traffickers, and have allowed police to use dogs to search travellers' luggage without probable cause.

In addition, police may search boats on inland waterways without probable cause, obtain search warrants based on anonymous tips, ignore "no trespassing" signs and barbed wire fences and enter private property without search warrants. When it comes to enforcing the drug laws police have broad powers resembling martial law.

Even the court system is taking on the characteristics of wartime courts. The Congress has limited the constitutional right to bail, authorized seizure of assets before conviction, required harsh mandatory sentences, limited appeal rights and is now talking of limiting habeus corpus. Courts have allowed lawyers to be subpoenaed to testify against their clients before grand juries, allowed seizure of assets to be used to pay an accused's legal fees, and allowed courts to prosecute foreigners kidnapped abroad or even brought to our courts after an invasion.

When Will We Learn The Lesson Of Ayatollah Khalkhali?*

Drug Czar William Bennett and other top federal officials are giving consideration to ideas for kidnapping or assassinating major foreign drug traffickers. Conceivably, such actions might also be directed against kingpins on American soil.

Even beheading has been discussed. On "Larry King Live," June 15, 1989, a caller to the national cable television show suggested to Mr. Bennett, "Behead the damned drug dealers." He replied, "I mean, what the caller suggests is morally plausible. Legally, it's difficult.... But...somebody selling drugs to a kid? Morally, I don't have any problem with

---

* Arnold S. Trebach, "When Will We Learn The Lesson of Ayatollah Khalkhali?" *The Drug Policy Letter*, July/August 1989, p.1.

that at all." Mr. Bennett reiterated his position the next day in a written statement that told drug dealers, "You deserve to die."

Many Washington experts look upon all of these assassination and beheading stories as non-stories; humorous, weird, but not worthy of serious comment. Yet, these are not jokes. Given our history and current drug war hysteria, some of these ideas could soon be implemented. Even official consideration of these ideas documents how continued pursuit of the current drug war and harsh enforcement of prohibition will destroy much that is precious about the great American experiment in democracy and decency. The essence of the democratic approach is to deal with wrenching social problems in a balanced, non-violent fashion that preserves the constitutional freedoms of all Americans, even the most despised ones.

On too many occasions throughout our history, however, the American government and people have lost their collective heads, egged on by demagogues in power, and violated that decent democratic credo. In every case, extreme actions were taken supposedly to preserve the nation from destruction. In many of the past cases — for example, the internment of loyal Japanese-Americans during World War II and the destroying of lives and reputations by McCarthyism during the 50s — it later became clear that the actions were morally wrong, illegal, and unnecessary. Fortunately, none of those past excesses ever involved a systematic campaign of assassinations and kidnapping during peacetime.

Meddlesome Legal Issue: Murder Is Murder

Under virtually all applicable law — that of the United States, most foreign nations, and international legal codes — the harsh actions being considered are illegal. Killings and kidnappings carried out by government officials, or at their direction, remain just that, killings and kidnappings. The fact that otherwise illegal acts are carried out in the name of a government or of a noble cause, as Oliver North has discovered, does not make them legal. Indeed, we are quick to label violent acts of the nature we are now contemplating as state-sponsored terrorism when carried out by countries we do not like.

The law of civilized nations for centuries has provided for two broad situations in which killings were legal. First, when a war had been formally declared or when a condition of open hostilities had existed between two nations. Second, Article 51 of the U.N. Charter confirms "the inherent right of individual or collective self-defense if an armed attack occurs against a Member of the United Nations...." It is this ancient right of nations that is now being invoked by hard-line legal experts, such as Maj. Gen. Hugh Overholt, the U.S. Army Judge Advocate General, to justify the killing of terrorist leaders wherever they may be found. The same logic is being applied by federal drug war zealots to major drug traffickers.

The self-defense argument posits that since President Reagan declared drug trafficking to be a threat to the national security of the country, killing or kidnapping major drug dealers, or "narcoterrorists," is justified under Article 51. The argument is, in a word, preposterous. In its essential core, the activity of drug sellers is to provide wanted products to willing buyers. It is doubtful that an impartial court would find that Article 51 applies. If, however, American officials or their agents ignore these cautions and operate in foreign countries under this new, tortured doctrine of international law, other nations could use it to legitimately send their hit squads to American soil for the purpose of "taking out" those American officials involved in the initial assaults. The narcoterrorists would also retaliate using the law of the jungle as justification.

Capital Punishment for Drug Dealers

Assume, however, that we are somehow, magically able to surmount all of the legal questions, that we grant the most committed drug warriors their fondest hopes and that we cow the American people and the world into accepting a tough new legal order providing the most severe punishment for drug dealers and users. What then?

There is little in the criminological history of the world to suggest that any form of capital punishment would have any significant effect on the use and abuse of drugs in the general society over the long haul. Even for murder cases, many advanced nations have concluded that capital punishment has no documented impact on the crime rate and demeans the society that uses it. Thus, capital punishment has been written out of their laws.

The United States retains capital punishment for murder and treason. The United States also has had legal provisions on occasion during this century providing for execution in cases of drug trafficking, but no such execution has ever taken place within our borders. No federal or state law now provides for any form of execution in cases of simple drug trafficking, as distinguished from homicides committed in the course of drug trafficking. A review of the laws and the legal literature suggests that no advanced, democratic country has the death penalty in drug trafficking cases today. Only 12 countries clearly do so: Algeria, Burma, China, Cuba, Egypt, Guinea, Iran, Malaysia, Singapore, Taiwan, Thailand and Saudi Arabia. Because the laws are not always clear, even this list is based upon some conjecture and other countries could probably be included.

Also unclear from the evidence is the impact of capital punishment in drug trafficking cases on the use of drugs in these nations. Indeed, there is much evidence that while highly publicized executions sometimes seemed to slow down drug activity temporarily, the usual pattern was that executions took place side-by-side with much trafficking and use. For example, admirers of China have claimed that in the late 40s a combination of the revolutionary spirit and mass executions of narcotic addicts stamped out the drug problem. While there may well have been a downturn in use, there have been persistent reports in recent years from Chinese government sources of trafficking through China and of executions for both drug sales and possession.

Many committed drug warriors have argued nevertheless that the brutal methods, for the most part, worked in China and that it is time for America to get just as brutal with drug dealers and users. However, in light of recent events, with mass upheavals against the dictators who rule the country and public executions, does any drug war zealot now want to argue that their system "worked" even in regard to controlling drugs?

> ### The Difficulties of Ayatollahs and Czars
>
> "If we wanted to kill everybody who had five grams of heroin, we'd have to kill 5,000 people, and this would be difficult."
> Ayatollah Sadegh Khalkhali, Tehran, July 8, 1980
>
> "Legally, it's difficult...But...somebody selling drugs to a kid? Morally, I don't have any problems with that at all."
> Drug Czar William Bennett, Washington, June 15, 1989, in response to a suggestion that drug dealers be beheaded

The Lesson of Ayatollah Khalkhali

It is, of course, difficult to obtain a clear picture of what is actually going on in any area of Chinese life. Somewhat more obvious is The Lesson of Ayatollah Khalkhali. With the advent of the Iranian revolution in the late 70s, it was ironic that heroin use boomed in the midst of Moslem fundamentalism. So did the use of other drugs, including marijuana and hashish. Millions of users were reported in the press. By the summer of 1980, officials of the revolutionary government responded to the growing crisis with some of the harshest actions in the history of drug control. They took action which their counterparts in western nations sometimes dream about on bad days.

The roving executioner of the revolution, Ayatollah Sadegh Khalkhali, sent out his hit squads, picked alleged drug traffickers and users off the streets, presided at brief trials, shouted "I shall exterminate you vermin!" and ordered summary executions that often were carried out within minutes. During a seven-week period, 176 people were executed for drug offenses, many shot standing near neighborhood walls where they had been caught.

Yet, drug trafficking and use flourished. The Ayatollah was criticized by his peers for not being effective enough in controlling the drug problem. On July 8, 1980, at a press conference, he defensively explained that there were practical limits even to his direct methods of dealing with drugs: "If we wanted to kill everybody who had five grams of heroin, we'd have to kill 5,000 people, and this would be difficult."

That is The Lesson of Ayatollah Khalkhali. Vast multitudes of Iranian citizens continued to violate the drug laws even in the face of immediate death sentences. Few national leaders or drug experts seemed to have learned this lesson.

Malaysian Model: Death and Detention

Certainly, Malaysian leaders have not learned the lesson. It is important to look at that nation because the Malaysian model for controlling drugs is cited time after time by drug war supporters in America. Malaysia plays an active role in promoting tough international campaigns against drugs. There is active cooperation between Malaysian police and the U.S. Drug Enforcement Administration. In 1985, Dr. Siti Hasmah, the prime minister's wife, participated in Mrs. Reagan's First Ladies Anti-Drug Conference in the United States.

Malaysia's drug laws are among the harshest in the world. Their Dangerous Drugs Act of 1975 demands a mandatory death sentence for drug trafficking. Mere possession of small amounts of drugs — 15 grams of heroin or morphine, 200 grams of marijuana — can and has put a noose around a human neck on the presumption that the drugs were being held for sale. From the beginning of 1975 through September 1988, 73 people were hanged for violation of the drug laws. (On a proportional basis, this would have been equivalent to at least 1,100 executions in the United States.) One hundred thirty-six drug offenders were awaiting execution on death row at the end of September, 1988.

A 1985 legal amendment allows the government to order two-year detentions without trial of persons suspected of being drug traffickers. At the end of 1988, the government had 894 people under such detention. A new law in 1988 provides for civil procedures to seize assets of suspected drug traffickers, apparently in imitation of American law.

Despite all of these draconian measures, official reports state that the use and abuse of drugs keeps rising. There was comparatively little documented drug abuse during the early 70s. By the early 80s, however, it was reported that at least 300,000 youth in this small country of approximately 16.5 million people were using drugs during school days. (They were not necessarily addicts.) The number of hard drug addicts was placed at 61,334, 80 percent of whom were men below 30 years of age. By 1988, Malaysian government experts estimated 90,000-100,000 active registered drug addicts; U.S. State Department experts estimated the total number of addicts in the society at 250,000, most on heroin and engaged in crime to support their habits.

This is not meant to pick on Malaysia or any country with drug troubles. Indeed, Malaysia is probably typical of many other nations which are less open and honest about providing information to the outside world. Yet, Malaysia must look anew at its drug policies which seem so well intentioned and yet so counterproductive.

And the United States must also look closely at the Malaysian model. If the hardliners in the Bush administration continue to receive encouragement from the president, the Congress and the American people, by the end of the century we will look like an expanded version of Malaysia. Perhaps the major difference will be that instead of the hangman's noose, the symbol of our modern drug control effort will be the headsman's axe.

Keep The Troops In The Barracks*

America is in real danger of turning its metaphorical "war on drugs" into a bloody reality. With the failure of every other enforcement effort, from crop eradication through border interdiction to street-level policing, a growing chorus of influential Washington policy makers is urging the ultimate escalation — sending U.S. troops to Latin America to battle traffickers.

The calls for military intervention are coming fast and furiously from Congress, where frustrated members from all points on the ideological spectrum share a conviction that only armed force will rid America of drugs. "We should engage in joint military and paramilitary operations, with congressional approval, including helicopter and air strikes on cocaine fields," Sen. John Kerry (D.-Mass.) told a Tufts University audience this year. Defending a similar proposal, Rep. Charles Rangel (D.-N.Y.), chairman of the House narcotics committee, said, "I have deeper commitment to fighting the drug traffickers than I did the North Koreans." Sen. William Cohen (R.-Maine) has argued that the only solution is to "go to the source," even if that means "taking out the machine-gun nest with troops."

Hit Drug Labs

Key officials in the Bush administration favor a similar approach. Drug czar William Bennett privately advocates the use of special operations forces to hit foreign drug labs and shipment centers. A National Security Council task force reportedly will recommend to President Bush that he greatly step up the military's role in fighting drugs overseas, including a possible combat role in fighting drugs overseas. Mr. Bush will be receptive: He told the Veterans of Foreign Wars in March that drugs represent "a threat no less real than the adversaries you have battled" and vowed to "combat drug abuse with...our nation's armed forces."

The major source of bureaucratic resistance to this groundswell is the Pentagon itself, which doubts whether the drug war is winnable and fears becoming embroiled in an endless, ill-defined commitment that detracts from its traditional mission.

The military has good reason to resist this call to arms. Given how many countries produce drugs, including the U.S. itself, the chances of winning are small compared to the likelihood of tearing apart the social and political fabric of countries in which the military intervenes.

The first problem for U.S. anti-drug expeditionary forces will be defining the enemy. Simply shooting a few known kingpins in Medellin wouldn't dry up the supply of either drugs or criminal entrepreneurs willing to run them across borders. Peasant growers and traffickers don't wear uniforms. Nor do they belong to a single, defined organization that can be forced to surrender. "There is a perfect textbook example of guerrilla warfare," Michael Perez, a Drug Enforcement Agency agent stationed in Bolivia, was quoted as saying earlier this year. "You never know who's who — who's a good guy and who's a bad guy."

U.S. troops would have to treat entire sectors of Latin American society as potential foes. More than half a million Bolivians live off the profits of coca and cocaine production. Tens of thousands of peasant cultivators are tightly organized into militant unions with powerful links to national worker organizations. Their roadblocks, mass demonstrations, strikes and other non-violent tactics have paralyzed government efforts to eradicate coca planting. Trying to conquer them with force would be no easy feat.

---
* Jonathan Marshall, "In the War on Drugs, Keep the Troops in the Barracks," *The Wall Street Journal*, July 27, 1989, p. A10.

To complicate matters, U.S. troops wouldn't know who their friends are, either. Corruption is so endemic in the drug-supplier nations that anyone up to presidents and army chiefs of staff can be on the traffickers' payroll. In Colombia, according to a recent Bogota television news report, traffickers appear to "have access to practically all confidential government information, such as minutes of cabinet meetings." The corruption ensures that the kingpins enjoy protection even as they use the local police and military to knock off upstart competitors.

Colombia, at least, has never been taken over entirely by the traffickers. Bolivia was, in 1980, during the famous "cocaine coup." The situation is not much better now that the corrupt generals and colonels no longer rule. Said a former American adviser to the country's narcotics police to an *Atlantic Monthly* writer, "I have to tell you I think that 100 percent of the Bolivian enforcement structure was corrupted." After the U.S. sent troops to Bolivia in 1986 — the model for current interventionist proposals — a Bolivian congressional investigation accused the interior minister who oversaw the whole operation of taking payoffs to protect the major drug lords.

Peru is no better. A recent staff report by the House Committee on Foreign Affairs observes that "corruption in all segments of the Peruvian government continues to impede meaningful anti-narcotics efforts."

Even honest segments of these societies loudly protest the introduction of U.S. forces in the drug war. The Latin allergy to anything smacking of "Yankee imperialism" ties the hands of even the most sympathetic leaders. The one exception to that rule is the 1986 U.S. anti-drug raid in Bolivia which damaged the otherwise-high popularity of President Victor Paz Estensoro's government. Today, Bolivian leaders state emphatically they will never permit such an operation again.

Latin leaders know that escalating the drug war risks not only their political future, but their nation's survival. In Peru, the army frankly confesses the reasons for its reluctance to take on the traffickers at the same time as it fights the fanatical Shining Path guerrillas. It needs popular support to fight terrorism — and it can't retain popular support if it tries to eradicate coca.

Unlike traditional counterinsurgency, which relies on winning the loyalty of peasants and isolating radical guerrilla forces, a military campaign

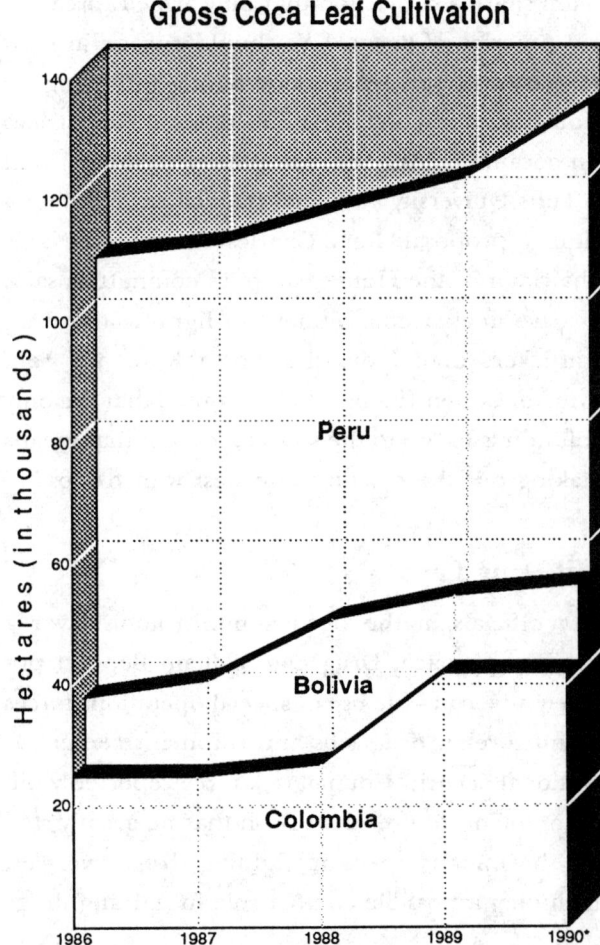

Source: International Narcotics Control Strategy Report, U.S. Department of State, March 1990
* projected

against the peasant economy in the Andean states could unite the entire rural population against the intruders. "It would create another Vietnam or another Central America," says Edmundo Morales, author of *Cocaine: The White Gold Rush in Peru.* Already, adds Peruvian journalist Gustavo Gorriti, "the Shining Path guerrillas have been able to maneuver both the Peruvian government and the Americans into doing exactly what they wanted. They have made the fight against eradication and punitive raids from police and helicopter-borne units piloted by Americans the cause to unite most of [the peasants]. Any kind of escalation of the current commitment will play nicely into their hands."

The Shining Path, although not yet successful at penetrating Bolivia, maintains strongholds on the border between the two nations. Its proximity may fuel concerns of the Bolivian government, expressed in a 1986 study, that the response of traffickers to military attack might result in "the emergence of a new and deadly guerrilla movement joining extremists, destitute peasants and drug traffickers."

"Narco-Terrorists"

Some proponents of military intervention ignore this danger by assuming traffickers, guerrilla insurgents and terrorists are one and the same — "narco-guerrillas" or "narco-terrorists" — despite their vastly different social and political agendas. Groups like the Shining Path derive some income from drug taxes but ultimately aim to impose a puritanical communist regime; most traffickers have no problem with democracy or capitalism as long as they are left alone. In Colombia as well as Peru, traffickers and guerrillas have waged bloody vendettas for control of territory. Yet, a foreign invasion that targets them both is likely to bring them together.

As long as U.S. demand for drugs swamps Latin American societies with narco-dollars, military intervention will succeed no better than any of the other failed strategies that have attempted to eliminate the supply at its source. Unlike them, however, it will risk substantial numbers of American lives abroad on an open-ended, exceedingly dangerous mission. Worse, it promises to inflame urban nationalism and peasant radicalism, social forces that together could destroy the fragile governments of any cooperating countries. So far no South American country has volunteered to commit suicide for the sake for the sake of the U.S.'s frustrated drug warriors. North Americans should be glad they haven't.

Overkill In Panama[*]

On the same day the United States invaded Panama last December, the Lithuanian Communist Party declared its independence from the overall Soviet party. In an article on Dec. 22, 1989, I pointed out that the news from Lithuania had been "little noticed among the headlines" about Panama.

In the same article, President Bush was urged to provide quick and "convincing evidence" in support of a major reason he had given for the invasion — "eminent danger to the 35,000 American citizens in Panama" from the government controlled by Manuel Antonio Noriega.

As usual, both in the press and in the public mind, the dramatic use of armed force in Panama was rewarded with greater attention (and an inflated poll standing for Mr. Bush) than were nonviolent and faraway political events. But more than three months later, it's clear that the first step in Lithuania's movement for national independence was of more lasting importance than any of the

---
[*] Tom Wicker, "Overkill in Panama," *The New York Times*, April 5, 1990, p. A29.

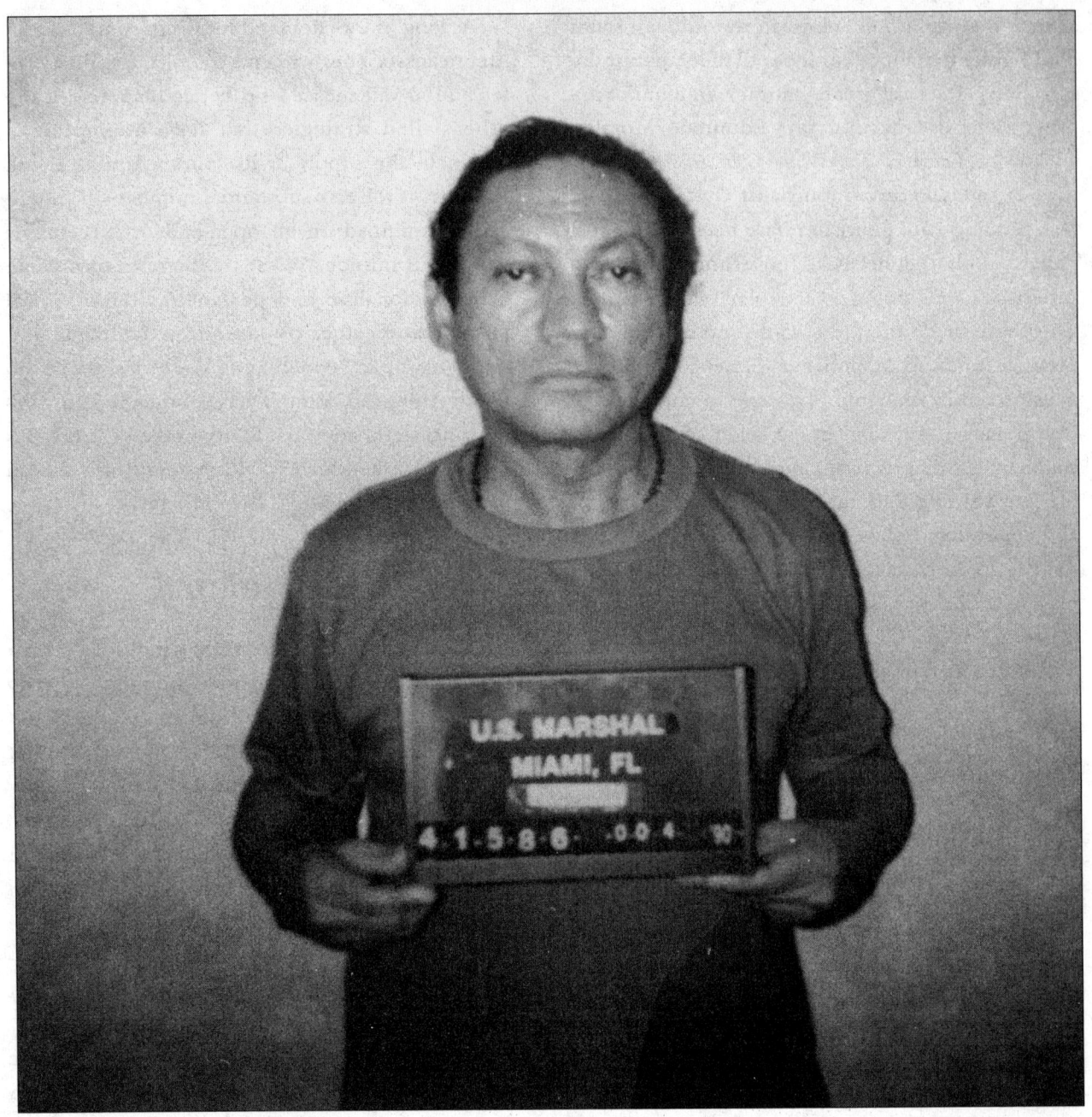

The Leader of Panama in U.S. Custody

sins and threats of General Noriega.

It's not so widely realized that Mr. Bush has not yet provided the evidence to prove his claim of "eminent danger" to Americans in Panama. In the continued absence of such evidence, or any White House effort to provide it, it's reasonable to conclude that there isn't any, or not much.

The trigger for the invasion was the killing of a single U.S. soldier while he was running a Panamanian roadblock in a restricted zone. That was deplorable but insufficient cause either to envision a real threat to the lives of 35,000 other Americans, or to warrant a costly military invasion of a sovereign nation.

Mr. Bush and administration spokesmen also spoke of danger to the Panama Canal. But Gen. Colin Powell, the chairman of the Joint Chiefs of Staff, has pointed out that 14,000 U.S. troops, a force "quite adequate" to defend the canal from General Noriega, were in Panama *before* the invasion. That force, on the face of it, also seems adequate to the defense of all American residents against whatever threat existed.

Nor was the operation a necessary anti-drug action. Even if General Noriega was up to his neck in illicit drug traffic as late as 1989, the huge dollar cost of a military operation involving 24,000 troops would have been better devoted to providing drug treatment slots in the United States. Now additional millions must be spent to make up for economic losses inflicted on Panama by the United States during and before the invasion.

No wonder, then, that William Webster, the director of Central Intelligence, has said that "we made a mistake in overemphasizing the importance of Noriega." And no wonder that lawyers for the dictator charge that Operation Just Cause — the ludicrous code name for the invasion — was "outrageous" and "the first time the United States has invaded a country and leveled it to arrest one man."

Such drastic "justice," they might have said, was never considered in the cases of the brutal Anastasio Somoza of Nicaragua, or any of the several murderous generals who have ruled Guatemala, or Papa and Baby Doc Duvalier in Haiti.

General Noriega's lawyers further claim that because of these circumstances all charges against him ought to be dismissed. But an illegal arrest — which is essentially what the defense contends the general suffered — has never been grounds for dropping charges against a defendant; and recently the Supreme Court ruled that the U.S. Constitution does not protect a foreigner against the actions of U.S. agents in a foreign country.

Sending 24,000 troops to bag Manuel Noriega nevertheless is likely to stand in the history of overkill higher even than Ronald Reagan's Grenada operation. This long after the invasion, for example, Washington is not able to state with any certainty how many Panamanian citizens died; some estimates range into the thousands and most of them substantially exceed the U.S. death count — 202 civilians and 314 soldiers.

Even taking the latter figures at face value, and adding the 23 American soldiers killed in the invasion, 539 people lost their lives as the primary human cost of putting handcuffs on one thug. But when a defense lawyer referred to "indiscriminate" U.S. firepower, Judge William M. Hoeveler protested that "a war was going on — why do you say it was indiscriminate?"

He did not say what word would have been better, or how a ham-fisted exercise in executive muscle-flexing could be distinguished as a war.

Waging War On America's Poor[*]

There is a new battlefront in the war on drugs — housing. U.S. Secretary of Housing and Urban Development Jack Kemp has promised a national public housing policy that will include house-to-house searches, identification cards and eviction of subsidized housing residents.

This is one more example of the new drug war strategy of punishment without reliance on the criminal law. Just as workers are being subjected to drug testing and thereby being punished, and boat owners are having boats seized through civil forfeiture, the housing attack results in punishment without the protections of the criminal justice system. This new strategy further highlights the drug war's destruction of constitutional protections and the trend toward creating a conflict between rich and poor, white and black in the war on drugs.

House-to-House Searches in Chicago

The most aggressive campaign has been in the public housing projects in Chicago. The Chicago Housing Authority has instituted "Operation Clean Sweep," which includes locking all the exits to a building and conducting unannounced, warrantless sweep searches of tenants and their guests. Under the guise of housing inspections police officers and security personnel have "inspected" dresser drawers, closets, bedding, personal items, kitchen cabinets, refrigerators, medicine cabinets and even Christmas presents of residents.

After the searches — that is what the "inspections" really are — the buildings are fenced in with security grates, and residents are required to present identification cards to security personnel. Guests cannot stay past midnight without special passes and security guards are stationed at building entrances 24 hours a day.

The best way to describe the events is through the eyes of some of the people living there. The following are some of the allegations contained in a lawsuit filed by the American Civil Liberties Union on behalf of tenants in the buildings:

- Rose Summaries was out of the building, but her brother was visiting her apartment. When he tried to leave to go to a job interview, he discovered that the doors to the outside had been barricaded and were being guarded by police officers. He was told he could not leave until his sister's apartment was searched and if he tried he would be arrested. Hours later, after her apartment was searched by four police and two housing officials, he was finally told he could leave. But he had already missed his job interview.
- Rose Summaries' daughter did not arrive home from school on time. When she was half an hour late, Ms. Summaries went to look for her. She discovered her daughter was standing outside in the December cold unable to return home because police officers would not let her in without a picture ID.
- Rose Summaries' sister planned to visit for Christmas with her two children. She planned to stay with Ms. Summaries because she could not afford a hotel. Housing authority officials told her that this would not be allowed because she could not have guests in her apartment after midnight.
- Jane Doe 1 was babysitting in her apartment for the three children of her sister at 11:55 p.m. Her sister was working until 2 a.m. A housing authority official knocked on the door and demanded that the children leave the building by midnight. Jane Doe 1 had to find

---

[*] Kevin B. Zeese, "Housing: The New Battleground in the War on Drugs," *The Drug Policy Letter*, July/August 1989, p. 4.

someone else to take the children at midnight.

- Jane Doe 2 lives in an apartment with her three children. A group of police and housing officers entered her apartment and searched under the cushions of the couch and inside the freezer. The officers picked the lock on her bedroom door and searched the room, including clothes in her dresser drawer. Later that day, Jane Doe 2 was returning to her apartment. Upon entering her building, police subjected her to a personal search, including her bags in which she was carrying Christmas presents.
- John Doe does not live in CHA housing but on weekends he visits his elderly parents, staying overnight to assist them and provide security. Police officers have stopped him on the street, told him he cannot stay overnight, and threatened him with arrest.

Mass Evictions in Washington

On May 16 an elite force of 50 black-uniformed U.S. Marshals, members of the Special Operations Group, met at a military base in Washington, D.C., to finalize plans to evict people from 300 apartments. Specially trained to handle civil disturbances and anti-terrorist strikes, the Marshals carried assault rifles and were joined by 20 D.C. police officers.

By the end of the day tenants had been evicted from 50 properties. The first day of raids resulted in three drug seizures, $250 worth of heroin, $1,000 worth of crack and a small amount of cocaine. By the end of the week-long strike the force had made 209 evictions.

The tenants were chosen for eviction because of alleged drug dealing. Marshalls reviewed 1,800 pending evictions, comparing them to information from landlords and the D.C. police to find properties suspected of drug dealing. There was not a high degree of confidence in the likelihood of finding drugs. As the assistant director of operations told *The Washington Post*, "This is a crapshoot."

As the evictions progressed there became more doubts. At one apartment there was confusion about the apartment number. When the eviction was completed and the Marshals left, the drug dealers were in the hall and tenants said: "Everybody here thinks they got the wrong apartment." In many cases tenants proclaimed they were fighting with their landlords about repairs and that was the cause of the rent dispute. The same landlords were the source of allegations about drugs.

There were also criticisms about the way the victims were handled. At least five evicted families, with a total of 15 children, turned up at the District's Department of Human Services pleading for assistance. D.C. Council Member H.R. Crawford said, "Someone should have been there to help those children. I don't like seeing babies being put out crying." Another complaint was that the evictions were allowed to proceed in pouring rain. Guidelines for evictions usually require suspension when there is a 50 percent chance of rain.

A National Housing Drug War Strategy

The D.C. and Chicago plans are the models for a national housing strategy. Secretary Kemp testified on May 15, before a subcommittee of the Senate Appropriations Committee that he wants to use recently appropriated housing operating subsidies "to implement local programs such as...'Clean Sweep' in Chicago." This could require huge sums across the nation; Chicago authorities report that securing one building cost up to $200,000.

At an earlier hearing Kemp described the Clean Sweep program with admiration:

"In Chicago I met an innovative public housing authority director, Vince Lane, who has developed Operation Clean Sweep. Vince has worked with the police to search every unit from the top to the bottom of the building and those who didn't belong were evicted. A security system was implemented in projects so that no outsiders could get in and residents were identified by picture IDs."

Chicago is not alone in its overly aggressive use of police power in trying to control drugs in public housing. In New York City a 2,200 person Housing Police Force has made 30 sweeps since 1986. Twenty-one officers work directly with the police department's Organized Crime Control Bureau and 12 officers are assigned to the Tactical Narcotics Team. New Orleans has created "drug-free zones," set up an urban squad specially trained to fight drugs, appointed a housing authority drug czar, issued tenant ID cards, and has a 24-hour hotline for anonymous tips. Orlando, Fla., has established three high-profile police substations in three housing projects, painted the police logo on the outside wall, and parked police cruisers at the buildings. In New Haven, Conn., apartments are used for sting operations and police arrest visitors for trespassing. Charleston, S.C., has erected an eight-foot high brick and iron fence around the housing complex.

Mr. Kemp has also moved to ease eviction proceedings. After a police officer was killed in a housing project in Alexandria, Va., it became a test case for eased eviction procedures. Drug-related evictions are consistent with the Anti-Drug Abuse Act of 1988, 21 U.S.C. 581 (a) (7), which permit evictions even if a mere guest of a public housing tenant is arrested for a drug-related crime.

The first test case of new, streamlined eviction procedures occurred on April 17, 1989, in Alexandria. With television crews recording the event for posterity, two families were evicted. The next day a photograph of Evalena Durham adorned the front page of *The Arlington (Va.) Journal.* She was surrounded by piles of her personal effects and sat clutching a folded American flag given to her 12 years earlier at the funeral of her husband, an Army veteran.

What to Do About Drugs in Public Housing

There is a significant drug and crime problem in public housing. A survey conducted by HUD this February reported 52 percent of projects in the eastern half of the country and 37 percent in the western half had drug problems.

Rather than repressive, police-state measures, we must consider more rational and effective approaches. For example, we should begin to stitch back together the safety net that had been shredded during the Reagan era. Public housing reached its current debilitated condition after years of neglect.

We should also emphasize positive steps that can be taken in public housing. In Omaha, Neb., the housing authority is attempting to promote a better life and dignity for tenants. The authority emphasizes education as the key to escaping poverty. It has created an award of a $100 savings bond for a year's perfect attendance in school. A self-help foundation of the housing authority has created a scholarship to three of Omaha's colleges. Five study centers have been established in the projects so students can get extra individual instruction.

We must find ways to get people out of public housing and integrated into society so that all of the poor are not grouped together in crime-infested, substandard shelters. Perhaps we should have a goal of ending public housing and instead moving toward integrated, subsidized housing.

House-to-house searches are not new. They have already failed in U.S. history. King George II approved Writs of Assistance in the 1750s authorizing warrantless searches for contraband. The writs were challenged in Massachusetts in 1761. Attorney James Otis declared that the writs were repugnant to the Magna Carta and fundamental principles of law which recognized the sanctity of the home. He argued they were "the worst instrument of arbitrary power, the most destructive of English liberty, and the fundamental principles of law, that ever was found in an English law book" since they placed "the liberty of every man in the hands of every petty officer." While the king's courts upheld the legality of the Writs of Assistance a youthful spectator in the courtroom, John Adams, wrote about Otis' eloquent argument: "Then and there the child Independence was born."

To prevent these kinds of abuses from ever happening again, the Founders created prohibitions against mass searches in the Constitution. Nothing in the Constitution has ever stated that its full protection does not apply to the poor whom circumstances force to live in public housing.

Rural Citizens Under The Guns And Helicopters[*]

You wake up in the morning, to the sound of the birds in the trees, in a home you built with your own hands. The doors don't have, or need, locks. You go to sleep to the sound of the frogs down in the pond. If any vehicles pass by your property within a mile or so you'll be sure to hear their faint sounds. The only aircraft which pass by are small private planes, at heights of a few thousand feet. (The airforce no longer conducts sonic boom tests in the area because a local activist who owns an aviary got a congressman to pay attention.) In the winter it rains a lot (maybe a hundred inches). Any rain between May and October is a rarity, so water is as precious as gold, both for plants and livelihood, and for fire protection. When you travel on the roads to go to town (the main town in the area has a population of 1,500 people) it is not uncommon to see no other vehicles for maybe as long as an hour of travel time. Most folks grow their own vegetables, have at least a few fruit trees, and raise a few animals. Many people maintain a few horses for riding. A substantial number of people do not want utility company electricity (and in fact some folks have actively and successfully resisted its encroachment). Subsequently, they use electricity produced from the sun, or water wheels and once in a while from the successful use of a windmill. The absence of telephones, or presence of wireless telephones, is quite common. Alternative toilets and outhouses are as common as septic tanks. People don't make a lot of money; they work in the woods doing firewood or logging. Some are ranchers; some fish Somerville, many have service jobs. People have characteristics typical of many rural areas: a slower pace; time for introspection and family; and a sense of independence and self-reliance. People also grow marijuana.

Starting in April, small private planes get lower. They start traveling in grids; the beginning of the annual hunt for the cannabis plant is underway. Law enforcement claims they stay a thousand feet off the deck with their airplanes. Even if this is true in most instances, the sound produced is anything but tranquil, especially when the grid patterns are followed for hours on end. Law enforcement has hundreds and hundreds of thousands of acres to search in the innumerable forested valleys that make up the most publicized area of marijuana enforcement in the country. This "Emerald Triangle" consists of portions of Humboldt, Mendocino and Trinity Counties in

---

[*] Ronald M. Sinoway is a lawyer in rural Humboldt County, California. He has taken a lead role in litigating against illegal government enforcement of the drug laws in his community and in other parts of the United States.

Northern California, an area comprising a 50-mile square. On the basis of a tip, busts by the local marijuana eradication teams, sheriff's departments, or local state-led drug task force units, can occur anytime. But they usually start in April or May and continue into the summer and come late July through the end of October, the hunters arrive en masse. The helicopter, airforce, and ground troops of the Campaign Against Marijuana Planting arrive and go out on daily search and destroy missions, disrupting daily activities of people within miles of the actual operation sites. Because of the raiders, past and flagrant abuses, helicopters have been restricted; a 500-foot bubble of privacy exists over persons, vehicles and structures. Ground troops also have to be restricted as they must remain away from curtilages and houses without properly authorized warrants from a magistrate. Thus, peoples' privacy, while restricted, is not ruthlessly and callously disregarded in its entirety.

The assault takes different forms and increases. Dogs are used for sniffing vehicles that are stopped on the roads, and the "marijuana profile" gives cause for the postal service to search even a light package securely taped, if it is from a "known marijuana growing county." However, both of these tactics have had substantial problems. The last time the postal service stopped and opened some packages fitting their profile, they found nothing but ceramics, and law enforcement may soon pay a price in court for overstepping its bounds last year.

Marijuana is eradicated wherever it can be found. A court order holds six hundred-odd law enforcement officers on a scene in check until at least the end of this year. On can feel the tension as the hunters have to obey rules they think are trivial and unimportant. Like the Vietnam body count, the numbers of plants "eradicated" are exaggerated. Although no CAMP troop has ever been hurt by a grower during any raids since 1983, they come armed to the teeth and ready for the kill, just looking for the opportunity to blow another human being away.

When the helicopters swoop down, the prop wash can be felt many times on the ground. In the early days helicopters actually stopped in front of windows of homes, chased people on horseback, and even blew toilet paper out of someone's outhouse. When the marijuana eradication program began, weapons were seized indiscriminately, and road blocks were used. Although neither occur anymore after a cry was raised in court, either could be reinstituted again. Water lines are still cut indiscriminately, whether they are connected to pot patches or not. Many of these marauders undoubtedly would cheer a devastating forest fire to do their work for them.

Prosecutions in federal court for small amounts of marijuana are draconian upon conviction; the mandatory minimum sentence is five years or more. Land forfeiture by the federales is a harsh reality, in some cases even for small amounts of marijuana. Asset forfeiture by the locals trying to make money

> *Although no CAMP troop has ever been hurt by a grower during any raids since 1983, they come armed to the teeth and ready for the kill, just looking for the opportunity to blow another human being away.*

is also a reality. People have moved away, both because they could not supplement their income as they used to, and because others did not want to live in a war zone any longer.

The economy of the area has gone downward dramatically, with people being busted and losing their assets. Those busted are not just hippies; they are loggers, ranchers, fishermen, usually people who have never done another thing illegal in their lives. They are honest people, often times Republicans, who are shocked to realize how few rights are left, and how the system is stacked against them.

Yet through all of this onslaught, the most massive in the history of American law enforcement, people continue to grow marijuana, and not only in small amounts. In fact, the police report numbers indicating as much as a five-fold increase in marijuana compared to last year. Moreover, last year in Mendocino County the numbers were way up from the first year they started in earnest, indicating the futility of the hunt. Speak to any marijuana law enforcement officer off the cuff and he or she will tell you that the battle can't be won. Regardless of different tactics used by law enforcement officers, Yankee ingenuity is staying two or three steps ahead of the cops. However, the cops must continue to do their job and follow orders from above. Speak to the U.S. Attorneys in charge of asset and forfeiture work informally and they'll tell you they feel a little bad about taking people's homes because they grow marijuana. But these prosecutors care not about the loss of civil liberties and individual rights; the new tools given them by the courts are just ways to do their jobs more efficiently, get their promotions, and build their own bureaucracies.

What does all of this mean? The rural lifestyle and independent nature of both the old-timers, and the people who have moved here in the last 20 years who have merged on many issues to form a strong vital community where an individual's opinion still counts, will continue. There is more marijuana being grown now (and there has been for a number of years) in many other parts of the country, but the publicity value of continuing to attack this area will go on and on until it is no longer politically advantageous to do so. More rights will be lost, more marijuana will be grown, more lives will be made miserable for no discernibly sensible reason. Someday, somewhere, after going over a public opinion survey, a serious candidate for state or national office will come out publicly with what he or she already knows in his or her mind: legalization, or at least medicalization and regulation, is the cost effective and sensible way to go. Remove the market and make some money on it (as they do with liquor and gambling), and look like a smart politician. This person or these persons won't care that the vital by-product of a rational and sensible approach may be a restoration of civil liberties, and allowing people who want to continue in their pursuit of happiness to do so without the government dictating their mores.

But more money won't buy more success. The war on drugs — is fruitless, in both senses of the word. It has not borne fruit; that is, it has not made the United States even close to drug free.

—*Kurt Schmoke*

When we have failed, we should have the courage and the stamina to think anew, to change, and in this instance to abolish the prohibition. It is time to recognize the truth and to end the lie that we have a successful policy.

—*Robert W. Sweet*

The burden of proof that anti-drug laws discourage use clearly rests with those who are pushing the drug war. So far, no convincing evidence has been forthcoming.

—*Richard E. Dennis*

Chapter 11

The Growing Army of Dissenters

Introduction

During a national television confrontation recently, Congressman Charles Rangel observed that the supporters of the Drug Policy Foundation "could fit into a telephone booth." The response from a Foundation official was that it would have to be a pretty big telephone booth.

Is it engaging in hyperbole, however, to call the loyal opposition to the war on drugs, whether or not they are actually members of the Foundation, a growing army, as we do in the title to this chapter? We think not. Based upon a series of public opinion polls, including one released by the Drug Policy Foundation, there is seemingly good evidence that the percentage of popular support for radical change in American drug policy has risen from single digits in the early 1980s to as high as 36 percent today. This could amount to as many as 64 million Americans. That is an army.

Of course, it is a minority army and a divided force. Most citizens of America (and other countries, we believe) support the existing martial approach to controlling drugs. The loyal opposition is split among those who, like many libertarians, favor outright legalization of all drugs, those who favor legalization of only a few drugs such as marijuana, and those who would keep all drugs illegal but who would ease up on drug-war extremism.

What cannot be denied is that those who have openly come out for drastic change now include some of the most prominent people in the society of America and other countries, such as former Secretary of the Treasury and former Secretary of State George P. Shultz. Much of the credit for the current interest in fundamental reform, though, started in April 1988, with the clarion call for a national dialogue on new ways of dealing with drugs from the mayor of Baltimore, Kurt L. Schmoke.

The Mayor Of Baltimore Continues His Challenge*

In 1984, Marcellus Ward, a Baltimore City police officer was killed — murdered — while taking part in an undercover drug sale. Officer Ward was wearing a wire and the entire deadly episode was captured on tape. As Baltimore City State's Attorney, and the person responsible for prosecuting Ward's killers, I had to listen to that tape many times.

However, I didn't need to hear the sound of Marcellus Ward being shot to know that there was something terribly misguided about expecting law enforcement officers to stop drug abuse and drug trafficking. Rather than convince me of our need for a new national drug policy, Officer Ward's murder simply confirmed it.

The United States has been spending nearly $20 billion a year doing the kind of work that got Officer Ward killed: investigating, watching, arresting, prosecuting and jailing drug law violators. And under the new National Drug Control Strategy recently proposed by President Bush and Secretary Bennett, still more money will be poured into the war on drugs in the years to come.

But more money won't buy more success. The war on drugs — as currently waged — is fruitless, in both senses of the word. It has not borne fruit; that is, it has not made the United States even close to drug free. Millions of Americans continue to violate our drug laws every year by using or selling illegal drugs. And, even more important, the war on drugs is fruitless in that it's doomed to failure.

Doomed, not for lack of effort, money, or good intentions (the latter still paving the road to hell), but because of the internal and inescapable contradictions posed by the war on drugs. These I'll discuss shortly.

When I speak publicly about the war on drugs — civil war on drugs would be a more apt description — I usually begin by posing three questions.

1. Have we won the war on drugs?
2. Are our current strategies winning the war on drugs?
3. Will doing more of the same allow us to win in the future?

Given the contentiousness of the war on drugs, the unanimity with which audiences respond "No" to each of those questions reflects a growing recognition that our current national drug policy is a failure.

---
* Kurt L. Schmoke, Mayor, Baltimore, Md.

If we haven't won, aren't winning, and won't win in the future by doing more of the same, it becomes legitimate, and perhaps even obligatory, to offer alternative strategies for stopping drug abuse and drug trafficking. That is what I've tried to do since April 1988 when I publicly called for a national debate on the merits of decriminalizing drugs. I have been arguing that law enforcement is incapable of ending drug abuse or drug-related crime, and that we should instead develop a public health strategy to the war on drugs. Making drugs illegal has not diminished the American appetite for these substances. That is because drug abuse is a disease. And like any other disease, it responds to medical treatment, not criminal sanctions.

What is decriminalization? It's not legalization of all drugs. Drugs would not simply be made available to anyone who wants them as is the case now with the drug nicotine. Decriminalization is in effect "medicalization," a broad public health strategy — led by the Surgeon General, not the Attorney General — designed to reduce the harm caused by drugs by pulling addicts into the public health system. Criminal penalties for drug use would be removed and health professionals would be allowed to use currently illegal drugs, or substitutes, as part of an overall treatment program for addicts. (Narcotics maintenance — giving drugs to addicts — is not a new idea. Heroin addicts have been maintained on methadone for many years). Drugs would not be dispensed to non-users, and it would be up to a health professional to determine whether a person requesting maintenance is an addict.

For purposes of this article, I'm going to focus on three reasons why medicalization would be a better national drug policy than our current one. They are: 1) the unprecedented levels of crime — much of it violent — that has accompanied drug prohibition; 2) the increased rates of HIV infection caused by addicts sharing contaminated needles; and 3) the social inequities that have resulted from the war on drugs.

Crime: The War on Drugs as a Self-Inflicted Wound

It's practically a truism that what frightens people most about drugs is not their use, but what results from the fact that they're illegal.

Random violence, unsafe streets, government corruption, young people working as lookouts and drug runners instead of being in school, money laundering, prison overcrowding, a criminal justice system near collapse: these are the problems that lead the public to tell pollsters and politicians that they want something done about drugs.

The irony is that something was done about nearly identical problems once already this century. Alcohol Prohibition was repealed in 1933 after it led to the same kind of chaos we're now experiencing with the war on drugs. (Actually we did more than repeal Prohibition; we unfortunately went to the other extreme and began promoting drinking as a social good. This promotion continues unabated with the alcohol beverage industry spending billions of advertising dollars each year to encourage people to drink).

The views of decriminalization foes notwithstanding, there are lessons to be learned from alcohol Prohibition. The most important one being that easy profits from the sale of mind-altering substances inevitably lead to the growth of criminal enterprises. And as we witness daily on television and in newspapers, these criminal enterprises will go to any length, sell to any person (children included), defy any law, murder any competition, bribe any official, and risk any punishment to protect their billions in ill-gotten gains.

We will never be able to prosecute our way out of drug-related crime. That's true for two reasons.

First, the volume of drug-related crime far exceeds the prosecuting capacity of the criminal justice system. For example, Baltimore has been under a court order to reduce its jail population. Through the judicious use of alternatives to incarceration, we are now under the capacity level mandated by the court. Nevertheless, Baltimore's jail and Maryland's penitentiary remain dangerously overcrowded because of the continued influx of drug law violators.

Nationwide the story is the same; prison overcrowding has become endemic. The inmate capacity of the federal prison system has already been greatly exceeded. Moreover, if current trends continue, in 15 years half of all federal prisoners will be incarcerated for drug violations.

Those favoring a law enforcement approach to drugs argue that the answer to prison overcrowding, as well as excessive plea bargaining, court congestion and revolving door justice, is to build more prisons. Doubtless new prisons are needed, but we could never build enough of them to keep pace with the growing number of drug arrests. One explanation is taxpayer resistance. The average cost of a prison cell is $50,000-$80,000. The average cost of incarcerating one prisoner is $18,000-$30,000 per year. As others have pointed out, it's cheaper to send a young person to Penn State than to the State Pen.

The other reason that we will never prosecute our way out of drug crime is because a law enforcement strategy ends up creating the very problems it is intended to solve. I was a prosecutor for seven years. My office put thousands of drug offenders in jail. I attended anti-drug abuse conferences, sat on anti-drug abuse task forces, participated in anti-drug policy studies, controlled large anti-drug budgets, and supervised large anti-drug undercover operations. I worked with very committed law enforcement officers on the federal, state and local level. As State's Attorney I could certainly have used more money; but, it is not a lack of money or dedication that has kept law enforcement from putting an end to drug abuse and drug-related crime.

We will never be able to prosecute our way out of drug-related crime.

Stepped-up prosecutions along with stepped-up interdiction efforts maintain or increase the black market price of drugs. These high prices — and profits — simply induce new traffickers to enter the trade. Thus, while the criminal law probably does deter some drug use, it does nothing to deter drug traffickers and drug-related violence. If traffickers willingly risk the violent internecine battles that are commonplace in the drug trade, it's not surprising that they continue to take the relatively small risk of being caught by the police and the even smaller risk of being successfully prosecuted.

Deeper involvement by the military in drug interdiction will simply raise the price in the illegal market, increase dealer profits and expand the number of points of entry for drugs. A recent GAO report says, "Department of Defense data show that in FY 1987, the Air Force designated 591 AWACS flying hours to drug interdiction, which resulted in six seizures and ten arrests. The incremental cost to DoD associated with this assistance was $2.6 million. In the first quarter of FY 1988, 154 designated AWACS flying hours, which represents an incremental cost of $678,000, resulted in two seizures and three arrests."

This is a near-perfect example of conventional wisdom at its worst. Using the military to fight drug smugglers sounds like a good idea, but it will be money and effort wasted. The nearly $3.3 million spent for the AWACS bought very meager results. The money would have been better spent on drug treatment and other substances abuse prevention efforts. The same can be said for the Navy and the Coast Guard who, together, spent $40 million in 1987 in order to seize 20 vessels and make 110 arrests, about a 2-day average in Baltimore.

How will medicalization reduce drug-related crime? First it will remove most of the illegal profits from the drug trade that keep the traffickers in business. Second, it will reduce much of the crime that addicts commit to get money for drugs. Instead of buying drugs on the black market, addicts will be able to turn to the public health system for treatment — treatment that will be much more widely available than it is now. The money for this increased availability of treatment will come in part from the transfer of resources from law enforcement to public health. Under a policy of harm reduction, addicts could be maintained and eventually weaned from drugs. Such a policy would mean safer drugs for the addict, and safer streets for everyone else.

One popular misconception about a public health strategy to the war on drugs is that it is a new, and even radical idea. Actually, decriminalizing drug use is not a new idea at all.

Prior to the passage of the Harrison Narcotics Act in 1914, private physicians and clinics could dispense drugs to addicts. The Harrison Act was interpreted by the Supreme Court to mean that private physicians could not prescribe narcotics for the sole purpose of keeping an addict comfortable.

In the intervening years since 1914, the original role of the medical profession in fighting drug addiction has been all but forgotten. In its place has come a policy of trying to end drug abuse through the force of law. It's a policy accompanied by martial rhetoric. It's a policy filled with righteous indignation. It's a policy that promises a civilization without drugs. But it's also policy bereft of reality and as non-existent as the Emperor's new clothes.

The question is, how much longer can we afford to keep our eyes closed to both the danger and the mythology of the war on drugs? With the AIDS epidemic the time has already passed.

AIDS is now the world's most dangerous communicable disease. In the United States, there are over 117,000 known cases of AIDS, and as of 1989 there were 68,441 deaths. The Centers for Disease Control estimate that as many as 1.5 million Americans are knowingly or unknowingly carrying the HIV virus. Furthermore, the number of AIDS cases is expected to soar to 365,000 by 1992, with 80,000 new cases in that year alone. Also by 1992, the CDC is projecting 263,000 deaths from AIDS in the United States. There is no known cure and no vaccine for AIDS.

On the other hand, this is known: intravenous drug use is now the single largest source of the new HIV infections. Taking Baltimore as an example, there were 908 cases of AIDS in Baltimore City as of Nov. 21, 1989. Of those, 45 percent were related to IV drug use, an increase of 4 percent just since May.

These statistics should have a sobering effect on those responsible for our national drug policy, but so far they haven't. Thus, instead of coming to grips with the frightening reality that thousands of people are contracting AIDS directly or indirectly through IV drug use (many of whom are infants born to infected mothers), our national leaders continue to condemn needle exchange programs or any other decriminalization policy that is designed to slow the spread of AIDS. A needle exchange program is a form of decriminalization because it requires the removal of criminal sanctions for the possession and distribution of syringes.

Einstein once said in reference to war that the atomic bomb changed everything except the way people think. We can now say the same about drug abuse: AIDS has changed everything except the way policymakers think.

The Social Inequities of Drug Abuse: The Price of Being Poor

There's always been something slightly Orwellian about the war on drugs. On the one hand, the war is often carried out in the name of children. On the other hand, children, especially those at-risk of failure, are some of its most frequent victims.

We used to think of "at-risk" children as poor children or children of teenage parents. That's still true. But now the definition must include teenagers who have found drug dealing to be a better road to prosperity than school; teenage bystanders caught in the middle of drug turf battles; children born to IV drug users infected with AIDS; crack-addicted children with no place to go for medical treatment; teenagers arrested on drug possession charges spending time in jail instead of school. All of these children are losers in the war against drugs.

And what about poor people generally? They fare no better. The fact of the matter is the urban poor — those among us with the least money, the least education and the least chance of achieving economic opportunity — year in and year out bear a disproportionate share of drug addiction, incarceration, drug-related crimes and now AIDS. This is a fundamental injustice, and it's been lost sight of in our effort to stop drug abuse through use of the criminal law.

But we can do something about this injustice. We can step back from the brink of losing millions of young people to illiteracy, crime and finally to jail. We can put an end to the corrupting influence on poor children of drug traffickers and their profits. And we can restore a measure of fairness to the victims of the war on drugs and even a measure of peace.

But to do that we need to recognize that drug abuse is a disease, impervious to coercion, but not to treatment. We also have to recognize that changing to a public health strategy with an emphasis on harm reduction is only part of the answer — the short-term part. In the long term, if we really want to turn people, especially young people, away from mind-altering substances, we need to turn them toward education, literacy, and economic opportunity. More of all three won't come cheaply. But they will save lives. They will promote justice. And they will reduce the number of people abusing drugs: claims that our law enforcement approach to drugs cannot make, even after 75 years.

Medicalization: The First Step

There's no clear path, no risk-free way, of changing from a drug policy that relies on law enforcement to one that relies on the public health system. That is why I have called for the establishment of a national commission to recommend how all drugs, legal and illegal, should be regulated. The commission would be made up of medical and legal experts and would be guided by the principle of harm reduction: The availability of any particular drug being based on the dangerousness of that drug. Under this scheme, marijuana could probably be sold in government stores to adults. On the other hand, cigarettes, which contain the drug nicotine and kill 350,000 people every year, would likely be more closely regulated than they are now.

In no case could narcotics legally be sold to children.

As much as I believe we need a national commission, I have to admit that there's been little public support for the idea. It, like so many other ideas tied to medicalization, is dismissed as surrender to the drug lords. Better, the conventional wisdom goes, to escalate the war on drugs by hiring more police, building more prisons and placing our civil liberties more at risk.

But the conventional wisdom is wrong. The way to win the war on drugs is to build more schools, not more prisons. To hire and train more treatment specialists, not more police and prosecutors. To be consistent in our approach to drugs, not to be hypocritical. Nicotine and alcohol kill hundreds of thousands of people every year but few, if any, advocate making them illegal. The drug traffickers know all this already. Their great fear is that those who write our drug laws might one day know it too.

A Federal Judge Enlists[*]

I have come to the conclusion that we must abolish the prohibition of drugs. The driving force behind drug abuse in our society is what drives all too much in our society — money, or the lack of it. Prohibition policies only fuel the engine of drug abuse.

I have reached this conclusion after 11 1/2 years as a federal trial judge, repeatedly sentencing people convicted for participation in this social phenomena and seeing our justice system overwhelmed and frustrated by its inability to control drug abuse. It also comes after serving as a federal prosecutor during the 1950s and 1960s and as a Deputy Mayor of New York City, under John Lindsay, when I tried to encourage alternatives to addiction — methadone and experimental treatment programs. It also comes from being a parent, a position I still happily hold.

End Drug Prohibition

Drug abuse has become an escape for those without a stake in society. Their sense of self is weakened to the point that they will knowingly risk self-destruction, addiction and incarceration, absent an alternative motivation. That is our real problem. If the driving force behind drugs is money, or lack of it, then I suggest it is time to abolish the prohibition, to cease treating indulgence in mind alteration as a crime, and to focus our resources on the underlying problems.

The first result of such a course would be the elimination of the profit motive, the gangs, the drug dealers. The second would be the identification of users, those who seek drugs, those who are at risk in the society. Finally, of course, some revenue should be produced to reinforce research, educational and treatment programs. As a result almost nine billion federal enforcement dollars could be rechanneled for prevention and rehabilitation. Obviously, the model is the repeal of Prohibition and the end of Al Capone and Dutch Schultz.

The method that might accomplish this is the legislative repeal of federal prohibition, the setting of federal standards for the dispensation of drugs and their taxation, the availability of funding and revenue to state and local governments which would undertake to identify users, to research blocking alternatives for the addict and to increase

---

[*] Robert W. Sweet, "Admit That the Drug War is not Successful; Abolish Prohibition," *The Drug Policy Letter,* November/December 1989, p. 5. The article was excerpted from a speech by Judge Sweet, who sits on the U.S. District Court for the Southern District of New York, to the Cosmopolitan Club in New York City on Dec. 12, 1989. Judge Sweet was the first federal judge in recent history to come out for the full repeal of drug prohibition.

therapeutic treatment centers. Perhaps making methadone available to all heroin users who now seek it instead of the relatively few for whom slots are presently available. Perhaps making residential treatment available for anyone who meets a certain defined level of addiction, permitting anyone beyond that threshold to obtain drugs only after medical intervention.

As to increased use — it must be anticipated, given the history of the repeal of Prohibition, although the picture is by no means as clear as one's first assumption might be. First, the reality is that today one who seeks to buy drugs has little difficulty in finding the marketplace and purchasing the product. I venture we could mosey over to Sixth Avenue and 43rd Street right now and buy whatever we want. The gamble would have to be that addressing the underlying causes, providing safe narcotics and treating the users, would ultimately result in a healthier America. If it is otherwise, it will be because our citizens have lost the capacity to act affirmatively and are unable to control their individual addictions. The present climate seems to me to be optimistic. There is emphasis on health, diet and what one ingests. If our society can learn to stop using butter, it should be able to cut down on cocaine. If it cannot, no prohibition can be effective.

As part of the specter of increased use there is the cry of genocide, that abolishing prohibition will destroy those least able to survive in the society. This challenge is real, and political dynamite. It must be carefully considered, otherwise someone like myself is accused of insensitivity, racism and worse.

Let us face that honestly and recognize that we must alter society to eliminate, or at least substantially reduce poverty and those conditions which result in drug abuse. It will take money, restructuring and maybe even increased taxes. Among the 23 industrialized nations, although our infant mortality rate is among the top four, our tax revenues as a percentage of gross domestic product are among the bottom three (Turkey and Japan) and we are number two in defense spending (Greece). Our commitment for jobs, education, health and housing must be enhanced. If we are not willing to become our brothers' keepers, then we will have to become our brothers' jailers — and that is not an acceptable alternative to a nation which professes to prize personal liberty.

Perhaps then this is a watershed issue, one of responsibility, responsibility by the individual for his or her life, responsibility of the society to provide the setting and the knowledge so that individual decisions can be made appropriately. Perhaps we must ask not what can we do to eliminate drugs but what we can do to eliminate, or at least reduce, the level of poverty and other causes of drug abuse.

Answers for Congressman Rangel

One of the most powerful voices questioning change in our present prohibitive program is Congressman Charles Rangel, chairman of the House Select Committee on Narcotics Abuse and Control. Last year Mr. Rangel challenged advocates of change to answer a series of tough questions. As he put it:

Press them, the advocates of change, about some of the issues and questions surrounding this proposed legalization and they never seem to have answers.... Those who tout legalization remind me of fans sitting in the cheap seats at the ball park. They may have played the game, and they may know all the rules, but from where they're sitting they can't judge the action.

Well, I don't consider myself a tout, nor is my seat a cheap one, but I'm not afraid to judge the action. In this particular ball park — so far it's been a no-hitter, everyone can see that. Drug prohibition is not making a safer or healthier society. Even though Mr. Rangel's questions were intended by their weight to sink the prospect of change, they do raise issues to be faced.

■ *What drugs should be covered?*

All mind-altering substances.

■ *Who would administer the dosage, the state or the individual?*

The state would set the amounts and prices, and the individual would be denied a lethal frequency of purchases. Otherwise purchases would be at will.

■ *Would the government establish tax-supported facilities to sell these drugs?*

Though the question is loaded, the answer is yes, and the support would be derived from the tax on the sale.

■ *Would we get the supply from the same foreign countries that support our habit now, or would we create our own internal sources and dope factories, paying people the minimum wage to churn out mounds of cocaine and bales of marijuana?*

Let's skip the minimum wage issue — the supply would be from pharmaceutical companies who are today manufacturing drugs of the same characteristics.

■ *Would there be an age limit?*

Yes, the same as alcohol.

■ *What would be the market price and who would set it, would private industry be allowed to have any stake in any of this?*

See alcohol.

■ *What are we going to do about underage youngsters?*

This is the toughest question, but we have to recognize that they have access to drugs as we speak. The part of the problem that is attitudinal may be altered. The education and training and morality of youth extends well beyond drugs, however, and must be our first priority for survival — see the "Forgotten Half."

■ *How many people are projected to become addicts?*

Maybe no more than today, given the reality of present availability. As Lester Grinspoon, M.D., of the Harvard Medical School has said: "We have to believe that in the long run, people will respond in a rational way to the availability of substances with a potential for destruction. There will always be casualties as with alcohol."

■ *Since marijuana remains in a person's system for weeks, what would we do about pilots, railroad engineers, surgeons, police, cross-country truckers and nuclear plant employees who want to use it during off hours? And what would be the effect on the health insurance industry?*

The short answer is "see alcohol." The premise of Mr. Rangel's first question is inaccurate. Marijuana does not stay in a person's system for weeks. Inactive metabolites that exert no psychoactive effect are all that remain after a short time.

Finally, the congressman refers to the problem as "this foreign-based national security threat." This is an internal issue of moral, educational and economic dimensions, to be solved not by guns and tanks and the paraphernalia of war, but rather with faith, moral suasion, family commitment and individual responsibility. Foreign adventure and enhanced prison terms will not provide hope and have not changed attitudes.

Prospects for Change

As to the likelihood of change, I am told by students of the repeal of Prohibition that the same conditions existed then. Those who live by public opinion will not act until a critical mass is perceived. The simple solution — jail the dealers — echoes other simple solutions of the past and remains appealing to many. But how about the cost of increased jails when it costs as much to keep a criminal in jail as it would to send him to Harvard. That particular equivalency appeals to me as an old Yalie.

If there is to be change it will be because at some point the rhetoric will prove hollow, and it will be apparent that the drug war with its present battle lines cannot be won, that our resources have been spent repressively and more significantly, unproductively. If the repeal of Prohibition is the model, researchers, civic organizations and concerned citizens will increasingly challenge the allocation of resources and the imposition of a social problem upon the criminal justice system. What seems today like a lost cause, a Berlin Wall if you will, may tomorrow achieve the critical mass necessary to motivate those who seek to discover and enact the public will.

It is time for change. President Kennedy said at the Berlin Wall: "Change is the law of life." When we have failed, we should have the courage and the stamina to think anew, to change, and in this instance to abolish the prohibition. In terms of Bill Moyers' recent program on another war, the Vietnam War, it is time to recognize the truth and to end the lie that we have a successful policy.

My message is then — we must abandon rhetoric and simplistic solutions and be willing to think anew, reallocate our resources and be willing to sacrifice so that dignity and capacity can alter the minds of our youth instead of crack, ice and heroin. In short, abolish prohibition.

The Anger Of A Retired Chief Detective[*]

I have been in and around the law enforcement field for 42 years. People find it strange that I support the legalization of drugs. As someone who has been on the front lines of the war on drugs I know it will never work. I also know that police are among the principle victims in the war on drugs.

The six plaques added last year to the New York City memorial of those killed in the line of duty were all commemorations of officers killed in drug enforcement situations. The Drug Enforcement Administration federal agent whose death brought President George Bush to console the bereaved family; the DEA agent tortured and murdered in Mexico; the Customs agent presumed dead when his helicopter crashed in the Bahamas last month while chasing a smuggler's boat; the federal agent and 6 contract pilots whose plane crashed into a Peruvian mountain with sabotage suspected, all represent federal officers who have literally given their lives for the drug war. Each year dozens more, serving at all levels of government, are seriously wounded.

To these casualties must be added the many undercover officers, who suffered psychological stress and injury from their assignments, and those who, engulfed by the milieu in which they were placed, succumbed to personal drug abuse. It has taken litigation to compel the government to agree that line-of-duty disability compensations are merited by the hazards of undercover drug assignments. Progressive police administrators have learned that personnel have to be rotated out of such assignments frequently because of the high risks involved.

---

[*] Ralph F. Salerno, "I am an Angry Man: My People, the Police are beingLied To," *The Drug Policy Letter*, November/December 1989, p. 11.

Such casualties have become so commonplace that they are now found in the last paragraphs of news stories, if they are even mentioned. These are some of the reasons I favor ending the war on drugs.

Another reason that I am involved in such efforts is that I am an angry man. The maturity of years has not deprived me of an excellent memory, and in the present war on drugs I am experiencing a tremendous sense of *deja vu*. I have been here before. The same war was being fought in the 1960s when the principal substance of abuse was heroin, a miniscule problem when compared to today. I was a Supervisor of Detectives in the New York City Police Department. Then the problem was the old French Connection, the Turkish poppy crop refined in laboratories around Marseille and pipelined into New York City for distribution by the mafia. We were told by our political leadership that if the Turkish poppy crop was destroyed, the purification mills destroyed and the major American mafiosi importers caught and convicted, there would be an end to the problem. While all of these things happened, the problem did not end.

The Turkish poppy crop was reduced and then virtually eliminated with American money used to eradicate the poppies and convert the farmers' efforts to other products. It quickly became apparent that poppies could be grown in other parts of the world. Within two years the Mexican share of the heroin supply jumped from 38 percent to 77 percent. Then the market spread to Southeast Asia and Afghanistan. Today the poppy crop is untouchable.

The French police destroyed the heroin mills, and we learned what a heroin mill really is. It is a chemist, brought together with $5,000 worth of equipment and a couple thousand dollars worth of chemicals. This combination can be put together anywhere in the world.

I worked hard with my colleagues to arrest and convict the American mafiosi and participated in the federal investigations of Vito Genovese, Carmine Galante and others who were sent to prison for very long prison terms. They were readily replaced by relatives, friends, and associates and nothing changed. Today La Cosa Nostra groups have a very limited role on the drug scene. New organized crime groups, the Jamaicans, Colombians, Los Angeles gangs and others have taken their places. The names of the players have changed but the game is exactly the same.

What angers me is that today, police officers and all other Americans are being told by our political leaders that if the coca crop in Peru and Bolivia can be curtailed it will all be over, ignoring the botanical fact that coca can be grown in many parts of the world. We are told that if the chemicals can be cut off from the purification plants in Colombia it will all be over. The chemicals are derivatives of the oil industry and there are wells in many parts of the world. We are told that if we can incarcerate the Medellin and Cali cartels it will all be over, and that is another lie. The Latin-American narco-traficantes will be replaced by others as easily as were the American mafiosi.

So I am angry because the people I have spent my entire life with, the law enforcement community, are being lied to, just as I was lied to 20 years ago.

Perhaps the greatest pain we suffer is the growing problem of corruption among my colleagues. This also is not a new problem. After the famous French Connection heroin bust we discovered that the heroin was stolen from the New York City police property clerk's office. The investigations of the Knapp Commission proved the corruption of the elite narcotics enforcement unit whose members had become "princes of the city." Today dozens of sheriffs have been convicted of drug corruption, local police officers, federal agents, prosecutors and even judges have been convicted of drug charges. Even the once incorruptible FBI has had its casualties. Enough!

The Despair Of The Foot Soldiers*

In preparing this text, my colleague and I were concerned that we properly express not only our particular viewpoint, but also, perhaps, speak for rank-and-file law enforcement personnel. Law enforcement personnel at a policy-making level are well-represented in centers of power, and are frequently called upon by the news media to express their opinions and ideas. But rank-and-file law enforcers, the ones responsible for actually executing the policies formulated by their bosses, are rarely if ever seen outside their role as the tools of our government policies. They are rarely asked their opinions and even more rarely give them. They are like walk-ons and extras in a drama written and staged by politicians. In virtually every law enforcement agency — police and investigative agencies, prosecuting agencies, correctional agencies — unsanctioned expressions of opinion are tantamount to treason. We make no claim to speak for *all* rank-and-file law enforcement personnel, merely that we are attempting to give voice to a view which is shared by others within law enforcement, a view which dare not be voiced aloud.

Indeed, one of the two bylines on this paper is a pseudonym. "Mr. McBride," because of his government employment, uses this pseudonym, out of concern that publishing or speaking out using his true name would subject him to retaliation, via transfer, demotion, or perhaps firing.

---

* Arthur McBride and John T. Shuler. Arthur McBride is a psuedonym for a front-line law enforcement officer who requested anonymity for fear of reprisals by his agency. John T. Shuler is an attorney in New York.

We have nothing but admiration and respect for the thousands of honest and hard-working law enforcement personnel, although we know that many disagree with some or all of our premises and conclusions.

For the politicians who have created the drug war, we have little but contempt. Those people, by exploiting the drug issue for their own ends, are displaying contempt for the dedication and courage of those who carry out their unworkable policies and reckless edicts at great personal cost. They also display a contempt for American citizens by carrying on the public debate about drugs in a hysterical and misleading manner.

Most law enforcement agency chiefs deserve little better. As the creatures of politicians, they often sacrifice the well-being of their subordinates and the communities they serve with shortsighted decisions. Both the hysterical anti-drug politicians and the law enforcement officials who truckle them have climbed to power over the bodies of dead police officers and citizens.

Similarly, we have little, if any, sympathy for narcotics traffickers, especially at the higher levels. Putting these people out of business is not the least attractive feature of decriminalization.

Decision-Making in Law Enforcement

A facet of prohibition which is rarely, if ever, publicly discussed is the day-to-day decision-making of law enforcement agencies.

The reality of law enforcement in the "war on drugs" is that policies and decision-making are tailored to political needs. These political requirements, in turn, lead to a concern with "keeping the numbers up" (that is, rising numbers of arrests, of amounts of illegal drug seizures, of indictments, and longer jail sentences). Politicians are eager to show they are meeting the challenge of the "Drug

Crisis," so they vote more money for law enforcement and for tougher sentences. Law enforcement managers, concerned with questions of reappointment, bureaucratic power struggles and budgetary fights, similarly "keep the numbers up" to show they are doing their jobs. This may not necessarily mean simply churning out numbers, but also staging raids and arrests which will garner press attention. Of course, those opportunities sometimes are generated fortuitously.

A few months ago, one of the authors of this paper participated in an investigation which resulted in the seizure of a large number of kilos of very nearly pure cocaine. While the subjects of the investigation were being interviewed, one of the investigators' supervisors, without consulting any of the other persons responsible for the investigation, telephoned the press relations office of his agency and arranged for news of the seizure to be released. While this was going on, the persons conducting the interviews were devising a plan to continue the investigation which was dependent on the "owners" of the "stash" being unaware of its seizure. Without divulging any additional details (the investigation, at the time of this writing, is still in progress), we can say that the persons initially apprehended were no more than two rungs underneath the Medellin Cartel's American management. The case investigators were startled to discover that listeners of at least one all-news radio stations already knew how much cocaine had been seized, and from where. The plan to move up the ladder of this particular drug organization had to be scuttled, at best delaying and at worst terminating a potentially fruitful opportunity. The need to score points with a public, (and politicians), hungry for proof that the "drug war" is being fought decisively won out over sensible investigative techniques.

The root causes of the problems we have discussed above must ultimately be laid at the feet of those who have sold us, and have perpetuated, the idea that law enforcement is the theater where the resolution of our national social problems must be played out.

In local police agencies, the "number" is usually that of arrests, for the DEA the number is kilograms seized, and for district attorneys' and prosecutors' offices the numbers are indictments, convictions, and conviction rates. These differing goals sometime create conflict between prosecutors, who want strong prosecutable cases, and investigators, who may be more interested solely in the number of arrests. For a prosecutor's office caught between an expanding caseload and public pressure for impressive conviction rates, stronger cases mean more wins at trial, and more leverage in plea negotiations, and therefore fewer trials. More leverage in plea negotiations translates into more guilty pleas and longer sentences. In areas where prosecutors must run for reelection in contested races, rates of conviction, and long sentences may mean the difference between winning and losing.

Police officials must justify their budgets (and

their positions), and are "expected" by the public and many political leaders to produce results, and that is particularly true where a controversial issue such as drugs are concerned. If the question asked of them is "how many people are you arresting?" The quality of those arrests recedes as soon as any political pressure to increase the numbers appears. Police bureaucracy may not be concerned with whether the arrests are prosecutable or not; they just need high numbers in order to show to the public that they are "doing their jobs."

This mania for "numbers" is one of the tenets of the "war on drugs." Like the daily body counts in Vietnam, it is the gauge of bureaucratic success. It is the way that public officials and bureaucrats can claim that they are "winning" (or "losing" if that is the point to be made) the war; the public has been taught after 20 years of listening to the rhetoric of the war on drugs that numbers are how victories and losses are declared. (However, it is possible to "unlearn" that lesson if empiricism — the conclusion that drug traffickers are ruining your neighborhood — teaches differently). If the "numbers" are up then we must be doing okay; if they are down we have to do something else to get them up again. But, bringing the numbers up is not that difficult, and it usually has little relationship to the strength or weakness of the drug trafficking economy as a whole. It's easy (relatively speaking) to go after street dealers since they are visible and plentiful; but actually disrupting the structure of the business itself requires long, painstaking, dangerous and unreliable investigations.

In New York, another popular method of increasing the "body count" is to count summons (tickets) in the same category as arrests. This means that when, at the end of the month, arrest totals look low, teams of narcotics investigators will be directed to issue summonses to marijuana possessors. Marijuana purchasers will be observed making their purchases, and will then be apprehended. The marijuana will be seized, and the buyer will then either be given a summons on the street, or brought into the station under arrest and given a desk appearance ticket, a more elaborate version of a summons.

Tactical and strategic decisions are often made primarily for the purposes of generating photo opportunities. The pictures are not unfamiliar: police brass and politicians standing behind a table on which are arrayed guns, drugs, money, scales and other paraphernalia; quotations are given regarding the so-called "street value" of the contraband seized. The other basic scenario has to do with depicting the arrests of defendants, and comes in two flavors: footage of defendants being walked into a court or police facility, often shielding their faces from the cameras, or footage of the actual raids and arrests.

The New York City Police Department (NYPD) has run several operations, code-named "GEMINI," in the Washington Heights neighborhood of Manhattan, an area with a large open retail and wholesale cocaine market. The GEMINI operations involved making a large number of undercover sales on a particular block, and then simultaneously executing a large number of search warrants and making many arrests. TV news crews are brought along in surveillance vans, and encouraged to videotape the ensuing chaos. (In one of the recent GEMINI operations, TV news personnel were seen on the street the day *before* the arrests. Many of the traffickers made themselves scarce until after the raids.)

The use of the news media in law enforcement isn't necessarily improper, or useless. The cause of deterrence may well served when news reports place offenders on notice that their conduct may be punished. Problems arise when, on the one hand, publicity becomes the tail which wags the dog of enforcement, or when the tough-talking publicity is in effect, a hollow threat. Nothing undermines deterrence more quickly than promises that can't be kept.

Occasionally the use of the news media for staged events has partisan political motives. In October of 1988, roughly one month before the presidential elections, the Bureau of Alcohol, Tobacco and Firearms (BATF) staged a series of arrests and raids against Jamaican-organized crime groups in New York City during a visit by then-candidate George Bush. The implication of the news pieces was that the arrests were the culmination of a large-scale investigation. According to several federal law enforcement sources involved in the operation, the BATF — an agency which has, with relatively few agents, made the best progress of any federal agency in attacking Jamaican organized crime groups — collected all of their outstanding arrest warrants against Jamaican offenders. They had then prevailed upon various units of the NYPD conducting Jamaican organized-crime investigations, and asked if the NYPD units had any open warrants that could be executed during Bush's visit. By "assisting" the NYPD, the BATF was then able to take credit for the execution of those warrants. Thus, an incumbent vice president looked tough on crime while in town making a campaign stop for President. We are unaware of any comment on this by the Dukakis campaign. More disturbing, no one in the New York or national press corps seemed either to be aware of or to care about the shameless manner in which they were being manipulated.

Please don't misunderstand our point. Most if not all of the offenders arrested were members of dangerous trafficking groups, groups dominated by sociopaths. But these arrests were not timed for their investigative value, nor to maximize their effect in terms of law enforcement purpose. They were done to make George Bush look tough. Police agencies do not stand alone with respect to this sort of chicanery. District attorney's offices routinely engage in equally cynical maneuvers. Prosecutors — and here we speak of prosecutor's offices in New York, although the same dynamic presumably operates similarly elsewhere — are just as concerned with the numbers they generate.

Thus, prosecutor's offices, where volume is a concern, are less than eager to conduct tedious and involved investigations of major offenders. This has, relatively, less to do with individual prosecutors than with their leaders. Individual prosecutors are often personally motivated to "go after the big guy," either out of a sense of fairness, efficacy, or personal pride. But for the managers of prosecuting agencies, it is imprudent to "waste" a young prosecutor on a case which may, for instance, take four or five weeks of attorney time when the same attorney can prosecute dozens of low-level street dealers.

What is not common knowledge — even among prosecutors — is that in New York State, District Attorney's offices have a second source of income, apart from direct funding from the municipalities or counties they serve: state funding based upon the number of indictments filed. This creates enormous pressure to maximize the number of indictments filed — the more indictments, the more money. In a period in which many local governments — and New York City's is certainly no exception — are hard-pressed financially, the temptation to orient prosecution to "mass-production," as it were, grows ever greater.

This concern with numbers can have life-threatening consequences for both police officers and the public.

In the first instance, any time that law enforcement resources are diverted from the apprehension and prosecution of violent offenders, we all suffer. Every prosecution of a nonviolent street offender is time wasted that could be spent on more difficult, more violent targets.

This brings to light a fundamental problem with almost all drug prosecutions: while drug prohibition is rationalized on the basis of the relationship between drugs, drug trafficking and violence, investigations and prosecutions of violent crime on the one hand and narcotics on the other hand are rarely, if ever, coordinated.

Productivity and safety are at odds at the most elemental tactical levels. The emphasis on "numbers" generation and productivity often means direct and indirect shortcuts with respect to safety. Having to produce numbers means shoddy investigations. Any shoddy investigation which leaves a potentially dangerous offender out of prison instead of in is a threat to society at large. It is also particularly dangerous if, during the course of a trial, that offender gets to see the face of an undercover police officer.

For instance, search warrant executions, which are extremely dangerous, are best and most safely conducted with planning, reconnaissance and rehearsal. Even the best-prepared raid can go awry, resulting in the deaths of offenders, officers, and bystanders. The execution of narcotics search warrants and other raids account for 32 percent of the fatalities related to narcotics among law enforcement officers over the period 1978-1988. Thorough preparation is immensely time-consuming. A day spent in planning for the execution of a search warrant may, for police managers, be a day "wasted" — a day not spent in generating enough information to apply for another search warrant, a day not spent in arresting more traffickers.

Pressure to produce numbers often also forces individual police officers, already engaged in stressful and dangerous work, into taking unconscionable risks. Officers newly assigned to undercover work with little or no experience may be directed to make purchases from dangerous sellers. In New York City, the pressure to produce numbers often results in narcotics officers working in smaller-than-normal teams, in order to produce a larger number of arrests per officer.

Hypodermic Prohibition

After pointing out these considerations of law enforcement deficiencies in the enforcement of drug laws, we do not accept the hypothesis that if deficiencies can be rectified, that somehow law enforcement could indeed wage a successful "war on drugs." In fact, our argument is the opposite, that in fact law enforcement cannot ever emerge "victorious" (whatever that may mean). These criticisms do not cite anomalies that can be rooted out by a zealous reformation of our law enforcement scheme. They are in fact NECESSARY CONSEQUENCES of our law enforcement approach. They are the inevitable policies that result from an ill-conceived premise: that law enforcement can and should be a primary tool for accomplishing political goals and altering the individual behavior of the citizenry. The root causes of the problems we have discussed above must ultimately be laid at the feet of those who have sold us, and have perpetuated, the idea that law enforcement is the theater where the resolution of our national social problems must be played out. If law enforcers must necessarily use and advocate unjust and undemocratic methods, and must increasingly jeopardize their own safety, in order to meet an arbitrary and illusory goal, then they do so because the values that created those policies are unjust, undemocratic and unmindful of the public good.

Perhaps the most stark example of misplaced values, and the dangerous policies generated thereby is the case of hypodermic needle prohibition and AIDS in New York City. The possession of hypodermic needles is criminally prohibited in New York State; a class "A" misdemeanor, hypodermic possession is punishable, in theory, by a sentence of up to one year in jail. While those sentences are rarely, if ever imposed, New York's criminal sanctions prevent IV drug users from purchasing hypodermics at pharmacies, and make them subject to arrest (and their needles to confiscation) if caught. Consequently, there is an illicit market in hypodermic needles. Anecdotal evidence suggests prices ranging from between one to $5 per syringe. Many IV drug users, however, share needles either to avoid the cost of purchasing them, or because they are not available. Since even inexpensive "disposable" syringes can be used repeatedly — albeit at great risk — the sharing of needles is widespread.

In 1985, a limited needle exchange program was proposed in New York City. Three years later, despite intense opposition from law enforcement and black and Hispanic leaders, the program started. The program became an issue mayoral campaign of 1989, when the two leading candidates, including the current mayor, David Dinkins, made opposition to needle exchange, even on an experimental basis, part of their campaigns, and the program has now been ended. This year, Mayor Dinkins and Health Commissioner Woodrow Myers attempted to terminate a feature of a city-funded program which conducted outreach with IV drug users and, among other activities, distributed small bottles of bleach with instructions on how to disinfect syringes using the bleach.

Although needle distribution has also come under fire from other quarters, it has been greeted with widespread derision and criticism by law enforcement officials.

At no point has any law enforcement official in New York ever publicly questioned whether the struggle to eliminate certain drugs from our society is worth the risk of the deaths of the citizens they are (in theory) trying to save.

To the best of our ability to investigate this matter, through contacts in most (although not all) of the law enforcement agencies in New York, no agency (outside the Health Department) ever gave any serious thought whatever to the epidemiological consequences of hypodermic syringe prohibition.

In the case of hypodermic prohibition and AIDS — as in the drug war generally — decisions are being made on a symbolic level, which is perfectly consistent if one sees law enforcement as a set of symbols rather than as a set of agencies involved in a more or less rational enterprise within the context of a democratic society. However, if one sees law enforcement agencies as involved in attempting to solve or mitigate stated social problems (for example drug use and misuse) the decision-making processes we've outlined have deeply troubling implications.

In public debates and all the public portrayals (fictional and journalistic) law enforcement is the genre in which we perform and observe our national passion plays. If one of Japan's metaphors for self-identity is the samurai, America's myths and fables about cops and robbers are the folklore through which we transmit and reinforce many of our values. The police officer or administrator, and, less frequently, the prosecutor, is the image of moral authority and icon of social control, and the values conveyed by those figures are generally implied rather than explicitly stated. With respect to symbolic value it matters not whether we generate those values through fictional television and movie characters or through press conferences and "live" TV news footage.

One of the difficulties is that our values as a national community are hardly homogeneous, despite attempts by dominant groups to transmit them, and that at best we are ambivalent about many of the actual issues raised by illegal drugs, illegal drug trafficking and illegal drug use.

How does this relate to the issue of hypodermic syringe distribution in New York City? It means that leading public figures can discuss the issue only in the vaguest of moral terms, and can almost entirely ignore the economic and public health implications of their unarticulated moral stance.

The moral argument made by anti-needle law enforcement officials is generally stated as an antipathy to "encouraging" or "sanctioning" IV drug use. New York's Mayor David Dinkins has said, "I do not wish to see people assisted in becoming addicted."

Since IV drug use is immoral because it is illegal and/or inherently immoral, the reasoning goes, allowing unfettered access to syringes or actively providing syringes to IV drug users is akin to providing a person a firearm with which to commit suicide, or to providing a person an instrument with which to break the law.

In the first instance it is consistent, *prima facie*, with moral approbation against IV drug use to oppose easily obtained syringes. If IV drug use is inherently immoral, and therefore illegal, there is a certain logic to obstructing IV drug use by limiting the ease with which one can obtain the necessary instrument, namely the syringe. At that point, the question must be asked: Which is the superior moral position, denying access to syringes to express society's opprobrium and disapproval of drugtaking behavior, or, using every likely means necessary to prevent the spread of a horrific public health disaster? Those who argue that needle distribution is encouraging drug abuse must accept the logical consequences of their position: IV drug users will die of AIDS in large numbers. Those IV drug users will in turn infect their lovers and children. Their lovers and their lovers' lovers will in turn infect others with AIDS. Proponents of needle prohibition must therefore be willing to accept the moral responsibility for the suffering and death from AIDS of persons who are not only not IV drug users, but who are *entirely unaware* of any IV drug use. To argue that death by AIDS is a public policy goal preferable to trying to maintain the status quo is to carry the "war on drugs" to absurd and almost inconceivable dimensions: that the "war on drugs" is more important than any other single social issue, even one that involves the potential almost certain deaths of thousands.

A large population of IV drug users, already HIV positive, will die unless treatments are devised. Public health policy should be directed at using whatever measures seem likely to help limit that number. Needle distribution is one of those measures.

At no point has any law enforcement official in New York ever publicly questioned whether the struggle to eliminate certain drugs from our society is worth the risk of the deaths of the citizens they are (in theory) trying to save. No law enforcement official in New York has ever expressed an opinion that was anything other than a testament to the creed of the "war on drugs": that certain drugs must be suppressed at all costs. This is the real folly of the "war on drugs." By regurgitating the standard litany of platitudes our law enforcement officials (and our politicians) have failed us; they have failed to illuminate all the issues confronting us, and have denied our society the chance to consider all the choices available and, most importantly, the consequences of those choices. Our law enforcement leaders have passed the test of the "war on drugs"; they are "tough" and "strong" and unequivocal in their devotion to the cause (and consequently have gained approval and stature). The tragedy is they have failed the test of honest and courageous leadership.

The paternalist rationale for needle prohibition is fallacious. The goal of drug (and needle) prohibition is to save drug users from themselves, from drug use. Abandoning IV drug users to AIDS says, in effect, that we don't really care about these people. The only conceivable defenses of this policy would be that AIDS as "punishment" for drug use will deter other drug users — somewhat akin to sacrificing quarantined sufferers of a contagious disease; and the brutal notion that the best way to deal with illegal drug users is for all of them to die. The public debate about hypodermic syringes would be well served if these ideas could make it into the open, so that we could discuss IV drug users as sentient beings capable of suffering, instead of as the abstract bearers of moral approbation. Needle prohibition disenfranchises IV drug users by making it difficult or impossible for them to act responsibly toward themselves and others.

Finally, no defense of needle prohibitions justifies their effects on the sex partners of IV users and the sex partners of sex partners of IV drug users, etc.

This is, in fact, the paradox of prohibition.

Prohibition is a policy which purports to act on behalf of the common good, but whose underlying assumptions are never examined in public, and are never examined carefully by those who create and implement it. Those policy-makers, rather than being motivated by the public good, are driven more by personal gain and political advantage than by the public good, which receives lip service and little else in the enforcement of laws against drugs.

The American People Are Starting To Question The Drug War[*]

The vaunted drug war may have faded temporarily from the headlines. Nonetheless, the Bush administration and Congress continue down this blind alley, even though a recent nationwide poll released by the Drug Policy Foundation finds that the American people believe present policies aren't working and that the drug war is unwinnable.

Despite legitimate questions about the wisdom and effectiveness of current policies, our paramilitary drug war strategy remains ascendant — largely by default. Unlike most government policies that are subject to debate, federal anti-drug strategies are pursued in a vacuum. Its proponents make hysterical statements about the dangers of legalization without any empirical evidence to support them. This has resulted in many mistaken public attitudes.

For example, 60 percent believe marijuana is physically addicting; 52 percent believe heroin makes people crazy, violent, and psychotic; 57 percent believe that marijuana is at least as addictive as alcohol and cigarettes; and 76 percent believe that marijuana use leads to stronger drugs.

---
[*] Richard J. Dennis, Chairman, Advisory Board, Drug Policy Foundation.

The drug warriors prefer to characterize public attitudes in the broadest of terms, without any reliance on polling data and scientific analysis. The mass media have compounded this conspiracy against reason by failing to ask the right questions. That is why I commissioned the most exhaustive poll on the drug issue to date, conducted by Targeting Systems, Inc. of Arlington, Va., This scientific survey polled 1,401 adult Americans in a random telephone sample Jan. 24-Feb. 4. The results comprise the largest and most comprehensive independent national opinion poll ever conducted on the drug issue.

The most surprising finding is a surge in support for legalization. Surely, by any measure of costs and benefits, legalizing drugs stands a better chance than current policy of solving our national drug problem. The major argument against legalization is that it will possibly lead to an increase in drug use and addiction. But by assigning reasonable costs to all aspects of the drug problem, it can be shown that the benefits of drugpeace are large enough to offset economic consequences of at least a doubling in the number of addicts.

Law enforcement at all levels costs us close to many billions a year. It will require additional billions to fight the narco-terrorists in Central and South America. And we forego billions of dollars in potential revenue by failing to legalize drugs and tax them. Obviously, proponents of legalization do not desire the increased use of drugs. But should drug use rise, the social costs would be at least partially offset by increased tax revenues.

Moreover, no one has documented that legalization leads to increased use. Drug Czar William Bennett and others have vociferously insisted that use under legalization would skyrocket. But the TSI poll shows that the drug warriors have exaggerated these fears to serve their interest in a continued drug war. Less than four percent of respondents said they were very likely to try legal marijuana, and less than one percent were very likely to try legal cocaine. Are we to believe that the American people are not only salivating for legal drugs, but also lying about it?

People understand that making drugs cheaper means that certain individuals will use more. What is equally true, but less understood, is that there is no economic incentive for dealers to push dirt cheap drugs. Thus, legalization may lead to less drug use instead of more, particularly by children and teenagers.

This means that the drug war is simply illogical; there is no good evidence that tough drug laws retard drug use. The TSI poll demonstrates that Americans implicitly acknowledge this: 88 percent of respondents believe that people will continue to obtain drugs no matter what the government does to stop them. The burden of proof that anti-drug laws discourage use clearly rests with those who are pushing the drug war. So far, no convincing evidence has been forthcoming.

Even if the war on drugs were able to end drug use, would it be worth the prospective cost to our values and liberties? The path down which the drug warriors would lead us is a slippery slope that threatens irreparable harm to our fundamental rights and constitutional protections. If we win the drug war, but lose the Bill of Rights, is that a good tradeoff?

Proponents of legalization aren't unaware or unfeeling about the personal destructiveness of drug use, and believe crimes against others committed under the influence of drugs should be vigorously prosecuted. And legalizers know that intemperate drug users cause indirect harm to loved ones and economic associates (among others), and set bad examples for kids. But to preserve our free society, we should think long and hard before criminalizing individual behavior that has no direct consequences for others. The fact that drug consumption is a bad idea tells us nothing about whether it should be punishable. And a jail term for setting a bad example is at once laughable and disgusting.

One of the glories of American life is that many things are legal that are not condoned by society-at-large, such as atheism, heavy metal music, and offensive speech. For example, it's clear that a majority of Americans think atheism is the belief of a diseased mind. It's not hard to imagine some theological equivalent of Bill Bennett making the case that the indirect harms (to society generally and children specifically) of godlessness require penalties for atheism. And we all know heavy metal music is the work of the devil. Why permit this indirect rending of the social fabric? Doesn't offensive speech just sicken us and make us feel hostile? It causes lots of distress.

The obliteration of the idea that there should not be laws against victimless crimes is at the heart of this confusion. We ought to re-establish it before criminality merely equals the sum of the whims of intolerant majorities. The propriety of individual behavior that doesn't clearly and directly endanger others is a moral or aesthetic judgement, not a matter for the courts. Otherwise, who defines the moral code for the state to enforce? Jesse Helms?

The drug warriors seek to place the force of law behind their crusade, because allowing for individual choice on drug use undercuts their moral restoration. But their strategy leads us inexorably toward a police state. Already, Fourth Amendment protections against unreasonable search and seizure have been weakened significantly. In the service of the drug war, our courts are reducing the standards for demonstrating probable cause, allowing the admission of illegally obtained evidence, and sanctioning property confiscation in advance of due process. Long prison sentences for trivial offenses like possessing small amounts of pot are the embodiment of cruel and unusual punishment. And the right to privacy — a fundamental American concept — has been placed in jeopardy by policies that allow for surveillance by helicopter and encourage children to report on their parents.

> *If we win the drug war, but lose the Bill of Rights, is that a good tradeoff?*

The current anti-drug strategy relies on the theory of enforcing "user accountability" through harsh criminal treatment for all drug users. But the TSI poll finds that a majority of Americans dissent from this approach. Respondents take a harsh view of drug dealers and want to get tough. But the truth is that tough drug laws don't discourage dealers. A recent Rand Corporation study of drug dealers in Washington, D.C., found that street dealers who sold drugs more than one day a week faced more than a one-in-five chance of being imprisoned for every year they sold drugs, a more than one-in-14 chance of being seriously injured, and a more than one-in-70 chance of being killed — a fatality rate 100 times greater than that of the general work force. When dealers aren't discouraged by jail time or even execution, the only drug war alternative is to target users.

But according to the TSI poll, a solid 68-21 majority believes that drug users should receive treatment and counseling instead of fines and imprisonment. This represents an implicit rejection of user accountability. Since effective law enforcement against drug dealers is impossible, and the public rejects enforcing user accountability, drug legalization is the only plausible alternative.

In releasing the TSI poll, the Drug Policy Foundation noted, "In rejecting the war on drug users and in choosing not to use drugs even if drugs were legal, Americans are saying 'make health, not war.' Americans want to help their neighbors who abuse drugs; they do not want to imprison them."

The Foundation added that the poll demonstrates "significant support for outright legalization of drugs. Americans are realizing that more jails, more arrests and more seizures will never solve the drug problem. When they also realize that the risks of legalization are small — less than one out of 100 Americans willing to try legal cocaine — then support for legalization will expand even more."

Of course, the Foundation was speaking of rational Americans whose overriding interest is solving the drug-crime problem. That goal is only peripheral for Drug Czar Bennett, whose primary interest is in a reactionary authoritarianism. Bennett has demonstrated time and again that his true agenda resides with the political and cultural implications of the drug war, not in pursuing policies like legalization that might actually solve the problem. The least we might expect is a czar whose primary interest is in reducing human suffering.

The most obvious evidence of Bennett's real priority is his commitment to a war on marijuana. This stems from a cultural clash of values rather than any drug policy imperative. The TSI poll indicates that most Americans take a much more reasonable approach to pot use. Only 17 percent of respondents believe that adults who smoke marijuana should be treated as criminals. Most respondents view pot's health effects as similar to those of tobacco and alcohol; 66 percent think cigarette smoking poses a health risk equivalent to or greater than marijuana smoking.

This national tolerance of pot users bodes ill for the war on drugs, which is likely to degenerate into a war on marijuana. Pot users don't carry Uzis. They can't hide millions of dollars worth of marijuana in small places. This makes them the easiest target for the enforcement of harsh drug laws. Already, pot users constitute more than a third of annual drug arrestees — most of whom were in possession of a small amount for personal use.

To justify the war on pot, drug warriors are forced to argue that it is a "gateway drug" whose legalization would lead users to more harmful and addictive drugs. While government studies have shown some correlation between pot use and cocaine addiction, they also show that tobacco and alcohol use correlates with drug addiction. Moreover, keeping pot illegal forces buyers into an illegal market where they are more likely to come into contact with other drugs. Most damaging to the gateway argument is that 61 million Americans have tried pot, but there are about one million cocaine addicts. If pot is a gateway drug, it's a narrow gate.

Whether focused on marijuana or other drugs, the Bush-Bennett user accountability strategy is based on a frightful denial of reality. Millions of Americans are paying a lot to take drugs, and are doing so knowingly and willingly. (An exception is children, who aren't old enough to make a voluntary choice; this is why they should be excluded from any legalization plan.) It is arrogant and, ultimately, counterproductive to base a national anti-drug policy on such a discredited ideology of social engineering. This policy is bound to fail the moment the troops are gone.

Some softer-core drug warriors attempt to maintain the fiction that drugs are going from dealer to user with no conscious choice involved.

The myth of the utter evil of dealers versus the benign participation of users does a grave injustice to those who deal drugs out of desperation. For example, the previously cited Rand Corporation study found that two-thirds of those charged with dealing drugs in Washington, D.C. held legitimate jobs that paid, on average, $9,600 annually. Those who sold drugs daily earned another $24,000 a year. The illicit earnings represent an income level far beyond their attainment through legitimate employment. The study also found that 7 out of 10 street dealers reported using drugs themselves; they dealt drugs at least partly to support their own habit. The predatory dealer and the victimized user are often one in the same person.

Bush, Bennett, and other politicians have gotten lots of mileage from demonizing drug dealers. But most dealers are simply pursuing the American dream in the absence of more legitimate opportunities. Like other Americans, they measure success by material wealth. Our current drug laws present an extraordinary opportunity for their enrichment. Legalization would remove the lure of easy money that beckons them and would greatly reduce the power of the drug-financed gangs that increasingly control domestic distribution. A decent society shouldn't tempt desperate people with the windfall profits that result from keeping drug illegal.

Demonizing drug dealers is only one example of the utter bad faith of the drug warriors. The degree of callousness reflected in current policies is most evident when considering the medical use of currently illegal drugs. Marijuana has proven useful in alleviating pain in some victims of multiple sclerosis, effectively reduces the nausea that accompanies chemotherapy, and may be helpful in treating glaucoma. Heroin has helped patients to deal with severe pain, and is legally prescribed for such purposes in Great Britain and Canada.

Yet, current drug policies make it virtually impossible to provide these drugs to patients who would benefit. Public attitudes in this area are more humane than current policy: 76 percent of poll respondents would allow physicians to prescribe heroin as a painkiller for terminally ill cancer patients, and 69 percent would allow marijuana use by glaucoma sufferers.

While the public may be rational about drugs and drug use, it unfortunately seems willing to jettison constitutional protections to advance the drug war. The poll found that 65 percent would allow the use of mandatory drug tests to keep their jobs, and 71 percent would grant police power to the military to fight drugs in their neighborhoods. But these statistics are less shocking when placed in the historical context of other government-sponsored assaults on the exercise of civil liberties. The post-World War I "red scare," the Word War II internment of Japanese-Americans and the McCarthy-era loyalty oath provide plenty of precedent for suspending the exercise of constitutional protections to deal with perceived national crises. We can all be grateful for the wisdom of our nation's Founding Fathers in requiring super-majorities to enact constitutional changes.

Much of the willingness to abandon these rights is attributable to how the drug policy debate has been managed. Drug warriors and the media have ruled out-of-bounds any serious discussion of less intrusive solutions. Americans understand intuitively that conventional law enforcement and court procedures stand no chance of retarding drug use. In the absence of serious debate about the merits of legalization, the only recourse they can see is militarization. They are willing to countenance this assault on their rights because of fear of drug-dealing gangs and foreign narco-terrorists. Ironically, legalization would instantly disempower those elements without sacrificing our most fundamental freedoms.

Despite their acceptance of militarization, Americans generally do not believe that more law enforcement is the answer to drug abuse. Fully 68 percent characterize it as primarily a health problem by supporting treatment and counseling as preferable to punishment. A plurality see the problem of drug abuse rooted in social ills; 46 percent think the government should focus its efforts and resources on tackling social problems which contribute to drug abuse, while 40 percent think the concentration should be on punishing drug users. In general, Americans do not believe that the government devotes enough money to treatment programs and education: 70 percent say it spends too little. When told that treatment and education programs may actually be less expensive than locking up all drug users, 74 percent want the emphasis on treatment, while only 13 percent favor widespread incarceration.

Finally, and unsurprisingly, views of the drug issue differ depending on life experience and education level. Those over 50 years of age are adamantly for tough approaches. Those under 40, particularly the 30 to 39-year-old group, are much more receptive to alternatives. Men are somewhat more favorable to alternatives than women. People with a high school education or less are much more likely to be hard-liners than those with a college education. And opinions in the Northeast and Pacific Coast regions are more lenient than in the South and the Mountain States.

Approximately one in four Americans is willing to consider drug legalization — a number far greater than the drug warriors care to acknowledge. This level of support for legalization is not surprising when the proposal is shorn of its political overtones and considered more directly on the merits. Keeping drugs illegal carries the price of providing sky-high profit for dealers and pushers; causes one-quarter of all new AIDS cases; requires $30 billion or more in annual law enforcement costs; and prevents the medicinal use of drugs for those who would benefit from them. These exceptionally high costs, combined with the limited risks of legalization, should give impetus to those in pursuit of more rational drug policies.

Support for Medical Use of Illegal Drugs

Should physicians be allowed to prescribe heroin as a pain killer for terminally ill patients?

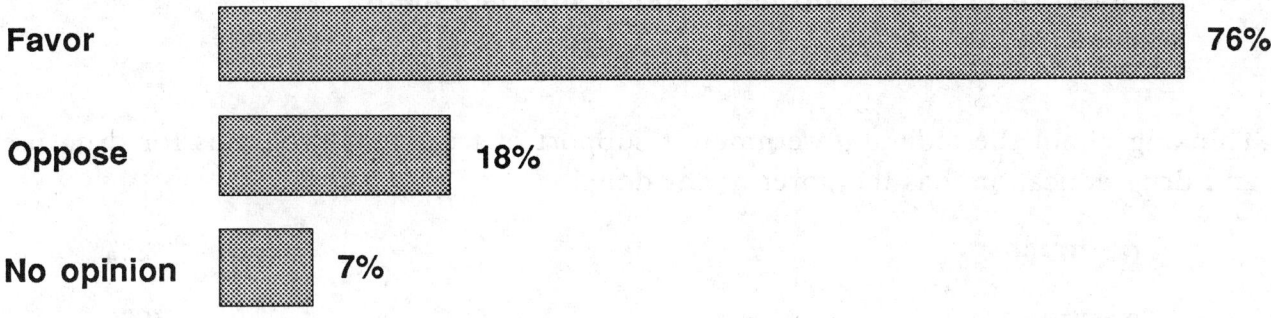

Should physicians be allowed to prescribe marijuana as a treatment for glaucoma, a condition that can lead to blindness?

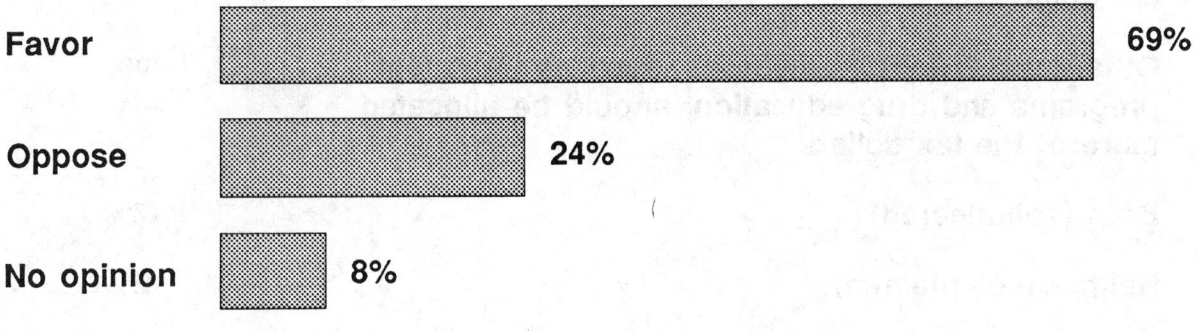

Source: DPF/Targeting Systems, Inc. Survey Jan.-Feb. 1990

Support for a Public Health Approach to Drug Abuse

Which do you think is preferable?

Providing treatment and counseling for drug users	**68%**
Punish drug users with fines and/or imprisonment	**21%**
No Opinion	**11%**

Thinking about the federal government's support of treatment programs for drug use and drug education, has the government done:

Too much	**2%**
Too little	**70%**
About the right amount	**23%**
No opinion	**5%**

The current law enforcement efforts to curb drug use cost taxpayers hundreds of millions of dollars per year, with an ever-increasing prison population reaching one million people in the U.S. Do you feel that:

Imprisoning all drug users is the best use of tax dollars	**13%**
Other less expensive methods, such as treatment programs and drug education, should be allocated more of the tax dollars	**74%**
Both (volunteered)	**7%**
Neither (volunteered)	**2%**
No opinion	**4%**

Source: DPF/Targeting Systems, Inc. Survey Jan.-Feb. 1990

Opinions on Legalization and Individual Choice

Finally, we'd like your opinion on two different approaches to today's drug problems...in you opinion, which approach is more likely to reduce the drug problem?

President Bush and drug czar William Bennett have stated their policy as a war on drugs through maximum government efforts. This includes more prison sentences for casual drug use, the use of the military (both at home and abroad) to fight the distribution of drugs, and more tax dollars spent on prisons to hold all of the people convicted or using or selling drugs.   **55%**

Lawmakers who criticize the current approach to the drug problem have stated that increased law enforcement won't end drug use, but will result in higher prices and demand for drugs, and more violence in urban areas in the United States. They believe that some people will use drugs no matter what the government policy is, and suggest that the government legalize and control the distribution of less serious drugs, while providing more drug treatment and better education programs. Drugs would only be available to adults, and anyone caught giving them or selling them would be severely punished.   **36%**

Neither (volunteered)   **5%**

No opinion   **4%**

Source: DPF/Targeting Systems, Inc. Survey Jan.-Feb. 1990

Opinions on Legalization and Individual Choice
(continued)

All drug use is immoral and should be illegal

Strongly agree	**46%**
Somewhat agree	**15%**
Somewhat disagree	**17%**
Strongly disagree	**18%**
No opinion	**4%**
Total agree	**65%**
Total disagree	**35%**

Adults should be allowed to make their own decisions about drug use.

Strongly agree	**17%**
Somewhat agree	**21%**
Somewhat disagree	**15%**
Strongly disagree	**46%**
No opinion	**1%**
Total agree	**38%**
Total disagree	**61%**

Source: DPF/Targeting Systems, Inc. Survey Jan.-Feb. 1990

How likely the Respondent Would Be to Try a Given Drug if it Were Legalized

(Among Those Who Have Tried it and Those with No Experience)

Have tried **marijuana** in the past:

	YES (35%)	NO (65%)	TOTAL
Likelihood of trying if legalized:			
Very Likely	8.5%	1.1%	3.7%
Somewhat likely	11.0%	3.1%	5.9%
Not very likely	13%	5.8%	8.3%
Not at all likely	66.8%	88.9%	80.5%
No opinion	08%	1.1%	1.6%

Have tried **cocaine** in powder form in the past:

	YES (11%)	NO (89%)	TOTAL
Likelihood of trying if legalized:			
Very likely	1.5%	0.5%	0.6%
Somewhat likely	7.5%	0.4%	1.1%
Not very likely	12.8%	3.1%	4.1%
Not at all likely	78.4%	95.1%	92.8%
No opinion		0.9%	1.4%

Source: DPF/Targeting Systems, Inc. Survey Jan.-Feb. 1990

The Research Advisory Panel suggests to the legislature that whatever we have been doing in the area of drug abuse should be immediately modified. Legislation aiming at regulation and decriminalization should be formulated as novel efforts that could be quickly modified if unsuccessful.

—*California Research Advisory Panel*

Chapter 12
Winding Down The War On Drugs

Introduction

The call for radical reform of the drug laws is, in essence, a prayer for an end to the hatred, demagoguery, crime, violence, and harm to personal health caused by the drug war. Reform advocates believe that while the currently illegal drugs are bad for our society, criminal prohibition in the American style is much worse.

Sooner than many clever politicians realize, a majority of the voters will demand change. In doing so, the electorate will not be voting sympathy for drug barons or approval of drugs but rather they will be coming out for peaceful compromise.

Reform should take place in two stages. The

first stage should include those steps which are urgent, which should be taken immediately, and which involve the fewest legal amendments. This is a medical approach to drug control and focuses on controlling two major recognized illnesses, AIDS and drug addiction. *The dominant philosophy should be that AIDS is a greater threat to society than drug abuse.* Because injecting narcotic addicts are the major cause for the transmission of AIDS, our supreme objective now, tomorrow morning must be to lure virtually every one of them into some form of treatment. While our health system does have many good programs for addicts, those programs are underfunded and over puritanical.

The dominant philosophy of American strategy now appears to be better dead from AIDS than alive addicted to injectable drugs.

If, however, we followed the models of a few other countries, Washington and every major American city would have a proactive, nonpuritanical health program. It would be replete with neighborhood clinics, trailers in drug areas, and an outreach effort to convince injecting addicts, prostitutes, and all those connected with the drug scene or at risk from AIDS to come in out of the cold for help. Radio ads and posters would imitate this bold message from a Liverpool, England poster, "Drugs Injectors and AIDS — Syringes, Needles, etc. and Condoms Are Available FREE — The Old Lodge, Church Rd — Tel 653-3871 — Strictly Confidential — No Appointment Needed."

The services offered would include politeness, compassion, a general health check-up, free needles within a needle exchange system, advice on safe injecting, condoms, advice on safe sex, and mental health counseling. In addition, there would be prescriptions from doctors for needed medicines, including for some patients medicinally pure oral and even injectable drugs.

There is nothing terribly new or even risky about the first stage because we can fly the experts across the oceans within a few days to start setting up tested programs. The risk is that we will delay their emergency commencement — and further risk the health and welfare of the entire nation. Current laws discourage most needle exchange programs and positively prohibit the prescription of injectable drugs. The necessary legal amendments must be made and funds reallocated so that such treatment facilities are available to every addict on demand.

Because so many political leaders oppose such health programs, it may be necessary for major law firms to work with enlightened medical leaders so as to clear a legal path through the ideological underbrush. As in the case of the civil rights movement, bigotry and ignorance sometimes cannot be fought only through political action and legislatures. Good lawyers and well-crafted legal actions then must move into the gap and start moving through the courts.

However these new health systems are achieved they should have a positive and immediate impact on the public welfare. Such systems competing with the illegal drug systems in, say, Washington, New York, or Detroit would mean that any addict or prostitute (sometimes the same person) would find immediate help at any one of many user-friendly clinics all over the city. Police stations, as in Amsterdam, would dispense needles to addicts and also advice on where to get rapid treatment, including legal drugs and more needles, as well as detoxification and drug-free programs. There would be fewer addicts in our prisons and more in clinics. These cities would not be drug-free or crime-free but they would be much healthier and safer communities in which to live.

When law enforcement does become involved, that involvement should be as part of the effort to provide assistance to people who need help. People violating drug laws should not be incarcerated. Instead, they should be provided the assistance needed to prevent anti-social behavior. Community service, job training, treatment or education should be supplied when it is needed. Intensive supervised probation should be used for most of those who must enter the criminal justice system so that they may be helped to become productive members of society. Incarceration should be reserved for the truly violent predators in our society.

Another immediate problem that should be faced in a more humane way is the availability of drugs as medicines. This includes marijuana for the treatment of nausea, muscle spasms, pain and glaucoma, as well as heroin and other narcotics, for the treatment of pain. While these problems are not as threatening as AIDS, they are a very immediate and real threat to hundreds of thousands of seriously ill Americans. Our failure to provide much needed medicine to seriously ill fellow citizens weighs heavily on the conscience of our nation and defines us in ways that should make us uncomfortable.

On a longer term basis, the real solutions to drug abuse do not depend so much on drug policy as they do on our economic, educational and social policies. We should look back to the presidential crime commissions of the 1960s and 70s. The recommendations made there are consistent with what we see as the solutions to drug abuse and crime today. Twenty years ago the National Commission on the Causes and Prevention of Violence compassionately observed: "To be young, poor male; to be undereducated and without means of escape from an oppressive urban environment; to want what society claims is available (but mostly to others); to see around oneself illegitimate and often violent methods being used to achieve material success; and to observe others using these means with impunity — all this is to be burdened with an enormous set of influences that pull many toward crime and delinquency. To be also black, Puerto Rican or Mexican-American and subject to discrimination adds considerably to the pull." The violence commissions summarized their recommendations in three words "neighborhood, family, employment."

That is where we should focus our resources. We need to encourage Head Start programs and after-school programs for children. We need to make it easier for families to stay together and grow together and we need to give people the hope and human dignity of a job that promises them a future. Unfortunately, as Judge Robert Sweet pointed out in his call for an end to drug prohibition, our society has been going in the other direction: "In 1986, 33 percent of families headed by persons under 25 were below poverty-level, a rate double that for 1967 and triple the 11 percent rate for all American families in 1986... Drugs have become an escape for those without a stake in society whose sense of self is weakened to the point that they will knowingly risk destruction and addic-

> *On a longer term basis, the real solutions to drug abuse do not depend so much on drug policy as they do on our economic, educational and social policies.*

tion absent an alternative motivation."

In the second stage, of reform, we must somehow confront the challenge of more rationally and peacefully providing drugs to those members of the general adult population who wish to purchase them. This stage is much more controversial than the first and would involve more sweeping legal changes. It will take more time to implement but its eventual adoption is inevitable. Many sensible, responsible officials believe that the way in which Americans dealt with alcohol is the way to deal with most illegal drugs. Joseph Galiber of New York, a black member of the state senate, has produced the most extensive legislative plan to date on this subject. It is contained in a bill he has introduced into the New York State Assembly. When Judge Robert Sweet made his historic speech in favor of legalization, he supported, without quite saying so, the Galiber model.

In essence, a state body would regulate the hours and conditions of the sale of all drugs. Thus, the rule of law would replace the law of the jungle. Sales would be restricted to adults. Drugs would be pure, properly labeled as to precise content, and the packages would contain health warnings on all of their dangers. No prescriptions would be required but, at least under the Galiber law, sellers would have to be licensed physicians or pharmacists. Places of sale could not be near schools or places of worship. The state authority would be encouraged to make all drugs available to adult residents of the state but the authority might decide to make some drugs (say marijuana, cocaine, and heroin) available legally but not others (PCP and crack.)

This broad approach would put many, if not most, street drug dealers and international barons out of business. Addict crime would be correspondingly diminished. As with alcohol, many problems would remain, including the commission of crime by citizens under the influence of drugs and drugged driving. Sadly we must accept their continued existence in minimal amounts as part of the reality of life.

In other words, with proper leadership Americans can be trusted to exercise moderation and temperance in regard to all manner of things. That is now the case, on the whole, with fatty food, with alcohol, and with tobacco. We Americans are abusing all of these substances less than in the past. There is no reason to believe that moderation and responsibility cannot be brought to bear on the currently illegal drugs once they are pulled within legal controls.

The power of such ideas was further demonstrated in recent months when the Research Advisory Panel of the California government came out with an historic report calling for an end to the war on drugs and a gradual repeal of drug prohibition. The radical report from this generally conservative official group of experts so shocked the state attorney general that he refused to provide state funds to publish the document. Individual members of the panel then proceeded to reproduce and distribute the report at their own expense.

We close this review of the latest thinking on the drug front with excerpts from that report of the California Research Advisory Panel for 1989. The most influential social trends often start in that frontier western state, which just became the most populous in the United States. The panel's recommendations could well become the launching pad for fundamental drug law reform in America and in many countries throughout the world. It is just possible that the United States could then begin to lead rather than lag in the development of humane and enlightened drug policies for the 21st century.

The Expert Report That The California Government Tried To Suppress*

Executive Summary

In previous annual reports the Research Advisory Panel has used the experience acquired during its operation to be critical of the research community and to summarize other problems of drug abuse important to the state of California. In this annual report, the panel presumes to suggest that the legislature act to redirect this state away from the present destructive pathways of drug control.

Our war on drugs for the past 50 years has been based on the principle of prohibition and has been manifestly unsuccessful in that we are now using more and a greater variety of drugs, legal and illegal. As with the "noble experiment" of the 18th Amendment, prohibition as opposed to regulation has not controlled drug use and a societal overreaction has burdened us with ineffectual, inhumane and expensive treatment, education and enforcement efforts. These efforts at reducing the social cost of drug use fail to distinguish between drug effects and associated criminal activity and fail to recognize that different drugs pose different problems and that we do not have one massive drug problem.

The Research Advisory Panel suggests to the legislature that whatever we have been doing in the area of drug abuse should be immediately modified. Legislation aiming at regulation and decriminalization (not "legalization") should be formulated as novel efforts that could be quickly modified if unsuccessful. The panel suggests that this legislation be formulated following four principles. First, separately consider the different drugs involved and not consider that there is one massive drug problem; second, distinguish between the effects of drugs and the associated criminal activity; third, design the legislation being aware that these are initial efforts subject to change with experience; and fourth, think of "drugs" as *including* alcohol and nicotine, not as being separate substances.

The first suggestions for demonstration legislation, rationalized and detailed herein are:

1. Permit the possession of syringes and needles
2. Permit the cultivation of marijuana for personal use
3. As a first step in projecting an attitude of disapproval by all citizens toward all drug use, take a token action in forbidding the sale or consumption of alcohol in state-supported institutions devoted in part or whole to patient care or educational activity.

Commentary

In previous annual reports the Research Advisory Panel has used the experience acquired during its operation to be critical of the research community and to summarize other problems of drug abuse important to the state of California. In this annual report, the panel presumes to suggest that the legislature act to redirect this state away from the present destructive pathways of drug control. The panel suggests that this legislation be formulated following four principles. First, separately consider the different drugs involved and not consider that there is one massive drug problem; second, distinguish between the effects of drugs and the associated criminal activity; third, design the legislation being aware that these are initial efforts subject to change with experience; and fourth, think of "drugs" as including alcohol and nicotine, not as being separate substances.

---

*Twentieth Annual Report of the Research Advisory Panel 1989, Commentary Section. Prepared for the Governor and Legislature.

Panel Qualification

The panel presumes to make these suggestions because of the long experience of panel members in activities relating to drug abuse, both in their role as members of the panel and also from their comprehensive experience outside of their panel function in areas related to the effects of drugs, the treatment of drug abuse and societal response to drug abuse.

The panel approaches the legislature differently from most advocates that appear before you. Such advocates have some conflict of interest, but that conflict is not always disclosed nor easily apparent to the legislature or to the persons themselves. It is not easy or pleasant, but it is essential, to acknowledge that even peace officers and workers in the drug abuse treatment industry (not to mention simple "legalization" advocates) have an interest in maintaining and initiating certain practices. With minor exceptions, members of the panel over the past 22 years have had no vested interest in drug treatment programs or sources of research support. Panel members are appointed by different agencies within the state and most receive compensation from their primary employment and are relieved of any tendency to react out of self-interest to suggestions for change.

After years of informed discussion and sensing a change in the attitudes of a large fraction of the population, panel members have agreed that we are mandated as an advisory group to the legislature to suggest that some legislation be attempted to reduce the damage to society now being imposed by drugs (always including alcohol and tobacco) and by inappropriate societal reaction to drug use.

Immediate Needs

Action must occur now. It is unnecessary to belabor the magnitude and importance of the problems of drug abuse as they are currently perceived by at least a fraction of the American public and by their elected representatives. The reaction is in part rational and justifiable, but is also colored by emotion and misunderstanding. The traditional activities by enforcement and regulatory agencies, however expanded by the long standing wars on drugs, whether directed at the individual drug user or small or large purveyor, have not been able to alter the course of the problems, of the extent of use, of individual damage or of the associated criminal activity. Even in the judgment of the enforcement agencies this traditional approach has accomplished little except possibly to increase price and encourage experimentation with alternate drugs. In spite of the sanctions imposed upon drug users, we have over the past 22 years seen massive epidemics involving high-dose intravenous methamphetamine, heroin, marijuana, hallucinogens, sniffed cocaine, synthetic narcotics, PCP, and now smoking freebase or crack cocaine. It appears incontrovertible that whatever policies we have been following over the past generations must not be continued unexamined and unmodified since our actions to date have favored the development of massive individual and societal problems.

Action must be innovative. Not only should the leaders of this state act now, but they must act differently. They must adopt actions unlike those we have tested and found wanting over past generations. The responsibility for initiating change appears to us to be passing at this moment from the intellectual and scholarly community to the legislature. There is more than an undercurrent of published discussion favoring radical change and questioning the efficacy of what, for convenience, we will call the "prohibition policy." Technical journals cited below and leading intellectual periodicals across the political spectrum have published carefully reasoned discussions establishing that our present policies are worse than useless. "Legalization" (not our term) has even been supported by conservative leaders such as William F. Buckley and Milton Friedman.

Basis of Derivation of Suggested Legislation

The panel believes that a rational approach to change should be based on three concepts that neither the public nor many legislators appear to be aware of or appreciate, however clear the distinctions are to researchers and practitioners in the area of drug abuse:

1) Differentiate different drugs and different routes of administration. There is no basis for progress in talking about *the* drug problem and looking for *one* magic solution to the massive problem as it is perceived by the public. The approach must be based upon a separate consideration of each of the several drugs involved. The various drugs involve different toxicities and different individual and social problems. The terrible lethal effects of cigarette smoking, that is, of inhaling tobacco smoke, are familiar. Some drugs, notably alcohol, cause, as a direct pharmacological effect, criminal or anti-social activity. Other drugs, notably heroin, are much less inherently dangerous either to the individual or to society, in spite of their high addiction liability, but they generate massive problems for the criminal justice system. The statement about heroin is not controversial or arguable. The California and federal legislatures have acknowledged that narcotics are not inherently prohibitively dangerous and have authorized programs to provide huge doses of methadone, a strong narcotic, to heroin users in lieu of their street drug.

We must then, not be naively permissive in our attitude toward alcohol and other depressants that disinhibit and cause inappropriate reactions. And we should not react emotionally against less harmful drugs in such a way that their regulation generates more problems than would their ungoverned use.

Eventually, although certainly not at this time, regulations, that is, societal reaction, will have to take into account different routes of administration as well as different drugs and recognize, for example, that cocaine in one form may be a minor hazard, whereas smoked cocaine may be highly addictive and require a more restrictive approach.

In our judgment, a first step in rationalizing our approach would be to further isolate marijuana from the other illegal drugs. This drug is widely used as a social drug, comparable to alcohol. More than half of the population has or will have had experience with this drug. Marijuana presents the same problems of responsible and irresponsible use as alcohol. However, no change in regulation would be acceptable if it leads to another industry comparable to the alcohol and tobacco industry.

2) Separate drug effects from associated criminal activity. Legislators and other political leaders must look objectively at the hazards claimed to result from drug abuse and differentiate damage caused by direct drug effects from damage engendered by societal reaction. For example, the population is not actually threatened by the behavior of the heroin user under the influence of this drug. The heroin user who is "coasting" after an injection is not given to violent activity. Yet those same heroin users, driven by their compulsion, will, in their efforts to maintain a supply of this drug, resort to income-generating criminal activities. These may be as minor as panhandling, may lead only to property and drug trafficking crime or, the personality of the user permitting, result in violent crime. Above the individual user is a stratum of heroin purveyors who operate as organized criminal activity and who will, the need in their opinion requiring, resort to the most violent acts. Obviously, to burden the individual user with the onus of organized criminal activity carried out by people who are rarely users themselves can lead to control of the problem only if the consumers are totally removed from the streets. This has not been accomplished even in the face of horrendous penalties, including briefly, in New York State under the so-called Rockefeller plan, the death penalty.

With a drug like marijuana, which enjoys popular approval in the face of legal prohibition, the associated criminal activity is regarded as nominal. And in the face of a refusal by a significant fraction of the population to support the laws against marijuana, it will be impossible to control the market in marijuana. Indeed, although the huge illegal market for imported marijuana may add significantly to our negative balance of payments, that market is not associated with drive by killings or other devastating criminal activity.

3) Awareness of Risk/Benefit Ratio of Any Chance. Suggestions for changes in the regulation of abused drugs should realistically take into consideration the possibility that any relaxation of regulation could lead to increased use. Any change effected should be evaluated over time to ensure that it does nothing, or the minimum, to encourage drug use. The term "legalization," should never be used in describing the approach we are advocating since we are not proposing to add an unregulated drug to the market or to permit the development of an industry which proselytizes for drug use. "Decriminalization" would be a legitimate description, but there is no intent to minimize the dangers or encourage the use of any drugs, always including those already in wide and damaging use, such as alcohol and tobacco.

A Stepwise Approach to Decriminalization

The panel does not pretend to be able to suggest an ultimate solution to the problem of drug abuse and does not suggest that an ultimate solution be sought at this time. Instead, we suggest a phased approach based upon the above principles of differentiating drugs and their problems that would initially achieve minor change but would demonstrate to the public that the minor change involved would not be accompanied by any significant increase in use or other damage. Since the panel does not pretend to have the ultimate solution it suggests that the outcome of such legislation be monitored closely.

Not only the traditional legislative responses, but most current proposals in the area of drug abuse legislation, are almost entirely in the direction of being increasingly more restrictive and vengeful. One can surmise this is a result of an apparent fear of being labeled "soft on drugs." Existing legislation, like prohibition itself, should be considered essentially a failure but one from which we can learn. Prohibition was characterized at the time as a "noble experiment," a judgment with which most of us would now agree. This noble experiment, however, was unsuccessful and after less than a generation was terminated. The intent of the 18th Amendment was beyond criticism and the effort was indeed noble, did accomplish a decrease in alcohol consumption, and could be used to justify additional experimental approaches. However, the experiment was unsuccessful in that the American public did not support enforcement and the illegal market generated an amount of associated criminal activity in the 1920s that was unacceptable to the public.

We are currently at a similar point in our history where much of the leadership and a considerable fraction of the public are coming to question whether prohibition is not equally unproductive in coping with the drug problems. Clearly the marijuana laws are unenforceable in the face of the attitudes and practices of a significant fraction of the population.

The panel then suggests areas in which initial steps can be taken to prevent individual tragedies and unclog our judicial system. Should any of the ideas prove less than optimal, the legislation can be modified as easily as the Volstead Act was terminated. If the changes are successful, they will serve to demonstrate to the citizenry of California that different drugs can be viewed differently, that some decriminalization may be beneficial to the general public, and that they can be developed without great or irreversible harm.

Suggested Legislation

Remove penalties for possession of needles and syringes. The statement that heroin is inherently not a dangerous drug has been somewhat weakened by the appearance in the community of the AIDS virus. This virus is transmitted, among other ways, by the use by one person of paraphernalia contaminated with the blood of an infected person. The AIDS virus has already spread through the drug-using community to an extent that varies with the sanitary practices of the local population. The prevalence of infection is much higher, for example, in New York City than in San Francisco.

There are two suggested methods of controlling the spread of this relatively new virus. The first, demonstrably ineffective, is to adopt a moralizing attitude, continue our current practices and simply add the individual tragedy and economic burden to the community of more AIDS patients. There is no reason to conclude that the additional threat of infection with AIDS has lead to a decrease in the use of injected drugs.

The other method of controlling the spread of the AIDS virus would be to encourage sanitary practices at the time of injection by making it possible for each heroin user to use his own "outfit," that is, syringe and needle, rather than accept the risk of using one contaminated with another addict's blood. This would become permissible as well as possible if the intravenous (IV) drug user were permitted to legally possess his own syringe and needle. The idea of providing or permitting the possession of the paraphernalia is controversial being viewed by some as offensive to the public morality. This attitude appears extremely shortsighted, in that making clean outfits available will not affect the prevalence of heroin use for the simple reason that syringes and needles are not difficult to obtain at this time. It follows that current experimental programs of needle exchange will be ineffective so long as the IV drug user fears harassment or arrest for carrying paraphernalia on his person.

Heroin users understandably try to avoid carrying supplies of their drug and their injecting paraphernalia any more than is absolutely necessary since the mere possession of the substance and the

> *A first step in rationalizing our approach would be to further isolate marijuana from the other illegal drugs. This drug is widely used as a social drug, comparable to alcohol.*

equipment is a punishable, although nominal, crime. The possession of paraphernalia is defined as a misdemeanor. Even though convictions under that complex section of the code are not easy to obtain if the charge is contested, the availability of the charge becomes a convenient means of harassing the addict and of subjecting him, in effect, to a three day jail sentence without trial. A person with a prior drug-related conviction must be especially careful since, in such a situation, even the possession of an ordinary spoon can be construed as possession of paraphernalia. As a result, users are reluctant to carry their own outfits and, their compulsion being upon them, are quite likely to use whatever equipment is available at the site of drug purchase. People driven by the compulsion that a heroin user feels, and given their choice between using someone else's outfit and doing without their drug will use the possibly contaminated equipment.

The panel urges an approach that would acknowledge the difficulty of treatment and accept a humane, rather than a punitive approach, and attempt the control of the spread of AIDS through the drug-using population by removing the prohibition against the possession of drug using equipment, which equipment is after all no different than that used by a diabetic or that available in the trash cans of some dozens of offices and hospitals in every city. The suggestion then, is that those sections of the codes (California Health and Safety Code sections 11364, 11364.5, and 11364.7 and Business and Professions Code section 4140) be revised to decriminalize possession of needles and syringes. Whether syringes and needles remain prescription items or not is a minor consideration in the spread of drug abuse, since this equipment or substitutes improvised out of plastic tubes and pacifiers are already easily available.

The result of this action would be to control to some extent the spread of the AIDS virus. Fortunately, in California the action could have significant impact since the incidence in drug users with HIV infection is still below 5 percent in cities other than San Francisco. Also, there would be important progress in controlling the spread of hepatitis, other infections, and local abscesses. Most important, it would provide experience and presumably evidence that liberalization of regulations would be followed by some gain in individual and public health rather than by a massive increase in drug use. There is no reason to believe that the availability or lack of availability of needles and syringes has anything to do with the recruitment of new heroin users. Except during the early years of the epidemics (1949-50 and 1970-71) the spread of heroin use to new users can be best understood by considering what older students in this area refer to as the "infectious disease model." New heroin users do not appear because of the availability of syringes, but because of their contact with established heroin users.

Allow cultivation of marijuana for personal use. Insofar as damage to the individual and society is concerned, the quantitatively most important drugs are alcohol and nicotine in the form of cigarettes. There remains, then, as the other quantitatively important drug, marijuana, which has become, for a large fraction of the population, a social drug comparable in pattern and approaching that of alcohol in extent of usage.

Marijuana is a disinhibiting drug used socially to relieve anxiety and as such has many liabilities in common with alcohol. We acknowledge that marijuana is not without its effect on the individual user and would not suggest any change that carried a significant risk of increasing the use of marijuana. We resist the use of the word "legalization" in relation to any drug, including marijuana. On the other hand, an objective consideration of marijuana shows that it is responsible for less damage to the individual and to society than are alcohol and cigarettes, the other social drugs mentioned above. A further consideration in forming a reaction to the wide use of marijuana is that it is a source of conflict between generations and of disrespect for the law.

Equally important is the economic and, to some extent, criminal activity associated with the marketplace of marijuana. At the moment, we are adding millions to our trade deficit, off of the books to be sure, by our purchases of marijuana in Colombia, Mexico, Thailand, and elsewhere. Yet, thanks to a previous action of the California Legislature, the product of this illegal activity may be possessed and used by the citizen with the possibility of only minor sanctions.

The legislature, some years back, did liberalize the regulations pertaining to marijuana in making the possession of a small amount (less than one ounce) an infraction, rather than a crime, calling for a citation and a nominal fine upon the first violation. This change has not lead to any disastrous consequences. On the contrary, it has reduced the tension between generations and decriminalized to some extent the generally sanctioned use of this new social drug by large numbers of people.

This new situation, for which we applaud the legislature, is however, not stable, in the sense that the failure to act in relation to the supply of the drug leaves unmet the question of the still illegal market and the economic problem that that entails. If this disparity could be resolved there would be economic gain and a great simplification of law enforcement which now devotes a considerable effort to seizing a small fraction of the illegal importations or cultivations.

The panel therefore suggests that the law be changed to permit cultivation for personal use. Such cultivation would be permitted only on property serving as the residence for the individual, that is, it would not authorize the cultivation of 50 plants on a national forest and it would not permit the possession outside of the home of more than the present one ounce, nor would it sanction the provision to others in or out of the residence whether by sale or in the form "parties". The change regulating the provision of this drug *must* be made in such a way that we do not see the development of another industry comparable to the alcohol or cigarette industry. This would require extensive revision of Health and Safety Code, Section 11358, which covers substances and matters other than the plant.

There are people who will express concern about whether such a change, however warranted by social and economic gains, would not also result in increased use. These justifiable concerns must not be dismissed out of hand. The panel insists that no attitude of approval of marijuana, or alcohol, or tobacco be projected. In fact, as we have said above, we all remain prohibitionists to the extent that prohibition will work. To the extent that prohibition creates a marketplace or social conflict, we suggest more flexible, practical, and humane policies. It appears that the use of marijuana has reached a plateau at this time, and that usage over foreseeable circumstances will remain about at its present level, as is the case with alcohol.

From the point of view of the younger members of the population, the problem becomes a matter of consistency which we should answer by saying marijuana is "just as bad as alcohol," rather than as the defenders of marijuana would probably say, "it's no worse than alcohol."

The resulting conflict between the proposed change in California Law and existing federal law is apparent, but the liberalization of state regulations would result in decreased enforcement activity at the state level, and federal enforcement activity is directed primarily at a level above the activity we are presently discussing. The success of a trial of this sort would provide leadership to other states and nationally. It would have no immediate effect on problems related to other more emotionally-laden drugs, except as it demonstrates the need to consider these problems separately and one by one with an awareness of risk/benefit ratios.

Reducing the Use of Drugs

The present status or effectiveness of education aiming at drug abuse prevention is obviously disappointing. The amount and variety of drugs with which younger people are experimenting and subsequently using have increased to its present level during the very period when this state had a required kindergarten through 12th grade anti-drug use curriculum in place. National efforts, in or out of the formal school situation, have been equally disappointing.

Not even the success in controlling cigarette smoking extends to the youthful population. However, it is from the successful imposition and acceptance of restrictions on smoking by the adult population that we must learn important lessons about which target population to focus on and about which arguments work and which do not. The successful campaign against smoking did not focus entirely on the user but engaged most of the population in making an aesthetic and personal responsibility issue out of smoking.

The abstract advertisements about cancer and other deadly issues were ineffective compared to the demonstration provided by intelligent community leaders and, laudably, doctors who publicly gave up tobacco and made an issue of passive smoking. In drug education we have focused on physical damage, which is not important to a young risk-taker. And we have focused on the population that we consider to be at-risk, that is, young people and some minority groups. The target population should be the total population and should examine the use of all drugs, including or even especially, the nominally legal alcohol, tobacco and prescription drugs.

In efforts to limit the use of quantitatively important drugs, we should act to influence the entire population so that an unambiguous attitude of disapproval is projected. Even those of us who continue to drink or smoke should be willing to do so without claiming that our practices are anything but bad. For a parent to decide that his children will never see him drink and that he will not keep alcohol in the home, even though he may drink socially elsewhere, is not hypocritical, but exemplary.

A major effort in changing the attitudinal climate will eventually have an effect on potential new users or judging from the experience with cigarettes, shorten the duration of their habit.

However, efforts at drug abuse prevention or limitation must be multiple in that populations exposed to hard drugs present separate problems. Certain populations, notably those in urban ghettos, have greater contact with smoked cocaine and injected heroin, drugs which by those routes of administration are highly addictive, that is, highly likely to be used compulsively. About these "hard drugs," there are two preliminary points:

1) Drug education among these high-risk populations proceeds at the level of individual experience and independently of our efforts. The loss of control in using certain drugs becomes recognized, and most people in these populations then resist their use. That is, some drugs do get a bad name. As a result, epidemics of such use are self-limiting to some extent, and, after these epidemics (of which we have now seen four: two

heroin, one high-dose IV-speed and one smoked-cocaine as crack), we see a residual number of users who have not matured out of their habit.

2) The spread of the habit from these established users to new recruits can be best understood by the infectious disease model mentioned above, and accounts for the relatively small number of new users after the initial period of high use. The number of people involved with these "hard" drugs is small compared to the numbers using the social drugs discussed above, and the problems, however destructive and however exaggerated in extent, are geographically limited and are typically associated with non-pharmacologic problems.

For the general public, effective drug education would consist of neutralizing advertisements (however disguised) that glamorize and proselytize for drug use. Instead, an aura of general disapproval of all drugs, including the common socially used drugs should be established.

Suggested Actions

Prohibit (legal) drug use in special state establishments. We have recently seen amazing progress in dissuading people from the use of tobacco. We will below suggest additional action in relation to alcohol, already a regulated drug, with at least some discipline applied. Overall, prohibition is not feasible but restricted use of alcohol in inappropriate places is justifiable and would be an essential step in projecting the attitudinal change desired.

The panel applauds the establishment of tobacco free areas in state institutions. As a condition of their funding the legislature should now insist that certain agencies within the state system not sell or provide alcoholic beverages within the confines of their campus or building. This should be immediately applied to any medical center campus or hospital. Doctors and other care-givers have a generally favored status and acquire with that a special responsibility to project an attitude of disapproval about the use of any disabling drug while they are accepting responsibility for a dependent patient. Certainly the state acquires a liability in providing alcohol to individuals who are then going to drive or see patients. More importantly, such use then projects an attitude totally at odds with that which we claim throughout our discussions as desirable.

Similarly, it is impossible to rationalize the use of a depressant drug, clearly shown to impair performance after small doses, on a university or state university campus dedicated to intellectual activity. The individual instructors, that is, teachers at all levels, should probably feel an obligation to neither drink nor smoke in public, but this is not a matter for legislation.

Counter ads. In addition to the emphasis on role modeling implied by the suggestion immediately above, there is an obvious need for counter promotion to offset the various advertising techniques that subtly, or explicitly, imply sexual or other social rewards for the use of products. The experience with cigarette advertising would suggest that counter ads placed immediately after the offending ad and providing an alternate view of the problem were more effective than current isolated, however cute, anti-drug ads. To what extent this policy could be initiated intra-state is a matter beyond our competence, but it would appear more than desirable.

References

The following section includes important articles, books, reports, court decisions, agencies, organizations and drug policy actors; it is arranged by chapter (and subchapter where needed).

Chapter 1

President George Bush, White House, Washington, D.C. 20500.

Office of National Drug Control Policy, Old Executive Office Building, Washington, D.C. 20500. (202) 673-2520. William J. Bennett, Director.

Office of National Drug Control Policy, National Drug Control Strategy, U.S. Government Printing Office, September 1989. (202) 783-3238. Fax (202) 275-0019. Order processing code #6705.

Office of National Drug Control Policy, *National Drug Control Strategy*, U.S. Government Printing Office, January 1990. (202) 783-3238. Fax (202) 275-0019. Order processing code #6782.

Office of National Drug Control Policy, *Leading Drug Indicators*, U.S. Government Printing Office, September 1990. (202) 783-3238. Fax (202) 275-0019. Order processing code #6899.

Majority Staffs of the Senate Judiciary Committee and the International Narcotics Control Caucus, *The President's Drug Strategy: One Year Later*, September 1990.

Domestic Council Drug Abuse Task Force, *White Paper on Drug Abuse*, U.S. Government Printing Office, 1975.

"The Drug Czar Derides the Intellectuals"

Below are the leading intellectuals who were derided by William Bennett in his Harvard speech.

William F. Buckley, *National Review*, 150 E. 35th St., New York, N.Y. 10016. (212) 679-7409.

Milton Friedman, Hoover Institution, Stanford, Calif. 94305-6010. (415) 723-1754.

Professor Ethan A. Nadelmann, Department of Politics, Woodrow Wilson School of Public and International Affairs, Princeton University, Princeton, N.J. 08544.

George P. Shultz, Hoover Institution, Stanford, Calif. 94305-6010. (415) 725-3492.

Chapter 2

Edward M. Brecher, *Licit and Illicit Drugs*, Little, Brown and Company, 1972.

Data Center and Clearinghouse for Drugs and Crime, 1600 Research Blvd., Rockville, Md. 20850. (800) 666-3332.

Drug Abuse Warning Network, Division of Epidemiology and Prevention Research, National Institute on Drug Abuse, 5600 Fishers Lane, Room 11A-55, Rockville, Md. 20857.

Katherine M. Jamieson and Timothy J. Flanagan, eds., *Sourcebook of Criminal Justice Statistics — 1987*. U.S. Department of Justice, Bureau of Justice and Statisics. Washington, D.C., U.S. Government Printing Office, 1988.

Katherine M. Jamieson and Timothy J. Flanagan, eds., *Sourcebook of Criminal Justice Statistics — 1988*. U.S. Department of Justice, Bureau of Justice and Statisics. Washington, D.C., U.S. Government Printing Office, 1989.

Ethan Nadelmann, "U.S. Drug Policy: A Bad Export," *Foreign Policy*, Spring 1988.

Ethan Nadelmann, "Drug Prohibition in the United States: Costs, Consequences and Alternatives," *Science*, September 1989.

Justice Statistics Clearinghouse/NCJRS, U.S. Department of Justice, User Services Department 2, Box 6000, Rockville, Md. 20850. (800) 732-3277.

National Criminal Justice Reference Library, 1600 Research Blvd., Rockville, Md. 20850. (301) 251-5500.

Arnold S. Trebach, *The Heroin Solution*, Yale University Press, 1982.

Arnold S. Trebach, *The Great Drug War*, Macmillan, 1987.

Arnold S. Trebach, "Why Not Decriminalize?" *New Perspectives Quarterly*, Summer 1989.

Chapter 3

Peter Cohen, IWA University of Amsterdam, Grate Bickersstraat 72, 1013 KS Amsterdam, Netherlands. 31 (20) 525-1246.

National Household Survey, National Institute on Drug Abuse, 5600 Fishers Lane, Rockville, Md. 20857.

Eddy L. Engelsman, Director of Alcohol, Drugs, and Tobacco, Ministry of Welfare, Public Health, and Cultural Affairs, P.O. Box 5406, 2280 HK Rijswijk, Netherlands. 31 (70) 340-6937.

E.C. Buning, *The Municipal Health Service and the Drug Problem: Facts and Figures*. Gemeentelijke Geneeskundige en Gezondheidsdienst, Amsterdam, 1990.

Peter Cohen, *Cocaine Use in Amsterdam in Non-Deviant Subcultures*, Institute for Social Geography, University of Amsterdam, 1989.

H.N. Plomp, H. Kuipers and M. Van Oers, *Smoking, Acohol and Drug Use Among School Students From 10 Years*, Amsterdam/Utrecht, 1990.

References

Prof. Dr. Frits Rüter, Director, Van Hamel Institute of Criminal Law, University of Amsterdam, Klovenierburgwal 72, 1012 CZ Amsterdam, Netherlands. 31 (20) 525 3375.

American Embassy, Lange Voorhoug, #102, 2514 EJ The Hague, Netherlands. 31 (70) 362 4911.

Chapter 4

Institute for Scientific Analysis, 2235 Lombard St., San Francisco, Calif. 94123. (415) 921-4987.

National Institute on Drug Abuse, *Women and Drugs: A New Era for Research*, Research Monograph Series 65, U.S. Government Printing Office, 1987.

Ira Chasnoff, et al., "Cocaine Use in Pregnancy," *New England Journal of Medicine*, Vol. 313, No. 11, Sept. 12, 1985.

Centers for Disease Control, *Morbidity and Mortality Weekly Report*, Vol. 39, No. 9, March 9, 1990. The report speculates about the causes, but does not mention drugs.

Gideon Koren, et al, "Bias Against the Null Hypothesis: The Reproductive Hazards of Cocaine," *The Lancet*, Dec. 16, 1989.

U.S. General Accounting Office, *Drug Exposed Infants: A Generation at Risk*, June 1990.

Narcotics and Drug Research, Inc., 11 Beach St., New York, N.Y. 10013. (212) 966-8700.

Neil A. Weiner and Marvin E. Wolfgang, *Pathways to Criminal Violence*, Sage, 1989.

Ralph A. Weischeit, *Drugs, Crime and the Criminal Justice System*, Anderson Publishing Co., 1990.

Bruce D. Johnson, Paul J. Goldstein, Edward Preble, et al, *Taking Care of Business: The Economics of Crime by Heroin Abusers*, Lexington Books, 1985.

Chapter 5

Dr. Lester Grinspoon, Department of Psychiatry, Harvard Medical School, Cambridge, Mass. 02139. (617) 277-3261.

Judge Francis L. Young, Drug Enforcement Administration, Opinion and Recommended Ruling, Finding *of Fact, Conclusion of Law and Decision of Administrative Law Judge*, Marijuana Rescheduling Petition, Docket No. 86-22, Sept. 6, 1988.

National Organization for the Reform of Marijuana Laws, 1636 R St., N.W., #3, Washington, D.C. 20009. (202) 483-5500. Donald Fiedler, National Director.

Robert Randall, Alliance for Cannabis Therapeutics, P.O. Box 2120, Kalorama Station, Washington, D.C. 20009. (202) 483-8895.

Steven Sallan, Norman Zinberg, Emile Frei, III, "Antiemetic Effect of delta-9-Tetrahydrocannabinol in Patients Receiving Cancer Chemotherapy," *New England Journal of Medicine*, No. 293, 1975.

Robert Randall, *Marijuana, Medicine and The Law*, Galen Press, Washington, D.C., 2 volumes, 1988.

Chapter 7

Drugs Branch, Home Office, 50 Queen Anne's Gate, London, England SW1H 9AT U.K. 44 (1) 273-3000.

Institute for the Study of Drug Dependence, 1-4 Hatton Place, London, England EC1N 8ND U.K. 44 (1) 430-1991.

Chemical Dependency Program Division 3823, Minnesota Department of Human Services, 444 Lafayette Road, St. Paul, Minn. 55155. (612) 296-4610. Carol Salkowski, AIDS Coordinator.

Mersey Regional Training Centre, 27 Hope St., Liverpool, England L1 9BQ U.K. 44 (51) 709-3511. Pat O'Hare, Director.

National Research Council, *AIDS, Sexual Behavior and Drug Use*, (Feb. 8, 1989), National Academy of Sciences, 2101 Constitution Ave., N.W., Washington, D.C. 20418. Sales: (202) 334-3313. Information: (202) 334-2138.

Charles Eaton, lecture at the Drugs and Society Seminar, Columbia University, New York, March 29, 1990.

Michael R. Kagay, "Poll Finds Antipathy Toward Some AIDS Victims," *The New York Times*, Oct. 12, 1988.

New York City Department of Health, "The Pilot Needle Exchange Study in New York City: A Bridge to Treatment," December 1989.

Todd Purdum, "Dinkins Decides to Cancel Needle Exchange Program." *The New York Times*, Feb. 14, 1990.

Dulcey Consuelo Davidson, Institute for Citizen Education in the Law, Puget Sound School of Law, Tacoma, Wash.

Ian Clements, Julian Cohen, Patrick O'Hare, "1987 HIV Infection Among Drug Injectors in England," *Druglink*, Vol. 3, No. 3.

Drugs and HIV Monitoring Unit, Mersey Regional Health Authority, "HIV Infection among Drug Injectors in England," *The International Journal on Drug Policy*, Vol. 1, No. 1.

Allan Parry, "Needle Swop in Mersey," *Druglink*, Vol. 2, No. 1.

J. Young, *The Drugtakers*, Paladin, London, 1971.

See also *The Great Drug War*.

Chapter 8

John Diaz, "Furor over Report of Teenaged Drug Use," *San Francisco Chronicle*, May 15, 1990.

Jonathan Shedler and Jack Block, "Adolescent Drug Use and Psychological Health: a Longitudinal Inquiry," *American Psychologist*, May 1990.

Michael Aldrich, Tod Mikuriya, Gordon Brownell, Jerry Mandel, *Fiscal Savings in California Marijuana Law Enforcement, 1976-85, Attributable to the Moscone Act of 1976*, Testimony to the California Senate Judiciary Committee, April 7.

Chapter 9

John Hurst, "Too Tough On Drug Abusers?," *The Advocate*, May 8, 1990, p. C1.

John Hurst, "Straight Faces Abuse Complaints, *The Advocate*, May 8, 1990 p. C1.

DeNeen L. Brown, "Va. Cites Drug Treatment Center For Not Reporting Alleged Abuse," *The Washington Post*, September 30, 1990, p. B8.

For additional information see *Fred Collins v. Straight*.

See also *The Great Drug War*.

Chapter 10

Florida v. Riley, No. 87-764 (Jan. 23, 1989).

Florida v. Royer, 460 U.S. 491 (1983).

Florida v. Rodriguez, 469 U.S. 1 (1984).

Illinois v. Gates, 462 U.S. 213 (1983).

Oliver v. United States, 466 U.S. 179 (1984).

Summaries et al. v. Chicago Housing Authority et al., 88C10566 (U.S. District Court for the Northern District of Illinois).

Texas v. Brown, 460 U.S. 730 (1983).

United States v. Place, 426 U.S. 606 (1983).

United States v. Villamonte-Marquez, 462 U.S. 579 (1983).

Ted Galen Carpenter and Channing Rouse, *Perilous Panacea: The Military In the Drug War*, Cato Institute Policy Analysis No. 128, Feb. 15, 1990.

References

Congressional Record 3579, 45th Congress, 2nd Session (May 20, 1878).

Milton Friedman, "An Open Letter to Bill Bennett," *The Wall Street Journal*, Sept. 7, 1989.

Stephen Halbrook, "Military Enforcement of the Drug Laws Under the Posse Comtatus Act," *Drug Law Report*, September/October 1984.

James Longo, "Tempers Rise During Face-Off Over Initiatives," *Army Times*, May 23, 1988.

Bureau of International Narcotics Matters, Department of State, *International Narcotics Control Strategy Report*, March 1989.

Arnold S. Trebach, *The Heroin Solution*, Yale University Press, 1982.

International Legal Defense Counsel, 111 S. 15th St., 24th Floor, Philadelphia, Pa. 19102. (215) 977-9982. Robert Pisani, executive director.

"Rural Citizens Under the Guns and Helicopters"

Ronald M. Sinoway, Esq., P.O. Box 1339, Redway, Calif. 95560. (707) 923-3905.

"Waging War on America's Poor"

National Tenants Organization, et al. v. Kemp. Civil Action 88-3134 (U.S. District Court, Washington, D.C., June 20, 1989, bench decision).

National Housing Law Project, 1950 Addison St., Berkeley, Calif. 94704. (415) 548-9400. David Bryson, staff attorney.

Chapter 11

The Hon. Kurt L. Schmoke, 250 City Hall, Baltimore Md. 21202. (301) 396-4889.

The Hon. Robert W. Sweet, 40 Center St., Room 2202, New York, N.Y. 10007.

Chapter 12

Steven Wisotsky, *Beyond the War on Drugs*, Prometheus Books, 1990.

National Research Council, *An Analysis of Marijuana Policy*, National Academy Press, 1983.

Select Committee on Narcotic Abuse and Control, House of Representatives, *Legalization of Illicit Drugs: Impact and Feasibility*, Part I, Sept. 29, 1988.

Index

A

ACT 83, 98, 100, 102-3
AIDS 4, 28-30, 38, 47-8, 49-50, 54-5, 63, 83, 104-6, 119, 125-6, 128-30, 132-40, 142-3, 145, 147-9, 203-4, 215-17, 222, 230-1, 237-8
alcohol 17, 25, 27-9, 36-7, 39-40, 47-9, 51, 53, 57-8, 97, 112, 114, 117, 120, 123, 133, 155, 156-7, 159, 167, 168, 174-5, 201, 205, 207, 213, 217, 220, 232-41
amphetamine 27, 32, 52, 234
Australia 126, 138-9, 141, 143

B

Barry, Marion 4
Bennett, William 3-4, 7-8, 14, 20, 23, 25, 28-34, 38, 41, 62, 71, 79, 80, 82, 126, 137, 146, 152, 164, 178, 182-3, 185, 187, 200, 218-21, 225
Bush, George 3-4, 7-8, 20, 24, 28-32, 38-42, 62-3, 69, 74, 81-2, 104, 126, 137, 152, 163-4, 174, 178, 180, 186-7, 189, 191, 200, 208, 213, 217, 220, 222, 225

C

cocaine 3-4, 7-10, 16-7, 20-1, 24-33, 35-6, 38-42, 46, 47-9, 52, 54, 58, 61-82, 114, 122-3, 132, 151-5, 157, 165-6, 172-3, 180, 182, 187-9, 193, 204, 206, 207, 208, 211, 212, 218, 220, 227, 232, 234, 235, 240, 241

D

DEA 1-2, 29, 39, 68, 84, 104-6, 155, 165, 180-1, 208, 211

E

Engelsmann, Eddy L. 45, 49
England 126, 141, 147, 178, 230

F

Friedman, Milton 178

H

heroin 7-8, 10, 16, 25, 27, 30, 33-6, 39, 41, 47-9, 52, 54, 57-8, 62-3, 67, 70-1, 78, 108-14, 119, 122-3, 126-8, 132, 142, 146-8, 151-5, 157, 185-6, 193, 201, 206, 208, 209, 217, 221, 223, 231-2, 234-8, 240-1

I

Iran 184-6

M

Malaysia 184, 186
marijuana 1-2, 16, 25-6, 28-37, 39-40, 47-9, 51-8, 72, 77, 79, 81-6, 88-106, 132, 140, 144-5, 151-162, 164-6, 178, 180, 182, 185-6, 195-7, 200, 204, 207, 212, 217, 218, 220-1, 223, 227, 231-9
Mersey Harm Reduction Model, Liverpool 141, 143
methadone 36, 48, 54, 70, 108, 110-11, 115-22, 134-5, 142, 147, 201, 205-6, 235

N

National Federation of Parents for Drug-Free Youth 165
Netherlands 46-53, 55-8, 125, 138
Noriega, Manuel 3, 181, 189, 191
NORML 83, 98-100, 102-3

O

opiate 27, 52, 110, 119, 165

P

Panama 3, 34, 177-8, 180-1, 189-91

Parents Resource Institute for Drug Education, Inc. 159, 164-6
Parry, Allan 141-2, 147-9
Partnership for a Drug Free America 21
PCP 7-8, 16, 30, 39, 157, 232, 234
Peru 166, 180-2, 188-9, 208-9

R

Rangel, Charles 45, 81-2, 187, 199, 206-7
Reagan, Ronald 9, 24, 30-2, 66, 78, 80, 82, 84, 116, 157, 163-4, 180, 184, 186, 191, 194

S

Shultz, George 23-4, 200
Straight, Inc. 163-75

T

Thatcher, Margaret 46, 138-9, 146
tobacco 26-9, 33, 39-40, 47-49, 53, 58, 67, 72, 74, 155-7, 159, 213, 220, 232, 234-6, 239-41